Fashion Marketing

Fashion Marketing
Contemporary Issues

Second edition

Tony Hines

and

Margaret Bruce

AMSTERDAM • BOSTON • HEIDELBERG • LONDON • NEW YORK • OXFORD
PARIS • SAN DIEGO • SAN FRANCISCO • SINGAPORE • SYDNEY • TOKYO
Butterworth-Heinemann is an imprint of Elsevier

ELSEVIER

Butterworth-Heinemann is an imprint of Elsevier
Linacre House, Jordan Hill, Oxford OX2 8DP, UK
30 Corporate Drive, Suite 400, Burlington, MA 01803, USA

First edition 2001
Second edition 2007

British Library Cataloging in Publication Data
A catalog record for this book is available from the British Library

Library of Congress Cataloging in Publication Data
A catalog record for this book is available from the Library of Congress

ISBN–13: 978-0-7506-6897-2
ISBN–10: 0-7506-6897-0

For information on all Butterworth-Heinemann publications
visit our web site at http://books.elsevier.com

Typeset by Charon Tec Ltd (A Macmillan Company), Chennai, India
www.charontec.com

Printed and bound in The Netherlands
07 08 09 10 11   10 9 8 7 6 5 4 3 2 1

Working together to grow
libraries in developing countries

www.elsevier.com | www.bookaid.org | www.sabre.org

ELSEVIER   BOOK AID
International   Sabre Foundation

Contents

Foreword

Fashion is driven by creativity, desire and aspiration. Consumers want to buy unique items that are expressive, personal to them and reflect their taste and status. Fashion designers and buyers have to provide clothes that meet these ever changing needs and are available at a given price point. Also, they define and reflect trends. Trend forecasting influences the colours, the styles and textures that are abundant in stores. However, if even the slightest hue or shade of colour or style fails to match consumers' tastes, then these items will not sell. So, it is challenging to predict and order volumes of clothes way in advance of when they are likely to appear in store. Technology drives innovation in textiles and is a dynamic force in fashion. Think about aromatherapy to enhance a sense of well-being delivered in clothes, think improvement in sports ware, etc. Price deflation, getting the quality and design to match consumers' desires, needs and tastes and managing the supply chain to provide innovation to the high-street make fashion marketing exciting and challenging.

As well as the fashion item, e-tailing and other ways of selling, promotion and managing the supply base are affecting the organisation and management approaches to fashion. Fashion leadership is only attained by being one step ahead in being aware of the multiple impacts on the fashion business, learning how these may improve the fashion business and implementing change at the right time.

This book addresses the key issues of fashion marketing. It demonstrates the complexity, challenges and fun of the business. It provides useful insights into the nature of the business of fashion.

Kate Bostock
Business Unit Director Womenswear & Girlswear
Marks & Spencer

List of contributors

Emma Banister is a Lecturer in Consumer Behaviour at Lancaster University Management School. Her first degree was in Politics and History at Newcastle University, and she completed her M.Sc. in Marketing at the School of Management in 1997. Her postgraduate dissertation was on the structure and transfer of meaning in the music industry, and specifically explored the consumption of imagery by adolescent consumers. Emma was later awarded her Ph.D. from UMIST where she conducted research into symbolic consumption and the rejection of products – specifically the notion that the 'undesired end state' functions as an incentive to avoid products with negative images. The research draws on social psychology and sociology in its examination of possible selves and product user stereotypes. A variety of methods were employed (including projective techniques) to generate both qualitative and quantitative data.

Margaret Bruce B.Sc., M.Sc., Ph.D., is Professor of Design Management and Marketing at Manchester Business School and where she is also the Director of the Centre for Business Research. She holds a Professorship in Design and Fashion Marketing at University of the Arts London and a Professorship of Strategic Design Management at ICN, University of Nancy 2, France. She holds an Honary Professorship at Xi'an Institute of Technology, China. Professor Bruce has published 10 books and her latest books are: 'Marketing Leadership by Design' (Butterworth-Heinemann 2005) and International Retail Marketing (Butterworth Heinemann 2004). She has published over 200 papers in the areas of fashion marketing, innovation and design. Professor Bruce has conducted a number of international research programmes in design and innovation. She is a member of Council of the British Academy of Management.

Steve Burt B.A. Ph.D., is Professor of Retail Marketing at the Institute for Retail Studies in the Department of Marketing, University of Stirling, and is president of the European Association for Education and Research in

Commercial Distribution. He has conducted research into retailing, with a particular interest in comparative and international retailing, since graduating from the University of Oxford in 1981. Sponsors of research projects include public and private sector organizations such as the Distributive Trades EDC, the European Community, Marks & Spencer, ICL, Safeway, Scottish & Newcastle Breweries, Esslette Meto and the European Travel Research Foundation. His academic publications have covered various aspects of retail strategy, European retailing and internationalization and have appeared in journals such as the *British Journal of Management, European Journal of Marketing*, and the *International Review of Retail Distribution and Consumer Research*.

Ranis Cheng B.A. (Hons)., MRes., is currently a doctoral researcher at Manchester Metropolitan University Business School. The focus of her doctoral research is the role of corporate identity within the fashion retail sector. She has presented research papers at a number of conferences, including the British Academy of Management, the Academy of Marketing and the European Academy of Management.

Alice W. C. Chu is currently Assistant Professor at the Institute of Textiles and Clothing, The Hong Kong Polytechnic. She teaches retailing management and is currently working within a research team examining the role of the accessories business in Hong Kong. She has also carried out research on imagery in retail promotion and the subject of store atmosphere.

Lucy Daly Ph.D., is a Research Business Manager for the Centre for Business Research at Manchester Business School and has worked on a variety of projects including business and market research, strategy development and product evaluation. She has published extensively and her PhD from the University of Manchester Institute of Science and Technology (UMIST)examined Supply Chain Management.

Anne Marie Doherty is Professor of Marketing at the University of Glamorgan. Previously, she held posts at the University of Wales, Aberystwyth and the University of Ulster. She holds a PhD in Marketing from the University of Strathclyde. Her research interests are in international retail marketing, particularly international fashion marketing and market entry mode strategy. Her work has been published in marketing journals such as the *European Journal of Marketing, Journal of Marketing Management* and the *International Marketing Review*. She has been guest editor of the *European Journal of Marketing* (2004), the *International Journal of Retail and Distribution Management* (2002) and the *International Marketing Review* (2000) on the topics of fashion marketing, retail franchising and the internationalisation of retailing respectively.

Ian Grime Ph.D., is a Principal Lecturer in Marketing at Manchester Metropolitan University Business School with research interests in brand identity. He completed his doctorate at Loughborough University and has published his work in the *European Journal of Marketing* on brand identity in the automobile industry.

Tony Hines B.A., Econ. (Hons), Ph.D., F.R.S.A., M.C.I.M. is Professor of Marketing at Manchester Metropolitan University Business School. He is Director of Doctoral Programmes and has research interests in supply chain strategies, marketing decisions, lifestyles, consumption and identity. He has led international consultancy assignments and funded research projects in these areas. He is the author of 16 books including *Supply Chain Strategies – Customer-Driven and Customer Focused* and *Management Information for Marketing Decisions* in addition to *Fashion Marketing – Contemporary Issues*, all published by Elsevier. Furthermore, he has authored and co-authored a number of academic journal articles most recently for the *European Journal of Marketing*, the *Journal of Marketing Management*, the *International Journal of Entrepeneurship and Management* and *The Textile Institute Journal*. He has also published a number of book chapters based on his research interests. Additionally, he has a number of international and prize-winning conference papers. He regularly contributes press commentary and is in demand as a commentator on contemporary marketing issues for both print and broadcast media.

Margaret K. Hogg is Professor of Consumer Behaviour and Marketing at Lancaster University Management School. She read Politics and Modern History at Edinburgh University, followed by postgraduate studies in history at the Vrije Universiteit, Amsterdam and then by an M.A. in Business Analysis at Lancaster University. She spent 6 years working in Marketing with K Shoes, Kendal. Prior to joining UMIST in September 1995, she completed a Ph.D. at Manchester Business School in Consumer Behaviour and Retailing. She subsequently worked as a Senior Lecturer in consumer behaviour at Manchester School of Management, UMIST before taking up her current post. Her research interests include consumer behaviour, retailing and marketing history. Her work has appeared in refereed journals, including the *Journal of Marketing Management*, the *European Journal of Marketing* and the *International Journal of Advertising*. She has presented papers at a number of international conferences, including US meetings of the Association for Consumer Research and the Society for Consumer Psychology.

Cynthia L. Istook is currently an Associate Professor, Department of Textile and Apparel Technology and Management at North Carolina State University. Dr Istook received her Bachelor's degree in Fashion Merchandising, Clothing, and Textiles from Texas Christian University in 1976. She worked for Sanger Harris (a Federated Department store) for almost 3 years in the management training programme as an assistant buyer and department group manager. Dr Istook obtained a Master's degree in 1989 and a Ph.D. degree in 1992 from Texas Woman's University. Her master's thesis research concerned the durability of Texcellana 80% Cotton–20% Wool fabric. Research for her dissertation was centred on Computer-Aided-Design (CAD) in the apparel industry. She has taught at Baylor University in Waco, Texas, the University of North Texas in Denton, Texas, and Texas Woman's University.

Tim Jackson is a Principal Lecturer in Marketing at the University of Arts, London College of Fashion responsible for leading research and teaching initiatives at Post Graduate level in Fashion Buying and Merchandising. His work both in retail management and in buying and merchandising for a number of leading fashion retailers, including, Dash, Jaeger and Burton, has allowed him to develop practical insights into the industry while conducting his academic research. Tim is co-author of the first UK text on fashion buying and merchandising with David Shaw, published by MacMillan in January 2001. The book has made a significant contribution to the study of fashion buying and merchandising in a UK context. More recently he has edited the *Fashion Handbook* with David Shaw published by Routledge in 2006. Tim is academically and professionally qualified in marketing, having gained an M.A. in Marketing and the CIM Diploma. He has undertaken considerable research into the fashion industry while based at the London College of Fashion. In addition to lecturing at the LCF, he has lectured at the University of Westminster and Surrey University. He is in demand as a regular contributor to radio and television programmes involved with fashion.

Christine Kratz is Head of the Academic Department of Marketing and Negotiation at the ICN Business School based in Nancy, France, which is part of the 'grandes écoles' of management bringing together the most prestigious French business schools. Christine Kratz holds a Master's degree in the Science of Management from the University of Nancy. As an Associate Professor at ICN, she is deeply involved in the Executive Center in the fields of lecturing and consultancy. The main themes she lectures on are marketing, innovation, design and product portfolio management. In order to create a tight link between lecturing and applied research, she has designed and led an ARTEM workshop – an innovative multidisciplinary approach bringing together students from the schools of business, engineering and art – in partnership with the French crystal producer DAUM. These workshops are intended to enable students to master change management through design and interdisciplinary thinking. Her most recent research in the field of Design is centred around sensorial and product configuration, particularly in the context of luxury marketing. She has conducted numerous studies in the sectors of champagne and crystal and has presented papers on these subjects at international conferences including *British Academy of Management* and *European Academy of Management*. She is currently working on a joint project with Professor Margaret Bruce of Manchester Business School conducting a comparative study of design strategies between UK and French companies.

M. C. Lam graduated from ITC in 1998. After graduation she worked in Next (Asia) Ltd as Assistant Merchandiser. She now works for the Hong Kong Government's Health and Environment Hygiene Department.

Beatrice Le Pechoux is currently a Post-Doc Research Assistant at North Carolina State University.

Trevor J. Little is currently Professor and Head of Department of Textile and Apparel Technology and Management at North Carolina State University. Professor Little received his Bachelor's degree in Textile Industries from the University of Leeds in 1971. He then went on to obtain a Ph.D. degree in 1974 from the University of Leeds. Professor Little's research interests include apparel manufacturing and management, production and assembly systems, design for manufacturability, automated manufacturing systems, handling systems, manufacturing simulation, human factors, technology development, and information technology.

Ruth Marciniak B.A. Hons, PgD, M.B.A., is a Senior Lecturer in Marketing and Retail Management at London Metropolitan University. She is currently completing her PhD thesis on e-commerce strategy planning processes employed by the UK fashion retail sector. Her research activities have provided her with the opportunity to access major UK fashion retailers. She has also published in the area of fashion retailing and e-commerce in refereed journals including the *International Journal of Retail and Distribution Management* and the *Journal of Fashion Marketing and Management*. She has presented academic papers at a number of national and international conferences, including EIRASS and EAERCD. In addition to lecturing at London Metropolitan University she has lectured at Manchester Business School and is an External Examiner at the University of Northumbria and the University of Paisley.

Christopher M. Moore is Professor in Marketing and Retailing at Heriot Watt University in Edinburgh. He is Director of the George Davies Centre for Retail Excellence. Previously, He was Professor in Marketing and Director of the Glasgow Centre for Retailing at Glasgow Caledonian University, Glasgow. He has published widely in the area of fashion marketing and the focus for his doctoral research was the international expansion of fashion retailers into the UK. He has consulted to a wide variety of fashion companies, ranging from Issey Miyake to Marks & Spencer. He is also a regular guest columnist on consumer issues for Emap media.

Lee Quinn B.A., M.Res., P.G.C.E., is a Lecturer in Marketing at Manchester Metropolitan University Business School. He was previously an ESRC supported Doctoral Researcher at Manchester Metropolitan University Business School. His research interests include managerial sensemaking, the discursive and linguistic construction of identity, and the development of philosophically grounded and methodologically critical research in the strategic marketing domain. These areas of interest largely emanate from his Ph.D. thesis in which he applied a social constructionist theoretical perspective to the study of market segmentation in a fashion-retailing context.

Martin Raymond is editor of *Viewpoint* magazine, a twice yearly trends, brands, intelligence and lifestyle predictions journal. He lectures in journalism and fashion lifestyle at the London College of Fashion, and is a regular contributor to *The Independent on Sunday* and BBC Radio 4's *Front Row* arts programme. He is also co-author of *100 Years of Change; Design and Style in the Twentieth Century* and creative director of The Future Laboratory.

Bill Webb is a Senior Lecturer in Marketing at the University of Arts, London College of Fashion and a member of the Management Research Group, as well as leading his own successful consulting firm. He has many years experience of working in the fashion industry and has held positions at senior level with responsibility for marketing. Bill was a main board director for Richards before it became part of the Arcadia Group and founding director of Management Horizons, a retail consultancy. Bill's research interests are related to branding, sizing, store location and e-commerce. He has recently worked with IBM as part of a small research team examining the impact of e-commerce on clothing retailers. He has published a number of papers related to fashion marketing in academic journals and at conferences, most recently at the University of California, Berkeley in the USA, and is a regular contributor to practitioner publications such as *Retail Week*.

Acknowledgements

Tony would like to thank Janice for giving her time, support and encouragement for this project.

Margaret would like to dedicate the book to Barbara, Chris, Thomas and Lydia Warren, Jasmine and Steve Glennon.

We would both like to thank Anna Fabrizio at Butterworth-Heinemann for her patience, and enthusiasm.

We are grateful to Delia Alfonso for her enthusiasm, encouragement and support for this project in its early stage and in bringing the first edition to fruition 2001.

Also many thanks to the contributors who have helped this project achieve its mission.

Finally, thanks to you the reader for choosing to spend your time reading our book we hope you find it interesting, motivating and useful.

Introduction

In this introduction to the second edition it is perhaps appropriate to reflect upon the impact of the first edition. The *European Journal of Marketing* editorial 38 (7) p744 commented that the first edition of *"Fashion Marketing"* made a significant contribution to a growing research agenda in the field. It has proved to be useful to a new generation of scholars and researchers developing their own research agendas in Fashion Marketing. It is to be hoped that the new edition will provide new ideas and stimuli for readers. The number of chapters has increased: (a) to reflect the changes in contemporary fashion markets; and (b) to address omissions identified by readers of the first edition. Some chapters that were included in the first edition have been replaced to bring the treatment of those topics up to date. Most of the chapters that appeared in the first edition have significant new content and some have been completely re-written to take account of contemporary issues of interest. This new edition has sixteen chapters whereas the first edition had twelve. There are completely new chapters on market segmentation; buying and merchandising; luxury brands; retail identity; approaches to research; supply chain strategies, structures and relationships; global markets and global supplies; and the international flagship stores of luxury fashion retailers.

Fashion is a global business. It is an exciting, dynamic and creative business. Fashion is about self-expression, emotion and identity. Fashion reflects *and* pushes cultural and social boundaries. The mix of aesthetic, technology and business makes fashion a special and fascinating industry. Fashion is big business and employs large numbers of people with different talents and skills to bring fashion apparel to the consumer. Designers, new product developers, textile producers, manufacturers, merchandisers, buyers, marketers, technologists, supply chain experts, logistics managers, strategists and retailers including front line customer service staff are all involved with delivering the best product to the marketplace in the fastest time, and at the most competitive price. The industry is concerned with every aspect of design, manufacture, marketing and distribution from concept to carrier bag. Overlaying this is the fact that these processes have to be managed through complex networks of suppliers, and the various intermediaries supporting production located throughout the world moving merchandise from producer to consumer. This is not easy – fashion changes constantly. The traditional seasons of spring, summer, autumn and winter may be less visible than they once were but they are still apparent, with frequent in-season changes. Colour, form, texture, label, etc. can be extremely short-lived. This makes forecasting, planning and marketing risky and complex.

The growth of the 'new economy' affects the structure of the fashion business. New dotcom companies offer fashion apparel via the Internet. But, are these operating as wholesalers or retailers? What 'added value' do they offer consumers? How do they deliver customer fulfilment and cope with distribution issues? Nonetheless, they pose a potential threat to the 'brick and mortar' retailers, in terms of being a new channel to market and, in many cases, offering cheaper prices for branded goods. The emergence of 'click and mortar' retailers – traditional retailers offering Internet sites – has stimulated Internet shopping. Boundaries between retailers, manufacturers and dotcom companies are becoming blurred. Alongside this re-organization of the industry, consumers are less loyal. Consumers do 'shop around' for the best deal, based on price, quality, convenience or brand awareness, but how they shop on the Internet for fashion is not predictable. It is in 'business to business' transactions where the new economy seems to be gaining a foothold. Ordering and shipping dyestuffs from Japan to factories in India, tracking the movement of goods as they are being transported from China to the UK and other similar business activities are where the e-commerce is beneficial. New partnerships and strategic alliances are being formed with e-commerce.

The 'old' paradigms of management thinking in the fashion industry are being challenged. Quick response, flexible approaches and the constant drive to offer innovative products to consumers have to be managed effectively. How can new design talent be spotted and given the opportunity to flourish? Fragmented markets make it difficult for retail marketers to identify prospective target markets and to segment customer groups. Retail organizations constantly renew and revitalize themselves and their identities through the science or is it the alchemy of marketing activities? Constant newness of design not simply in their products but in their store-designs, merchandising displays and theatrical approaches to retailing refresh their brand identities. Witness the variety of developments in the marketing of fashion merchandise through non-traditional outlets such as supermarkets and opportunities for expansion into different segments e.g. Reiss from men's wear into women's wear and from domestic to overseas markets. And yet there is still a place in the highly complex, competitive fashion market for the traditional or classic retail offering.

Since the first edition of this reader there have been important changes in the way retailers offer fashion to consumers. The phenomenon of 'fast fashion' in a retail context has become very important for many in the industry. However, although many retailers use the term 'fast fashion' it can mean different things to each organization. There has also been a rapid growth in supermarket fashion taking a larger market share. Many traditional retailers have felt the pinch as supermarkets have steadily eroded their markets particularly in categories such as children's clothing and leisurewear. Having said this it is now possible to pick up a man's two-piece suit for under £40 in your local supermarket. Ten years ago this would have been unthinkable. Fashion can be cheap and it can be expensive so why does this paradox exist? Fashion futures are influenced by new materials and advanced technologies. These will present new challenges and create new aesthetics and sensibilities. Seamless garments offer a comfortable fit; partly finished garments may be bought and then 'finished' by a local micro-manufacturer based at a local supermarket; dyeing a garment may be available at the 'touch of a button' and be another programme offered on a domestic washing machine. How can the needs of the 'green consumer' be met?

There are often press reports about exploitation in the industry. For example, clothing manufactured in the undeveloped parts of the world is exported to markets in the developed world to be sold at very high prices. Workers in these factories often exist on subsistence wages. Their employers are a part of a global supply network to satisfy demand in markets in the developed world. How can consumers be ethical in making fashion purchases?

This book covers the main themes that affect marketing in the fashion world. The first two chapters by Tony Hines outline the dynamics of the global fashion industry and the machinations of the supply chain. The shift of apparel manufacture to lower labour cost countries, for example in the Far East and Eastern Europe is shown and the importance of global brands is stressed. New approaches to supply chain strategy are discussed – the iceberg theory – is advanced to explain some of the problems in global sourcing strategies and the implications of e-commerce for supply chain management are mapped out. Margaret Bruce and Lucy Daly examine the challenges of fashion buying and merchandising in Chapter 3. Tony Hines and Lee Quinn turn their attention to market segmentation and its role in fashion marketing in Chapter 4 recognising consumer complexities and the challenges facing retailers. A number of problems with existing approaches to segmentation are discussed and a clear proposal is made to develop better theoretical understanding by broadening world-views acknowledging contributions and requirements of practitioners. Christopher Moore and Steve Burt embellish the theme of globalization in Chapter 5 with their focus on the problems fashion retailers face with expanding internationally. Chapters 6 considers retail brand marketing in fashion retail. William Webb identifies three issues that fashion retailers have to address: culture, strategy and operations. In Chapter 7 Margaret Bruce and Christine Kratz examine competitive marketing strategies of luxury brand retailers. Chapter 8 explores store image and atmospherics, Alice Chu and M. C. Lam discuss the situation in Hong Kong for fashion retailers. In Chapter 9 Tim Jackson describes the process of trend forecasting in the fashion industry. Chapter 10, by Beatrice Le Pechoux, Trevor Little and Cynthia Istook discusses innovation management and creativity within the fashion industry. They develop a Product Development Framework, which incorporates Consumer

Needs and links this with the requirement of retailers to have a stream of successful products. The next two chapters focus on identity. Negative self-identity is the theme of Chapter 11 by Emma Banister and Margaret Hogg. They note that the user images and stereotypes that accompany negative selves may explain why consumers reject fashion items and avoid shopping in certain retail environments. Tony Hines, Ranis Cheng and Ian Grime explore retail identities in Chapter 12 looking at desired and perceived identities in two specific cases involving fast fashion retail, Zara & Hennes and Mauritz. In less than a decade the world of electronic retailing has been created and it has become a significant growing channel of distribution for fashion merchandise. Ruth Marciniak and Margaret Bruce discuss who sells online, who buys on line, what makes a good website and they show how consumer value can be leveraged through E-tailing in Chapter 13. Christopher Moore and Anne Marie Docherty provide a number if insights into international flagship stores and luxury brands in Chapter 14. Capturing the zeitgeist Chapter 15 by Martin Raymond reveals different fashion marketing futures that are appropriate for the global world of fashion. The final contribution by Tony Hines discusses alternative approaches to research in fashion marketing and completes the 16 chapters in this edition.

1

Globalization: global markets and global supplies

Tony Hines

Introduction

This chapter provides an overview of the impact of globalizing markets and globalizing production centres throughout the world. In this context, it is essential to understanding the competitive landscape for this important international industry before examining some of the key themes and contemporary issues that consume time and effort of policy-makers, managers, consultants and researchers. The chapter begins by examining meanings of fashion markets and fashion marketing in the context of this text before examining in detail the changing business environment. Globalization is then explored through two key industries that underpin fashion markets: textiles and clothing. Structures and conditions that have caused the phenomenon of globalization are examined and it is defined before moving on to identify consequences for fashion markets. The interconnectedness of these markets and supply networks at both the local and global level is demonstrated through discussion of UK retail markets.

Fashion markets and fashion marketing

The textile, apparel (clothing)[1] and footwear industries are what many consider to be elements of a fashion industry. Textiles in the shape of home furnishings, fabrics, curtains, various upholstery, wall and floor coverings are considered by many to be fashionable items, as indeed are clothing and footwear. However, the term fashion can be used more broadly and cover a much greater range of goods. A glance at any contemporary style magazine would lead one to conclude that fashion could equally apply to food, housing, music, automobiles, perfumery and beauty products. Indeed, modern lifestyles and consumerism rely heavily on and are influenced by these wider fashion trends. Nevertheless, much of the focus for this book in terms of products and markets will remain with two important industries that underpin fashion markets: textiles and clothing.

World trade in textiles and clothing is around US $350 billion. Textile and clothing industries worldwide represented 7 per cent of total world exports in 2004. Between 1997 and 2004 clothing exports grew at 5.9 per cent and textiles at 3 per cent. This hides the disparities between different economies and the reliance placed on these industries. For example, in Bangladesh clothing represents 76 per cent of total exports, in Sri Lanka 51.6 per cent, Cambodia 80 per cent whereas in China it is only 11.9 per cent. Textile exports represents 47.7 per cent of Pakistan's total exports, China 6.3 per cent and Sri Lanka 4 per cent (ILO, 2005).

Employment figures range from an estimated 19 million people employed in Chinese Textile and Clothing Manufacture in 2004 up from 14 million in 1995 to 76,963 in Mauritius. Worldwide there are estimated to be 40 million people employed in these industries. The majority of people employed in the clothing sector are women. Although figures vary from country to country, it is estimated that over 70 per cent of all employment is in this industry is female.

There has been a declining trend in global employment in the clothing sector – from 14.5 million workers in 1990 to 13.0 million in 2000, partly as a result of a consolidation process of this production group and a more intensive use of capital. Likewise, employment in textiles declined from 19.7 million workers in 1990 to 13.5 million in 2000 (ILO, 2006). Nevertheless, both textiles and clothing manufacturing employment remain significant and in many developing economies it is the most important sector. In addition to the reported numbers employed directly there are significant numbers of indirect workers who rely on these industries. Table 1.1 indicates employment in clothing manufacture in selected countries between 1995 and 2005 and their relative importance to the particular country's economy as a percentage of manufacturing industry.

---

[1]Apparel is a term used by many US commentators and industry reports to describe the clothing industry. It comes from the French word for clothing. These terms may be used interchangeably in this book.

Table 1.1 Trends in employment and share of clothing as a percentage of manufacturing employment, selected countries; 1995–2005 *Source*: ILO (2005).

	Year	Employment	Share (%)	Year	Employment	Share (%)
Bangladesh[1]	1998	1,049,360	49.9	2004	2,000,000	n.a.
Cambodia	1995	–	n.a.	2005	250,000	38.2
China[1]	1995	14,710,000	6.2	2004	19,000,000	18.9
India	1998	398,618	5.0	2001	463,319	6.2
Pakistan[1]	1996	26,915	4.8	2001	2,300,000	42.9
Sri Lanka	1997	154,542	34.9	2000	165,388	34.2
Mexico	1997	72,660	5.2	2005	460,000	12.3
Guatemala	1997	66,800	n.a.	2005	104,464	23.0
Romania	1997	286,300	14.1	2002	403,400	25.3
Turkey	1997	142,554	12.6	2000	164,353	14.6
Mauritius	1997	69,423	65.6	2001	76,963	65.8
Morocco	1997	131,995	16.1	2002	176,894	17.8
Madagascar[1]	1999	83,000	44.9	2001	87,000	44.8

n.a. = Not available. – = Insignificant.

[1] Recent data from Bangladesh, China, Pakistan and Madagascar are for clothing and textiles. China's textiles and clothing share based on 2003 data. Manufacturing employment in 2003 based on estimation.

Sources: UNIDO: Industrial Statistics Database (INDSTAT) 2003 and 2005, Rev. 2 and 3; Cambodia: *Better Factories Cambodia Project,*China: *China Textile Industry Development Report 2005* for textiles and clothing and *China Statistical Yearbook 2004* for manufacturing employment; Pakistan: Textiles and clothing employment for 2001 from Institut Français de la Mode (IFM) et al.: *Study on the implications of the 2005 trade liberalization in the textile and clothing sector* (Paris, Feb. 2004). manufacturing employment from the Federal Bureau of Statistics; Bangladesh: Bangladesh Garment Manufacturers' and Exporters' Association (BMGEA) for 2004 data; Guatemala; Association Gremial de Exportadores de Productos no Tradicionales; Madagascar Ministry of Labour and Social Law.

Table 1.2 Employment in the USA (textile and clothing sector), seasonally adjusted (thousands) *Source*: ILO (2005).

	Jun. 04	Dec. 04	Jan. 05	Feb. 05	Mar. 05	Apr. 05	May 05	Jun. 05
Textile mills	239.3	233.2	231.5	230.1	228.7	225.5	225.4	224.7
Textile product mills	178.5	178.0	178.1	177.9	177.9	177.7	178.3	176.7
Apparels	285.9	271.9	269.3	267.2	262.8	262.2	258.5	256.0

Source: Bureau of Labour Statistics.

China, Pakistan and India have the largest number of people employed in the textile sector.

Employment in the US textiles and clothing sector (Table 1.2) fell by about 7.7 per cent from June 2004 to June 2005. Since quotas were lifted on 1 January

2005, about 25,000 jobs have been lost in the sector as a whole, most of them in apparel manufacturing.

World textile and clothing markets are truly international networks of supply and demand. If one considers human basic needs, food and clothing come near the top of the list. Food and clothing provide for our biological and physiological needs. They are amongst the oldest markets in the world. Europe has been a leading exporter of clothing in recent times. In 1980 the EU (15) had a world market share of exports equivalent to 42 percent of the total market for clothing but by 2003 this stood at around 26 per cent (WTO, 2004). During this same period China increased its market share from 4 per cent in 1980 to 23 per cent in 2003.

Table 1.3 illustrates the major regional flows of trade in clothing. The annual percentage change shows the shift in value by percentage year on year in the final two columns or over the period from 2000 to 2004 in the first column for annual percentage changes. Intra-European trade is by far the largest share at US $80.2 billion.

Table 1.3 Major regional flows in world exports of clothing, 2004 (Billion dollars and percentage)

	Value	Annual percentage change		
	2004	2000–2004	2003	2004
Intra-Europe	80.2	11	21	11
Asia to North America	45.9	5	11	10
Asia to Europe	30.9	8	19	13
Intra-Asia	29.7	5	12	16
South and Central America to North America	11.9	4	5	15
Commonwealth of Independent States (CIS) to Europe	1.1	9	14	15

Source: WTO (2005).

Table 1.4 shows the leading clothing exporting and importing regions and countries and their share of world markets in 2004. The EU 25, China and Hong Kong China are the leading exporters significantly higher than the others in the table. China together with Hong Kong China is the largest exporter. The EU 25 and the US are the largest importers of clothing products. China and Hong Kong China being relatively small as importers. This illustrates the large trade balance surplus for China. Earnings are significantly higher than expenditure.

Exports of textiles and clothing in the world in 2004 represented $195 billion and $258 billion respectively (WTO 2005).

Table 1.4 Leading exporters and importers of clothing, 2004 (Billion dollars and percentage)

	Value	Share in world exports/imports				Annual percentage change			
	2004	1980	1990	2000	2004	2000–2004	2002	2003	2004
Exporters									
EU (25)	74.92	–	–	27.0	29.0	9	6	18	9
Extra-EU (25) exports	19.13	–	–	6.9	7.4	9	4	13	11
China[a]	61.86	4.0	8.9	18.3	24.0	14	13	26	19
Hong Kong, China	25.10	–	–	–	–	1	−4	3	8
Domestic exports	8.14	11.5	8.6	5.0	3.2	−5	−10	−2	−1
Re-exports	16.96	–	–	–	–	4	−1	6	13
Turkey	11.19	0.3	3.1	3.3	4.3	14	21	24	12
Mexico[a,b]	7.20	0.0	0.5	4.4	2.8	−4	−3	−5	−2
India[c]	6.62	1.7	2.3	3.1	2.8	7	10	10	...
USA	5.06	3.1	2.4	4.4	2.0	−12	−14	−8	−9
Romania	4.72	...	0.3	1.2	1.8	19	17	25	16
Indonesia	4.45	0.2	1.5	2.4	1.7	−2	−13	4	8
Bangladesh	4.44	0.0	0.6	2.0	1.7	3	−7	13	0
Thailand[b]	4.05	0.7	2.6	1.9	1.6	1	0	1	12
Vietnam[b]	3.98	...	...	0.9	1.5	22	41	35	12
Korea, Republic of	3.39	7.3	7.3	2.5	1.3	−9	−8	−8	−7
Tunisia	3.27	0.8	1.0	1.1	1.3	10	4	1	20
Pakistan	3.03	0.3	0.9	1.1	1.2	9	4	22	12
Above 15	206.32	–	–	78.6	80.3	–	–	–	–
Importers									
EU (25)	121.66	–	–	39.9	45.0	10	7	19	14
Extra-EU (25) imports	65.86	–	–	20.9	24.4	11	7	20	15
USA	75.73	16.4	24.0	32.4	28.0	3	1	7	6
Japan	21.69	3.6	7.8	9.5	8.0	2	−8	11	11
Hong Kong, China	17.13	–	–	–	–	2	−2	2	7
Retained imports	0.17	0.9	0.7	0.8	0.1	−44	−16	−38	−83
Russian Federation[b]	5.46	–	–	1.3	2.0	19	27	25	13
Canada[d]	5.22	1.7	2.1	1.8	1.9	9	2	12	16
Switzerland	4.34	3.4	3.1	1.5	1.6	8	7	15	9
Korea, Republic of	2.75	0.0	0.1	0.6	1.0	20	38	13	8
Australia[d]	2.67	0.8	0.6	0.9	1.0	9	11	20	22
Mexico[a,b,d]	2.58	0.3	0.5	1.7	1.0	−8	−5	−9	−15
Singapore	2.06	0.3	0.8	0.9	0.8	2	7	8	6
Retained imports	0.56	0.2	0.3	0.3	0.2	0	18	−7	12
United Arab Emirates[b,c]	2.05	0.6	0.5	0.7	0.8	...	15	15	...
Norway	1.67	1.7	1.1	0.6	0.6	7	10	13	8
China[a]	1.54	0.1	0.0	0.6	0.6	7	6	5	8
Saudi Arabia[c]	1.03	1.6	0.7	0.4	0.4	...	6	13	...
Above 15	250.61	–	–	93.7	93.0	–	–	–	–

[a] Includes significant shipments through processing zones.
[b] Includes Secretariat estimates.
[c] 2003 instead of 2004.
[d] Imports are valued free on board (f.o.b.)
Source: WTO (2005).

The growing impact of China on world textile and clothing markets

China has an estimated 40,000 textile and garment manufacturing firms and 24,000 textile mills with 19 million people employed in textile and clothing manufacture and a forecast growth rate of 17 per cent per annum to increase its capacity further (WTO 2004, 2005 and World Bank Report, 2005). China's clothing imports into the UK stood at £1.7 billion in 2002 and they are expected to increase to £2.8 billion by 2005 when 20 per cent of all clothing purchases by UK consumers will have been made in China. China produced 20 billion garments in 2002 enough for each person on the planet to have four garments from China in their wardrobe. China had a positive textile and clothing trade balance with the rest of the world at $54.6 billion (US) with $50.4 being clothing and $4.2 being textiles. Perhaps it should be no surprise that the country with the most people is so dominant in a labour intensive industry such as clothing. Pure labour economics on the basis of supply and demand might lead us to conclude thus.

China's clothing exports to the USA stood at just around $9 billion in 1990, $25 billion in 1995 and they are forecast to rise to $70 billion by the end of 2005. This acceleration in growth is fuelled by the demise of the multi-fibre arrangement (MFA) quota system. Trade liberalization will also have the effect of lowering the price of goods by 46 per cent in the US market and by 42 per cent across the EU increasing further retail price cuts. The Chinese economy has grown fast over the past 20 years but average income is still only one twenty-fifth that of France and there are over 100 million people living in absolute poverty according to Oxfam (2005).

According to ILO (2005) China's clothing exports reached US $61.62 billion in value in 2004, while its import of fabrics, raw materials and textile machinery from other countries reached US $24.02 billion. China is the world's third largest textile importer, just behind the EU and the USA. The Chinese textile industry is the world's largest importer of raw cotton. China is also among the top importers of wool in the world (220,000 tons in 2004) and the world's largest importer of textiles machinery and parts (importing US $4.48 billion in 2004, of which 43.1 per cent, or US $1.95 billion, came from the EU).

India's expected growing share of the world market

India is also a beneficiary of the removal of the MFA and is expected to increase its share of the global textile business from 3 per cent to 15 per cent by 2010 according to the World Trade Organization (WTO). The textile industry in India employs 35 million people and accounts for nearly one-quarter of India's exports. The impact that trade liberalization will have may be illustrated by one company's (Matrix) reported expected growth from US $17 million turnover to around US $60 million by 2010 slightly lower than that expected for the Indian sector as a whole but nevertheless a significant increase. Indian cotton exports are predicted to grow from US $12 billion in 2005 to about US $40 billion by 2010. Indigenous experts are critical of the optimistic estimates and point to the threat of China's increasingly dominant position in world markets. Although they agree that there will be growth they argue that India must develop its logistics capability if it is to compete against China. This requires significant public investment in the road, rail and other transport infrastructure. Pakistan, Egypt and Turkey will also benefit from the expected growth of cotton exports as a consequence of the demise of the MFA.

Textile and clothing together represent 14 per cent of the country's total industrial production, nearly 30 per cent of total exports, and is the second largest employment generator after agriculture. Commentators predict that the end of quotas will increase India's current 4 per cent share in world trade in this sector and the creation of more than 1 million jobs between 2005 and 2010. It is a complex picture. India recorded a 28 per cent growth in textile exports for the period January to March 2005 in comparison with the same period the previous year. (ILO 2005).

MFA 1974–1994

The 30-year period preceding the introduction of the MFA in 1974 had been a period governed by the General Agreement on Tariffs and Trade (GATT). GATT was originally negotiated in the 1944 Bretton Woods Meeting to aid reconstruction of world economies after the 1939–1945 World War. The Uruguay Round marked the end of the 20-year agreement on textile and clothing quotas that were negotiated bilaterally and governed by the rules of the MFA. The MFA provided for the application of selective quantitative restrictions when surges in imports of particular products caused, or threatened to cause, serious damage to the industry of the importing country. The MFA was a major departure from the basic rules and particularly the principle of non-discrimination. On 1 January 1995 it was replaced by the WTO Agreement on Textiles and Clothing (ATC), which provided for a transitional process for the ultimate removal of these quotas by 1st January 2005.

The WTO ATC 1995–2004

The WTO stated that 'the ATC is a transitional instrument, built on the following key elements: (a) the product coverage, basically encompassing yarns, fabrics, made-up textile products and clothing; (b) a programme for the progressive integration of these textile and clothing products into GATT 1994 rules; (c) a liberalization process to progressively enlarge existing quotas (until they are removed) by increasing annual growth rates at each stage; (d) a special safeguard mechanism to deal with new cases of serious damage or threat thereof to domestic producers during the transition period; (e) establishment of a Textiles Monitoring Body (TMB) to supervise the implementation of the agreement and ensure that the rules are faithfully followed and (f) other provisions, including rules on circumvention of the quotas, their administration, treatment of non-MFA restrictions and commitments undertaken elsewhere under the WTO's agreements and procedures affecting this sector.'

The product coverage, listed in the Annex to the ATC, covers all products, which were subject to MFA or MFA-type quotas in at least one importing country. The MFA provided the teleoaffective structures (i.e. rules) under which the world markets for textiles and clothing trade needed to comply with during this period. However, like all rules the parties engaged in industry practice were constantly circumventing them both wittingly and unwittingly. When quotas were full in producing countries products were often moved to countries where quota was available for no other reason than to get around the rules of the MFA and later the ATC. This illustrates one key economic argument against protectionism which is it is often the cause and supporter of economic inefficiency and is wasteful of scarce resources. Table 1.5 illustrates how complex the agreement to free textiles and clothing from the MFA over the 10-year period was.

Table 1.5 Schedule for freeing textiles and garments products from import quotas

Step	Percentage of products to be brought under GATT (including removal of any quotas)	Percentage of products to be brought under GATT (including removal of any quotas)
Step 1: 1 Jan. 1995 (to 31 Dec. 1997)	16% (minimum, taking 1990 imports as base)	6.96% per year
Step 2: 1 Jan. 1998 (to 31 Dec. 2001)	17%	8.7% per year
Step 3: 1 Jan. 2002 (to 31 Dec. 2004)	18%	11.05% per year
Step 4: 1 Jan. 2005	49% (maximum)	No quotas left

(a) *Full integration into GATT (and final elimination of quotas)*
(b) *ATC terminates.*
The actual formula for import growth under quotas was: by *0.1 × pre-1995 growth rate* in the first step; *0.25 × Step 1 growth rate* in the second step and *0.27 × Step 2 growth rate* in the third step.

Source: WTO (2005).

The schedule for freeing textiles and garments products from import quotas (and returning them to GATT rules), and how fast remaining quotas had to be expanded. The example is based on the commonly used 6 per cent annual expansion rate of the old MFRA. In practice, the rates used under the MFA varied from product to product.

Ten countries most restricted by textile and clothing quotas, 2004 (quota impact indica

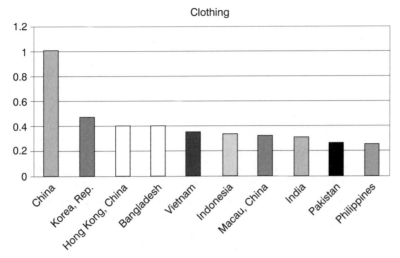

Figure 1.1 Impact of textile and clothing quotas. *Source*: ILO (2005).

Figure 1.1 shows exporting countries that were most affected by import quotas established by the USA, the EU and Canada. A quota impact indicator has been designed to measure the extent to which a country has actually used the quota to its limit and how many quotas have been applied to each country. China is most affected by quotas. In clothing, the Republic of Korea's exports were also significantly constrained by import quotas, followed by other main exporters from Hong Kong, China and countries in South Asia and South-East Asia. Other exporters affected by order of importance were Thailand (11th place), Malaysia (12th place), Taiwan China (13th place), Sri Lanka (16th place), Turkey (18th place) and Cambodia (20th place). Despite restrictions under quota clothing exports grew at an average rate of 5.9 per cent between 1997 and 2004. The textiles industry recorded an average growth rate of 3 per cent in the same period. Developing countries now account for half of world textile exports and almost three-quarters of world clothing exports.

Free trade vis-à-vis fair trade

Contemporary notions of free trade are anchored in Adam Smith's discussions within 'An Inquiry Into The Nature And Causes Of The Wealth of Nations' 1776. At this juncture some readers may wonder why I am discussing a text written over 330 years ago to discuss contemporary global fashion markets but as will be revealed in this discussion it is these discourses that greatly influence the way we think about notions of free trade. Free trade is a powerful concept, highly politicized and of great influence in contemporary society for the ways in which we structure markets and its impacts on the ways in which buyers and sellers in those markets act. Producers of textiles and clothing merchandise, retailers, consumers and governments are engaged in interactions subject to the laws of economic behaviours observed and reported by Smith (Sutherland, 1993). Thus the patterns of thought and behaviours constitute a link between structures, social practices and social action, it is the *'habitus'* concept that Bourdieu referred to (Jenkins, 2002).

Free trade is essentially a system of trading without recourse to tariffs, quotas and export subsidies. Prior to the introduction of free trade in Britain in the 18th century a system referred to as *'mercantilism'* had been adopted to afford certain goods protection from an open trading system which may have been damaging to the particular trade. Mercantilists were often merchants with a vested interest in promoting their own well-being but the overriding argument was simple their aim being to ensure that exports exceeded imports and hence the balance of trade was favourable. Maintaining the trade balance would require government intervention through a system of tariffs and quotas. The purpose was to ensure economic growth through such protection (Barber, 1967). Modern discourse revolves around free trade but the practices remain mercantilist. For example, the WTO is responsible for managing the international trading system and as such is charged with ensuring that trade barriers are removed in an orderly way. The purpose of such a managed system is to protect the interests of all parties who are members. However, there are numerous disputes about quotas, tarrifs and other protections between members states.

WTO rules in practice: an illustrative case

The following example is taken from my own research. One episode is reported here to illustrate how even the most rigid rules can be made flexible. It emerged in an interview with Mr. Dian Gomes, the CEO of Slimline; a key Sri Lanka clothing manufacturer employing 3,200 workers in 2002. Slimline is located in Pannala, a 2-hour journey from Sri Lanka's capital, Colombo. The Gan Island group which is referred to in the episode is a former Royal Air Force (RAF) site, situated at the southerly tip of the Maldives archipelago approximately 700 miles from Pannala. At the time of this research the MFA imposed particular rules and regulations with regard to export quantities on the Sri Lanka clothing industry. The MFA quota system established in 1974 by GATT and later superseded by the WTO was designed to support a number of developing export countries by guaranteeing an export market despite severe competition from more efficient producers who were controlled through quota. Sri Lanka was allocated quotas by categories of clothing allowing it to export into the developed world markets. This allocation had a significant impact on the development of the industry, growing from a zero base in 1979 to almost 50 per cent of national industrial production in 2001 (Central Bank of Sri Lanka, 2001). However, the labour intensive apparel sector faced heightened competition in particular from countries that underbid Sri Lanka's already low hourly labour costs of US $0.41 such as Bangladesh (US $0.31), China (US $0.28) and Pakistan (US $0.26) (SLAEA, June 2002). The MFA was in place throughout this research and was abandoned in January 2005 which subsequently further increased competition. The clothing buyers are almost exclusively located in Western countries with the US representing the single most important market for output from Sri Lanka, accounting for 65 per cent of total exports in 2001. The EU was the second largest market for exports at 30 per cent in 2001 with the UK capturing 64 per cent of EU exports (SLAEA, June 2002). Slimline produces underwear and lingerie for Marks and Spencer, Victoria's Secret, Lerner, Express, BhS and Hanro of Switzerland. In the following I present the episode as a quote from the interview in full:

Dian Gomes, CEO of Slimline:

> 'Last year [2002] with associated companies with quota [MFA export quota] in this category we had around 700,000 dozens of quota available to us because they did not produce in the category. Suddenly this year I ran short of quota because these associated companies were also producing garments in the 652 category [women's underwear] and I was not aware. I simply assumed we had sufficient quota to deal with our orders. This is how we had always operated and we didn't compare the notes. Come June I suddenly realised I am not going to get any support from my other associate companies because they need the numbers. So suddenly I've got stock for about $3 million in the warehouse and I need to do 200,000 dozens of panties and didn't have the quota. Now I would be dead in that kind of situation if I had to go back to the customer and say that you got all the materials in but I did not have the quota to do it. You might as well shut the plant down. So a unique threat got me to go in front of my workforce [of] 3,200 people. A week previously I had flown to the Maldives to the Gan Islands where we have another plant Linear Clothing. Next to that plant was an abandoned plant shut down by another Sri Lanka clothing company. Everything was perfect. The plant was perfect. Air conditioning worked and the general condition was good. I came back and I had to tell the people what had happened [with regard to quota and what the implications were]. So I said to the good native Singhalese [employees] this is the current situation. I need 300 volunteers to take a flight to the Gan Islands work for one year and to make it happen [overcome the quota restriction]. One thousand people volunteered because we had a culture or a mindset, which was aggressive enough to take on a challenge. Now what we did was send 350 [manufacturing] machines. Right the girl with her own machine. It's like a soldier having their own gun the tool for performance is a machine. Men, women and machine were loaded into the freighter [aeroplane] and they were all flown to the Gan Islands to deliver the goods. Then I suddenly realised a threat was turned into an opportunity. I had an opportunity to do a million dozens from Gan which is non-quota into the same customer. So all these 'screw-ups,' I would say, you need to convert into an opportunity and talk to the customer to do that. Then some of my

other colleagues went to other parts of the world and delivered them. Sometimes the fear of failing and the threat of the customer walking out make you do things that you never thought of before. Think out of the box. I think post 2005 a lot of Sri Lankans will think out of the box because if they don't they will be pushed over the cliff. Currently for us it is quota restriction that stops our growth.'

The quoted episode emphasizes that apart from profit, one overall end pursued in the Sri Lanka clothing industry is to cultivate and intensify the ties to the Western customers, largely by means of complying with and adapting to demands. This is also highlighted by Mahesh Amalean, Chairman of MAS Sri Lanka; the holding company of Slimline:

'The only way Sri Lanka can survive in the textile business against lower wage countries such as China and Brazil is if it moves up the quality ladder, and produces better goods for large global retailers. Racing to the bottom with Bangladesh is a no win game. The only way to build long-term relationships with large global brands is to produce higher and higher quality under improving working conditions. Retailers demand not only better prices and quality, but also better conditions for workers. Sri Lankan manufacturers must tie themselves to big Western Retailers to survive, and factory standards and compliance is one of the first things they ask about. They have to because their customers are asking them.'

One end (teleology) of the clothing practice is thus compliance and adaptation. This can be linked to the economic dependence on the income generated by garments (apparel) in Sri Lanka. The apparel sector is the largest single export earner and contributor to Sri Lanka's Gross National Product, employing more than 300,000 workers directly (SLAEA, June 2002). However, the propensity and ability to cooperate closely with Western companies and to adapt and comply accordingly is not merely a unique feature of the clothing practice that is born out of economic necessities. Instead it is deeply rooted in the culture and history in which it is embedded. Sri Lanka, known as Ceylon prior to 1972, has a long history of colonial rule since the 16th century by the Portuguese, the Dutch and the British only gaining independence in 1948. The Sri Lanka clothing practice is thus interspersed with more general customs, or styles with reference to adaptation to and compliance with foreign customs and demands, embedded in cultural–historic roots. Similarly, the large number of workers volunteering for the Maldives assignment cannot only be linked to economic considerations but also to the primary status of the family, clan or community and the significance of the collective over the individual that is part of many Asian cultures (Hofstede 2001), in particular Sri Lanka's dominant Buddhist community. The full case with a more detailed commentary about the practices is reported in Hines and Zundel (2006).

The globalization phenomenon

The term 'globalization' has been coined to represent the ways in which markets have converged throughout the world and the ways in which production poles have shifted geographically to satisfy global consumers. It is a trend. It is not to assume that we have arrived at the destination yet. It is rather that in this world economic system there are identifiable influences and trends that are developing new and emerging patterns of economic behaviour that can be clustered under one theme, hence, globalization. Other writers have defined the term in different ways which include claims that globalization is a defining feature of human society at the start of the 21st century (Beynon and Dunkerley, 2000). Globalization has a hegemonic role in organizing and decoding meaning of the world (Mattelart, 2000). Others define globalization as power relationships, practices and technologies that characterize and shape the contemporary world (Schirato and Webb, 2003). The convergence trends identified in markets, products, consumer behaviour and society encapsulate only one aspect of globalization the other perspective is one of growing divergence.

Approaching 20 per cent of the world population lives in poverty. This is defined by the World Bank as people living on less than US $1 per day. Supporters of globalization are believers they stress the benefits, they are optimistic and they see it as the culmination of revolutionary structural change. Sceptics view it as evolutionary change, continuing the trend of colonial expansion that was at its height between 1870 and 1914. They are more pessimistic than the protagonists. Indeed some commentators view the concept of 'laissez-faire' globalization as no more than a market liberal ideology denying the possibility of resource scarcity (Gray, 2002). The underpinning economic arguments of this approach are that new technology and the price mechanism will ensure the supply of resources in sufficient quantities. Thus 'necessity is the mother of invention' as one resource becomes scarce technology through innovation will ensure timely renewal of alternative resources to achieve the same end. This places an overriding emphasis on science and may explain the UK and other Western government's emphasis upon developing the scientific research agenda. For example, policies to develop alternative sources of energy focus upon conservation on one side of the equation and on investment in scientific research on the other to provide suitable alternatives. It is exemplified by Schumacher's statement that 'One of the most fateful errors of our age is the belief that "the problem of production" has been solved' (Schumaker, 1993).

International trade is nothing new. We have engaged in international trade since mankind has been able to walk even before the development of nation states, as we now know them. The 'Silk Road' from east to west is an early example of a supply route transporting products from where they were made in China through to the markets of Europe where they were sold.

Value creation, information and powerful brands

Companies who want to achieve dominance in their chosen markets are shaping competitive market landscapes throughout the world. These organizations want to leverage their powerful brands in order to transcend local domestic markets. These organizations need to satisfy their customers by understanding their needs better. They are developing powerful information systems that provide their owner(s) with vast databases that they can mine to identify market trends and utilize for targeted-promotional activity. New product innovation and creativity to leverage both the brand and the vast arrays of information that these global brand owners have at their disposal requires them to think in new ways about their business and the competition they face. Owning assets is no longer as important a consideration as owning customers. This belief is evidenced by recent trends to restructure organizations and to outsource many of the functional and traditional activities previously regarded as essential to the well-being of the organization. Efficient and effective supply chains are required to manage customer demand and brand operations. Customer relationship management is supported through e-commerce. Back-office support activities are more focused on satisfying customers and fulfilment of the marketing promise is critical to the organization's future. Organizations are focused on value creation rather than merely short-term profitability. Creating value streams is important as markets, marketing processes, supplier networks and operations throughout the globe become integrated through e-linkages in a complex chain moving parts, products and information around the network in order to meet customer demand. Different strategies are required to pursue this goal as time and distance shrink (Cairncross, 1998). Internet strategies present opportunities to integrate complex supply chains from concept design to store, and on to the final consumer. Markets and market opportunity may be both local and global. Organizations will be managing networks to leverage brand values and this can be achieved using global communication systems from anywhere in the world.

According to Dicken (1998, p. 283), the textiles and clothing industries were the first manufacturing industries to take on a global dimension and are the most widely dispersed industries across the developed and developing world.

> Indeed, global shifts in the textiles and clothing industries exemplify many of the intractable issues facing today's world economy, particularly the trade tensions between developed and developing economies. These changes continue to cause intense political friction.
>
> Dicken (1998, p. 283)

Globalization defined

Ghoshal and Bartlett (1998, p. 18) refer to companies that are multinational, international and global in the context of developing key strategic capabilities.

Multinational companies build a strong local presence through sensitivity and responsiveness to national differences. *International* companies exploit parent company knowledge and capabilities through worldwide diffusion and adaptation, whereas *global* companies build cost advantages through centralized global-scale operations. The turbulent economic environments of the 1970s and 1980s had led to a rash of reports, studies and recommendations to managers offering prescriptions to run their businesses more effectively in the new 'global' environment. As Ghoshal and Bartlett (1988, p. 21) comment, globalization became a term in search of a definition. *The term* was interpreted in a variety of ways and given new meanings. A *Newsweek (1986)* article offered advice to managers to reorganize and streamline their businesses by offering standard global products and managing operations through a centrally co-ordinated home office, a method, it was stated, that the Japanese had used for years. However, many managers and academics remained unconvinced by this formula of standardization, rationalization and centralization. It was true that for some Japanese companies the formula had worked, but it was equally true that for others it had not. Ghoshal and Bartlett (1998, p. 22) give a number of examples where the formula had failed in Japan for companies such as NEC and Kao, whereas some European and US companies not working to any prescribed formulas had been successful (Unilever, Ericsson and Procter & Gamble). The quest for global formulas was replaced by a search for fit. The dominant strategic requirement of the business and the development of strategic capabilities to match the requirement were seen as important. Nevertheless, the forces of global change act very differently on different industries, and any analysis of global strategy and organization must begin with an understanding of where the industry is placed.

Levy (1995, p. 353) provides an economic definition for the phenomenon of globalization as follows:

> To economists globalization is seen as the increasing internationalization of the production, distribution and marketing of goods and services.

Govindarajan and Gupta (1998, p. 3) provide a number of different ways to define globalization, but at the level of the specific country they refer to:

> The extent of the interlinkages between a country's economy and the rest of the world.

They state that the key indicators defining globalization of an industry are:

- the extent of cross-border trade within the industry as a ratio of total worldwide production;
- the extent of cross-border investment as a ratio of total capital invested in the industry;
- the proportion of industry revenue accounted for by companies that compete in all major regions.

In this respect, the textiles and clothing industries would score highly against all the criteria given. This will become clearer as the chapter unfolds. Dicken (1998, p. 5) views globalization as a complex of inter-related processes rather than an end-state, and in taking such a process-oriented approach he makes an important distinction between the processes of internationalization and globalization:

> Internationalization processes involve the simple extension of eco-
> nomic activities across national boundaries. It is, essentially, a quan-
> titative process which leads to a more extensive geographical
> pattern of economic activity . . . Globalization processes are quali-
> tatively different from internationalization processes. They involve
> not merely the geographical extension of economic activity across
> national boundaries but also and more importantly the functional
> integration of such internationally dispersed activities.

Globalization and its impact upon supplies

Globalization as a phenomenon is itself a consequence of competitive pressures that have led textile and clothing producers towards an endless search for ways to lower production costs, first through efficiency measures often internal to a single organization or network of organizations locked in a continuous supply chain. Second, the search for lower cost sources of supply shifts production and organizations controlling production to offshore locations throughout the globe, where conditions are more favourable than in the home market where the products will be sold and consumed. Often, these global shifts have a devastating impact upon domestic markets, where production jobs are lost, investment declines and the trade balance worsens. Investment declines not simply as a consequence of production erosion, but also in relative terms for those organizations that remain locked into industrial decline, because investors and governments are unwilling to take the financial and political risks that investment in the future requires. This reduction in investment is a consequence of perceived increasing uncertainties.

For retailers, the future requirement that they become large is predominant in the 'psyche' of major retail groups. Being large when markets are saturated in domestic economies requires retailers to develop beyond their own geographical boundaries. For the very large retailing groups it is a matter of who can get to the future first. Who can dominate market share. These large retail groups have enormous purchasing power and are able to extract economies of scale from their operations and economies of scope from their existing and developing supply chains. Globalization is not only identified through economic shifts, but also through cultural and social change that has been hastened by rapid communication and transportation infrastructures. Consumer behaviour has changed as markets have converged. Consumer behaviour patterns are also shifted not simply by consumers themselves, but by the professional purchasing and procurement officers of retailing groups who exert enormous influence over consumer choice. For example, designers, range selectors, sourcing decisions and decisions about what merchandise to stock or replace will paradoxically limit consumer choice. Adopting an integrated marketing approach is a necessary condition to achieving consumer satisfaction. Supply chain structures, strategies and processes are interdependent upon and a corollary of consumer-demand patterns identified through market intelligence and marketing information. Supply chains are in effect the corollary of demand chains.

The phenomenon of globalization, conditions that give rise to it, and shape the structure, strategies and consequences are probably more transparently evident in the textile and clothing industries than in many other sectors. Markets from Manchester to Manchuria and suppliers from Singapore to Sacramento are subject to the phenomenon of global forces and global shifts. This is what makes fashion markets and fashion marketing an exciting area to study.

The textile and clothing industries are both international and global in nature. It is clear that by any current definition of globalization these industries qualify. Let us now turn attention to the place of the UK within this global market and first examine market definition. For example, how do we define markets and what implications does this have for what we know about them?

Market definition

Standard Industrial Classification (SIC) codes are used by the Department of Trade and Industry within the UK to define the scope of an industry. This is done according to product characteristics. The SIC codes were redefined in 1992, making some statistical comparisons to earlier periods more problematic, since some codes were merged and aggregated differently. SIC(92) 18 encompasses the various sectors making up the UK Apparel Industry (DTI, 1998). Companies that comprise the industry tend to specialize in a sector: menswear, ladieswear, childrenswear, knitwear, lingerie, street fashion, designerwear or accessories (scarves, ties, hats and gloves). SIC codes such as those used by the UK government are important and provide a mechanism for gathering statistics and supplying information about an industrial grouping. Definitions about the types of organizations comprising the group are important if accurate statistical data are to be available. Similarly, in other countries there are similar mechanisms for gathering statistics relating to these industries. Trade bodies also gather statistics about the industry and they too use government data. For example, the British Clothing Industry Association (BCIA), The National Textile Center (US), American Apparel Manufacturers Association and Korean Federation of Textile Industries, to name but a few organizations. Statistical data are useful for making comparisons between different competing countries comprising an industry, although one has to be careful in drawing comparisons 'like with like'. It has already been stated that there may be difficulty in comparing data from different time periods when classification codes change. However, it is also the case that it is difficult drawing comparisons across different countries or regions of the world when the definitions of firms comprising the industrial groupings differ. Furthermore, it may also be difficult when statistical data collection methods differ and estimates become less accurate.

Large retailers and their influence on trade

Fortune 500 lists leading corporations annually in 2004 the largest US corporation was Wal-Mart Stores with annual turnover of US $288,189 million up 9.6 per cent on 2003 when it was also the largest US corporation. It had annual profits of over US $10,267 million in 2004. The company has 3,500 stores in the US alone and each store employs as many as 500 workers per store, and handles a rotating inventory of 100,000 plus items, delivered by a 6,300 fleet of trucks travelling over a billion miles in a year from 110 distribution centres. Wal-Mart is listed as general merchandising store meaning that it sells mixed ranges of clothing, food and home-ware. It is nevertheless, the largest seller of clothing by volume and value within the USA. The nearest competitors in the category are Target (US $49,934 million) ranked 27, Sears-Roebuck US $36,099 million ranked 45 and JC Penney US $25,678 million ranked at 74. To give some idea of how enormous the company is Nordstrum with US $7,131 million and SAKS with US $6,437 million are ranked 294 and 320, respectively. Fortune 500 also identifies fastest growing industries by revenue growth and profit growth. Apparel was number 32 in the list of fastest growing industries by the revenue measure and 19th by profit measure. The best 5 and 10 year return-on-investment list showed apparel ranked 12th and 6th respectively. It is worth noting that Asda-Wal-Mart the UK holding of Wal-Mart became the largest retailer of clothing in the UK by volume in 2004 taking over the number one position from Marks & Spencer who still retained the number one position by value.

Clothing sales in the UK for 2003 and 2004 as shown in Table 1.6.

Table 1.6 Clothing sales in the UK for 2003 and 2004

Retail sales £ millions	2003	2004
All retail sales	212,293	221,807
Annual % change	2.4	4.5
All non-food retail sales	112,332	117,434
Annual % change	1.5	4.5
Clothing specialists' sales	**27,464**	**28,792**
Annual % change	5.4	4.8
As % all retail sales	12.94	12.98
As % of non-food retail sales	24.45	24.52

Source: Adapted from CSO & Mintel 2005.

Clothing specialist sales represents 12.98 per cent of total retail sales in 2004 and 24.52 per cent of the non-food retail sales. The UK clothing specialist sector at retail values is worth around US $40 billion in 2004. To put it another way it is just above the Sears-Roebuck turnover and just below Target turnover in our listing of Fortune 500 retailers. If the UK specialist clothing industry comprised a single retail group it would come in at around 35 in the list of large US corporations. The UK industry represents about 14 per cent of Wal-Mart's turnover in the same financial year.

All UK consumer spending in 2000 stood at £603 billion and clothing accounted for 5.15 per cent. The total market for clothing was £31 billion. In 2004 the market for clothing had grown to £36.96 billion and all consumer spending had risen to £726 billion and now represented 5.09 per cent of consumer expenditure. All retail sales had risen from £186.65 billion in 2000 to £221.81 billion by 2004 clothing had remained fairly stable as a proportion at 16.6 per cent during the period. It is worth noting that the footwear market adds a further £5.95 billion to clothing in a total market for clothing and footwear of nearly £37 billion in 2004.

Table 1.7 indicates the relative fall in prices of clothing and footwear over a 10-year period from 1995 to 2004 when simultaneously prices for all goods have risen. Looking at a base year 1996 all prices rose by 11.2 per cent while clothing and footwear fell 25.3 per cent.

Table 1.7 The relative fall in prices of clothing and footwear from 1995 to 2004

Year	All price index	Clothing and footwear index
1995	97.6	103.3
1996	**100.0**	**100.0**
1997	101.8	97.5
1998	103.4	93.8
1999	104.8	88.8
2000	105.6	82.3
2001	106.9	76.2
2002	108.3	70.7
2003	109.8	68.0
2004	111.2	64.7

Source: 'Consumer Trends' CSO (2005).

UK retail structure

There are a number of different retail formats through which fashion is sold within the UK. The relative importance of these formats is illustrated by the data displayed in Table 1.8. While clothing multiples have maintained their market share as a percentage of the sales volume at near to 18 per cent it is significant that discounters represent the major sales channel approaching 24 per cent and perhaps more significantly the fastest growing channel is

Table 1.8 Data of different retail formats sold in UK

Total clothing retailer shares – sales volume (%)	2003	2004	2005
Clothing multiples	17.1	17.8	17.6
Clothing independents	4.5	4.3	4.3
General stores	19.1	17.6	16.7
Dept stores	5.0	4.7	4.6
Mail order	5.3	4.7	4.2
Discounters/C&C	23.7	24.2	23.3
Sports shops	4.8	4.8	4.9
Supermarkets	14.3	15.9	19.4
Others	6.2	6.0	5.0
	100.0	100.0	100.0

Source: Hines (2006). From composite data.

supermarkets having over taken clothing multiples in 2005 and second only to discounters. The implications are considerable. Supermarkets and discounters together now account for nearly 43 per cent of the total volumes sold in 2005. This might suggest a number of possible alternative plausible explanations. For example, has fashion become less important than price in the mind of the consumer? Well possibly it has in terms of consumer expectations. Perhaps consumers simply expect better value for their money and the discounters and the supermarkets present that option. Alternatively, perhaps discounters and supermarkets are competing not simply on price but perhaps they are meeting the needs of consumers by introducing more fashionable clothes but at more affordable prices by exercising their retail muscle to achieve purchasing economies that they are able in part to pass on to consumers. Whatever the explanation it is having an impact upon other retail channels as they struggle to compete particularly mail order, department stores and general stores.

UK retail market size and market shares

The most influential retail organizations in the UK clothing sector in terms of market shares is given in Table 1.9.

Companies owned by Philip Green listed in the table account for 7.9 per cent of the market in 2005. Green's clothing empire is worth more than the three leading supermarket chains together, almost worth all the department stores together and approximately 75 per cent of the leading clothing retailer by value Marks and Spencer. Supermarkets are an interesting market development in the past 5 years since the first edition of this book was written they have increased their market shares consistently. Asda now part of Wal-Mart with their George offer in particular, Tesco with Cherokee and

Table 1.9 Market share as a percentage of sales values

Market shares (%)	2003	2004	2005	04 versus 05
Clothing multiples	**27.3**	**29.0**	**29.2**	**0.2**
Dorothy Perkins	1.5	1.5	1.3	−0.2
Evans	1.3	1.2	1.1	−0.1
Burtons	1.3	1.1	1.0	−0.1
Top Man/Top Shop	1.6	1.7	1.8	0.1
New Look	2.2	2.0	2.1	0.1
Next	4.8	5.4	6.1	0.7
The Gap	0.9	1.1	0.9	−0.2
River Island	1.1	1.2	1.3	0.1
Clothing independents	**10.1**	**9.4**	**10.1**	**0.7**
General stores	**18.1**	**17.6**	**16.8**	**−0.8**
Bhs	2.9	2.8	2.7	−0.1
Littlewoods	1.6	1.3	1.3	0.0
Marks & Spencer	12.8	12.7	12.2	−0.5
Woolworth	0.8	0.8	0.7	−0.1
Department stores	**8.8**	**8.4**	**8.7**	**0.3**
Debenhams	3.5	3.7	3.8	0.1
House of Fraser	1.6	1.2	1.3	0.1
John Lewis	0.9	0.9	1.1	0.2
Total share of market	**64.3**	**64.4**	**64.8**	**0.4**
Mail order	**7.8**	**7.0**	**6.6**	**−0.4**
Discounters/C&C	**11.2**	**11.5**	**11.2**	**−0.3**
Bon Marche	0.8	0.9	0.8	−0.1
Peacocks	1.0	1.1	1.1	0.0
Primark	1.5	1.7	1.7	0.0
TK Maxx	1.0	1.2	1.4	0.2
Matalan	3.6	3.6	3.4	−0.2
Sports shops	**7.6**	**7.3**	**7.4**	**0.1**
Supermarkets	**5.1**	**5.7**	**6.6**	**0.9**
Asda	3.1	3.3	3.6	0.3
Tesco	1.4	1.8	2.2	0.4
Sainsburys	0.2	0.3	0.4	0.1
Total share of market	**31.7**	**31.5**	**31.8**	**0.3**

Source: TNS 2005 (data for 52 weeks ending 9th January).

Sainsbury with Tu have all developed their own successful clothing brands. Sainsbury although small relative to both Asda and Tesco have doubled their market share by value in 2 years and proportionately are growing faster than the other two supermarkets by this measure. However, interestingly it is both Tesco and Asda-Wal-Mart that have grown volumes at a faster rate than any other organization in clothing retail. Asda's share of the market by volume has increased from 7.1 per cent in 2003 to 9.2 per cent in 2005. In the same period Tesco increased its volumes from 4.1 per cent to 7 per cent.

The growth of supermarket fashion

During the past 5 years the phenomenon of supermarket fashion has emerged as a significant market trend in the UK. Why should this be the case?

Supermarkets were previously regarded as a place to buy basic clothing often selling socks, underwear, limited offers on shirts, T-shirts, women's casual tops own brand jeans and limited ranges of children's clothing often to capture particular markets like back to school. Since the first edition of this book in 2001 the landscape for clothing has changed and supermarkets have captured a small but growing significant market share from traditional clothing outlets. Three major players have grasped the opportunity of growing supermarket fashion including accessories (jewellery, bags, gloves, hats and shoes): Asda, Tesco and Sainsbury (in order of importance) putting investment into finding ways of taking more money from the same consumer base. As high street stores wrestled with their identities in the minds of consumers focusing their efforts on branding and brand development many consumers were becoming more interested in how they could become 'fashion cheats' buying some more expensive items and mixing them with lower priced disposable fast fashion purchased at low price points. For the consumer there is no longer the stigma attached to buying fashion in a supermarket. Consumers know and like a bargain when they see it. The 'fashionistas' and fashion snobbery hasn't completely disappeared and there are some consumers who would not want to buy or at least be caught out buying in a supermarket. Perhaps the latter point being more important than the former. The one fact that becomes clear from Tables 1.10 and 1.11 is that supermarkets are increasing their volume share at a much faster rate than their value share and this means in simple terms that they are selling more for less offering consumer's good prices.

Table 1.10 Supermarket share of clothing market % sales volume

Supermarket shares	2003	2004	2005
Asda	7.1	7.6	9.2
Tesco	4.1	5.3	7.0
Sainsburys	1.0	1.0	1.0
	12.2	13.9	17.2
Other supermarkets	2.1	2.0	2.2
All supermarkets	14.3	15.9	19.4

Supermarket share of the clothing market by volumes has increased significantly over the 3 years 2003–2005. Tesco increased volumes by more than 70 per cent and Asda-Wal-Mart by 30 per cent. Sainsbury maintained their volumes at 1 per cent. A number of smaller supermarkets combined account for around 2 per cent by volume. In value terms supermarkets accounted for nearly 7 per cent of the market in 2005 up 2 percentage points on the 2003

Table 1.11 Supermarket share of clothing market % sales value

Clothing sales by value	2003	2004	2005
Asda	3.1	3.4	3.7
Tesco	1.4	2.0	2.3
Sainsburys	0.2	0.3	0.3
	4.7	5.7	6.3
Other supermarkets	0.4	0.3	0.3
All supermarkets	5.1	6.0	6.6

Source: TNS.

figure. Some of the biggest losers in the rise of the supermarket as a serious clothing competitor have been some of the major high street specialist names like The Gap, Evans, Burtons and Dorothy Perkins. The rapid growth of some of the discounters has also been halted with Matalan, Bon Marche and to a lesser extent Primark all feeling the chill wind of supermarket competition in some categories. Marks and Spencer, Woolworths, Littlewoods and C&A have also lost ground in some categories to the growth of the supermarket. Both C&A and Littlewoods withdrew from the UK retail clothing market in 2002 and 2003 respectively. Independent retailers have also lost out in the rise of supermarket fashion. Supermarkets have in many respects taken a fresh look at where they can extract value from their existing customer base. They have then set about the task with the same efficiency they apply to sourcing and procurement of most other products.

The average age of the supermarket consumer buying women's clothing in the UK is between 35 and 55 years but this does not mean that people younger or older are excluded. One significant trend identified in the last few years is the notion of 'perceived age' as opposed to chronological age. People over 50 years old often have a much lower self-perceived age and this influences purchasing behaviour. It would have been unthinkable just 20–30 years ago for mothers shopping for clothes with their daughters for fashion-wear, but today this is not so. Similarly, the increasingly active older person is buying more casual wear for holidays and various activities they engage in. None of this has gone unnoticed by supermarket buyers and merchandisers keen to fill their increasingly larger retail spaces with more non-food ranges that potentially offer greater profitability.

Figure 1.2 illustrates the average age profile of customers in the UK Womenswear retail sector and the average price points (indexed). For example John Lewis customers are aged between 50 and 60 years and an average price index just under 2.1 relative to H&M customers average age just under 30 years and an average price index around 0.7. It is possible to profile particular patterns from such data. This type of data is used to segment fashion markets with the aim of targeting marketing communications.

This section has given an overview of the UK retail clothing sector and demonstrated its interconnectedness to world markets through sourcing and

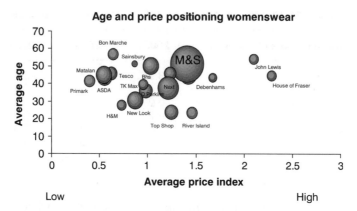

Figure 1.2 Average age and price point positioning. *Source*: Hines 2006.

purchasing strategies adopted by large retail organizations. These topics are dealt with further and in more detail in the next two chapters. However, it is worth examining briefly the impact of global sourcing strategies in the context of the removal of quota restrictions.

Global production networks: global sourcing

Prior to the removal of the ATC quota restrictions in January 2005, the sourcing of clothing was mainly influenced by quotas held in the sourcing country and availability of raw materials was a secondary consideration. Now that quotas are removed the availability of raw materials and a country's capacity to process and transform them into product will become more important. Vertical integrated production of textiles and clothing will provide an important comparative advantage to clothing exporting companies and countries. The vertical integration will have to be either real or 'virtual' if the country or enterprise concerned is to be able to develop national or international partnerships to increase supply chain efficiency and satisfy the quick response requirement. Rapidly expanding 'full package' sourcing solutions deliver speed to market. They usually involve all stages from initial concept, product development ending with the delivery of finished products. New global supply networks are being established by many of the larger savvy supply organizations with full packaged sourcing in mind. These global organizations want to manage all operations in the very way that Li and Fung pioneered. Essentially the retail buyer goes to the full package operator who determines appropriate suppliers (raw materials, components, manufacture, logistics, quality services, pre-retail services including labelling and packaging) according to price, quality and capacity. For the retail buyer they only have to deal with one organization and the full package sourcing organization deals with the co-ordination problems of the various suppliers.

As a consequence of this trend some major retailers and brand names have already announced a drastic reduction in the number of their supplying countries and partners. For example, Gap, which sources in 50 countries, have also indicated that in the future they will be able to choose their suppliers more freely and more carefully and to develop partnerships with them, focusing in particular on the improvement of labour practices (ILO, 2005).

Summary

This chapter has given the reader an overview of some of the complexities and insights into the interconnectedness of your local high street retail stores with the global economy. It began by defining fashion markets and fashion marketing. It discussed the relative importance of textile and clothing manufacture in the context of the world economy. Importance measured by size of regional and country trade flows, employment and individual country earnings from exports and the cost of imports. It moved on to examine the impact of China with its phenomenal capacity to produce textiles and clothing. China's growth rate as the leading exporter is a cause for concern for many other manufacturing countries that were previously protected under quotas but now the gloves are off, in the battle for markets worldwide. India too is of great importance in this market place. The demise of the controlled market under WTO rules was discussed in some detail and an example was given to illustrate how rules, in any case, are often circumvented. Globalization as a phenomenon was discussed in detail and illustrated the different perspectives that various commentators have towards a concept of globalization. Interconnectedness of the global to the local domestic economy of the UK retail sector was then examined. Particular trends were discernable which have come into being since the first edition of the book such as the rise of supermarket fashion and its growing importance. Finally the connection was made to global sourcing and the trend towards developing global production networks. Importantly these networks are increasingly managed by 'full package sourcing' organizations external to the purchasing organization (it is an outsourced function). The next chapter moves on to discuss supply chain strategies, structures and relationships in this connected world.

References

Barber, W. J. (1967). *A History of Economic Thought*. Harmondsworth: Penguin.
Beynon, J. and Dunkerley, D. (2000). *The Reader*. London: Athlone Press.
Cairncross, F. (1998). *The Death of Distance*. London: Orion Business Books.
Central Bank of Sri Lanka (2001). *Central Bank Report*. Colombo: Sri Lanka.
Dicken, P. (1998). *Global Shift*. London: Paul Chapman.
DTI (1998). *The UK Clothing, Footwear and Textile Industry An Overview*. London: Department of Trade and Industry.

Ghoshal, S. and Bartlett, C. A. (1998). *Managing Across Borders The Transnational Solution*. London: Random House Business Books.

Govindarajan, V. and Gupta, A. (1998). Setting a course for the new global landscape. *Financial Times*, 30 January, Section 1, 35.

Gray, J. (2002). *False Dawn: The Delusions of Global Capitalism*. 2nd Edn. London: Granta.

Hines, T. and Zundel, M. (2006). Notions of practice: the case of the Sri Lanka Textile industry. In *The Second Organization Studies Summer Workshop: Return to Practice: Understanding Organization As It Happens*, Mykonos.

Hofstede, G. (2001). *Culture's Consequences: Comparing Values, Behaviors, Institutions, and Organizations Across Nations*, 2nd edition. Thousand Oaks: CA, Sage.

ILO (2005). *Promoting Fair Globalization in Textiles and Clothing in a Post MFA Environment*. Geneva; ILO.

ILO (2006). *Global Employment Trends*. Geneva: ILO.

Jenkins, R. (2002). *Pierre Bourdieu*. Revised Edition, London: Routledge.

Levy, B. (1995). Globalization and regionalisation: toward the shaping of a tripolar world economy? *The International Executive*, July/August, **37** (4), 34971.

Mattelart, A. (2000). *Networking the World 1794–2000*. Minneapolis MN: University of Minnesota Press.

Newsweek (1986). Rebuilding Corporate Empires: A New Global Formula 14 April.

Oxfam (2005). Press Release EC decision to block Chinese clothing is bad for development Oxfam press release, 6 April 2005.

Schirato, T. and Webb, J. (2003). *Understanding Globalization*. London: Sage.

Schumaker, E. F. (1993). *Small is Beautiful: A Study of Economics as if People Mattered*. 2nd Edn., London: Vintage.

SLAEA (2002). *Five Year Strategy for the Sri Lankan Apparel Industry*. Colombo; Sri Lanka: Sri Lankan Apparel Export Association.

Sutherland, K. (Ed.) (1993). *Adam Smith Wealth of Nations*. Oxford: Oxford University Press.

TNS (2005). *Supermarket Clothing Statistics*. London, TNS.

World Bank Report (2005). *Annual Report*. New York, World Bank.

WTO (2004). *International Trade Statistics*. New York, WTO.

WTO (2005). *International Trade Statistics*. New York, WTO.

2

Supply chain strategies, structures and relationships

Tony Hines

'Supply chain management is seen as a critical factor in managing contemporary fashion businesses' (Hines 2001b). Probably even more so today than it was in 2001 when the first edition of this book appeared.

This chapter examines supply chain strategies, structures and relationships. It does so in the context of the international fashion industry and the developing concepts and meanings of supply chain management. The emergence of the supply chain as a focal point for research, study and to develop both knowledge and a better understanding of the industry dynamics has developed further since I wrote about globalizing supply chains in the first edition of the book (Hines, 2001a; 2001b). This chapter begins with the antecedents for supply chain management. It traces the roots back to operations management, economics of production and later the emergence of supply chain concepts within the discipline domains of marketing and strategy all of which are influenced by and have influenced the contemporary views of what supply chains and supply networks are in practice.

Supply chain strategies per se are more a recent phenomenon and although historically, these may have been implicit in managerial thinking today they are more explicit and have become an important feature of managing organizational systems that span boundaries of any single organization. Supply chain structures are an important element of supporting the strategies. Arguments prevalent in the early strategic management literature as to which comes first, strategy or structure are as relevant today in a supply chain context as they were nearly 50 years ago in strategic management (Chandler, 1962). For example, if the strategy is to achieve supply flexibility then what kind of supply chain structure is required? In formulating strategies and in developing appropriate structures to support strategies it becomes apparent that relationships are a further important consideration.

Antecedents of supply chain management

Supply chain management was a phrase first coined in the early 1980s to describe the range of activities co-ordinated by an organization to procure and manage supplies (Oliver and Webber, 1982). Initially, the term referred to an internal focus bounded by a single organization and how they sourced and procured supplies, managed their internal inventory and moved goods onto their customers (Macbeth and Ferguson, 1990). The original focus was later extended to examine not simply the internal management of the chain (Harland, 1995). It was recognized that this was inadequate and that the reality in managing supplies meant that supply chains extended beyond the purchasing organization and into their suppliers and their supplier's supplier (Christopher, 1992). It is recognized that there may be tiers of suppliers. Additionally it is recognized that the organization may have a customer who has other customers where their supplies are incorporated into other products or bundled in a particular way to provide a different product.

Four main descriptions of the *term supply chain management* have been reported in the literature (Harland, 1995) which are:

1 The internal supply chain integrating business functions involved in a flow of materials and information from the point of entry to a business to the point of exit.
2 The management of a dyadic or two party relationship with immediate suppliers.
3 The management of a chain of businesses including a supplier, the supplier's supplier, a customer and the customer's customer and so on.
4 The management of a network of interconnected businesses involved in the ultimate provision of products and services required by the end customer. (*Note*: the word constellation and a constellation diagram has been used by some to depict this relationship.)

A useful contemporary working definition of a supply chain is:

> 'The supply chain encompasses all activities associated with the flow and transformation of goods (products and services) from initial design stage through the early raw materials stage, and on to the end user. Additionally, associated information and cash flows form part of supply chain activities.'
>
> (Hines, 2004)

There are a number of different perspectives we can observe in relation to the development of the concept of supply chain management, as we understand it today. The first and earliest modern management approach to managing supply chains was clearly internally focused on improving productivity. The second wave of development was also mainly internally focused and an extension of the first concern with productivity to improve operations. The third wave developed in the transport and distribution literature concerned with moving goods efficiently and this is now mainly synthesized and reported in the logistics literature. The first three perspectives of managing supply chains concern themselves with efficiency and search for ways to improve efficiency. Latterly supply chains have been viewed as demand chains and the focus has shifted from the supplier towards the customer and what the customer requires. Within this latter view it has been recognized that the network metaphor and nomenclature with its non-linear perspective may be better suited than that of a chain.

Supply networks have developed, become more complex and as a consequence so too the boundaries of organizations have become less discrete and somewhat blurred (Barney, 1999). Some commentators have gone further to suggest that this blurring of boundaries may mean that it is not organizations that are in competition any more but rather supply chains (Christopher, 1996). Hitherto functional structures have become historical straightjackets rather than practical functional divisions and 'functional silos' have restricted intra-organizational and inter-organizational developments necessary to compete in the modern business environment (Slack et al., 2001).

Supply chains as a means of improving productivity of the firm

The earliest concerns of management were focused on improving productivity of the single firm. This strand of management thought was developed in what we now recognize as 'scientific management' and early practices were observed in the Ford Automobile plant in the USA (Taylor, 1911). Firms were seen as bounded systems in the economics literature. Within these systems it is desirable to maximize outputs from a given set of resource inputs. Hence productivity is an important economic measure of performance. One only has to view current government thinking to see that productivity is still an important focus for the UK economy and by association the firms that make up the economy (DTI, 1998; 2003; 2005). Related to productivity was the growth of interest in quality, productivity and competitive position (Deming, 1986).

Supply chains as operations management

Continuing the theme of productivity has been the focus of much of the supply chain literature found in operations management. Much has been written on the efficiency of operations and the associated lowering of inventories that can be better managed if operational improvements are made.

Focus on inventories: peaks and troughs

In the 1960s a precursor to the supply chain literature that would later concern itself with the effect of demand was the work of Jay Forrester examining the impact of demand amplification at stages in the supply chain and the impact this could have upon inventories (Forrester, 1961). Industrial management and purchasing and production management had a clear focus on inventory management. For most manufacturing organizations inventories represented a significant proportion of their Balance Sheet value (50–60 per cent or more). Thus organizations that could reduce their inventory-holding cost could improve their competitiveness (Jones and Riley, 1985). It has been demonstrated (Wikner et al., 1991) that improvements to the supply chain dynamics can be achieved by:

- 'fine tuning' the existing ordering policy parameters;
- reducing system delays;
- removal of the distribution echelon;
- changing the individual echelon decision rules;
- better use of information flow throughout the supply chain.

Complexity may be a function of product variation, non-standard production, increased system delays, number of linkages in the supply chain, complicated decision rules or simply changing decision rules, that is different sets of decision rules, and poor use of information for whatever reasons (e.g. timeliness, poor integration and communication). Furthermore, interactions between any of the actors in the supply chain may higher or lower complexity.

Volume volatility adds to the complexity within supply chain systems. In commodity markets where standard goods are exchanged this is less of a problem because demand is easier to predict. Where volume volatility is most prominent in markets where fashion is a key element of demand. Customers in these markets demand non-standard goods often in smaller volumes than would be the case for standardized products. For example, it is easier to predict demand for tins of baked beans than for a particular style of dress with associated colour and size variations adding to the volatility of volumes. Thus in mass markets with limited variety of offer to the customer the dynamics of supply chain systems may be easier to predict (Hines, 2004).

Supply chains as logistics

Towards the end of the 1980s the clear focus on operations alone was surpassed by a growing interest in distribution (Oliver and Houlihan, 1986). In the early 1990s moving towards this perspective became popular. In this construction of supply chain management it was about managing performance, productivity and market supply through distribution (Christopher, 1992; 1996).

Supply chains as a means of meeting customer demand

It was not until the mid-1990s that commentators began to think of supply chains in terms of front-end market demand (Fisher et al., 1994). Nevertheless, the dynamics of supply chain interactions still receive attention from researchers some 40 years after Forrester's original work on the topic (Fransoo and Wouters, 2000).

A capability to manage supply chains can prove to be a core competence for an organization. There are numerous examples of business success and failure being dependent on supply chain capabilities. Amazon.com is a relatively new e-retailing organization whose very survival and growth has been built around technical and organizational developments related to managing the virtual store and fulfilling customer orders. One important aspect of their development has been their ability to build relationships with organizations external to Amazon who already possessed capability to fulfil their promotional promises.

The shift in analytic focus over time is illustrated in Table 2.1.

Table 2.1 Analytic focus

From (pre-1990)	To (post-1990 to present)
Predominantly internal focus	Predominantly external (dyadic, chain, network)
Operations (internal efficiency)	Strategies (external market orientation)
Exchange /transactional focus	Relationship/structure focus
Functional processes (silo mentality?)	Integration
Cost efficiency (inputs/outputs)	Value added (outputs/inputs)
Physical processes	Financial, informational and virtual processes
Product quality (only major concern)	Service quality and total quality approaches
Simple (e.g. dyadic structures and relationships)	Complex structures e.g. networks
Traditional linear supply chains	Digital supply chains (value nets)
Inventory management	Information and customer service

Source: Purchasing and supply chain literature from 1930s to present day (after Hines, 2004).

Supply chain strategies

Supply chain strategies are either based on reducing cost and improving efficiencies or they focus on doing things differently to become more effective in serving the customer and creating added value. For a much thorough discussion of supply chain strategies see Hines (2004).

Strategic sourcing decisions

Sourcing centres on supplier selection, planning: design, specifications, purchases, manufacturing and deliveries. Delays in any of the elements of the sourcing process have implications for the throughput in the supply chain. Sourcing is the first stage of any supply chain cycle. Sourcing precedes any procurement and is part of the procurement cycle. Supplier selection and purchasing are an important part of any supply chain strategy. Strangely, however, there is a paucity of literature relating to sourcing decisions in relation to fashion given its significance to managing supply chains. It has been noted that retailers often use existing suppliers to design and develop new products (Lui and McGoldrick, 1996). Sourcing in a fashion context necessarily means global influences are strongly evident. There have been a number of different theoretical propositions that purport to explain sourcing in terms of international trade, foreign direct investment (FDI), offshore production, product life cycles and strategy (Swamidass, 1993). The value chain has also been used as one approach to make sourcing decisions (Kotabe and Omura 1989). However, none of these theoretical models sufficiently explains the complex nature of modern sourcing by fashion retail organizations. Lui and McGoldrick (1996, p.13) suggest that any new theory must introduce the dimension of product attributes. They conclude that it is a combination of low factor cost and product attributes that determine sourcing decisions. This statement, however, appears to ignore strategies that require quick response (QR). Nevertheless, maybe it reflects practice since the most prevalent reason for making a sourcing decision given by retail buyers in the UK is cost price. My own research in this area reveals that even in circumstances where they mention other reasons they are of secondary importance. This is especially the case in price sensitive markets. Market conditions usually imply that the apparel has low design content or alternatively the purchaser does not pay the full price for the design element. For example, there have been a number of high profile disputes between high street retailers, supermarket retailers and the originators of design concepts. These are known in the trade as 'knock-offs'. In instances where merchandise is essentially non-fashion market rules are governed simply by commodity trading (i.e. price is where supply and demand are in equilibrium). However, the contemporary paradox of fashion markets is that fashion is not necessarily expensive. There are all types of fashion, which consumers can choose, to suit their 'pocket', their 'taste', their image and their lifestyle. Fashion can be bought at Tesco, Sainsbury, Primark, Matalan and Asda as easily as it can at M&S, Next, Reiss, DKNY, Dolce and

Gabbana, Gucci and Chanel. Consumers are not afraid to mix and match either, no sense of customer loyalty here.

So where to source: local or global?

Well the answer to this question depends on the strategy. If your strategic focus is to achieve lowest cost you would need to source from a supplier who would help you do that. It may not matter where in the world the supplier is located or would it? Well not if you simply specify a contract price the supplier has to meet, along with delivery schedules the supplier has to meet too. However, there may be more uncertainty and there may be higher risk involved. For example, not as easy to get to the source if it is located geographically half way round the globe, if the plant managers don't speak your language and don't engage in practices that you have come to expect of your local supplier who you have now ditched because you have been able on paper at least to lower cost. Nor is it easy to know about or overcome disruptions to supply – strikes, tsunami, customs impounding merchandise, tariff disputes, accidents on the high seas, delays, other problems of manufacture. Things are always more difficult to manage at a distance even in the age of the Internet and advanced information communication systems. One manager told me it is easier, faster and cheaper to transmit errors but it still takes time to sort them out because it usually involves face-to-face interaction. Maybe distance is not dead after all (Cairncross, 1998). If on the other hand your strategic objective is to satisfy customers and earn a reasonable profit in so doing it may be appropriate to source closer to market to catch a trend. Hence it may be appropriate to source more locally. The premise here would be that what you incur by way of higher cost is set against faster lead times for delivery of the product. Thus if time is an important part of achieving your competitive advantage then it would be sensible to make the trade-off. Uncertainties may be lower from local supply sources because you may be in more regular contact. Hence establishing relationships may lead to improving competitiveness. Nevertheless, for each of these arguments I am putting forward you could equally present the opposite argument and you might be right given the particular circumstances. This is why the herd-like decision-making that takes place in many retail organizations is problematic. Supposing a group of twenty-something buyers just happen to meet at a business/social occasion in Corks Winebar, London. Inevitably the subject of what they do, how well they are doing, how much they get paid, what fun they had on their last buying trip to Vietnam or Bangladesh and so on comes into the conversation and for all they may deny it maybe they let slip who they buy from, prices paid and how good such and such is or don't touch supplier X may creep into the conversation. The discourse of many retail organizations has been about lowering intake cost to improve retail margins. No question here about being a better retailer in terms of knowing their customer and how to meet their needs better. Not much marketing here! However, catching a trend, buying cheap and hope you sell through is probably a relatively good description. However, if everyone follows suit and we have a high street full of 'me to' retailers it is very difficult for the customer to make a choice on anything but price. Thus the herd-like obsession with low cost decision instinctive approaches is problematic for most and it has major consequences for other organizational stakeholders: suppliers, shareholders and maybe ultimately the retail employees. This is a plea for strategic difference. If fashion suggests difference then why are so many fashion retail organizations oblivious to it?

The iceberg theory of costs and opportunity

The focus on offshore sourcing has increased during the past 15 years as a way to lower costs. However sourcing offshore may be ignoring some key data relevant to the decision-making process. This myopia would seem to be overlooking an 'iceberg' of costs many of which have been identified within my own research (Hines, 1998). The Iceberg beneath the waterline contains a number of hidden costs that are often ignored (the view from the bridge). These hidden costs could be substantial. Furthermore, these costs are often disguised or never traced back to the stock-keeping units (SKUs). Examples of some of the hidden costs are given in the model. Costs include: procurement, management time consumed in acquisition and monitoring progress or in re-work. More importantly something that is hardly ever measured is lost sales due to late delivery or incomplete delivery (wrong-size ratios, style mix, colour mix).

Procurement costs

Evidence from a number of retail fashion buyers who spend a significant amount of their time travelling abroad to search for new products suggests that the cost is not unimportant. Buyers often spend 2 or more months travelling to source merchandise during any given year. The cost includes airfares, hotel bills, telephone calls and subsistence payments not to mention the human cost of broken relationships, loneliness and fatigue measures that reflect in staff turnover measures. Furthermore, if one considers the time spent against orders placed there will be times when the cost of procurement is extremely expensive and significantly more than the final invoiced bought in price, which may be the only cost that is measured. Thus procurement costs may never be traced back to products. Such costs are more likely to reside in an overhead category of large organizations. What is more such costs may be allocated or apportioned arbitrarily to products that did not incur the costs, if they are allocated or apportioned at all.

Management time

Management time is consumed communicating with suppliers before acquisition, during acquisition and post acquisition. The number of managers involved and the amount of time spent can be significant. Major retail organizations have teams of managers that co-ordinate activities with offshore suppliers. The management team frequently visit the plants to monitor and plan production, to resolve operational difficulties and to help improve efficiencies. The time spent is not always traced back to the products that are consuming this resource.

Opportunity cost of lost sales

By far the greatest cost and perhaps the most significant part of the iceberg could be the opportunity cost of lost sales. If merchandise is not available within a store at the time the consumer wants to buy it the sale is lost. Not to worry you will have the lowest-cost merchandise in your warehouse when it finally arrives. Although consumer behaviour theory might suggest substitution of one product for another this may not happen within the same retail store. Substitution may unwittingly help competitors to achieve a sale. This part of the iceberg is where an offshore supplier is at greater disadvantage. Onshore suppliers are closer to market and a short delay in production will not necessarily result in late delivery or incomplete delivery, whereas a delay in production from an overseas source would more probably result in missing a shipping date. This may require drastic action to airfreight goods, adding significantly to cost and it is a cost that has not been built into the retailer's price point. Typically it takes 8–12 weeks to source from a far eastern source whereas it will be 4–6 weeks from the UK and perhaps just one week more from Morocco, Portugal, Egypt and Eastern Europe.

Figure 2.1 illustrates the iceberg costs together with potential areas whereby UK suppliers could build competitive advantage. Assuming that the iceberg costs for a UK supplier are less significant than for an overseas supplier would suppose that UK suppliers could build on strengths that an overseas source would find it difficult to achieve.

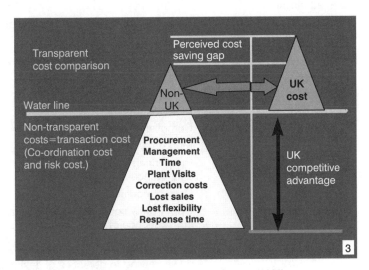

Figure 2.1 The iceberg theory of cost comparison. *Source:* © Hines (1998).

Sources of competitive advantage

The iceberg theory offers a number of possibilities that would enable local or near suppliers achieve competitive advantage vis-à-vis a more distant overseas supplier. It may be better to source onshore in particular circumstances.

However, it is not simply the iceberg but the size of the iceberg that will determine the relative advantage. In some cases an iceberg may exist but it may not be sufficiently deep to allow the UK supplier to exploit it. The stronger the relationship is between a supplier and a UK retailer the less likelihood of a large iceberg lurking. Conversely the weaker the relationship is between a UK retailer and a supplier the more likelihood of a larger iceberg that may be exploited by an alternative supplier.

Transaction costs are generally represented by two major components (Clemens et al., 1993):

$$\text{Transaction costs} = \text{Co-ordination costs} + \text{Transaction risk}$$

Co-ordination costs are those incurred exchanging information and incorporating information into decision-making processes. In sourcing or purchasing decisions it might include product information, prices, availability, design changes, shipping and so on. Transaction risk is the cost incurred as a consequence of other parties evading their responsibilities. For example, missing delivery dates, lowering quality or simply supplying incorrect quantities, colours or styles (Table 2.2).

Table 2.2 Transaction costs

Co-ordination costs	Risk costs
Procurement costs (informational costs, sourcing, administration)	Delays (unexpected)
Management time troubleshooting problems and dealing with supplier issues (beyond those normally expected for iceberg costs)	Exchange rate costs (not budgeted)
	Taxes – hidden duties (not budgeted)
	Unplanned Inventory storage costs (beyond those budgeted)
	Compliance costs
	Mark-downs
	Re-working and Rectification after acceptance of merchandise
	Design modifications
	Opportunity costs of lost sales as a consequence of other risk factors such as delays in receiving goods, longer production lead times than planned, unexpected mark-downs owing to defects e.g. design faults

Source: Hines, 2005.

Three issues debated in the transaction cost literature have been: asset specificity, uncertainty, and markets and hierarchies (Grover et al., 2003). Asset specificity recognizes that an asset may have been acquired for a specific contract and may not be transferable to other transactions. For example, a supplier may purchase a particular machine to produce garments for a specific retail customer and the machine has little or no value beyond that contract. Two types of uncertainty, may occur: environmental uncertainty, for example changes in technology that cause obsolescence or demand volatility (volumes and variety) maybe caused by fashion trends. Finally, markets and hierarchies focus on the ability of markets to co-ordinate demand and supply and governance issues. For example, in buyer–supplier relationships does the market allocate resources efficiently and secondly can these flows be controlled without recourse to ownership of the value chain? Before considering these last two questions it is important to examine the total ownership costs since it is influenced by transaction costs incurred by the purchaser.

Total cost of ownership

The total cost of ownership (TOC) has three central components: pre-acquisition costs (sourcing) + acquisition cost (purchasing) + post acquisition cost (storing, distributing and possibly writing off costs). It has been noted that 'choosing low cost not low price suppliers' is critical to any decision (Kaplan and Cooper, 1998). The purchase price is only one component that makes up the TOC. A supplier may deliver at the best price but they may not be the lowest-cost supplier. There are a number of possible reasons why this can be so. A low cost supplier is a supplier who is lower in total ownership cost terms than their competitors. A supplier may achieve a competitive advantage over their low price competitor for some or all of the reasons listed below:

- Transparent and timely information flows enable the retail buyer to determine more accurate delivery dates and avoid losing sales by being late to market.
- Suppliers using electronic data interchange over virtual private networks or via web-based systems are able to provide better levels of customer service that help retail buyers with their decision-making (e.g. avoid costly stock-outs or overstocking by having early warning information (two way) about demand and supply).
- Zero defects are a buzz-phrase in manufacturing operations especially in the automobile sector where they have implemented sigma six as a means of eliminating defects. However, retailers in this industry had a limited understanding of these concepts and the benefits they could bring for their organization longer term.
- Just in time supplies lowering inventory-holding (storage) costs.
- Vendor managed inventory (VMI) can create system efficiencies for purchasers who are able to have stocks as required to meet their customer demand. For suppliers, they acquire a better understanding of their forward

order book and it enables them to manage production flows more efficiently and to meet their retail customer demand.

- Co-ordinated category management from suppliers (e.g. skirts, tops and matching accessories arrive in store simultaneously).
- Collaborative product development may reduce retail and supplier costs.
- Electronic document exchange (EDE) reduces time in process (purchase orders, invoices, specifications) and retailers were beginning to see some benefits, as were suppliers. EDE helped transactions conducted at a distance.
- Electronic fund transfer increases cash flow for good suppliers encouraging them to achieve results on the retail buyer's behalf.

Organizational goals vis-à-vis individual managers goals have been noted as a source of difference in the seminal text on the topic (Cyert and March 1963).

Some transaction costs will be known in advance, for example, the purchase price. However, this analysis concerns itself only with those costs not known in advance of transactions for example, at the time sourcing and purchasing decisions are taken. In such cases the transaction costs are in effect 'iceberg costs' because their depth (how many?) and breadth (how much?) are unknown. Thus these transaction costs are uncertain.

$$Tc = Ic \qquad\qquad (1)$$

If, and only if, costs were not recognized at the decision-making point

$Tc = $ *Transaction costs,* $Ic = $ *Iceberg costs*

$$Ic = f(Cc, Rc) \qquad\qquad (2)$$

$Ic = $ *iceberg costs,* $f = $ *function,* $Cc = $ *co-ordination costs,* $Rc = $ *Risk costs*

Iceberg cost comparisons may be made after transactions are completed. They may be regarded as part of a firm's key performance measures. If such costs can be identified they can be used to inform future decisions taken in respect of supplier selection for future contracts.

Taking the analysis a stage further TCO is a useful concept to establish measures of comparison between different supplier efficiencies.

$$TCO = A + PV \sum_{i=1}^{n} (Ic_i - R_n) \qquad\qquad (3)$$

Where: $A = $ Acquisition cost, $PV = $ Present value, $Ic_i = $ Iceberg costs in year i, $R_n = $ Residual value in year i, $\sum_{i=1}^{n}$ *sum each relevant period's costs to obtain a* TOC.

Implications and contribution of the iceberg theory

Transaction cost theory is useful to identify 'iceberg costs' ex post. It is potentially most useful in examining supplier efficiencies and their impact on the retail organization's performance. Ex ante transaction costs are not necessarily known and therefore as a decision tool for first time supplier selection the iceberg theory has a more limited usefulness to practitioners. However, supplier efficiencies may be compared using the iceberg model and sourcing decisions based on it are made transparent as a consequence. TCO concepts extend the usefulness of TCT by identifying TCT within the concept of TCO to construct a full cost for doing business with any supplier for comparative purposes. Over time TCO offers a useful performance measure for the assessment of sourcing and purchasing decisions.

Time to market

Quick Response (QR) was a phrase coined in 1985 by Alan Hunter, a professor at North Carolina State University as a method of improving response time in the textile pipeline (Fernie, 1994). Hunter's original conceptualization was concerned with improving the response times of textile suppliers in the face of severe price competition from developing countries. The term has since evolved over time to represent a method of improving response time from the selection of a garment by a retailer to its replenishment by a manufacturer. It has therefore expanded in meaning to reflect the responsiveness of the whole clothing supply chain. Ko and Kincade (1997) 12 years on, define QR as being a business strategy to optimize the flow of information and merchandise between channel members to maximize customer service. In order to accomplish QR, retailers must employ a variety of technologies. Electronic Point of Sale (EPoS), barcodes and EDI are all classified as enabling quick response technologies (QRT). From a retail point of view the ultimate aim is to provide their customers (the consumers) with what they want to buy, when they want to buy it and at a price that attracts and persuades them to make the purchase. Retailers and contemporary retailing literature refers to Efficient Consumer Response (ECR) whereas manufacturers refer to QR. A critical aspect of this buying decision is for retailers to make sure they have sufficient stock to meet the demand. If stock is not available immediately within a clothing store it is likely that the customer will either substitute a product that is available immediately either from the same retailer or from a competitor. The substitute product may be a lower price offering even if bought from the same retailer. Either way the retailer risks losing business.

Many of today's supply chain practices are an attempt to replicate the external resource management model pioneered by Toyota. This is often referred to as 'lean thinking'. The predominant orthodoxy of supply chain management thinking has been devoted to 'discovering tools and techniques that provide increased operational effectiveness and efficiency throughout the delivery channels that must be created internally and externally to support and supply existing corporate product and service offerings to customers,' (Cox 1997). Cox goes on to attribute this thinking to studies of the Japanese Automobile industry in the 1970s and 1980s by Womack et al. (1990). Contrast this view with Fearne (1998) which emphasizes the importance of the customer and building relationships – 'a philosophy of doing business'. These two approaches highlight the differences between product push and market led strategies. Historically apparel retailing has adopted product push strategies and some organizations still do. Large retailing giants have adopted a monolithic planning approach to filling their stores with product volumes at the lowest cost. They have ignored customers at their peril and many have paid a high price in terms of lost customers and reducing profitability and in a few cases market withdrawal. Witness recent withdrawals from UK markets C&A, Littlewoods, and Ciro Citerio to mention a few. Contrast these retailers with 'the new kids on the block' Zara, New Look, George at Asda. These companies have been more responsive to customer needs and they have developed sourcing and supply chain strategies focused on their customers. These organizations claim to have products from design to in store within 3 or 4 weeks.

Recent practices observed in the USA and Western European Retailing organizations that have been adopted from practices in the automobile supply chains have focused on time compression and include:

- Reducing the numbers of suppliers in order to increase supplier dependency and to provide the retailer with increased dedication and flexibility.
- Eliminating agents except where they are deemed to add value by bringing in suppliers who have special capabilities. Superior technology, innovation and design are examples.
- Increasing application of Internet technologies to source or develop products faster, to obtain better prices through bidding or to search for specialist suppliers without the need to have agents.
- Shift responsibility to the supplier through VMI systems, pre-retailing services (ticketing, labelling, steaming, pressing, packaging for store ready display) and devolving responsibility for quality – hence lowering costs for stock-holding and other services.

The fast fashion phenomenon

The term *'fast fashion'* has slipped into common usage by apparel retailers, suppliers and commentators in the last 5 years. The concept is not new. The roots can be traced back to the development of QR techniques in the late 1970's and throughout the 1980's as US textile and apparel suppliers encountered severe competitive pressures from Far East and other lower-cost supply countries. However, the way in which fast fashion concepts have been implemented successfully by a very small number of retail organizations has been perceived within the industry as giving those firms (adopting the concept and successfully implementing it) a competitive advantage. Zara a retail brand owned by Inditex the Spanish parent was seen by many as an innovator in this retail genre. Zara entered the UK high street in 1997 with its first experimental store being opened in Regent Street, London.

Antecedents of fast fashion

From the earliest initiatives in the US Textile and Apparel Supply Chain (or Pipeline as it was called back in 1984) large integrated textile companies such as Milliken became interested in reducing process times through a technique called 'QR'. The initial results were impressive: reduced lead times and a claimed saving of 25 per cent of the total textile supply chain cost in the USA (Hunter, 1990). Throughout the 1980s and 1990s QR gained wide acceptance as computing power increased, making it possible to process the large amounts of data to run QR programs. Many supplier firms viewed QR as a way of increasing their own competitive position within the supply chain (Slack et al., 2001). 'They may not be the cheapest but they can respond the fastest', was the principle. It is well documented in the literature, for example, that Benetton, the Italian Knitwear retailer, has been able to respond quickly to demand 'in-store' through its QR policy of 'piece dying' garments in the colours that are in demand (HBS, 1984). The EpoS data from the retail store transmits colour, size and style data back to the production centres located in Italy who act quickly to respond and then deliver anywhere in the world where the product is required within, at most, seven days (Bull et al., 1993). However while QR promised much to domestic supply firms in the USA in the 1980s, a view has also emerged in the 1990s that it had not delivered all it promised (Hunter, 1990; Fisher et al., 1994; Fiorito et al., 1995; KSA, 1997; Lowson et al., 1999). The main problems identified were implementation issues, technological incompatibility (e.g. bar code standards) and a failure to integrate supply chain processes between organizations. It has been recognized that it was not simply QR tools and techniques that were essential capabilities needed by retailers and suppliers but competence to manage a network of suppliers to provide flexibility (Camuffo et al., 2001). Relationship management competence became paramount. This flexibility translates into business benefits which allow retailers and their suppliers to manage volume shifts through better capacity management and equally, if not, more importantly allows supply chain networks to postpone production closer to the actual demand period.

Time compression and responsiveness

Most of the emphasis in QR was focused on 'pipeline' modelling to reduce time throughout the supply chain (KSA, 1987). However, in practice much of the controllable element was dyadic between the organization initiating demand and their immediate supplier (Iyer and Bergen, 1997). In some respects it could be argued that the success of QR might be dependent on a number of dyadic relationships that are co-ordinated effectively. Questions arise over who can effectively co-ordinate and who is allowed to? Time compression reduces costs by making each process cycle shorter. Shorter lead times in procurement, manufacturing, replenishment, customer purchasing and consumption result in faster throughput times in the supply chain system. Figure 2.2 illustrates the supply chain process cycles.

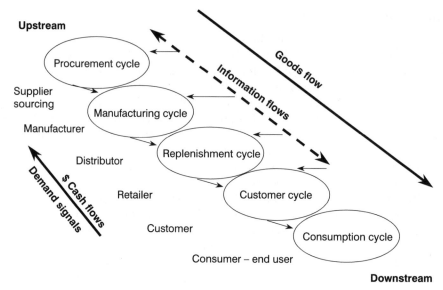

Figure 2.2 Supply chain process cycles. *Source:* Hines (2004).

Time compression in any cycle reduces holding cost, processing cost and inventory risk.

Today fashion retailing is itself a fast moving business. Where once retailers may have bought clothes for at most four seasons in a year today, buyers for many high street stores work on much shorter cycles. This reduces the opportunity for the buyer to achieve significant economies of purchasing through scale. This is an obvious point overlooked by many commentators. For example, if you buy store merchandise for a 6-week selling period you expect to turnover inventories perhaps 8 or 9 times in a year. Previously when operating a four season model you might expect to turnover the merchandise stock (inventory) in 12 or 13 weeks. Thus selling periods are greatly reduced when fashion is the key determinant of the buying decision. If retailers continue with their traditional purchasing model they will simply buy smaller volumes more regularly and lose their ability to achieve lower input costs through economies of scale since the order volumes and hence the production volumes do not justify lower unit costs. Of course they try to insist on lower prices through offering annual volumes and capacity filling for suppliers. This shift in purchasing practice has resulted in a number of key changes to the 'fast fashion' business model, which is listed in Table 2.3.

Emerging from the many interviews I conducted with those espousing the virtues of 'fast fashion' it became clear that it is retailers in the main who refer to fast fashion whereas suppliers often referred to QR. So what is the difference between the two constructs? Similarities exist in so far as both are forms of time-based competition. They rely on improving process cycles. QR is a supplier

Table 2.3 Differences between traditional and fast fashion business model

Characteristics	Traditional apparel retailing business model	Fast fashion retailing business model
Supply strategy	Efficiency-driven large volumes planned at lowest total cost.	Responsive to customer demand. Small- and medium-sized volumes in response to customer demand identified by store data.
Manufacturing operations	Outsourced to a number of different supplying contractors based on best prices (often globally). Do not own their supply chain but need to try and control it through standardized systems, policies and procedures. Larger organizations are able to exert pressure.	Backward vertical integration enables organizations like Zara to manage closely the different supply chain operations from design through to store. Owning much of their supply chain. What they do not own is closely controlled and relatively local in Spain, Portugal and Morocco with short lead times.
Lead times	Long lead times 12–16 weeks fabric, 6–10 weeks apparel production, 2–3 weeks shipping times.	Short lead times 8–10 days on some lines, most within 15 days including store shipment.
Demand based on	Forecasts well in advance of the selling season.	Forecast much closer to season and heavily influenced by real time demand data transmitted from stores.
Replenishment	Inventory levels trigger automatic replenishment orders from suppliers at pre-agreed contract prices.	No replenishment – when it's gone it's gone and move onto the next hot fashion.
Designs	Based on trend forecasts 18–24 months in advance of selling seasons.	Based on current catwalk shows. Digital photography and information and communication technology used to transmit visual data back to in-house design team to sample and cost. 'Knock-offs' as they are called in the trade for obvious reasons.
Fabrics (textile chain)	Various fabrics produced to specification by Textile Mills 12–16 weeks lead times, production has to be booked well in advance.	Mainly standard 'greige' fabrics piece dyed to seasonal colours in demand.

Source: Hines (2004).

construct that describes and explains methods of reducing production cycles to deliver product faster. It is built around having efficient systems of production. Similarly, 'fast fashion' is a construct that describes and explains retailer desires to satisfy consumer demand more efficiently and effectively. Efficient in the sense that time is reduced. Effective meaning that fashionable items are in store to meet demand. Supply chain integration and relational management is important to the success of both approaches.

However, it is the differences that reveal more than similarities about what exactly 'fast fashion' is. It is a marketing tool to drive retail footfall. It allows retailers to make up-to-date product offers to their customer base frequently. Thus, customers are driven to stores more frequently to view and buy 'fast fashion', which also tends to be young fashion. The target market for 'fast fashion' are mainly in the younger age groups, typically described as 16–24 year olds and more importantly gender biased towards female customers simply because they tend to purchase clothing more frequently and spend more on clothes. Volumes for each line produced tended to be smaller than traditional supply quantities for low fashion content clothing and perhaps more importantly most retailers when talking about fast fashion commented that unlike many traditional lines which were continuously replenished within season, 'fast fashion' lines tend not to be replenished. 'When it's gone, it's gone and that drives customers in to our stores more frequently because they don't want to miss the latest trend.'

Smaller volumes also minimize risks of obsolescence for retailers, that is fashion risk. Finally, one of the most important issues to emerge in discussion was that in order to produce fast fashion it was important to use stock fabric or greige fabric rather than specialist fabric. Although this appeared revelatory in the analysis one should not really be surprised and from a business point of view to develop clothes using specialist fabric requires greater time to source, specify and produce which is not what fast fashion is about. Fast fashion is disposable. It is for immediate consumption. It is to capture the look of the moment. It is not to linger in the wardrobe. It is definitely not durable. It is not built to last. It is not commodity clothing. It is not the 'beige (or even fawn) cardigan'. It is for immediate wear. It is at an affordable price. It does have in built obsolescence and therefore happily for retailers customers will need to repurchase within a short-time frame.

Figure 2.3 illustrates Zara's fast fashion business model. It demonstrates six key interaction stages from creation through to the customer. Importantly store information feedback into inventory management and new product development.

This business model carries advantages for Zara in managing inventory and associated costs whilst being able to ensure that products are in demand when they are in store. This advantage becomes clearer when Zara is benchmarked against the industry averages in Figure 2.4.

Figure 2.5 illustrates the production–market problem. Production is either complex or simple in this abstraction of reality and markets are either stable or dynamic. Stable markets are relatively easier to manage since demand

Zara supply model

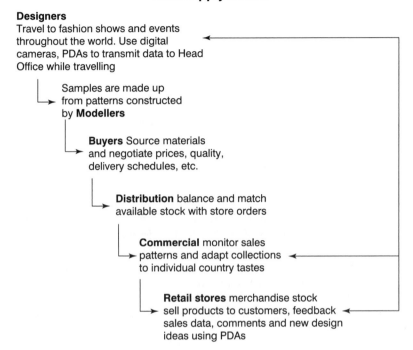

Figure 2.3 Zara's key interactions in bringing product to store.

Benchmarking Zara's inventory against the industry average

Confirmed stock	Zara (%)	Industry average (%)
6 month pre-season	15–25	45–60
Start of season	50–60	80–100
In season	40–50	0–20

Source: Zara UK, 2006.

You can see from this inventory model that Zara do not order as much in advance of season as conventional retailers. They operate more flexibly with a high proportion of in season adjustment. Essentially closer to a make to order model of inventory reducing stock-holding. This enables the company to reduce their mark-downs and maintain full prices.

60% of fabric is produced within the organization and 40% outsourced. The picture is the same for manufactured clothing lines 60:40 in-house to outsourced mainly from Europe and Asia. Distance is an important consideration and standard lines rather than fast fashion tend to be at greater distance.

Figure 2.4 Zara vis-à-vis industry averages.

patterns are less volatile. Production operations may be either simple or complex. In markets where the conditions are both simple in terms of production operations and relatively predictable demand patterns occur, risks are low and there is less uncertainty (e.g. tins of baked beans). The only shock to the supply system is likely to be endogenous that is, self-induced through say promotional activity or through an externality such as new research findings

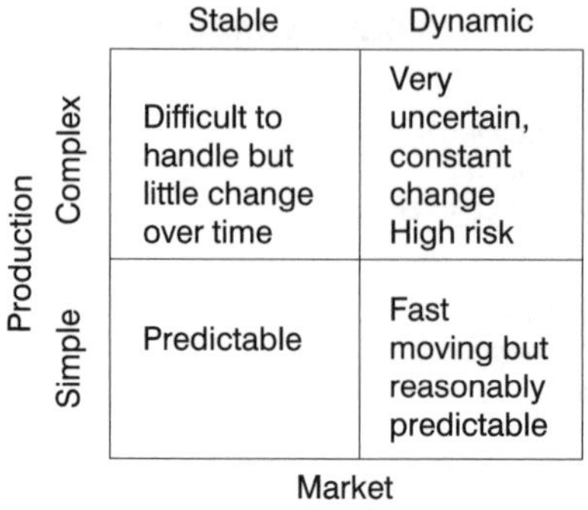

	Stable	Dynamic
Production Complex	Difficult to handle but little change over time	Very uncertain, constant change High risk
Production Simple	Predictable	Fast moving but reasonably predictable

Market

Figure 2.5 Typology of apparel merchandise.

report baked beans stave off the ageing process. In market conditions where there is rapid change such as fashion markets and especially when production operations become more complex (extra design content, special fabric sourced, offshore manufacture – longer lead times, transport and tariffs), risks are higher because demand is more volatile and more complex production may cause delays or incur additional costs.

Traditional supply strategies may only work in stable market conditions. Different strategies are required to cope with dynamic markets and this is illustrated in Figure 2.6.

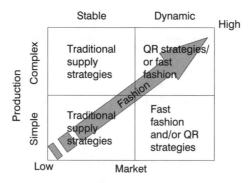

Figure 2.6 Typology of apparel supply strategies.

Supply chain structures

Metaphors have historically been adopted to describe these supply chain structures' organizational structures. In practice journals in the apparel sector throughout the 1970s and 1980s the term 'pipeline' was used to discuss the flows of raw materials through manufacturing processes and onto the final customer (KSA, 1987; Hunter, 1990; Hunter et al., 1993; Hunter and Valentino, 1995). In the 1990s 'supply networks' became fashionable (Christopher, 1996). 'Commodity chains' have also been used to describe global production networks (Gereffi, 1994). More recently demand chains and value nets (being short for value networks) have been coined to describe supply chains.

Degree of vertical integration

A further way to explore the structure of supply chains is to examine the nature of integration. Historically, it was assumed that each separate organization linked in a chain from the start of the process through to the customer (Williamson, 1971).

Hierarchy and governance are at the centre of this approach (Williamson, 1975). Historically, vertical integration was achieved through ownership and control of the vertically integrated firms in the system. For example, primary producers of wool or cotton would supply (secondary producers) textile mills and they in turn supply clothing manufacturers who in turn supply (tertiary) retail outlets and all these firms would be linked through ownership of the vertical chain. The agricultural producer, the textile mill, the manufacturer and the retailer all owned by a single entity. This governance structure ensured control over the supply chain. Nowadays control is achieved in other ways without the necessity of ownership of the vertical supply chain. For example, market power of large retail organizations with significant market shares can give retailers control over suppliers without recourse to ownership. This is achieved in a number of ways:

1 Retail control of channels to market means that producers need to establish their routes to market through building relationships with retailers able to act as intermediaries between the producer and the final customer.
2 Suppliers must comply with retailer demands if they are to remain a supplier in the longer term. For example, retailers measure supplier performance against competitor suppliers on variables such as: on time deliveries, complete deliveries, faults and service quality.
3 Suppliers often become reliant on their retail customers for routes to market. One often reads press articles reporting the power relationships exerted by retailers. For example, when a long established supplier to a retail organization loses contracts or relationships breakdown it emphasizes the power that modern retail organizations possess without the necessity of owning the supplier organization.
4 The removal of ownership but the maintenance of control provides the retail organization with greater flexibility to switch supplies without incurring the high costs associated with divestment of assets (selling buildings, plant, machinery and paying redundancy to the workforce). Supplier firms are often made aware or left in little doubt of the nature of the highly competitive market place they face when retailers negotiate supply contracts.

Thus benefits of control of the supplier network may be achieved without the necessity to vertically integrate in the traditional economic sense of the term. There are of course risks to this strategy especially if supplies or suppliers are temporarily limited. However, most markets adjust to imbalances in supply and demand in the medium term as has been noted in the economics literature (Smith, 1910 [1776]).

Supply chain relationships

A number of different aspects of supply chain relationships have already been discussed throughout this chapter. However, it may now be useful to synthesize and re-emphasize some of the underlying reasons and identify the genesis of the ideas from which the motives to examine relationships were drawn.

Quality focus

The influence of the quality movement may be highlighted drawing on Deming's fourth point of his fourteen points on quality he advocates that organizations' work more closely with fewer suppliers (Deming, 1982). This is a practice that has been adopted by many fashion-retailing organizations throughout the 1990s following practices adopted by automobile manufacturers a decade earlier.

Buyer–supplier focus

Buyer–supplier co-operation has received a great deal of attention in the literature and frequency of contact has also been viewed as a necessary precondition of relationship building (Heide and Miner, 1992).

Purchasing and supply focus

The literature on relationships in the supply chain discusses the traditional 'arms length' approach of purchasing in which adversarial relationships are a common feature on one pole and the 'partnership' approach which often adopts the analogy of marriage at the other pole. Often the focus of these studies examines the relationships existing between firms rather than the key business relationships within a supply chain context. Examples of the first category focusing on firm relationships would be strategic collaboration (Kanter, 1994), the value chain approach (Porter, 1980), evolution of relationships (Axelrod, 1984), make or buy decisions (Ford and Farmer, 1986) and study of purchasing relationships (Chao and Scheuing, 1992). A turning point in the literature was recognizing that supply chain relationships and purchasing negotiations went beyond the adversarial discussions focused on price alone (Carlisle and Parker, 1989). It was further recognized that these relationships could be much more complex and introduced the concept of networks to explain the types of relationships existing between suppliers and buyers to deliver products and services to the end customer (Ellram, 1994). A number of researchers were examining Japanese supply chain practices in the automobile industry discussed earlier (Womack et al., 1990). The notion of tiers of suppliers, together with the 'lean supply' concept was introduced during the early 1990s to explain relationships (Lamming, 1993). It was suggested that companies adopting a partnership approach performed better than those that did not (Sako, 1992). Lean supply with its emphasis on efficiency developed into agile supply in the 1990s as managers and commentators focused not simply on efficiencies but also required flexibility and this in turn required agility. Agility means being able to switch production flows on and off and possessing capability to respond to customer demand more effectively. More recently the term leagile has been coined to emphasize the two aspects: efficiency (lean) and effectiveness (agile).

Globalization focus

The changing dynamics of globalization and the shift of power from manufacturer to retailer have caused suppliers to re-think how they work with other companies in their customer value chain (Kuglin, 1998). More recently the rhetoric of partnership has been a pronounced discourse in the supply chain literature (Hines and McGowan, 2005).

Supply chain research

A number of important themes have been examined within this chapter. The themes selected are my interpretation of important developments that have brought us to where we are today. From roots firmly located in purchasing, supply and operations the concept of 'supply chain management' as we now understand owes much to developments in other disciplines – strategy, economics, marketing, organizational behaviour and information technology. It is the integration of these disciplines in terms of thinking and applications in terms of practice throughout the management process that is important in helping to understand the current issues and the future directions that research can take.

Integration is the key to managing these complex processes both internally and externally between firms that co-exist in the numerous supply chains that each organization has. The delivery of a single garment to a retail store may have a network of suppliers stretching around the globe and that is only one supply chain configuration that the retailer has to manage within a range, within a store, within all its stores. The variety of contact points and the number of different relationships that exist in this business to fulfil customer needs are highly complex. An important point to remember is that they are business arrangements and business relationships driven by the motive for profit through exchange. Therefore, examining the exchange processes and how they are managed has much to offer to gain a better knowledge and understanding of how these processes work and change through time. Also to assess the impact of global sourcing and purchasing strategies on both the supplying country and their population and the purchasing country population adds an important new dimension considering ethics and green issues. Longitudinal studies, quantitative research, ethnography, phenomenology and social interactionism are all methods that could be usefully employed in this context.

Comparisons drawn between different types of supply chain are always interesting. In this respect comparative case study research has much to offer. Why have Benetton chosen to take greater control of their supply chain by vertically integrating operations and expanding the number of production centres overseas. This is not simply a cost reduction exercise although that may be an important outcome. They have taken this decision to gain control over the supply chain to minimize risks as much as anything and to establish centres close to where they think their markets may expand. Fashion and fads in retail strategy could be explored to examine if the decisions taken are influenced by patterns of development elsewhere in the sector. For example, were Benetton influenced by Zara's success in establishing new markets in Europe outside of Spain quickly and effectively because they were a vertically integrated company applying 'fast fashion' concepts (never repeating) and adopting QR tools. Have other retailers copied or are they copying aspects of the ways in which these companies manage their supply chains or do they do things differently and if so what? We already know from the literature that many of the ideas and supply chain concepts have developed in manufacturing and in particular in automobile manufacture. Is managing the supply chain in the retail sector different to managing an automotive plant or an electronics plant? Is customization more or less important in fashion retail supply chains than in the computer industry where companies like Dell have led the way? What is different and what is similar about these organizations, their supply chains, their business operations, their marketing and their businesses? These are all interesting questions that when answered we would all learn something from that would help explain different aspects of supply chain management. Comparative research and research conducted that is interdisciplinary would offer some useful insights in this context.

Whatever aspects of supply chain management researchers' examine it is evident from the discussions within this chapter that supply chain management is critical to the successful business management of retail organizations. Researchers from different disciplines have much to offer in contributing to these debates.

References

Axelrod, R. (1984). *The Evolution of Co-operation*. London: Penguin.

Barney, J. B. (1999). How a firm's capabilities affect boundary decisions. *Sloan Management Review*, **40** (3), 137–145.

Bull, A., Pitt, M. and Szarka, J. (1993). *Entrepreneurial Textile Communities – A Comparative Study of Small Textile and Clothing Firms*. London: Chapman and Hall.

Cairncross, F. (1998). *The Death of Distance*. London: Orion Business Books.

Camuffo, A., Romano, P. and Vinelli, A. (2001). Back to the future: Benetton transforms its global network. *MIT Sloan Management Review*, **43** (1), 46–52.

Carlisle, J. A. and Parker, R. C. (1989). *Beyond Negotiation: Customer–Supplier Relationships*. Chichester: Wiley.

Chandler, A. D., Jr. (1962). *Strategy and Structure*. Cambridge, MA: MIT Press.

Chao, C. N. and Scheuing, E. (1992). An examination of the relationships between levels of purchasing responsibilities and roles of those in purchasing decision making. *First PSERG Conference*, Glasgow.

Christopher, M. G. (1992). *Logistics and Supply Chain Management Strategies for Reducing Costs and Improving Services*. London: Financial Times/Pitman Publishing.

Christopher, M. G. (1996). *Marketing Logistics*. Oxford: Butterworth-Heinemann.

Clemens, E. K., Reddi, S. P. and Row, M. C. (1993). The impact of information technology on the organization of economic activity: the, 'move to the middle' hypothesis. *Journal of Management Information Systems*, **10** (2), 9–35.

Cox, A. (1997). *Business Success: A Way of Thinking About Strategy, Critical Supply Chain Assets and Operational Best Practice*. Lincolnshire: Earlsgate Press.

Cyert, R. B. and March, J. G. (1963). *A Behavioural Theory of the Firm*. Engelwood Cliffs: Prentice Hall.

Deming, W. E. (1982). *Quality, Productivity and Competitive Position*. Boston: MIT Press.

Deming, W. E. (1986). *Out of the Crisis: Quality, Productivity and Competitive Position*. Cambridge: Cambridge University Press.

DTI (1998). White paper: our competitive future: building the knowledge driven economy (Cm. 4176). Available from: http://www.dti.gov.uk

DTI (2003). White paper: UK competitiveness: moving to the next stage. DTI economics paper No. 3. Available from: http://www.dti.gov.uk

DTI (2005). White paper: UK productivity and competitiveness indicators 2005. Available from: http://www.dti.gov.uk

Ellram, L. M. (1994). A taxonomy of total cost ownership models. *Journal of Business Logistics*, **15** (1), 171–191.

Fearne, A. (1998). Editorial. *Supply Chain Management Journal*, **3** (1), 4.

Fernie, J. (1994). Quick response – an international perspective. *International Journal of Physical Distribution and Logistics Management*, **24** (6), 38–46.

Fiorito, S. S., May, E. G. and Straughn, K. (1995). Quick Response in retailing: components and implementation. *International Journal of Retail and Distribution Management*, **23** (5), 12–21.

Fisher, M., Obermeyer, W., Hammond, J. and Raman, A. (1994). Making supply meet demand in an uncertain world. *Harvard Business Review*, **72** (3), 83–93.

Ford, I. D. and Farmer, D. (1986). Make or buy – a key strategic issue. *Long Range Planning*, **19** (5), 54–62.

Forrester, J. W. (1961). *Industrial Dynamics*. Boston, MA: MIT Press.

Fransoo, J. C. and Wouters, M. J. F. (2000). Measuring the bullwhip effect in the supply chain. *Supply Chain Management*, **5** (2), 78–89.

Gereffi, G. (1994). The organization of buyer-driven global commodity chains: how US retailers shape overseas production networks. In Gereffi, G. and

Korzeniewicz, M. (Eds.), *Commodity Chains and Global Capitalism*. Westport Conneticut: Greenwood Press, pp. 95–122.

Grover, V. and Malhotra, M. K. (2003). Transaction cost framework in operations and supply chain management research: theory and measurement. *Journal of Operations Management*, **21**, 457–473.

Harland, C. M. (1995). *Supply Chain Management: Relationships, Chains and Networks*. Sheffield: British Academy of Management.

HBS (1984). *Benetton*. Harvard Business School Case Study 6-985-014.

Heide, J. B. and Miner, A. S. (1992). The shadow of the future: effects of anticipated interaction and frequency of contact on buyer–supplier co-operation. *Academy of Management Journal*, **35** (2), 265–277.

Hines, T. (1998). The iceberg theory of cost comparison – overseas versus UK sourcing dilemma. *Drapers Record Apparel Challenge Conference*, London Bloomberg.

Hines, T. (2001a). Globalization: an introduction to fashion markets and fashion marketing. In Hines, T. and Bruce, M. (Eds), *Fashion Marketing: Contemporary Issues*. Oxford: Butterworth Heinemann, pp. 1–24.

Hines, T. (2001b). From analogue to digital supply chains: implications for fashion marketing. In Hines, T. and Bruce, M. (Eds), *Fashion Marketing: Contemporary Issues*. Oxford: Butterworth Heinemann, pp. 26–47.

Hines, T. (2004). *Supply Chain Strategies: Customer Driven and Customer Focused*. Oxford: Elsevier.

Hines, T. (2005). *Making Sense of Increasing Overseas Sources of Supply in the UK Clothing Sector*. British Academy of Management, Said Business School Oxford University.

Hines, T. and McGowan, P. (2005). Supply chain strategies in the UK fashion industry: the rhetoric of partnership and realities of power. *International Entrepreneurship and Management Journal*, **1** (4), 519–537.

Hunter, N. A. (1990). *Quick Response in Apparel Manufacturing*. Manchester: The Textile Institute.

Hunter, N. A., King, R. E., Nuttle, H. L. W. and Wilson, J. R. (1993). The apparel pipeline modelling project at North Carolina State University. *Journal of Clothing Science and Technology*, **5** (3/4).

Hunter, N. A. and Valentino, P. (1995). Quick response – ten years later. *Journal of Clothing Science and Technology*, **7** (4), 30–40.

Iyer, A. V. and Bergen, M. E. (1997). Quick response in manufacturer–retailer channels. *Management Science*, **43** (4), 559–570.

Jones, T. C. and Riley, D. W. (1985). Using inventory for competitive advantage through supply chain management. *International Journal of Physical Distribution and Materials Management*, **15** (5), 16–26.

Kanter, R. M. (1994). Collaborative advantage: the art of alliances. *Harvard Business Review*, **72** (4), 96–108.

Kaplan, R. S. and Cooper, R. (1998). *Cost and Effect – Using Integrated Cost Systems to Drive Profitability and Performance*. Boston, MA: Harvard Business School Press.

Ko, E. and Kincade, D. H. (1997). The impact of quick response technologies on retail store attributes. *International Journal of Retail and Distribution Management*, **25**, 90–98.

Kotabe, M. and Omura, G. S. (1989). Sourcing strategies of European and Japanese multinationals: a comparison. *Journal of International Business Studies*, **20** (Spring), 113–140.

KSA (1987). *New Technology for Quick Response: How US Apparel Manufacturers Can Capitalize on Their Proximity to the US Market, Getting Started in Quick Response*, Technical Advisory Committee AAMA.

KSA (1997). *Womens Wear Daily reprint in WDinfotracs*. New York, USA: KSA.

Kuglin, F. A. (1998). *Customer-Centred Supply Chain Management*. New York: Amacom.

Lamming, R. (1993). *Beyond Partnership Strategies for Innovation and Lean Supply*. Hemel Hempstead: Prentice Hall.

Lowson, B., King, R. and Hunter, A. (1999). *Quick Response – Managing the Supply Chain to Meet Consumer Demand*. Chichester: Wiley.

Lui, H. and McGoldrick, J. (1996). International retail sourcing: trend, nature and process. *Journal of International Marketing*, **4** (4), 9–33.

Macbeth, D. K. and Ferguson, N. (1990). Strategic aspects of supply chain management. *OMA-UK Conference on Manufacturing Strategy – Theory and Practice*, Warwick.

Oliver, J. and Houlihan, J. B. (1986). Logistic management – the present and the future. *Proceedings of 1986 BPICS Conference*.

Oliver, R. K. and Webber, M. D. U. (1982). Supply chain management: logistics catches up with strategy. *Outlook*.

Porter, M. E. (1980). *Competitive Strategy: Techniques for Analyzing Industries and Competitors*. New York: Free Press.

Sako, M. (1992). *Prices, Quality and Trust: Interfirm Relations in Britain and Japan*. Cambridge: Cambridge University Press.

Slack, N., Chambers, S. and Johnston, R. (2001). *Operations Management*, 3rd Edn. London: Financial Times Prentice Hall.

Smith, A. (1910 [1776]). *The Wealth of Nations*. London: Dent.

Swamidass, P. M. (1993). Import sourcing dynamics: an integrative perspective. *Journal of International Business Studies*, **24** (4), 671–691.

Taylor, F. W. (1911). *The Principles of Scientific Management (Special Edition Distributed to the Members of the American Society of Mechanical Engineers)*. New York: Harper & Brothers.

Wikner, J., Towill, D. R. and Naim, M. M. (1991). Smoothing supply chain dynamic. *International Journal of Production Economics*, **22**, 231–248.

Williamson, O. E. (1971). The vertical integration of production: market failure considerations. *American Economic Review*, **61**, 112–123.

Williamson, O. E. (1975). *Markets and Hierarchies*. New York: Free Press.

Womack, J. P., Jones, D. T. and Roos, D. (1990). *The Machine that Changed the World*. London: MacMillan.

3

Challenges of fashion buying and merchandising

Margaret Bruce and Lucy Daly

Introduction

The fashion industry has undergone considerable change over the years, with increasing global competition and the move towards a global supply chain impacting on lead times and supply chain management. The fashion retail buyer plays an important role in this process through supplier selection and product decision-making, and the role is arguably changing from purely operational to a much more strategic one. The complex nature of buying is demonstrated, as this focuses on management of a portfolio of suppliers, relationship building, as well as interfacing effectively with internal activities, especially merchandising. These activities are generic, but will vary according to the context in which they takes place. For own-branded fashion, the buyer will be involved with product development decisions and trend forecasting to ensure that the season's collections match with consumer expectations. The role of the buyer in product development is not discussed in detail, in this chapter.

This chapter covers the following:

- The dynamic context in which fashion sourcing occurs.
- The role of fashion buying in sourcing and managing a portfolio of supplier relationships.
- Interface with key activities in fashion retail, especially merchandising.
- The key skills of a fashion buyer.

Dynamics of fashion sourcing

The supply chain for fashion is complex, with many different parties being involved. Fashion and textiles is a volatile industry, and getting the right product in the right place at the right time can be difficult to achieve (Christopher and Peck, 1999). As a result relationships between organizations are an essential aspect of supply chain management as they facilitate communication within an industry operating on a global basis. A recent example of the challenges facing fashion buyers was the removal of worldwide quotas on 1st January 2005. This resulted in a fear of cheap imports flooding the UK market and impacting on employment in the UK textile and apparel manufacturing sector. Limits on imports from China were subsequently re-imposed later in the year, limiting growth in 10 categories until 2008 as a result of a surge in imports. However, this resulted in the so-called 'bra wars' that occurred in the EU and US during the summer of 2005, as by this time retailers had placed significant orders with Chinese manufacturers, and found that millions of garments were refused entry into the EU and held up at European ports (*Daily Telegraph*, 2005), so leading to a looming crisis and shortage of products in the stores. Other forces affecting fashion sourcing and buying are discussed here.

Impact of fast fashion

The fashion retail market also has become increasingly turbulent over the years. Supermarkets are moving into apparel retail, selling branded goods at discounted prices by taking advantage of the grey market (Mintel, 1999; Mintel, 2002a; Mintel, 2002b). This has resulted in the clothing retail market becoming split into a number of segments – luxury, high street and supermarket/out-of-town discounter. In addition to this, the fashion buyer may be responsible for product development for own-brand lines, rather than sourcing private label collections. Gannaway (1999) suggests that 'supermarkets are racing to make apparel an even smarter cash generator'. Asda and Tesco are at the forefront of this move and are investing heavily. In 1999 Asda sales of George apparel saw an increase of 16% on the previous year. Retailers are beginning to develop new approaches in order to remain competitive against such moves by retailers. The year 2000 saw the introduction of the Per Una range by George Davis into Marks and Spencer stores worldwide. The use of designer ranges for high street stores is a growing trend with Debenhams,

Marks and Spencer and New Look all taking advantage of consumer pre-occupation with designer brands. The entrance of supermarkets into the clothing market has increased competition and redefined how customers shop for clothing, with time-starved customers able to purchase cheap fashionable clothing as part of the weekly shop, rather than visiting the high street. Indeed, fast fashion is a growing phenomenon in the UK.

In recent years, there has been a shift towards low wage countries for the manufacture of consumer goods (Mattila et al., 2002) with products sourced from the Far East, and also from Italy, Portugal and Turkey (Vinhas Da Silva et al., 2002). In 2004 developing countries accounted for nearly 75% of all clothing exports (*The Financial Times,* 22 Oct. 2004), and more recently, with the removal of trade quotas, companies have greater opportunity to take advantage of cheaper goods from low-cost overseas manufacturers. China and India have been the major beneficiaries of the elimination of quotas, whilst the losers have been South Korea, Taiwan, Africa, the Americas and Europe. China has seen a 23 per cent rise in clothing exports, giving it a 28 per cent of the global clothing trade (*The Financial Times,* 25 Oct. 2005). However, the level of exports from China into Europe and the US has prompted the reintroduction of quota agreements with China, with the US agreeing quotas on 34 categories of clothing accounting for 46 per cent of China's imports into the US until the end of 2008 (*The Financial Times,* 9 Nov. 2005). Imports into Europe from China of standard clothing items including stockings, socks, blouses, bras and T-shirts were valued Euro 1.1 billion in the first quarter of 2005, and imports of pullovers grew by 534 per cent (*The Financial Times,* 35 Apr. 2005). The arising dispute resulted in large stockpiles in China of clothing destined for export, and tens of millions of garments in warehouses in Europe as they subsequently exceeded newly imposed quotas, resulting in some retailers taking action to recover money lost (*The Financial Times,* 20 Aug. 2005) and many facing shortfalls of stock in autumn collections (*Sunday Telegraph,* 21 Aug. 2005). India has been able to benefit from the reintroduction of quotas to China, with a rise in the number of orders from European and American retailers of 25 per cent between June and September 2005 (*Sunday Telegraph,* 11 Sep. 2005). However, the counter-argument to the reinstating of quotas is the case of European clothing retailers and importers. The EU clothing retailer sector, which benefits from sourcing garments cheaply from countries such as China, employs twice as many people as the EU garment manufacturing sector, which currently employs 2.5 million workers, a figure which has been declining for some years. It is believed that reintroduction of quotas may cost jobs in the retail sector, as retailers attempt to reduce costs elsewhere (*The Financial Times,* 19 May 2005). Many retailers are now moving production to Eastern Europe, Turkey and India, prompted not only by the problems faced with imports from China, but also in response to competition from retailers such as Primark, Zara and New Look, who are able to push the latest trends quickly by sourcing closer to home and so meet the demands of fast fashion, where in-seasonal changes occur frequently. This means that for some high street retailers, they are sourcing and buying on a weekly basis to introduce new fashionable items and to replenish stock. As a consequence, the retail fashion buyer is managing a complex portfolio of suppliers to meet speed, fashion and cost parameters. Companies moving production include Next and Debenhams (*The Financial Times*, 30 Aug. 2005).

Hidden costs often remain out of view in the decision to source globally, which is made without consideration of the true costs associated with such a move (Mattila et al., 2002). Hines (2001) poses the Iceberg Theory, which identifies a number of hidden costs associated with overseas sourcing, including travelling and subsistence costs of buyers; increased time taken by managers pre-acquisition, during acquisition and post-acquisition; and the cost of lost sales as a direct result of late delivery of merchandise. In addition, transportation delays, costs and quality issues are also problems associated with international sourcing (Lui and McGoldrick, 1996; Popp 2000). Long-lead times mean that companies have to rely heavily on long-term forecasts, which may be inaccurate. It is estimated that levels of merchandise sold at mark-down price has grown to in excess of 33 per cent, and that one in three customers is unable to find the goods required in stock. It is estimated that errors in pre-season forecasts may be as high as 50 per cent, and that in comparison, forecasts based on observations of 20 per cent of sales had errors as low as 8 per cent (Fisher and Raman, 1996, cited in Mattila et al., 2002). Errors in forecasting can result in lost sales and excess inventory. Hence, the experience of constant price reductions and sales in stores to get rid of unwanted stock quickly and to replace this with more fashionable items. Products where demand can be accurately predicted should be differentiated from those where demand is difficult to determine, and forecasting and sourcing strategies should be applied accordingly (Mattila et al., 2002). Consequently the role of the buying team is essential to a retailers' success.

Fashion buying cycle

The traditional fashion buying cycle occurs 1 year before a season, with leads for orders placed 6 months prior to product launch. Thus buying is based on long-term forecasts based on historical sales (Birtwistle et al., 2003). However, there is a risk of such forecasts being inaccurate as a result of out-of-date data and difficulties in predicting popular sellers, resulting in out-of-stock best sellers and excess stock poor sellers, requiring mark-downs and reduced margins (Birtwistle, 2003). When product is manufactured in low-labour cost countries such as the Far East replenishment/re-manufacture is not practical due to long-lead times. Many companies now use a combination of manufacturers for supply, with low-cost basic lines supplied by the Far East, fashion lines supplied by North Africa and Eastern Europe, and replenishment/re-manufacture from UK manufacturers (Birtwistle et al., 2003). Such a sourcing strategy results in higher overall costs, but reduced excess stock/mark-downs and out-of-stock/lost sales. Fashion buyers are managing a complex array of suppliers to achieve and deliver this sourcing strategy.

Traditionally, fashion sourcing focussed on sourcing product with the cheapest landed cost, usually overseas sourcing with a single delivery prior to the sales period (Mattila et al., 2002). The buyers' plan, which is developed up to 8 months prior to the selling season, was used to determine the volume and assortment of goods. However, companies are now recognizing that a quick response (QR) strategy can result in forecast accuracy as high as 95 per cent, with 95 per cent sell-through and goods delivered directly to store (Mattila et al., 2002).

An off-shore/local sourcing mix is one sourcing strategy a retailer may adopt. Although offshore sourcing may appear to be the optimal strategy when considering gross margin as a result of lower product costs, such a strategy often results in increased mark-downs at the end of the season (Mattila et al., 2002).

Companies in the fashion industry are increasingly using time as a factor for enhancing competitiveness. In addition, reductions in lead-time facilitate companies in addressing an increasing demand for variety. Development cycles are becoming shorter, transportation and delivery more efficient and merchandise is presented 'floor ready' on hangers and with tickets attached (Birtwistle et al., 2003). Companies are taking advantage of lower-priced products from overseas in an attempt to improve competitiveness, and discounts can be between 15 and 35 per cent for products sourced from Asia and Africa (Lowson, 2001). However, distance is key in today's turbulent fashion market, and goods from China can have a shipping time of 22 days, compared to 5 days from Turkey (*The Financial Times*, 30 Aug. 2005). This means that companies such as New Look, Tesco and Primark often look to source fast-fashion items, which need to be highly responsive to market demand, from countries that are closer to the UK.

Fast fashion has become an important factor within the UK clothing industry, and the objective of getting clothing to stores within the smallest lead time possible is of paramount importance to companies. This has resulted in an increasing number of 'seasons', and shipping times from suppliers needs to be taken in to consideration at sourcing (Mintel, 2002). Retailers are now moving as much of their sourcing away from the Far East, where shipping times can be as long as 6 weeks, to Eastern Europe, where shipping times can be as little as 2 to 3 days. However, fast fashion does not apply to the whole range in stores, and as much as 80 per cent of goods may be core and basic lines, with fast fashion accounting for up to 20 per cent (Mintel, 2002). Zara is an important example of a fast-fashion retailer, with repaid stock turnaround and vertical integration creating greater control over product lifecycles.

Companies in the Far East are becoming increasingly adept at moving from manufacture of commodity products to incorporating design and branding. For example, Episode, the women's clothing chain, is owned by the Fang Brothers Group, which is based in Hong Kong, Giordano, and Hong Kong based brand now has 200 stores in Hong Kong and China, and a further 300 stores throughout South East Asia and Korea (Jin, 2004).

QR

QR approaches to supply chain management were developed by the apparel manufacturers in the US during the mid-1980s in order to maintain competitiveness with offshore manufacturers through reduced lead times and accurate forecasting (Birtwistle et al., 2003). By using QR companies are able to reduce both excess stock holding in the supply chain and risk associated with forecasting. Suppliers, manufacturers and retailers establish long-term supply relationships in order to see reductions in time in manufacturing and distribution processes. Trusting and co-operative relationships between buyers and suppliers are important factors in such a strategy. When operating by QR methods the buyer schedules production time but product specifications are not finalized until nearer to delivery. This is as a result of the QR focus on demand rather than forecasting, which requires close partnerships between the retailer and its suppliers (Birtwistle et al., 2003).

Fashion supply chain

The retailers source globally for their textiles and apparel products to acquire cost benefits and in time to meet their fast moving and demanding consumer needs. The trend for offshore sourcing has led inevitably to a decline within employment in industrialized nations for textiles and apparel. However, global sourcing does not always suffice to meet retailers' demands, particularly if they need to replenish a well-selling stock mid-season, and so local suppliers are used in tandem with those offshore. Managing the logistics and supply chain for textiles and apparel suppliers and retailers has to be synchronized and is driven by the exigencies of the dynamic patterns of demand, especially for fashion items. A number of approaches can be taken to supply chain management and these are classed as: lean, agile and leagile. Each of these approaches is discussed here and they provide the context in which fashion retailers are choosing to select suppliers and manage a portfolio of supplier relationships.

Lean supply

The focus of lean supply management is the elimination of all waste including time to enable a level schedule to be established (Naylor et al., 1999). Abernathy (2000) proposes a model for a lean management of the supply chain for the textiles and clothing industry. He argues that lean retailers require rapid replenishment of products, and shipments need to meet strict requirements in terms of the delivery times, order completeness and accuracy. Key to this is the use of bar codes, EDI and shipment marking.

Agile supply

The Iacocca Institute (1991), argued that an enterprise could thrive in an environment of rapid and unpredictable change, through acting in an agile manner, and by responding effectively to constantly changing and highly competitive business environments. The agile supply chain is applicable to situations where minimal lead times are required to address volatile consumer demand with high levels of availability (Hiebelar et al., 1998). The agile supply chain has a number of distinguishing features. It is market-sensitive with the ability to respond to actual real-time changes in demand. Organizations must acquire capacity capability in order to be able to react to possible volatile fluctuations in demand. The use of information technology to share data between buyers and suppliers is crucial for agile supply (Harrison et al., 1999) as it will improve visibility of requirements and reduces the amount of stock (Hewitt, 1999). Information sharing between supply chain partners is important to support activities such as joint product development. Childerhouse and Towill (2000) argue that the adoption of the lean principles are appropriate for commodity products where demand can be predicted and agile principles are relevant for innovative products such as fashion garments where demand is unpredictable and product life cycles are short.

Leagile supply

The concept of 'leagile' supply chains has been suggested (e.g. Van Hoek, 2000; Mason-Jones et al., 2000; Naylor et al., 1999). 'Leagile' takes the view that a combination of lean and agile approaches should be combined at a decoupling point for optimal supply chain management. Mason-Jones et al. (2000) argue that agility will be used downstream and leanness upstream from the decoupling point in the supply chain. Thus, leagile enables cost effectiveness of the upstream chain and high service levels in a volatile marketplace in the downstream chain. However, Van Hoek (2000) argues that although a leagile approach to supply chain management may work in an operational sense, it makes no sense to fundamentally challenge the concept of agility, as it has to fit with an agile approach to supply chain management in order to be applied properly.

Textiles and fashion is characterized by volatile markets, short product lifecycles and high product variety (Fernie, 1999). The sector has low-profit margins and thus holding small quantities of stock is often not a viable option. Often, fashion companies combine agile and lean supply chain management methods to respond to changing markets in order to provide quick replenishment.

Managing a portfolio of supplier relationships

The fashion buyer plays a key role in developing and managing relationships between the company and its suppliers. A company will have a variety of types of relationships with different suppliers ranging from close partnerships with key suppliers to develop products and to generate the best outcome for both parties, through to distant relationships where it may be a one-off purchase and the emphasis is on getting the lowest price (Table 3.1). Often buyers will have a portfolio of relationships with manufacturers worldwide, and long-term relationships will involve a degree of social and personal relationships, as well as formal and contractual relationships between the organizations involved. As well as direct contacts between supplier and fashion retailer, agents and intermediaries are common and these serve to source suppliers and manage third-party relationships on behalf of the retailer and/or manufacturer.

Cultures vary widely from country to country and so a key consideration for the fashion industry is its global nature. Fashion buyers need to be sensitive to cultural differences when managing business relationships and some companies hire buyers with language skills when building relationships with foreign suppliers.

Relationships can be either formal or informal on all spectrums, and also long term or short term, although as companies become closer to being in a partnership their relationships are more likely to be longer term. Some relationships will be longstanding with buyers taking over existing relationships from the buyer before them. How do new suppliers get in to the company in such a situation? In a partnership the emphasis is not on price, but instead on trust and the long-standing relationship between the two companies. Often

Table 3.1 Types of relationships

Relationship	Characteristics
Strategic alliance Co-operative	• Integrate core competencies and add value to the relationship • Equality • Information is shared • A more efficient supply chain
Operational partnership	• A partnership based on one partner benefiting from the other's core competence • Partners may not benefit equally • More risk for one of the partners • Information sharing is selective
Opportunistic partnership	• One party performs activities that the other no longer will • Power inequality • One party gains at the expense of the other • Risk for one partner • Information rarely shared
Arms length Adversarial Conflictual	• Short term • Competitive • Price focussed • Low quality

such relationships are more important than paying the lowest price for a product, as companies need to feel confident that products will arrive when required and of an acceptable and consistent quality.

> 'If it was only cost we would go out of business tomorrow because as far as the customer is concerned they go to Marks and Spencers because they can trust it. 'I might not always find what I want but at least the quality is going to be good irrespective of where that product is manufactured', and with the same ethical quality that you would expect in the UK'.
>
> Menswear Buyer, Major Department Store A

> 'We tend to work direct with factories as much as we can, we don't, we try not to work through agents. That's really so that we can have, not necessarily the best prices but we can have as much one on one contact, therefore we've got quite a tight supply base but it's a supply base that we've known for a long time, they understand what the company is all about, they've been with us for the last 5 years, right from the beginning, and that's very important, the relationship that we have with them'.
>
> Buying Manager, Major Department Store B

However, is there a trade-off between price and quality? This presents considerable risk for the company, and the buyer, when considering a new supplier, as levels of trust between the two organizations have not yet been built.

Vendor selection

The increasing size of retail organizations and homogenization of merchandise has meant that vendor selection is a key buyer activity (Moin, 1986; Levy, 1987; Mayer, 1987; Feinberg, 1988; cited in Wagner et al., 1989). Many vendor selection criteria are particular to the retail industry, such as the role of the buyer in meeting company profit objectives, and that the goods purchased are intended for re-sale rather than for use in production. Consequently retail buyers use information regarding sales history and merchandise fashionability in vendor selection procedures (Wagner et al., 1989). Also, ethical sourcing is another dimension affecting choice of supplier (Shaw and Tomolillo, 2004). Fashion retailers do not wish to be tainted with claims of running sweat-shops and using child labour. Vender selection and approval of vendors can be a complex process and may involve a number of parties in the retailer and supplier. It is a contractual arrangement between the organizations concerned.

Fashion buying decision criteria

Across the consumer product spectrum as a whole, buyers consider quality characteristics including design, finish, durability, dependability, safety, taste and texture (Shipley, 1985). Wagner et al. (1989) cite Hirschman (1981) argue that buyers use manufacturer reputation, brand name, price, manufacturer size, selling history, merchandise quality, product innovativeness and product marketability factors in vendor selection. In a study of retail buyers from US department stores, Wagner et al. (1989) identified three criteria that dominate in vendor selection:

- selling history
- mark-up (the relationship between purchase price and selling price)
- delivery.

Important factors of negotiation for buyers include price, time of payment, stock keeping, co-operative activities, volume, delivery times and physical distribution, product quality and specifications and manufacturer assortment (Bowlby and Foord, 1995; cited in Hansen and Skytte, 1998; Lindqvist, 1983). For fashion buyers, responsiveness to requests is crucial (Da Silva et al., 2002). Also, Fiorito (1990) argues that a fashion buyer's decision to select a particular supplier is based on its ability to offer new products, an extensive variety and knowledge of the fashion industry. In addition, brand and country of origin are important dimensions. It is likely that the fashion buyer makes trade-offs between a number of factors, especially price, packaging, assortment and delivery (Dandeo et al., 2004).

Buying processes

However, it is not just external relationships that are important, but also internal ones between the different members of the buying team. Within retail buying are buying decisions and assortment decisions, with assortment decisions acting as a more comprehensive group than buying decisions – all buying decisions are assortment decisions, but not all assortment decisions are buying decisions (Nilsson and Host 1987 cited in Vinhas Da Silva, 2002). Assortment decisions relate to the rearrangement of current products to optimize sales, including decisions of product retention and deletion. The following quote from a merchandiser in a high street fashion retailer illustrates this point well:

'So, it's really the merchandisers who once the stocks in place, and you've got delivery dates on it, it's really the merchandisers role to make sure that they're (Buyers) still happy with those lines coming in. I mean often the buyer has to get involved because a lot of it's about styling and colour, but for example you know white's not working and we've got 2 more lines coming in and I'd be like should we still be doing them and is there any opportunity to change it, you know anything like that'.

(Interview Merchandiser, 24.2.05, Buckley, 2006)

Fashion buying is a strategic decision for the organization and affects the product assortment available to consumers. Such a process is likely to involve considerable information search, including market trends and consumer behaviour (Johansson, 2002) and also longer-term trends in the supply market such as concentration and switching costs (Jennings, 2001). Such information is often not forthcoming internally and thus has to be externally sourced. By contrast, standardized and modified re-buys often require internal and operational information, such as sales and cost figures (Johansson, 2002). Thus, fashion buying has strategic implications for the retailer. If the buyer makes wrong decisions, then this can have disastrous consequences for the reputation of the retailer and its economic performance.

The buying process includes a number of activities and steps (Johansson, 2002):

- Problem recognition (resulting from either internal or external stimuli)
- Product specification
- Supplier search
- Supplier choice
- Evaluation.

Such activities are conducted either by the buyer and/or input from other internal stakeholders in the process, such as merchandisers, design, etc. and, where appropriate, external wholesalers and producers who contribute to trend forecasting, and so on (Johansson, 2002). This chapter has addressed issues of supplier search, selection and choice. Using Johansson's terms, now it will focus on issues affecting problem recognition and product specification.

Fashion buying is a key role and it has been suggested that all of the different functional activities of the retailer are used to facilitate and assist the buyer to purchase merchandise that satisfies consumer demand (Rachman, 1979, cited in Fiorito, 1990). Typically, the buyer will liaise closely with merchandising and design in order to optimize the process (Table 3.2).

The buyer works closely with design functions to ensure a fit between trend forecasting and the consumer profile for the organization. The relationship with logistics and supply chain is also particularly important in determining accurate information for ticketing, labelling, warehousing and the flow of goods to store.

The buyer's role is multi-faceted, involving market evaluation, supply chain management, identification of trends and effective team working. Fashion buyers have to be able to work financially and be numerate, as they are working

Table 3.2 Buying, merchandising and related function: brief definitions (Adapted from Jackson and Shaw, 2001)

Role	Responsibilities
Buyer	• Decides on styles to be bought • Negotiates production with suppliers
Merchandiser	• Works with buyers planning the stock mix • Manages budget • Controls stock deliveries and allocation to stores
Designer	• Provides creative direction • Produces product designs for the buyer to select from
Garment technologist	• Provides technical (fabric and construction) advice • Controls sample development
Quality controller	Monitor product quality. This involves visiting suppliers and checking for adherence to company set product specifications.
Visual merchandiser	Manage the in-store presentation of product ranges. Often they use guidelines set by the buyers when developing presentation plans.

out volumes of product to purchase, and the cost of these. They also need to determine the retail price that the garments will achieve and the contribution made to the retailer. Whilst negotiating with the supplier, they need to be able to make these calculations rapidly and effectively. Such calculations will need to be made across different currencies too. Fashion buyers are judged in terms of profitability (Ettenson and Wagner, 1986). An effective fashion buyer is able to assess the product range and purchase according to customer needs and market trends; negotiate the highest profit margin on goods bought and sold; and ensure delivery on schedule. This is a tough set of demands to satisfy.

Fashion buyers require a broad range of hard and soft skills, including:

Garment buyer skills	Soft skills
	IT-orientated
To develop and buy a range of merchandise that achieves the profit margin and is consistent with the retailers buying strategy	Analytical
To source and develop products from an effective supplier base	Detail concisions
To be responsible for the negotiation of product prices including delivery and payment terms	Numerate
To research and evaluate all relevant products and market trends	Multitasking flexibility
To communicate effectively with suppliers, product teams and senior management within the company	Logical, rational
To work within the constraints of merchandise planning	Assertive
To effectively manage and develop the buying team	Retentive memory

The fashion buyer needs to interface effectively with merchandising to ensure that the collection is ready for display in store, as required. The buyer and merchandising roles need to dovetail and in some retailers they are organized in the same functional area to facilitate communication and understanding of each other's roles and responsibilities. Merchandisers likewise require hard and soft skills, as shown:

Merchandising skills	Soft skills
To estimate sales and plan stock levels to achieve the planned sales and margin for a specific garment	Commercial with creative flair
To provide regular analysis and progress reports referring to stock levels, sales performance and stock purchases to senior management	Multitasking flexibility
To work with the buyer on range planning to maximize commercial opportunities for products	Mental agility
To manage intake and commitment to accommodate the stock requirements of the business at any given time and the open to buy requirements of the garment type	Tough but fair
To manage stock distributions to stores optimizing customer demand, available selling space and seasonal selling opportunities	Self-motivated
To effectively manage and develop the merchandising/distribution team	Task-orientated Negotiation skills Fashion awareness Commercial awareness Planning skills Action-centred approach

Fashion buying cycle

The fashion buying cycle is short, with buyers now purchasing new goods as frequently as every 6 weeks (Kline and Wagner, 1994). However, in companies with a focus on fast fashion, this can occur even more frequently, even on a weekly basis (Buckley, 2006).

> ' . . . so there'll always be something being bought every week, whether it'll be one line or 20 lines. It depends on what stage they're at in their placing order stage. You know, from a buying point of view, they wouldn't say oh I'm . . . ., and sit down and place all their orders, it's not like that. It's just very ad hoc, it's just reacting'.
> (Interview Merchandiser, 24.2.05, Buckley, 2006).

In sum, the role of the fashion buyer can consist of between 18 and 25 different activities including studying market research reports and analysing post-sales records to identify levels of demand for different products (Fiorito, 1990). In

Fashion retail buying

Case study: Departmental store

Company background

Company A is a major high UK retailer, with over 375 stores nationwide, and a further 155 franchised stores overseas in Europe, the Middle East, Asia and the Far East. The company has a turnover of £7.3 billion, and in 2003 saw a profit of £822.9 million before exceptional items, an increase of 6.5 per cent on the previous year.

The company employs just below 66,000 people in UK stores and head office, and it is estimated that 10 million people shop in UK stores every week. Clothing retail accounts for the largest area of the business, constituting 50.1 per cent of retail sales in the UK. In 2003 the company held an 11 per cent share of the clothing retail marketplace, and the turnover for the year for clothing retail was £3958.1 million.

The buying function

Buying is a crucial activity for Company A's clothing departments, and is well represented at Board level, with Executive Directors of the various strategic business units. The structure for the buying operation is flat, with the buyer/product developer reporting to the director for their department, who then reports to the executive director. This allows decisions to be made rapidly, which is essential in a fast-moving market such as clothing retail.

There are both operational and strategic elements to the buyer's role. Operational work includes activities such as liaising with current suppliers, but at the same time the team is thinking more strategically about how the company should be repositioning its sourcing to optimize the combination of product, speed to market and cost.

The buying function is split into departmental teams, rather than operating as a central function. The benefit of this is that the buyer is able to work closely with the merchandiser and the technologist for that product area. However, it does mean that the company does not aggregate orders for product types across the business, in order to leverage scale.

The buying process

The buying teams are multi-functional, with the buyer, merchandiser and garment technologist working closely together to determine budgets, build ranges and source products.

The buying process is complex and the buyer undertakes a number of activities, beginning with analysing the sales figures for the current season to identify strengths and weaknesses. The buyer visits New York, Paris and Milan on trend shopping trips and to see the fabric and garment shows, and also conducts comparison-shopping in the UK in order to identify competitor activity. At the same time the merchandiser works to develop the buying budget, deciding on the number of UPCs that can be merchandised in stores, and on the total quantities of products required.

Finally the team then work with suppliers to define the production programmes, including pre-production, production planning, capability planning and delivery to stores.

Sourcing

Company A sources 45 per cent of its product from Europe, Eastern Europe, Turkey and Morocco, and the other 55 per cent from India, Sri Lanka and China. Decisions regarding sourcing location are based on whether the product is classified as core or fashion, and are conducted by the buying team. Demand for a core product is much more stable and easily forecast, and therefore is more suitable for manufacturing in a low-labour cost country with long lead times than a fashion product with unpredictable demand.

Company A categorize suppliers into two types – full service vendor and direct factory, depending on the working relationship between the two companies, and also the nature of the work being conducted. The buying team makes the decision as to whether a product is manufactured in a full service vendor or a direct factory, and this is based on capability available. Company A will always choose to manufacture in a full service vendor if they are able to produce the garment at the right quality and price, to the right design, and the correct lead time. However, if there is no full service vendor that meets these requirements the product will be produced in a direct factory.

The full service vendor category accounts for most products produced, and plays an important role for the company's success. Full service vendors play an active role in collaboratively designing the product alongside the buying team, and take responsibility for managing the manufacturing process. The full service vendor will then source the components required for manufacture, manage the manufacturing process (this may be in-house, out-sourced or as a joint venture), ship products to the UK and warehouse the products before they are sent out to stores. Company A only pay a full service vendor for the goods as they are moved into store from the supplier's warehousing facility.

The company will use a direct factory only if there is no full service vendor capable of producing the product required. The relationship between this type of supplier and Company A is much more arms length. Company A will design the product in-house at and develop the pre-production package, which is then passed to the factory for sampling and production. Once the product has been manufactured Company A will arrange for a logistics operator to transport the goods to a Company A-owned warehouse to be called into stores. Direct factories are paid free on board (f.o.b.).

When manufacturing fast-fashion goods, planning and communication within the supply chain is essential. As the order size is much smaller, it is important to know that a supplier will have the capability to change lines rapidly.

Information sharing

Within the buying function as a whole there is a mix of bottom-up and top-down information sharing, depending on the type of information to be shared.

The buying team takes a bottom-up approach with regards to sharing trend information. This information and information on sales is shared with the top 15 suppliers, which account for some 80 per cent of the total supply base. One of the most important considerations for the team is accurately defining the customer and matching the product range to that customer.

The board level share information regarding strategic considerations such as future aims and strategies of the business downwards with the buying team. This then allows the buying team to take account of such considerations when developing collections.

Summary

The role of buying has strategic and operational aspects in fashion retailers. The buying team conducts operational activities on a daily basis, and is also involved in strategic activity regarding future sourcing strategies. The buying team is also provided with strategic information from the board and this is integrated into the operational activity. The flat hierarchical structure aids the transfer of strategic and operational information throughout the whole of the buying function ensuring a good mix between strategic and operational activity.

The supplier plays an active and important role in the product development process, collaborating on product development and planning to ensure that information is accurately shared between companies. This is essential to ensure that consumer requirements such as product available and an exciting product mix are met to achieve competitive advantage.

addition the buyer will analyse and examine economic conditions, and industry and trade journals, in order to purchase the best products at the lowest cost. As discussed previously, relationship building is also argued to be a key aspect of a buyer's role (Wingate and Friedlander, 1978; Packard, Winters and Axelrod, 1983; cited in Fiorito, 1990).

Conclusions

The emphasis has been on the role of the fashion buyer on managing a portfolio of supplier relationships to meet rapidly changing consumer needs and market demands to provide an attractive assortment of fashion products on time and within acceptable price parameters. To do so is complex. It requires fashion buyers to possess a blend of hard and soft skills, particularly financial ability, people skills and a passion for the product. Interfacing with other activities, particularly design and merchandising is crucial too. The strategic role of the fashion buyer has been underplayed, but with the dynamic market context in which fashion retailers are placed, demands that this role is re-examined and its impact on strategy recognized.

Acknowledgement

The authors would like to thank Dr Susan Fiorito, Florida State University, for her contribution to this piece of research.

References

Abernathy (2000). Retailing and supply chains in the information age. *Technology in Society*, **22**, 5–31.

Birtwistle, G., Siddiqui, N. and Fiorito, S. (2003). Quick response: perceptions of UK fashion retailers, *International Journal of Retail and Distribution Management*, **31** (2), 118–128.

Bruce, M., Moore, C. and Birtwistle, G. (Eds.) (2004). *International Retail Marketing: A Case Study Approach.* Butterworth-Heinemann: Oxford, UK.

Childerhouse, P. and Towill, D. (2000). Engineering supply chains to match customer requirements. *Logistics Information Management,* **13** (6), 337–345.

Christopher and Peck (1999). Fashion logistics. In Ferine, J. and Sparks, L. (Eds.) *Logistics and retail management, Insights into current practice and trends from leading experts,* London, UK: Kogan Page Ltd. Chapter 5, pp. 88–109.

Daily Telegraph (2005). Bra wars deal gets EU off the hook for a year. 6, September 2005.

Da Silva, R., Davies G. and Naude P. (2002). Assessing the influence of retail buyer variables on the buying decision-making process. *European Journal of Marketing,* **36** (11/12), 1327–1343.

Dandeo, L., Fiorito, S., Guinipero, L. and Pearcy, D. (2004). Determining retail buyers' negotiation willingness for automatic replenishment programs. *Journal of Fashion Marketing and Management,* **8** (1), 27–40.

Ettensson, R. and Wagner, J. (1986). Retail buyers' saleability judgements: a comparison of information use across three levels of experience. *Journal of Retailing,* **62** (1), 41–63.

Fernie, J. (1999). Relationships in the supply chain. In Fernie, J. and Sparks, L. (Eds.), *Logistics and Retail Management, insights into Current Practice and Trends from Leading Experts.* London, UK: Kogan Page Ltd, Chapter 2, pp. 23–46.

Fiorito, S. (1990). Testing a portion of Sheth's theory of merchandise buying behaviour with small apparel retail firms. *Entrepreneurship Theory and Practice,* **14** (4), 19–34.

Gannaway (1999). Checkout Chic. *Grocer.*

Hansen, T. and Skytte, H. (1998). Retailer buying behaviour: a review. *The International Review of Retail, Distribution and Consumer Research,* **8** (3), 277–301.

Harrison, A., Christopher, M. and Van Hoek, R. (1999). Creating the agile supply chain, *School of Management Working Paper,* Cranfield University.

Hewwit, F. (1999). Supply or demand? Chains or pipelines? Co-ordination or control? *Proceedings from International Symposium In the Information Age,* Florence, pp. 785–790.

Hiebelar, R., Kelly, T. and Katteman, C. (1998). *Best Practices Building Your Business with Customer Focussed Solutions.* Simon and Schuster: New York, NY.

Hines (2001). From analogue to digital supply chains: implications for fashion marketing, *Fashion Marketing, contemporary issues,* ED Tony Hines and Margaret Bruce, Chapter 2, pp. 34–36, Butterworth and Heinemann: Oxford.

Iacocca Institute (1991). *21st Century Manufacturing Enterprise strategy. An Industry-Led View. Volumes 1 and 2,* Bethlehem, PA: Iacocca Institute.

Jackson, T. and Shaw, D. (2001). *Fashion Buying and Merchandising Management.* Palgrave: Hampshire.

Jennings, L. (2001). Thorntons the vertically integrated retailer, questioning the strategy. *International Journal of Retail and Distribution Management,* **29** (4), 176–187.

Jin, B. (2004). Apparel industry in East Asian newly industrialised countries. *Journal of Fashion Marketing Management,* **8** (2), 230–244.

Johansson, U. (2002). Food retail buying processes – a study of the UK, Italy and Sweden. *International Journal of Retail and Distribution Management,* **30** (12), 575–585.

Kline, B. and Wagner, J. (1994). Information sources and retail buyer decision-making: the effect of product specific buying experience. *Journal of Retailing,* **70** (1), 75–88.

Lowson, R. (2001). Analysing the effectiveness of European Retail Sourcing Strategies. *European Management Journal,* **19** (5), 543–551.

Lui, H. and McGoldrick, P. (1996). International Retail Sourcing: Trend, Nature and Process. *Journal of International Marketing,* **4** (4), 5–32.

Mason-Jones, R., Naylor, J. and Towil, D. (2000). Engineering the leagile supply chain. *International Journal of Agile Manufacturing Systems,* Spring 2000.

Mattila, H., King, R. and Ojala, N. (2002). Retail performance measures for seasonal fashion. *Journal of Fashion Marketing and Management,* **6** (4), 340–351.

Mintel (1999). *Womenswear Retailing,* March 1999.

Mintel (2002a). *Clothing Retailing In the UK,* April 2002.

Mintel (2002b). *Womenswear Retailing,* March 2002.

Naylor, N. and Berry (1999). Leagility: Integrating the Lean and Agile Manufacturing Paradigms in the Total Supply Chain. *International Journal of Production Economics,* **62,** 107–118.

Popp, A. (2000). Swamped in information but starved of data: information and intermediaries in clothing supply chains. *Supply Chain Management: An International Journal,* **5** (3), 151–161.

Shaw, D. and Tomolillo, D. A. C. (2004). Undressing the ethical issues in fashion: a consumer perspective. In Bruce, M., Moore, C. and Birtwistle, G. (Eds.), *International Retail Marketing: A Case Study Approach,* Oxford, UK: Butterworth Heinemann.

Shipley, D. (1985). Resellers' supplier selection criteria for different consumer products. *European Journal of Marketing,* **19** (7), 26–36.

Sunday Telegraph (2005). *Europe's Indian shopping spree.* 11 September p. 7.

The Financial Times (2004). Textile producers weave a web to restrict China: less efficient poor nations fear they will lose rich world trade when the global quota system ends this year, 22 October p. 10.

The Financial Times (2005). China and India gain from end of quotas. 25 October p. 9.

The Financial Times, (2005). Beijing Agrees to Curb clothing exports to the US. 9 November p. 11.

The Financial Times (2005). EU reveals surge in imports of textiles from China. 25 April p. 8.

The Financial Times (2005). Quotas on Chinese textiles 'would hurt' EU retailers. 19 May p. 10.

The Financial Times (2005). Textile quotas force shift in Chinese production. 20 August p. 7.

The Financial Times (2005). Retailers move production from China in response to demands of 'fast fashion'. 30 August p. 1.

Van Hoek, (2000). The thesis of leagility revisited. *International Journal of Agile Management Systems*, **2** (3), 196–201.

Vinhas Da Silva, R., Davies, G. and Naude, P. (2002). Assessing customer orientation in the context of buyer/supplier relationships using judgemental modelling. *Industrial Marketing Management*, **31**, 241–252.

Wagner, J., Ettenson, R., Parrish, J. (1989). Vendor selection among retail buyers: an analysis by merchandise division. *Journal of Retailing*, **65** (1), 58–79.

4

Segmenting fashion consumers: reconstructing the challenge of consumer complexity

Tony Hines and Lee Quinn

Introduction

The primary focus of this chapter concerns one of the most widely debated concepts in marketing theory and practice. Market segmentation implicitly lies at the core of most, if not all, strategic marketing initiatives facilitating the identification and satisfaction of an organization's most profitable customers (Dibb et al., 2005). In a fashion context a central measure of performance for managers adopting a market segmentation strategy lies in their ability to successfully address the following issues:

1 Identify the customer in a meaningful way.
2 Satisfy individual customer requirements profitably.

3 Implement the segmentation concept in ways that provide manageable solution. Particularly in view of today's increasingly fragmented and volatile consumer societies.

Whilst the first two of these issues are likely to be important for any customer-focused organization the final one in particular has become significantly relevant and inherently problematic in the context of fashion consumption and fashion retailing. Therefore, in order to address this fundamental concern, which is often highlighted in contemporary debates on market segmentation, the purpose of this chapter is threefold: first, to provide an overview of the antecedents and key chronological developments in segmentation research and theory development during the past 50 years; second, to highlight a number of criticisms which have been raised to question the usefulness of the segmentation concept in dynamic market contexts; and finally, to move beyond what can be described as an impasse in the development of the segmentation concept to present a theoretical commentary which accounts for the dynamic and complex nature of much social interaction and consumption as it occurs in a fashion context. The identification and importance of recognizing multiple self and social identities is highlighted as a key point of reference in order to present a number of important theoretical and practical implications which have so far been overlooked within critical debates on market segmentation.

Global interest in market segmentation

The topic of segmentation is highlighted as a top tier research priority for marketing according to the US Marketing Institute (2005) and in the UK, the Academy of Marketing's recently established Special Interest Group on the subject (Academy of Marketing, 2005) provides further evidence of its importance as a fundamental aspect of contemporary marketing theory. The value of marketing segmentation to practitioners cannot be underestimated and it has been widely viewed by managers as a means of adopting relatively efficient use of marketing resources (McDonald and Dunbar, 2004). Its effectiveness, however, is determined by the ability of managers to identify appropriate segments and implement strategies to reach target groups and individuals identified through analysis and interpretation.

The cited benefits of market segmentation

The underpinning principles of market segmentation can be traced to economic pricing theory, which suggested that discriminatory pricing could be used to maximize profits amongst different customer groups (Stigler, 1942). However, Wendell Smith (1956) has become widely cited as having written the seminal paper describing and labelling the concept of market segmentation. His argument was based upon changes in consumer market demand requiring a rational and more precise adjustment of product, on the supply side, to meet that demand. This balancing process to match supply to demand requires more co-ordination of marketing effort. It is suggested that segmentation can enhance marketing effectiveness and develop or maintain an organization's ability to benefit from identifiable marketing opportunities (Weinstein, 1987). This resource-based approach to managing organizations suggests that segmentation can help businesses allocate financial and other resources more effectively (McDonald and Dunbar, 2004). It is also suggested that it leads to a better understanding of groups of customers, which can assist in the design of more suitable marketing programmes (Dibb et al., 2002).

Research developments in the history of market segmentation

Following Smith's seminal proposals, research attention within the marketing literature initially concerned the selection of appropriate base variables that could also be utilized for the purpose of identifying market segments (Martineau, 1958). In its embryonic stage as a concept, market segmentation research began to gather pace during the 1960s. The central focus of numerous research efforts at this time maintained the pursuit of more suitable variables from which to segment customers (e.g. Webster, 1965; Pessemier et al., 1967; Bass et al., 1968) and these developments eventually led towards the development of increasingly sophisticated lifestyle-orientated models where customers' interests and activities could be correlated to individual socioeconomic characteristics as a means of objectively identifying homogeneous customer groups. However, as a result of these developments, questions were also raised as to whether multivariate techniques could successfully be applied in an attempt to clearly define segments with several researchers questioning the validity of identified segments (Green and Wind, 1973; Blattberg et al., 1976).

The 1980s saw concerted academic and practitioner efforts to develop a truly generalizable psychographic segmentation model. One of the key projects at this time was SRI International's 'Values and Lifestyles' (VALS) proposal and subsequent development of a VALS 2 model (Mitchell, 1983). Due to their increased complexity, however, these developments were also surrounded, as one might expect, by much research attention concerning the reliability of psychographic measures (Burns and Harrison, 1979), psychographic validity (Lastovicka, 1982) and the predictive validity of segmentation outputs (Burger and Schott, 1972; Novak and MacEvoy, 1990). In view of the trend towards such complex segmentation models it is perhaps not surprising that practical implementation difficulties were widely noted during the 1990s (Littler, 1992; Piercy and Morgan, 1993; Dibb and Simkin, 1997).

From around the mid-1990s the segmentation concept was further critiqued from a postmodern perspective and debates in the marketing literature highlighted a concern that consumer markets were becoming increasingly fragmented and consumers in the process were less predictable (Firat and Venkatesh, 1993; Brown, 1995; Firat and Shultz, 1997). Global changes in life-style, income, ethnic group and age continue to broaden the diversity of cus-tomer needs and buying behaviours (Sheth et al., 2000) and some observers suggest that market segmentation approaches are becoming less effective and efficient as a result (Firat and Schultz, 1997; Sheth et al., 1999). This is particu-larly evident in fashion markets where the benefits derived from products and brands are inherently varied and dynamic. Consequently, simple segmenta-tion frameworks adopting measures of social class, chronological age and gen-der are widely acknowledged as less useful descriptors of consumer attitudes, tastes and behaviours than they were even 10 years previously. Evidence from marketing practice supports this view.

> 'The area of demographics, you know, the A, B, C1 . . . that area of segmentation, is not as important anymore, particularly with fashion. You can't look at it in the same way that you used too, especially as people mix things up a lot now.'
>   (Marketing Manager: Supermarket Fashion Retailer)

The industry response to this problem has seen an increased popularity of seg-mentation approaches based on behavioural characteristics and increasingly complex segmentation frameworks (e.g. The Experian Consultancy's 'Fashion Segments,' 2004). However, in the dynamic context of fashion, problems with this approach remain and it is therefore important for us to closely examine the underpinning foundations of contemporary segmentation debates before offering an alternative and potentially fruitful alternative perspective.

Market segmentation: the evidence

Whilst critics have long argued that there are many managerial and practical problems to be encountered when considering how to segment markets and target consumers it is helpful to deconstruct the basis of such claims. The cen-tral concern behind several criticisms of the managerial approach to market segmentation focuses upon the notion that the process delivers outcomes that are neither robust nor stable. Clearly this would certainly appear to be the case in a dynamic market context such as fashion retailing. However, any manager implementing a segmentation strategy makes two undeniable assumptions concerning the nature of social world we make sense of: first, that the cus-tomer can be recognized through time as a major source of variability, and also that customers can be consistently aggregated in ways which can be correlated to other descriptor variables (Wensley, 1995). An objective understanding of the managerial segmentation approach might therefore overlook the acknow-ledgement that 'every [segmentation] model is at best an approximation of reality' (Wedel and Kamakura, 2002, p. 329). Clearly, therefore, one can argue that a major area for concern here lies in the ontological development of the segmentation concept. The identification of homogeneous consumer groups by means of an approximation of reality suggests the belief in an objective social reality where consumer understandings, preferences and behaviours may be objectively aggregated. This view of being in the world represents an understanding that determines a segmentation process by which attempts are made to reflect ontology upon method. Measurement of some objective reality that exists independently of social market interactions is the dominant view of reality adopted in this approach. Many, if not all, segmentation models appear to reveal this realist ontological assumption.

> 'I think there are definitely groups, without doubt. I think that there are these groups and I think that they'll pretty much be set. It would be a complete nightmare really if the segments did keep changing. If that was the case you would never be in the position of proper information . . . should we act on it or not because it may be changing?'
> (Marketing and Research Executive: Large UK Fashion Retailer)

To validate the segmentation argument in this vein would typically require empirical testing. However, the fundamental problem here is crudely exposed as Wensley (1995, s. 66) observes: '. . . neither assumption seems to stand empirical testing except at the very gross level such as more affluent people buy more expensive cars. We can neither assume consistent behaviour in terms of response to marketing actions such as price or advertising or with respect to previous behaviour except again in the sense that, in general, heavy buyers in a particular category tend to remain heavy buyers.'

Furthermore, despite inevitable differences between individual views on the nature of social reality, we also have to remember that managerial decision-making remains very much a human process characterized by intuitive and tacit ways of behaving (Curran and Goodfellow, 1990). It is further suggested that, because implementing a segmentation approach involves a number of managerial assumptions and arbitrary decisions, market segmentation is essentially nothing more than an arbitrary process (Hoek et al., 1996). Yet, even if it were possible to consistently aggregate customer groups through time, Wright and Esslemont (1994) argue that many unintended individuals are likely to be exposed to any tactical marketing messages aimed towards the target segment. As the results of this exposure are unknown, they conclude that there is no reason to expect that a targeted approach will provide better results than a mass marketing effort.

Making sense of the segmentation paradox

It is apparent that there is a need to make sense of the segmentation concept given the problems outlined. However, accepting the highly complex nature of contemporary consumer societies and the managerial difficulties involved in the implementation of a segmentation strategy, we would not suggest that empirical testing provides the only basis for 'validating' the segmentation concept. It is clear that a challenge to the future success of the market segmentation concept lies, paradoxically, in a broadening of the heterogeneity that the approach was designed to handle (Dibb, 2001). It is also apparent that context is important in representing contemporary social realities. Indeed, as Baudrillard (1994, p.79) observes, 'we live in a world where there is more and more information and less and less meaning.' The fashion retail sector provides a relevant context in which to explore the segmentation paradox as fashion markets are characterized by volatile demand where factors such as age, personal disposable income, lifestyle and culture all appear to influence a specific and increasingly fragmented market context (Hines, 2001). Retailers can often be seen to target offers towards specific groups of customers (Bevan, 2002; McGoldrick, 2002), which should lead us to conclude that they are successful by the criteria established within the marketing segmentation literature. However, potential customers are not always easy to identify and this is evidenced by perennial markdowns and unsold stock. Clearly there is much disagreement as to what should or should not be acceptable as a segmentation approach and the normative view – upon which most understandings of the concept are based and communicated through in the marketing literature – demonstrates that realist assumptions form the very basis of the normative segmentation approach. However, because segmentation is essentially dependent on the managers' view of any particular socially mediated consumption situation this suggests that it would be wise to accept a broadening of the normative view to accept alternative perspectives. The question is: how?

When social worlds collide

'As soon as you start to put numbers on people it starts to give a spurious sense of robustness and accuracy. Instead of having product range planning meetings there were people arguing about who was the classic customer and who wasn't. There was this temptation to over use it just because it was numerical.'
(Head of Marketing and Research: Large UK Fashion Retailer)

Although market segmentation clearly has its exponents and its critics, the nature of social identity has been largely overlooked in the debate so far. Jenkins (1996) highlights two important reasons why the concept of identity is important in the sociological literature: first, the identity of self, where we may wish to affirm and communicate to ourselves, and second, the identity of group, or social identity, where we communicate to others. These issues are also central to any proposed segmentation of consumer markets. A number of writers have addressed the notion of social identity with reference to the postmodern condition (see Table 4.1 for a brief overview of postmodern conditions) where consumption is a central activity in the facilitation and communication of identity (Giddens, 1991, 2002; Gergen, 1999). However, as Gergen

(1999, p.30) observes the chief problem is that the critiques are so powerful that they almost destroy themselves and the result is a standoff between critics and targets, with no obvious means of resolution.

Table 4.1 A description of postmodern conditions

Postmodern conditions	Brief descriptions
Openness/tolerance	Acceptance of difference (different style, ways of being and living) without prejudice or evaluations of superiority or inferiority
Hyperreality	Constitution of social reality through hype or simulation that is powerfully signified and represented
Perpetual present	Cultural propensity to experience everything (including the past and future) in the present, 'here and now'
Paradoxical juxtapositions	Cultural propensity to juxtapose anything with anything else, including oppositional, contradictory and essentially unrelated elements
Fragmentation	Omnipresence of disjointed and disconnected moments and experiences in life and sense of self – and the growing acceptance of the dynamism which leads to fragmentation in markets
Loss of commitment	Growing cultural unwillingness to commit to any single idea, project or grand design
Decentring of the subject	Removal of the human being from the central importance she or he held in modern culture – and the increasing acceptance of the potentials of his/her objectification
Reversal of consumption and production	Cultural acknowledgment that value is created not in production (as posited in modern thought) but in consumption – and the subsequent growth of attention and importance given to consumption
Emphasis on form/style	Growing influence of form and style (as opposed to content) in determining meaning and life
Acceptance of disorder/chaos	Cultural acknowledgment that rather than order, crises – and disequilibria are the common states of existence – and subsequent acceptance and appreciation of this condition

Source: Firat and Shultz (1997, p. 186).

Brands in particular are seen as particularly powerful symbolic resources in the construction of social identity (Elliot and Wattanasuwan, 1998). Moreover, in contemporary consumer societies social identity cannot be described as a static affair. Put simply, consumers are free to construct and re-construct their identities and group affirmations in an infinite manner, fluidly and not bound by time. In this sense segmentation solutions which effectively force individuals into groupings according to pre-determined constructs are understandably rejected by an increasing number of writers (e.g. Maffesoli, 1996; Cova, 2002).

'I think in a different sort of business I might believe in it [segmentation] but I think you've got to accept that's not the way this business operates and I'm realistic enough and pragmatic enough not to try and impose something that simply cannot be used.'
(Head of Marketing and Research: Large UK Fashion Retailer)

In many organizations segmentation is a default activity. It is not possible to target everyone and some criteria have to be applied to split consumers into manageable chunks. However, 'segmentation is not the holy grail of accountability and effectiveness that it is sometimes held up to be' (Hackley, 2005, p. 15).

'Obviously you do need to be somewhat targeted and to try and figure out who the customer is. What I want to know is who am I selling to and who am I not selling to and how do I start selling to those people. You can't rely on segmentation but it is useful and it helps you make decisions, it informs decision-making and lots of the time it's almost like security.'
(Marketing Manager: Supermarket Fashion Retailer)

The rational view provides a strategic aim of market segmentation as focusing scarce organizational resources towards groups with homogenous characteristics, thus ensuring that organizational resource utilization is efficient. Taking the normative view of the segmentation process in fragmented market conditions to its logical conclusion and pursuing the 'segment of one' (Dibb, 2001) would focus these resources on the individual customer. However, in light of the concept's economic foundations, a number of critical questions arise for the process of production and consumption if we assume that a segment of one is economically viable. First, customers would have to search for, or discover, products that satisfy their requirements since it may often be economically unviable for producers to identify single customers. Pursuing this proposition to its extreme position might lead us to conclude that market segmentation is unnecessary and that it is more important for customers to segment their suppliers. Second, to satisfy a single customer is necessarily more costly than to supply multiple customers, which in turn means individual customer servicing costs may be higher. One of the authors recalls a conversation with the senior management at VF corporation in the US when they reported that they were not interested in pursuing an e-business consumer model because it would be too expensive. 'Why deal with the individual consumer when we can deliver large quantities to WalMart' was the retort of the marketing director when faced with a question about e-business strategy. Obviously, for managers devising segmentation strategies these are important concerns. Managers are limited by budgetary constraints and geographical limitations (Hackley, 2005) so if we assume that customers make their product choices either consciously or unconsciously it becomes important to understand the processes by which decisions are made.

In this instance, views of identity that have become prominent in the sociological literature are important to facilitate our discussion. Hines and Quinn

(2005) contrast a number of alternative theoretical perspectives regarding the nature of self and social identity highlighting the significance of these arguments for the concept of market segmentation. Initially they draw upon the work of Lacan (1979) who argued that a key aspect of the unconscious mind can be likened to the construct of language. It operates symbolically, suggesting that language constructs meaning through culture but recognizing that the development of identity is more socially constructed than biologically determined (Berger and Luckmann, 1966). Therefore, at a conscious level, identity may be characterized by language and meaning. However, at an unconscious level, assuming the Cartesian notion of an inner mind, symbolism is deemed more important in determining action. Drawing reference to 'optimistic' and 'pessimistic' views of identity that became prominent in the sociological literature it is suggested that in its 'optimistic' sense of meaning that individuals may be motivated to self-actualize (e.g. Maslow, 1967), thus discovery of an inner self not artificially imposed by some traditional perception. The psychoanalytic path to identity, espoused by Freud (1940), supports the view that individuality equates with difference. Akin to the pessimistic view held in the psychodynamic tradition is of mass society estrangement, whereby the trend towards selfishness and self-absorption manifests itself through fragmentation. However, although in our everyday social worlds we present ourselves as individuals an alternative perspective offers that we do so within one of the multiple, socially mediated roles that we have constructed. In essence these constructions can be presented metaphorically as 'masks,' which serve to prevent us revealing what we do not want to reveal (Goffman, 1959). 'Identity management' may manifest itself in modified attitudes and behavioural patterns of individuals. What we see is not necessarily who they (consumers) are (as individuals or collectively).

Marketers attempt to understand consumer and customer similarities rather than differences and, in effect, this premise is what makes the segmentation concept operational. Relative to the concept of market segmentation this argument presents a further important dimension. Segmentation tools and methods rely on the identification of individuals and groups whose consumption needs can be satisfied by producers. Ultimately marketers may know where you live, how old you are, your gender, your religion, your income bracket and so on. However, they do not know your other, context-dependant, multiple selves, which we assume determine your preferences, and how you will decide to allocate your income. In practice, therefore, traditional segmentation tools assume a static dimension, attempting to identify particular characteristics at a point in time. Highlighting the nature of socially constructed and therefore multiple consumer realities, on the other hand, enables us to identify consumers themselves as being as dynamic as the societies in which they negotiate meaning. One implication is that conscious consumer behaviours or attitudes traditionally captured through a survey may only be revealed at a point in time, implicitly suggesting static market conditions. Metaphorically speaking, we suggest that in this context consumers construct and reveal behaviours and attitudes consciously to those 'looking into the mirror' (Strauss, 1997). For the observer it is a Gestalt 'moment of truth.' For the unquestioning manager, this provides a handle from which to interpret complexity, which in turn reinforces the normative segmentation model.

As Hines and Quinn (2005) maintain, this argument suggests that segmentation strategies are most useful for conditions in which markets are static (ordered) and consumer behaviour is consciously predictable. They are less useful in conditions where markets are dynamic, or rather, where individuals construct plausible versions of the context-specific social reality they experience in such a way that they become less predictable. Unfortunately for marketers, fashion markets are becoming increasingly dynamic (i.e. less ordered, more complex and increasingly diverse). More importantly, if self and social identities are fluidly re-constructed through societal fragmentation then perhaps social identities are moving closer to self-identities. Ultimately therefore, categories such as 'high spender,' 'average spender' and 'low spender' may be more meaningful constructs from which to address the everyday customer. If not, it therefore becomes more important to either understand markets in terms of socially constructed spaces, or through examining social discourses, rather than to simply analyse past behaviours. Essentially, past behaviour patterns in this sense may provide little indication of future behaviours.

Social encounters of a third kind

This position leads us then to an impasse where the concept of segmentation is undoubtedly held up as a useful tool in some respects but, ultimately, its limitations are all too clear.

> 'We only ever intended these typologies to be a working tool. It was a way of just providing a common view of the customer. That's all we were trying to do. I very quickly recognised that there were certain areas of the business where, I wouldn't say segmentation couldn't help at all, but where because of the nature of research because it can be quite slow moving, it's imperfect, it can attempt to rationalise the irrational in lots of ways in terms of fashion.'
> (Head of Research and Planning – European Fashion Wholesaler)

However, in the fitting words of Kenneth Gergen (1999, p. 30), 'But one final turn must be made in this story. For many it is a downward turn that leaves a deposit of despair. As the arguments unfold not only do the traditions seem groundless ... but so do the critiques. The critiques initially seem to offer moments of insight, new ways of understanding, possibly some positive alternatives. And yet, if this is the termination of the dialogue we end in a sorry state. It is on this soil of critique and dead-end despair that social constructionism takes root. For many constructionists the hope is to build from the existing rubble in new and more promising directions. The postmodern arguments are indeed significant, but serve not as an end but a beginning. Further, if we are careful and caring in the elaboration of the constructionist alternative, we shall also find ways of reconstituting the modernist tradition so as to retain some of its virtues while removing its threatening potentials. We move then from prevailing despair to more positive possibilities – from deconstruction to reconstruction.'

The social construction of identity

Social constructionists might argue that the social world is an interpretive network of human beings brought together through time, place, utility and form. Identification of particular segments is therefore fraught with problems that emanate from the four dimensions discussed in the last sentence. Meaning is derived and interpreted through culture (Geertz, 1983, p.4) and knowledge merges through and into localized culture as meanings are assigned (Gubrium, 1989). Groups, formal organizations and everyday life conditions encountered help people make sense of their worlds (Douglas, 1986). It is apparent in this position that individuals have their own identities as individuals, as part of a family group, as part of formal organizations they engage in and as part of a region, nation and world community (Jenkins, 1996). They interpret their own identities in these different contexts whereas traditional segmentation strategies entail that others impose identities externally through an assessment of characteristics, class, nationality, status and memberships amongst other things.

An interesting view of decision-making applicable in a segmentation context is supported by Weick's (1995) sense-making notion. Weick challenges the perception that environments are objective entities and subjective differences are only drawn because human information processes differ between individuals making interpretations. It is through interactions between object and subject that environments are shaped. For example, retail spaces and places are shaped through consumer interactions and mediations. Retailers invest heavily in property portfolios and store designs to encourage individuals to engage in an exchange process of cash for a bundle of goods and services. In terms of identity retail brands populate particular spaces to encourage footfall through their carefully designed spaces. Consumers making choices between brands are encouraged through their mediation within these socially constructed spaces that convey meaning through brand recognition. Essentially retailers make a statement through space and place that says: we know who we are; do you identify with us strongly enough to make a choice and a decision to buy? Consumers make choices between brands through identity processes. These interactions between subject and object are important shapers of the socio-economic process of consumption.

The inevitable challenge for practitioners may then be to accept that using more and more data inevitably leads to more and more segment possibilities. This is a situation which could compound the already reported difficulties to be encountered when competing in complex, fragmented and dynamic markets. Table 4.2 provides a useful summary of critical points of difference and

Table 4.2 Theoretical perspectives in market segmentation

Characteristic	Realist	Postmodern	Constructionist
Individual identity	Universal, definitive through measurable characteristics	Not universally definable but typically: fragmented, decentred, hyper-real, playful and paradoxical	Not universally agreed but continuously negotiated and agreed between actors
Group identity	Universal, definitive through measurable characteristics	Characterized through fragmentation	Socially constructed and negotiated within, through and by group interactions
Identifiers	External imposed by analysts using data from different sources to model behaviours and actions	N/A – To impose any identifiers would be un-postmodern	Within the specific context through interaction (Internal)
Dominant paradigm In segmentation research	Yes	No	No
Judgements	Objective	N/A – Highly critical of realist assumptions	Subjective
Context	Static – reliant on snapshots in time through data collection instruments usually survey/census data	Dynamic and highly fragmented – continuous change and by its very nature indefinable	Dynamic – continuous change model of identification through negotiation and interaction
Method	Static – Statistical analysis (e.g. cluster analysis)	Difficult to propose one	Anthropological and ethnographically appreciative approaches Focus on social discourses

similarity between the three ontological and theoretical perspectives pertinent to the identification of individuals and groups.

Implications for fashion marketing

A greater understanding of underpinning theoretical arguments in market segmentation is important for fashion marketers attempting to make sense of consumers' social identities. This discussion therefore makes a conceptual contribution to contemporary theoretical debates on market segmentation, which accounts for the dynamic nature of social interaction. It is not, however, akin to current standpoints in market segmentation, as merely a static classification, particularly as it fundamentally bears upon dynamic issues, which are magnified in a fashion context. It becomes important to understand the limitations of the segmentation concept in light of this dimension.

Managerial approaches to the segmentation problem although not socially constructed in the sense described above do just this applying pre-conceived notions of behaviour based upon externally identified determinants. A mathematical model of expected behaviour through specific, scientific group identities is the purpose for much managerial segmentation modelling. One could argue that some data in the analysis of identity is drawn from individuals themselves through the completion of census data or other personal data offered by the individual in different contexts (e.g. loyalty cards). However, most segmentation interpretations are made externally to the subjects and often through macro-modelling approaches. This in itself can be problematic in terms of assumptions developed to make interpretations about particular types of people let alone in the identity of their assumed behaviours.

> 'We're aware that we need to be that next step ahead and the only way we can do that is through understanding our consumer and finding out what we need to do to move with them and for them to stay with us so they don't go elsewhere.'
> (Marketing and Research Executive: Large UK Fashion Retailer)

To facilitate this move towards a socially constructed understanding of market segmentation strategy entails research methods from anthropological and ethnographical theoretical perspectives which examine how people actively, creatively and socially use brands, advertisements and mediated consumption in their own lives to symbolically realize their wishes and fantasies, and to produce a sense of social identity (Hackley, 2005). Only when these opportunities are realized can we move beyond the limitations of market segmentation and accomplish strategic goals in the dynamic and problematic contemporary world of fashion marketing.

References

Academy of Marketing (2004). Market Segmentation (Special Interest Group). Available, http://www.academyofmarketing.info/sigsegment.cfm

Bass, F., Tigert, D. and Lonsdale, R. (1968). Market segmentation: group versus individual behavior. *Journal of Marketing Research*, **5**, 264–270.

Baudrillard, J. (1994). *Simulacra and Simulation*. Ann Arbor: The University of Michigan Press.

Berger, P. and Luckmann, T. (1966). *The Social Construction of Reality: A Treatise in the Sociology of Knowledge.* London: Penguin.

Bevan, J. (2002). *The Rise and Fall of Marks and Spencer.* London: Profile.

Blattberg, R., Buesing, T., Peacock, P. and Sen, S. (1976). Identifying the deal prone segment. *Journal of Marketing Research,* **15** (August), 369–377.

Brown, S. (1995). Postmodern marketing research: no representation without taxation. *Journal of the Market Research Society,* **37** (3), 287–310.

Burger, P.C. and Schott, B. (1972). Can private brand buyers be identified? *Journal of Marketing Research,* **9** (May), 219–222.

Burns, A. C. and Harrison, M. C. (1979). A test of the reliability of psychographics. *Journal of Marketing Research,* **16** (February), 32–38.

Cova, B. (2002). Tribal marketing: the tribalisation of society and its impact on the conduct of marketing. *European Journal of Marketing,* **36** (5–6), 595–620.

Curran, J. G. M. and Goodfellow, J. H. (1990). Theoretical and Practical Issues in the Determination of Market Boundaries. *European Journal of Marketing,* **24** (1), 16–28.

Dibb, S. (2001). New millennium, new segments: moving towards the segment of one?. *Journal of Strategic Marketing,* **9** (3), 193–213.

Dibb, S. and Simkin, L. (1997). A program for implementing market segmentation. *Journal of Business and Industrial Marketing,* **12** (1), 51–65.

Dibb, S., Simkin, L. P., Pride, W. and Ferrel, O. C. (2005). *Marketing: Concepts and Strategies,* 5th Edn. New York: Houghton Mifflin.

Dibb, S., Stern, P. and Wensley, R. (2002). Marketing knowledge and the value of segmentation. *Marketing Intelligence and Planning,* **20** (2), 113–119.

Douglas, M. (1986). *How Institutions Think.* Syracuse, NY: Syracuse University Press.

Elliot, R. and Wattanasuwan, K. (1998). Brands as symbolic resources for the construction of identity. *International Journal of Advertising,* **17** (2), 131–144.

Experian UK (2004). Fashion Segments. *Internal Documentation and Ongoing Dialogue,* presented courtesy of Mr Patrick Gray, October 27th.

Firat, A. F. and Shultz, C. J. (1997). From segmentation to fragmentation: markets and marketing strategy in the postmodern era. *European Journal of Marketing,* **31** (3/4), 183–207.

Firat, A. F. and Venkatesh, A. (1993). Postmodernity: the age of marketing. *International Journal of Research in Marketing,* **10** (3), 227–249.

Freud, S. (1940). *Outline of Psychoanalysis,* Vol. XXIII, London: Hogarth Press.

Geertz, C. (1983). *Local Knowledge: Further Essays in Interpretive Anthropology.* New York: Basic Books.

Gergen, K. J. (1999). *An Invitation to Social Construction.* London: Sage.

Giddens, A. (2002). *Runaway World.* London: Profile.

Giddens, A. (1991). *Modernity and Self-identity: Self and Society in the Late Modern Age.* Cambridge: Polity Press.

Goffman, E. (1959). *The Presentation of Self in Everyday Life.* London: Penguin.

Green, P. and Wind, Y. (1973). *Multivariate Decisions in Marketing: A Measurement Approach.* Illinois: Dryden Press.

Gubrium, J.F. (1989). Local Cultures in Service Policy. In Gubrium, J. F. and Silverman, D. (Eds.) *The politics of Field Research: Beyond Enlightenment*, Newbury Park, CA: Sage, pp. 91–112.

Hackley, C. (2005). Communicating with the fragmented consumer. *Admap* (March) 13–15.

Hines, T. (2001). Globalisation: an introduction to fashion markets and fashion marketing. In Hines, T. and Bruce, M. (Eds.) *Fashion Marketing: Contemporary Issues*, Oxford: Butterworth-Heinemann, pp. 1–25.

Hines, T. and Quinn, L. (2005). Socially constructed realities and the hidden face of market segmentation. *Journal of Marketing Management*, **21** (5/6), 529–543.

Hoek, J., Gendall, P. and Esslemont, D. (1996). Market segmentation: a search for the Holy Grail? *Journal of Marketing Practice: Applied Marketing Science*, **2** (1), 25–34.

Jenkins, R. (1996). *Social Identity*. London: Routledge.

Lacan, J. (1979). *Four Fundamental Concepts of Psychoanalysis*. New York: W. W. Norton & Company.

Lastovicka, L. (1982). On the validity of life style traits: a review and illustration. *Journal of Marketing Research*, **19** (February), 126–138.

Littler, D. (1992). Market Segmentation. In Baker, M. J. (Ed.) *Marketing Strategy and Management*, London: MacMillan, pp. 90–103.

Maffesoli, M. (1996). *The Time of the Tribes: the Decline of Individualism in Mass Society*. London: Sage.

Martineau, P. (1958). Social classes and spending behavior. *Journal of Marketing*, **23** (October), 121–141.

Maslow, A. H. (1967). Self actualization and beyond. In Bugental, J. F. T. (Ed.) *Challenges of Humanistic Psychology*, New York: McGraw Hill.

McDonald, M. and Dunbar, I. (2004). *Market Segmentation: How to do it. How to Profit from it.* Oxford: Elsevier Butterworth-Heinemann.

McGoldrick, P. J. (2002). *Retail Marketing*. London: McGraw Hill.

Mitchell, A. (1983). *The Nine American Lifestyles: Who We Are and Where We're Going.* New York: Warner.

Novak, T. P. and MacEvoy, B. (1990). On comparing alternative segmentation schemes: list of values (LOV) and values and lifestyles (VALS). *Journal of Consumer Research*, **17** (1), 105–109.

Pessemier, E., Burger, P. and Tigert, D. (1967). Can new product buyers be identified? *Journal of Marketing Research*, **4** (November), 349–354.

Piercy, N. F. and Morgan, N. A. (1993). Strategic and operational market segmentation: a managerial analysis. *Journal of Strategic Marketing*, **1** (June), 123–140.

Sheth, J., Banwari, M. and Newman, B. (1999). *Customer Behavior: Consumer Behavior and Beyond*. New York: Dryden.

Sheth, J., Sisodia, R. and Sharma, A. (2000). The antecedents and consequences of customer-centric marketing. *Journal of the Academy of Marketing Science*, **28** (1), 55–66.

Smith, W. (1956). Product differentiation and market segmentation as alternative marketing strategies. *Journal of Marketing*, **21** (July), 3–8.

Stigler, G. (1942). *The Theory of Price*. London: MacMillan.

Strauss, A. and Corbin, J. (1990). *Basics of Qualitative Research: Grounded Theory Procedures and Techniques*. London: Sage.

The Marketing Science Institute (2005). 2004–2006 research priorities – research priorities for the customer management community. *The Marketing Science Institute*, Cambridge, MA (available, <http://www.msi.org/msi/rp0406.cfm#RP-CMC>).

Webster, F. (1965). The deal prone consumer. *Journal of Marketing Research*, **2** (May), 186–189.

Wedel, M. and Kamakura, W. (2000). *Market Segmentation: Conceptual and Methodological Foundations*. Boston: Kluwer Academic Publishers.

Weick, K. E. (1995). *Sensemaking in Organizations*. London: Sage.

Weinstein, A. (1987). *Market Segmentation*. Chicago: Probus Publishing.

Wensley (1995). A critical review of research in marketing. *British Journal of Management*, **6** (Special Edition), S. 63–82.

Wright, M. J. and Esslemont, D. H. B. (1994). The logical limitations of target marketing. *Marketing Bulletin*, **5**, 13–20.

5

Developing a research agenda for the internationalization of fashion retailing

Christopher M. Moore and Steve Burt

Introduction

While fashion retailer activity is essentially a domestic market-based activity, now for a significant minority of fashion retailers, operating within a foreign market is essential to their reputation and makes a significant contribution to their overall turnover. Foreign market expansion is not a new phenomenon, however. For example, Liberty opened their first store in Paris in 1890, while Burberry opened their first store in the French capital in 1909. However, it is true to say that in the past two decades, the international expansion of fashion retailers has been unprecedented, and has been fuelled by a variety of facilitating factors, the most notable of which has been the emergence of fashion retailer super-brands (examples of which include The Gap, Benetton and Gucci), whose image positioning makes them appealing to customers across the globe, regardless of their cultural background and ethnic origin.

Consequently, fashion retailers are now identified as amongst the most important international companies.

Hollander (1970), in his review of the internationalization of retailers in general, noted that fashion retailers were amongst the most prolific and successful when it came to foreign market expansion. Dawson (1993) identified a number of factors which he suggested serve to explain why internationalizing fashion retailers enjoy considerable success abroad. These various factors are listed in Table 5.1.

However, despite the international success of fashion retailers, there has been little reference to that success within the literature, and consequently, there has been insufficient consideration of their international strategies and activities. Therefore, the purpose of this chapter will be to explore in depth the pan-national expansion of fashion retailers.

Akehurst and Alexander (1996) proposed an agenda for future research in the area of retailer internationalization in general. The details of their agenda are provided in Table 5.2.

Table 5.1 Factors enabling the internationalization of fashion retailing

Factors

- Small format requiring limited capital and management set-up costs
- Ease of entry and exit compared to manufacturing
- Single brand format enables internationalization
- More suited to franchising than food formats
- Economies of replication

Source: Dawson (1993).

Table 5.2 Future agenda for the study of the internationalization of retailing

Six questions of retailer internationalization	Key issues to be addressed
What is the internationalization of retailing? Who are internationalizing?	Development of a definition Identification of the key determinants which identify categories of international retailer
Why are retailers internationalizing?	Examination of the motivations for internationalization
Where are retailers developing international operations?	Identification of the direction of international expansion
How are retailers developing international operations?	Examination of the methods of foreign market entry
When does internationalization occur?	Examination of the conditions in which internationalization occurs

Source: Akehurst and Alexander (1996).

These research questions readily apply to a consideration of the international expansion of fashion retailers, and these will be addressed here and will serve as a structure for the remainder of this chapter.

What is the internationalization of fashion retailing?

The internationalization of fashion retailing is apparent in three ways. The first to be considered, and ostensibly the most prevalent, is the sourcing of products from foreign markets. Sourcing raw materials and finished and unfinished product from abroad has been a long-established feature of the British and European clothing sectors. Buying from foreign markets is largely motivated by economic and competitive considerations, as retailers seek to take advantage of low labour costs within underdeveloped economies. A further motivation for foreign market sourcing relates to the power of country of origin as a factor, which influences consumers' perception of the style, reliability and quality standards of a garment. For example, the Italian fashion industry has recognized that consumers worldwide perceive products originating from Italy as superior in style and quality, and has therefore adopted the 'Made in Italy' mark as a means of further exploiting these positive perceptions.

Furthermore, as a result of the advent of the global fashion brand, many fashion retail buyers are forced, as a response to consumer demand, to stock the world's most successful brands, such as those created by Ralph Lauren, Calvin Klein, DKNY, Lacoste and Diesel. The 'pulling power' of these brands is such that the fashion buyer has little choice but to stock these brands, often at the expense of lesser known brands from their home market.

Within the context of the British fashion market, it has to be recognized that the disintegration of the country's textile manufacturing sector has also made it increasingly difficult for British fashion retailers to source products of an acceptable quality standard and at an acceptable competitive price within the UK. Furthermore, because the British textile industry has suffered from a chronic lack of investment over the past 30 years, buyers who seek to offer a differentiated product range must source from abroad because of the lack of sufficient technical expertise within the domestic market.

The second dimension of fashion retailer internationalization relates to the internationalization of 'management know-how'. This 'know-how' may be in the form of expertise in particular trading methods, marketing techniques or technological competence. With the international flow of management personnel from one company to another, improvements in management intelligence gathering and the advent of multi-market participation by fashion retailers, it is increasingly the case that ideas, techniques and policies adopted in one country are soon replicated by another retailer in another country. One has only to consider the speed by which fashion retailers copied the just-in-time design to manufacturing processes of Benetton in the 1980s and the 'brand as communicator' advertising of The Gap in the 1990s to appreciate the extent of inter-company influence within the fashion sector.

Finally, the third and easily the most obvious aspect of fashion retailer internationalization is the operation of retail shops by fashion retailers within foreign markets. A number of questions arise as a result of this direct form of participation within a foreign market by a fashion company, and these relate to such issues as the reasons for opening stores abroad, the direction of that opening, as well as the operating methods that companies adopt in order to operate stores abroad. These various questions are the focus for the remainder of this discussion.

Who are the international fashion retailers?

To definitively identify which fashion companies operate stores abroad is highly problematic for a number of reasons. The first is that no international database appears to exist which has tracked the international activities of fashion companies. Secondly, if such a database did exist, then it would be impossible to ensure its accuracy, since this is a dynamic and fast-changing market sector; retailers enter and exit from national markets at great speed, for as Dawson (1993) identified, the replication of a fashion retailer's trading format abroad is limited in terms of capital and management costs, and their single brand format lends itself to economies of replication.

However, despite the difficulties of locating exactly who are the international fashion retailers, it is possible to identify categories of fashion retailer likely to engage in foreign market expansion. This can firstly be done on the basis of country of origin.

Studies undertaken by Corporate Intelligence on Retailing (1997) found that, within a European context, the most prolific international fashion retailers, in terms of the number of European countries to be entered, and the number of stores operated within these markets, originated from France, Italy, the US, The Netherlands, Germany, Denmark and the UK. No clear explanation is provided as to why these markets should produce such internationally oriented retailers, but possible suggestions include the recognition that these countries have long been established as reputable exporters of clothing products and their fashion retailers are expert in product and brand development, distribution management and information technology.

A further categorization of international fashion retailers drawn from an analysis of the most prolific fashion retailers is provided in Table 5.3, and identifies their product focus, the number of stores and their size, their market positioning and target customer groups.

Where are fashion retailers developing international operations?

Studies which examine the direction of fashion retailers' foreign market expansion are limited, both in terms of the volume and the breadth of companies

Table 5.3 The four types of international fashion retailer

1 **The product specialist fashion retailers**: These are companies that focus upon a narrow and specific product range, such as Hom Underwear, La Senza, Tie Rack, Nike, Sock Shop and Jacadi and have a clearly defined target customer group either based upon demography (such as childrenswear), gender (such as La Senza and Hom Underwear) or a specific interest (such as sport and Nike and Reebok). While there are some obvious exceptions, such as Nike Town, these retailers typically operate small-scale stores either within busy customer traffic sites, such as adjacent to airports/railway stations or major mass market shopping areas, such as Oxford Street in London and Fifth Avenue in New York.

2 **The fashion designer retailers**: Fernie et al. (1997) provided a clear definition of the international fashion designer retailers which states that these have an international profile in the fashion industry as evidenced in their having a bi-annual fashion show in one of the international fashion capitals (i.e. Paris, Milan, London and New York) and have been established in the fashion design business for at least 2 years. These firms retail merchandise through outlets bearing the designer's name (or an associated name) within two or more countries and market their own label merchandise.

Company examples of this group include Gucci, Valentino and Chanel, who normally locate within premium locations within capital and other important cities.

3 **The general merchandise retailers**: Corporate Intelligence on Retailing (1997) identified these as retailers that include a mix of fashion and non-fashion goods within their merchandise offer. Examples include department stores such as Marks & Spencer, Harrods and Sogo. These foreign stores are often located within key shopping centres and tourist locations, the merchandise offer increasingly extends beyond two trading floors (Corporate Intelligence on Retailing, 1997).

4 **The general fashion retailers**: Unlike the product specialist fashion retailers which tend to concentrate upon one or two fashion product groups, the general fashion retailers are described by Corporate Intelligence on Retailing (1997) as offering a broad range of fashion merchandise and accessories, either to a broad (e.g. The Gap) or highly defined target segment (e.g. Kookai). This group are typically low to mid-priced and locate in 'city centre' locations so as to allow maximum access for mass market customers (Corporate Intelligence on Retailing, 1997).

Source: Hollander (1970), Fernie et al. (1997; 1998), and Corporate Intelligence on Retailing (1997).

considered. Those studies which examined the direction of expansion of specific fashion retailers have found that the choice of market to be entered is largely determined by the market positioning of the retailer concerned. For example, Lualajainen (1992) found that the luxury goods retailer Louis Vuitton focused its international expansion upon the world's leading centres, specifically the capital cities of the most prosperous nations.

Hollander (1970) found that a focus upon capital city expansion was a common trait of the internationalizing luxury fashion retailers and he termed this expansion strategy the 'New York, London, Paris syndrome'. He explained that luxury fashion retailers adopted this strategy of opening flagship stores within the world's leading centres in order to create an allure and sophistication for their organizations. As such, the operation of a flagship store in Paris, Rome or the like communicated to consumers that the company was cosmopolitan, successful and accessible to the world's richest and most beautiful people.

While the luxury fashion retailers typically focus their expansion upon geographically disparate foreign markets, other studies have found that general fashion retailers have tended to concentrate their expansion upon the markets that are geographically and culturally proximate to their local market. Again, drawing from the work of Lualajainen (1991), the international expansion of Hennes & Mauritz of Sweden attests to the fact that those retailers which seek to serve the broad mass market typically opt to enter those markets which are culturally and geographically close, so as to minimize the associated risk and maximize their control over their operations there. It is only when this adequate coverage is achieved within adjacent foreign markets that consideration is given to entering into markets that are culturally and geographically distant from the home market.

Moving from the firm-specific level, a series of patterns relevant to the geographic expansion of fashion retailers can be identified as follows:

- European fashion retailers typically confine their foreign market entry to other European markets, as well as the North American market.
- American retailers typically enter into Canada, followed by the markets of Western Europe, specifically the UK.
- European designer retailers have extended their international participation into the Japanese and Pacific Rim markets.

In the 1990s, partly as a consequence of the highly competitive conditions within the European Union and as a result of the opportunities afforded by the demise of the USSR, fashion retailers have reorientated their international expansion to include Russia and the other markets of Eastern Europe. Furthermore, the previously underdeveloped markets of South America and the Middle East have emerged as the new centres for fashion retailers' foreign market expansion (Fernie et al., 1998).

When does fashion retailer internationalization occur?

Drawing from the international expansion of European fashion retailers provided by Corporate Intelligence on Retailing (1997), it is possible to identify distinct time periods within which the international expansion of retailers has occurred. The period 1990–1995 can be identified as the most significant in terms of number of fashion retailers entering a foreign market for the first time, followed by the period 1985–1989. In contrast, the period 1980–1984 is identified as a lean period, unlike the late 1970s, when a significant number of companies went abroad for the first time.

In many respects these fluctuations very broadly mirror the changing economic conditions of the respective periods, whereby, for example, the growth in international participation by fashion companies in the late 1980s appears to have been precipitated by the positive economic conditions of the period. However, economic conditions alone fail to account for the variations in foreign market participation levels. For example, the unprecedented growth in international expansion within the early 1990s occurred within the context of a significant international economic recession. Therefore, other explanations must be found in order to explain the timing of fashion retailers' expansion into foreign markets.

On the one hand, embarking upon an expansion strategy during a recessionary period is sensible, since the associated costs are likely to be less. However, financial reasons alone cannot account for the volume of expansion. Instead, consideration must also be given to social factors which facilitate the global expansion of a fashion retailer's brand. Dimensions such as the emergence of a more cosmopolitan, better informed fashion consumer precipitate the demand for products abroad, and the availability of pannational advertising media, the Internet and an increased convergence in global lifestyles has enabled fashion retailers to communicate cost-effectively with consumers from a wide variety of foreign markets.

The issue of the timing of fashion retailer internationalization is also concerned with the range of preconditions which may facilitate and encourage foreign market expansion, as well as the obstacles which inhibit a retailer from achieving success abroad. The advantages of a strong brand image with associated values of cosmopolitanism, exclusivity and design excellence have been identified as a key factor contributing to the success of the international fashion design houses (Fernie et al., 1997). In a similar vein, the international success of such companies as Hennes & Mauritz of Sweden and Kookai & Morgan from France has been attributed to their ability to offer product ranges which are distinctive and perceived to be value for money, within retailer environments which are memorable and capable of easy replication across a variety of markets (Lualajainen, 1991; Moore, 1997; 1998). Furthermore, the international success enjoyed by fashion retailers has also been attributed to their ability to develop internationally appealing brands, such as in the case of Benetton and The Gap (Simpson and Thorpe, 1996), and serve customer segments inadequately catered for by indigenous retailers, or to create segments where none had previously existed (Johnson and Allen, 1994; Sternquist, 1997).

Scant attention has been given to the problems that internationalizing fashion retailers may face. Hollander (1970) argued that the major obstacles that mass market fashion retailers face within foreign markets are more likely to be cultural than technical. The importance of cultural affiliation and understanding was seen to impact upon the decision to enter, as well as avoid, certain countries on the part of retailers such as Hennes & Mauritz of Sweden (Lualajainen, 1991). Corporate Intelligence on Retailing (1997), while recognizing that internationalizing fashion retailers may face problems related to supply chain inefficiencies, the activities of local competition, and the control and management of foreign operations from a distance, stated that the main reason for failure within foreign markets was because fashion retailers often underestimate the cultural differences that exist between foreign and domestic markets. As such, these retailers invariably fail to make necessary adjustments to their offer in order to suit local market conditions.

Given the inextricable relationship between cultural context and the very notion of what is deemed fashionable, it is perhaps surprising that greater consideration has not been given to the role of culture within the process of fashion internationalization. No study would appear to have considered the critical factors that foreign fashion retailers require for success, or the obstacles that such firms potentially face, when entering the UK market.

Why do fashion retailers internationalize?

Of the research areas related to retailer internationalization, those that consider the reasons for retail firms' involvement within foreign markets has arguably attracted greatest attention (Hollander, 1970; Jackson, 1976; Waldman, 1978; Kacker, 1985; Salmon and Tordjman, 1989; Treadgold, 1990/1991; Alexander, 1994; 1997; Tordjman, 1995; Crewe and Lowe, 1996). Variously described as driving forces (Treadgold, 1990/1991), international inducements (Hollander, 1970) as well as strategic motivations (Alexander, 1994), all of these terms relate in some way to those factors that encourage retailers to consider international market involvement as a strategy for growth (Williams, 1992).

Alexander (1997) noted that 'push' and 'pull' factors have emerged as an important method for interpreting retailers' motives for expanding into foreign markets. Derived principally from the work of Kacker (1985), the 'push–pull' dichotomy seeks to explain why retailers are pulled towards a foreign market and/or are 'pushed' out of their home market in order to further their growth objectives. Based upon a review of the expansion activities of European retailers into the American market, Kacker (1985) claimed that these two sets of factors were the key drivers for the significant growth in European retailer acquisition of American firms from the early 1970s to the mid-1980s. Accordingly, European retailer activity was prompted by 'push' factors evident in the various home markets and by 'pull' factors in the American market.

Alexander (1997) provided a comprehensive, but not exhaustive, listing of the significant 'push' and 'pull' factors associated with retailers' international expansion. In addition, he also emphasizes the fact that these factors do not exist in isolation, but are mutually inclusive. Indeed, these factors serve to delineate the political, economic, social, cultural and retail structural conditions of the period. Table 5.4 summarizes the key 'push' and 'pull' factors, and sets these within their wider environmental context.

Other than the 'push' and 'pull' factors, the literature also acknowledges the importance of facilitating factors which support and enable retailers to successfully internationalize. Among the facilitating factors identified are those which relate to corporate philosophy and the vision of senior management to succeed abroad, the accumulation of in-company expertise, financial stability and capability, and expertise in communication and data technologies (Treadgold and Davies, 1988; Treadgold, 1991).

Table 5.4 Push and pull factors behind retailer internationalization

Boundary	Push	Pull
Political	Unstable structure, restrictive regulatory environment, anti-business culture dominant, consumer credit restrictions	Stable structure, relaxed regulatory environment, probusiness culture dominant, relaxed consumer credit regulations
Economic	Poor economic conditions, low growth potential, high operating costs, mature markets, small domestic market	Good economic conditions, high growth potential, low operating costs, developing markets, property investment potential, large market, favourable exchange rates, depressed share prices
Social	Negative social environment, negative demographic trends, population stagnation	Positive social environment, positive demographic trends, population growth
Cultural	Unfamiliar cultural climate, heterogeneous cultural environment	Familiar culture reference points, attractive cultural fabric, innovative business/retail culture, company ethos, homogeneous cultural environment
Retail structure	Hostile environment, high concentration levels, format saturation, unfavourable operating environment	Niche opportunities, company owned facilities, 'me too' expansions, favourable operating environment

Source: Alexander (1997).

Other studies have provided classifications of the inducements which encourage retailer internationalization, and these are clearly founded upon the 'home market push' and 'foreign market pull' premise. Tordjman and Dionisio (1991) classified retailer motives in terms of constraints and opportunities, the former relating to issues such as market saturation and legislation aimed at restricting growth, and the latter to the opportunities that a foreign country can provide for the development of an international image and increased profitability. Tordjman (1995) provided a refinement of the earlier classification by identifying external motives, such as the emergence of homogeneous consumer tastes, saturation of national markets, improvements in logistics and international information exchange, and internal motives which include the exploitation of brand image and corporate know-how over a wider range of markets.

Fragmentary accounts can be found within the wider motivational studies on retailer internationalization which include reference to fashion retailers (Hollander, 1970; Salmon and Tordjman, 1989; Treadgold, 1990/1991;

Dawson, 1993; Alexander, 1994; Sternquist, 1997), or from the very limited literature which considers the international migration of individual fashion retailers (Lualajainen, 1991; 1992; McHarg et al., 1992; Johnson and Allen, 1994).

Identifying the 'commercial objectives' which induce international expansion by retailers, Hollander (1970) suggested that luxury fashion houses developed international chains for reasons of prestige, while department store retailers went abroad because of saturation in the domestic market. Other studies which have considered the internationalization of high fashion and luxury brand retailers have suggested that the motivation to expand into foreign markets has been premised not so much upon the need to escape from home market restrictions, but instead upon the desire to exploit the potential of distinctive brands and innovative product offerings within receptive markets (Lualajainen, 1992; Fernie et al., 1997).

The adoption of a proactive approach to internationalization is not necessarily restricted to the activities of exclusive fashion design houses. As part of a general review of the features of retailer internationalization, Treadgold (1990/1991) maintained that specialist fashion retailers (focusing upon specific product types), such as Damart, Tie Rack and High & Mighty, all have entered foreign markets in order to maximize the opportunities afforded by their respective merchandize expertise and specialization. Similarly, according to trade press sources, there is evidence to suggest that other clothing firms with a highly focused product offering (such as the lingerie retailer, La Senza of Canada, and ski-wear specialist, Helly Hansen of Norway: Murphy and Bruce, 1999; Moore and Murphy, 2000) have engaged in foreign market expansion in response to foreign market demand for their products. In addition, retailers focusing upon highly specific customer segments, such as young female fashion retailers Kookai & Morgan of France, have been reported as stating that the decision to engage in foreign expansion was motivated primarily by the desire to exploit the opportunities afforded by underdeveloped competition in markets.

It cannot be assumed, however, that the international expansion of all clothing retailers serving clearly defined customer segments can be attributed to proactive motivations. For example, the entry into Spain by British childrenswear retailer Adams in the mid-1990s has been described as a reactive response by the company to imminent market saturation and increased competition within the domestic market (Johnson and Allen, 1994). Similarly, Lualajainen (1991) concluded that home market saturation within Scandinavia encouraged the expansion of youth fashion retailer Hennes & Mauritz of Sweden into the UK.

Research which has considered the internationalization of general merchandize retailers (Whitehead, 1991; McHarg et al., 1992) pays scant attention to the motives which have led to their cross-border expansions. Assuming that Laura Ashley can be categorized as a clothing retailer serving a broader market through varied ladies' and childrenswear collections, Treadgold (1991) argued that the firm's motivation for foreign market development was essentially proactive, determined by a brand and retail formula with a cross-market appeal. In contrast, Sternquist (1997) identified a clear relationship between the expansion of American clothing retailer The Gap into Canada, the UK, France and Germany and the saturation of the domestic market, and of opportunities within regional shopping malls in particular.

Furthermore, the literature has acknowledged that no one motivation or set of motivations for internationalization could be regarded as dominant over time, either for a specific company or sector (Alexander, 1994). Of those studies identified above, it would appear that none has considered how time and differing circumstances may serve to influence a fashion retailer's motivation and attitude towards foreign market participation.

It has been suggested that an examination of a retailer's motivation(s) for international expansion potentially provides rich insights into the nature of the company's strategic decision-making and its ability to interpret and respond to operating environments (Hollander, 1970; Alexander, 1994). By implication, the fact that only a perfunctory understanding of the reasons why fashion retailers have internationalized into the UK or elsewhere is available also means that our understanding of how these fashion retailers assess, understand and respond to their operating environments (as evidenced in their strategic decision-making) is essentially limited.

How are fashion retailers developing international operations?

The 'how' of retailer internationalization is a complex concept, and is essentially concerned with the alterations that a retailer makes with respect to their marketing mix elements in response to local market conditions. Furthermore, the 'how' of retailer internationalization also involves those entry methods that retailers adopt in order to facilitate the opening of stores abroad. Both dimensions will be considered here within the context of the international expansion of fashion retailers.

Sparks (1996) suggested that the strategies that retailers adopt for internationalization and the methods of foreign market entry that they use reflect the variations in the degree of direct involvement and control required by the retailer and the level of knowledge and transfer borrowing, in relation to management expertise and business ideas, that may exist between the entering retailer and associates within the local market. Similarly, the internationalization strategy and the market entry strategies that are adopted are linked to the place of decision-making for the retail business operating within the host country (Dawson, 1993).

Treadgold and Davies (1988) identified a range of strategic options available to a retailer seeking to operate within a foreign market and suggested that the manner in which a company entered a market and conducted operations served to reflect the availability of resources for foreign market development and the degree of operational control they sought to retain over foreign operations. Recognizing that a high degree of control implies a high cost entry strategy and that a low cost entry approach necessitates a consider-able loss of control, Treadgold identified three strategic options for the devel-opment of foreign operations. The first is a high cost/high control strategy, adopted mainly by firms with limited foreign market experience, which can be achieved through organic growth or the outright acquisition or dominant shareholding of a company currently operating within the foreign market. The alternative approaches include a medium cost/medium control strategy, achieved normally by joint venture arrangements, or a low cost/low control strategy, achieved through a franchise arrangement.

The themes of resource availability, the degree of control required by the internationalizing retailer and the extent of their experience in foreign mar-ket trading, identified by Treadgold (1991), are also apparent in the review of retailer internalization strategies provided by Salmon and Tordjman (1989). Without doubt, their work has proved to be highly influential to the under-standing of the strategic approaches adopted by retailers in respect of inter-nationalization (Dawson, 1993; Sparks, 1996).

Salmon and Tordjman (1989) identified three strategic approaches to retailer internationalization, *international investment*, *global* and *multinational*, and sug-gest that a retailer's choice of strategy is ultimately dependent upon the trad-ing characteristics and internal competencies of the company. The *international investment strategy* involves the transfer of capital from one country to another, with the aim of acquiring part-share or total shares in another operating com-pany. Retailers typically adopt this approach in the early stages of their international involvement in order to diversify their business for reasons of financial and political risk, to gain rapid market share within countries where the organic development of a chain of outlets would involve high risk and high cost, as well as to obtain the trading advantages inherent to that market.

Accordingly, Salmon and Tordjman (1989) assert that the type of retailer likely to use this type of international growth strategy would typically be large, highly diversified within their own domestic market (although this was clearly less evident among internationalizing British grocery retailers: Burt, 1993; Wrigley, 1997; 1998), and are committed to exploiting the growth opportunities available within foreign countries, mainly through the part or full acquisition of existing retail chains and other businesses. Within a fash-ion retailing context, the acquisition by the Paris-based LVMH Group of com-panies including Christian Dior, Givenchy, Loewe, Christian Lacroix, Fendi, Kenzo, Guerlain and Gant underlines their adoption of an international invest-ment strategy which seeks to spread their corporate risk across a number of different brands serving disparate customer segments. Consequently, should the LVMH conglomerate find that any one brand falls out of fashion favour, then the company has an alternative brand to promote and therefore an alter-native source of income.

The internationalizing fashion retailer typically must respond to two con-flicting pressures. The first is to adapt to local market conditions in order to fully respond to the needs of consumers, while the second is the desire to bene-fit from operational scale economies (Salmon and Tordjman, 1989). Following from Levitt's (1983) assertion of the worldwide convergence of consumer needs and wants, retailers who follow the second of Salmon and Tordjman's strategies, *the global strategy*, do so on the basis that they have access to consumer groups with shared lifestyle characteristics and purchase requirements, independent of their place of residence. A global strategy is therefore defined as a faithful replication of a trading concept abroad, and involves the standardization of the fashion marketing mix and the faithful replication of the same product range, communications methods, corporate identity, service and price levels within all stores, regardless of their geographical location.

The fashion retailers that use this strategy typically have a clearly defined corporate image and market positioning, often with a strong own-brand and possibly with a unique product range or trading format. Companies that replicate a standardized marketing strategy include general fashion chains such as The Gap, the designer companies including Gucci, Prada and Kenzo, and specialist fashion retailers like Lacoste and Nike. Product exclusivity, the influence of a founding personality (such as Laura Ashley within her company), the interplay between the product on sale and the store environments within which they are sold, all serve to shape the distinctive characteristics which are central to the success of a global strategy. In addition, Salmon and Tordjman highlighted the significance of an integrated supply chain, and suggested that the most successful global fashion retailers exert considerable influence over the design and quality standards of their products so that the reputation of their corporate brand can be managed and controlled at all times. Consistency in terms of all dimensions of the retailer's positioning is highly significant for the global retailer and can only be achieved through high levels of centralization. Consequently, successful global fashion retailers seek to retain and centralize tactical and strategic decision-making, and the standardization of their activities provides for economies of scale through the consistent replication of store format elements, marketing communications, product development and management control systems. In order to facilitate this centralization, global fashion retailers must invest in computerized management information systems in order to monitor and control the flow of stock and information.

There are also disadvantages associated with such centralization, and these are identified by Salmon and Tordjman (1989) as those related to inflexibility in responding to local market needs, which may result in the non-identification of market trends, demotivation and a lack of commitment among local management, as well as the danger of being associated with a particular specialization which may leave the company vulnerable in the face of competitor attack or changes in consumer attitudes.

A variety of studies have examined the utilization of globalization strategies by retailers in general and have questioned the extent to which this approach is viable within a retailing context. Waldman (1978) argued that environmental differences, such as those related to consumer culture, competitive conditions and economic and legal restraints, made standardization of the retailer's marketing mix across a range of markets impossible to achieve. Similarly, Martenson (1987) suggests that, while a retailer may be able to achieve a pannational replication of their core trading values and philosophy, it is unlikely that they will, at the same time, be able to achieve the successful implementation of a standardized trading approach.

The third internationalization strategy identified by Salmon and Tordjman (1989) is *the multinational strategy*, which seeks to preserve a basic trading concept or image across a range of geographically dispersed markets, but also adapts the formula to fit local market conditions and the expectations of local customers. Salmon and Tordjman identify C&A as an example of a multinational retailer. In all of the countries in which C&A trades, the company operates the same basic strategy of offering recognizable ranges of clothing for men, women and children, inexpensively. However, at a national level, the firm's marketing mix elements are adapted to suit local needs. As a result, each country has its own range of products, pricing and margin policy, while advertising and promotions methods are adapted to suit local market conditions.

While C&A are identified as a retailer that adapts their positioning mix to best suit national characteristics, French hypermarket chains, with representations across Europe, are identified by Salmon and Tordjman (and latterly by Dupuis and Prime, 1996) as having adapted their marketing mix elements at a regional level and increasingly at store level. This allows local managers the flexibility to select products and adjust prices in response to near trading environments. In order to respond to local conditions, multinational retailers develop decentralized management control structures, based upon a clear demarcation of responsibilities, whereby strategic decision-making resides with the parent company and is undertaken in the home country. Tactical and operational decisions are delegated to local management teams, either at national, regional or local level. This devolution of power to the host nation requires a management team that is able to identify local market trends and credibly respond to these through their marketing mix decisions. However, while this may suggest a loosening of centralized control on the part of the internationalizing retailer, Salmon and Tordjman emphasize that firms still retain control over the original business concept, using formal and informal communications channels, such as through the deployment of parent company personnel to co-ordinate and 'head-up' local operations. In such cases, the devolvement of power from the retailer's central administration can prove to be somewhat limited.

As a result of pursuing a multinational strategy, Salmon and Tordjman (1989) have identified three principal strategic consequences. The first is that the scale of investment (both in terms of time and financial resources) required in order to open each new shop, adapt the offering to suit local market conditions and recruit management capable of undertaking such initiatives is so significant that it invariably limits the speed of replicating such formats. Secondly, because of their adaptive techniques, multinational fashion retailers fail to benefit from the economies of scale associated with retailing, supply and advertising to the extent that is achieved by global fashion retailers, although those retailers that develop a large local presence within one country or region may benefit from scale economies within these markets. Thirdly, but not to their disadvantage, the multinational retailer, through the range and diversity of their market involvement and experience, may be able to integrate the know-how techniques and best practice found within foreign markets into their domestic and international business strategies.

Salmon and Tordjman predicted that the multinational retailers would gain market share within markets where the international procurement of goods is inhibited by the physical characteristics of the products, such as in relation to size or perishability. As such, the multinational retailer is expected to grow in significance within the food sector and other product categories that are less subject to abrupt changes in consumer tastes and lifestyle features. However, it is also their contention that it is the global strategy that will realize the greatest growth rate, which is partly attributed to the increased homogenization of consumer groups around the world and the homogenization of standards which will serve to facilitate the distribution of products between countries. Treadgold (1991) also predicted that the multinational approach would increase among retailers who seek to satisfy the requirements of local consumers while maintaining cost and scale economies where possible.

Dawson (1993), in a review of Salmon and Tordjman's typology, and specifically their choice of C&A as a classic example of a multinational retailer, argued that, while C&A may seek to adapt their marketing mix to suit local market conditions, any changes that are made happen in the context of a corporate brand framework that is both highly defined and uniform in its application. The elements of C&A's brand identification, store interiors and corporate colours are consistent across all countries, and while products may vary across markets in terms of their type and design, there is nevertheless a constancy in their styling and quality that is in keeping with the overall image of the C&A brand and their market positioning. Any devolvement in power is likely to be operational and possibly tactical in nature, and the flexibility that does exist is constrained by the prescriptive nature of the C&A brand identity.

Therefore, Dawson proposed that there is a case to be made which sees globalization and multinationalization not as two discrete and mutually exclusive approaches to transnational expansion, but instead as a continuum which marks the extent to which a fashion retailer's proposition is both capable and required to adapt to the needs of the foreign market. This continuum extends between the extremes of a standard global identity and a locally tailored one, and where a retailer is positioned on this scale is dependent upon the nature and importance of the retailer as a distinct brand entity, both at corporate and product level. Where the brand is regarded as central to the identity of the retailer and is clearly positioned within the mind of the actual and potential consumer, then the retailer is more likely to follow a global strategy. However, even within such a prescriptive strategy, there is the possibility that the operational and tactical elements of the retailer's positioning may be altered to suit the trading environment of the non-domestic market. As such, Dawson proposed that Salmon and Tordjman's (1989) classification must be 'loosened' and perhaps not taken as literally in order to adequately reflect the reality of international retailing.

Concluding comments

Fashion retailers are the most international of retailers, as was noted by Doherty (2000), who recognized that the international expansion of fashion retailers in Europe far outweighs the foreign market activities of retailers operating within other product sectors. However, despite the prominence of fashion companies as international retailers, the attention invested by researchers in this area has largely been perfunctory, and our appreciation of the nature and characteristics of the internationalization of fashion retailing remains largely incomplete.

The application of Akehurst and Alexander's (1996) research agenda to fashion retailer internationalization not only provides a clearer direction and focus for research activity within the area, but also highlights the many dimensions which seek to differentiate the process of internationalizing fashion retail operations.

In summary, the internationalization of fashion retailing is distinguished by its clear emphasis upon the exploitation of the brand as the fundamental driver for foreign market expansion and the fact that the possibilities for future expansion show little signs of abatement in the near future.

References

Akehurst, G. and Alexander, N. (Eds.) (1996). *The Internationalisation of Retailing*. London: Frank Cass.

Alexander, N. (1994). UK retailers' motives for operating in the single European market. *Proceedings, Annual Conference of the Marketing Education Group: Marketing Unity in Diversity*, Vol. 1, pp. 22–31.

Alexander, N. (1997). *International Retailing*. London: Blackwell.

Burt, S. (1993). Temporal trends in the internationalization of British retailing. *The International Review of Retail, Distribution and Consumer Research*, **3** (4), 391–410.

Corporate Intelligence on Retailing (1997). *Clothing Retailing in Europe*. London: CIG.

Crewe, L. and Lowe, M. (1996). United colours? Globalization and localization tendencies in fashion retailing. In Wrigley, N. and Lowe, M. (Eds.), *Retailing, Consumption and Capital. Towards the New Retail Geography*. London: Longman, pp. 271–83.

Dawson, J. (1993). The internationalization of retailing. In Bromley, R. D. F. and Thomas, C. J. (Eds.), *Retail Change. Contemporary Issues*. London: UCL Press, pp. 15–40.

Doherty, A. M. (2000). Factors influencing international retailers' market entry mode strategy. *Journal of Marketing Management*, 16, 223–45.

Dupuis, M. and Prime, N. (1996). Business distance and global retailing: a model for analysis of key success/failure factors. *International Journal of Retail and Distribution Management*, **24** (11), 30–8.

Fernie, J., Moore, C., Lawrie, A. and Hallsworth, A. (1997). The internationalisation of the high fashion brand : the case of Central London. *Journal of Product and Brand Management,* **6** (3).

Fernie, J., Moore, C. and Lawrie, A. (1998). A tale of two cities: an examination of fashion designer retailing within London and New York. *Journal of Product and Brand Management,* **7** (5).

Hollander, S. C. (1970). Who are the multinational retailers? In *Multinational Retailing,* pp. 14–53. Michigan State University Press.

Jackson, G. I. (1976). British Retailer Expansion into Europe. Unpublished Ph.D. Thesis, UMIST, Manchester.

Johnson, M. and Allen, B. (1994). Taking the English 'apple' to Spain: the Adams experience. *International Journal of Retail and Distribution Management,* **22** (7), 39.

Kacker, M. P. (1985). *Transatlantic Trends in Retailing: Takeovers and Flow of Know-How.* Connecticut: Quorum Books.

Levitt, T. (1983). The globalisation of markets. *Harvard Business Review,* 16 (3).

Lualajainen, R. (1991). International expansion of an apparel retailer – Hennes and Mauritz of Sweden. *Zeitschrift fur Wirtschaftsgeographie,* **35,** Heft 1, 1–15.

Lualajainen, R. (1992). Louis Vuitton Malletier – a truly global retailer. *Annals of the Japanese Association of Economic Geographers,* **38** (2), 55–70.

Martenson, R. (1987). Is standardisation of marketing feasible in culture bound industries? *International Marketing Review,* **4** (3), 7–17.

McHarg, K., Lea, E. C. and Oldroyd, M. (1992). *European Market Entry Strategies of UK Clothing Retailers.* Working Papers Series, University of Sheffield.

Moore, C. (1997). *La Mode Sans Frontiers? – The Internationalisation of Fashion Retailing.* Working Paper, Institute for Retail Studies, University of Stirling.

Moore, C. (1998). La mode sans frontiers: the internationalisation of fashion retailing. *Journal of Fashion Marketing and Management,* **1** (4), 345–56.

Moore, C. and Murphy, R. (2000). The strategic exploitation of new market opportunities by British fashion companies. *Journal of Fashion Marketing and Management,* **4** (1).

Murphy, R. and Bruce, M. (1999). The structure and organisation of UK clothing retailing. *Journal of Fashion Marketing and Management,* **3** (3).

Salmon, W. J. and Tordjman, A. (1989). The internationalisation of retailing. *International Journal of Retailing,* **4** (2), 3–16.

Simpson, E. M. and Thorpe, D. I. (1996). A conceptual model of strategic considerations for international retail expansion. In Akehurst, G. and Alexander, N. (Eds.), *The Internationalisation of Retailing.* London: Frank Cass, pp. 16–24.

Sparks, L. (1996). Reciprocal retail internationalisation: the Southland Corporation, Ito-Yokado and 7-Eleven convenience stores. In Akehurst, G. and Alexander, N. (Eds.), *The Internationalisation of Retailing.* London: Frank Cass, pp. 57–96.

Sternquist, B. (1997). International expansion by US retailers. *International Journal of Retail and Distribution Management,* **19** (4), 13–19.

Tordjman, A. (1995). European retailing: convergences, differences and per-spectives. In McGoldrick, P. J. and Davies, G. (Eds.), *International Retailing. Trends and Strategies*. London: Pitman.

Tordjman, A. and Dionisio, J. (1991). Internationalisation strategies of retail business. Commission of the European Communities, DG XXIII, Series Studies, Commerce and Distribution, 15.

Treadgold, A. (1990/1991). The emerging internationalisation of retailing: present status and future challenges. *Irish Marketing Review*, **5** (2), 11–17.

Treadgold, A. (1991). Dixons and Laura Ashley – different routes to inter-national growth. *International Journal of Retail and Distribution Management*, **19** (4), 13–19.

Treadgold, A. and Davies, R. L. (1988). Forces promoting internationalization. The *Internationalisation of Retailing*, Chapter I. Oxford: OXIRM/Longman, pp. 9–19.

Waldman, C. (1978). *Strategies of International Mass Retailers*. New York: Praegar.

Whitehead, M. (1991). International franchising – Marks and Spencer: a case study. *International Journal of Retail and Distribution Management*, **19** (2), 13–19.

Williams, D. E. (1992). Motives for retailer internationalization: Their impact. structure and implications. *Journal of Marketing Management*, **8** (3), 269–85.

Wrigley, N. (1997) British food retail capital in the USA – Part 2. Giant pros-pects. *International Journal of Retail Distribution Management*, **25** (2–3).

Wrigley, N. (1998) Market rules and spatial outcomes. In Barnes, T. and Gertler, M. (Eds.), *Regions, Regulations, and Institution: Towards a New Industrial Geography*. London: Routledge.

6

Retail brand marketing in the fashion industry

Bill Webb

Introduction

The 21st century may see retail marketers, like Cordwainers or Fletchers, con-fined to the annals of history. For the present, they are still with us, although their average length of job tenure is less than 18 months and many experts predict that the writing is already on the wall. This chapter looks at the role and prospects for the retail marketing of consumer goods and services. It will not attempt a comprehensive review of the most recent marketing initiatives and techniques, as so much other contemporary literature has done, but rather look for a rationale for the continued existence of a distinct retail marketing function, and discuss what this might be. It will examine:

- Changes in the nature of consumer demand.
- The retail response to date.
- Conclusions for retail brand marketing.

It will concentrate on the UK, with occasional international references. Mar-keting dominated commercial thinking in the second half of the 20th century. The idea has predominated that the proliferation of product choice meant that successful retailers had to identify, measure and understand their 'market', and target a specific segment within it with a 'unique selling proposition', that is something that provided more 'added value' to that particular group of customers than any available alternative. This was a step on from the previous 'selling era', when retailers simply put on offer the products produced, ever more cheaply, efficiently and to higher standards, by modern, automated manufacturing plants, and waited for customers to form queues to purchase them. The three keys to success in retail marketing were famously said to be 'location, location and location', that is having your store near to where large numbers of your chosen customers live or shop. Many retailers maintained that, with shops in the right locations, there was no further need for marketing the shops would do that for themselves. Some worked with other, additional, elements of the so-called 'Retail Marketing Mix' besides 'place' (location) (i.e. product, price, people and promotion). This Anglo/American process became the textbook model for consumer goods marketing. It spawned numerous methods of identifying specific groups from 'ABC1s' to, more recently, 'Dinkies' and 'Yuppies'. It developed a plethora of persuasive tools and programmes from Tiger Tokens or Greenshield Stamps to, more recently, 'Computers for Schools' and 'reward' loyalty card schemes. It has been extended first into Western Europe and the old Commonwealth, and more recently into the developing countries of Eastern Europe, Asia and South America. It has supported the growth of a global consumer society beyond the wildest dreams of those charged with reconstructing shattered economies after World War Two. In whatever way retail marketing activities are classified (above/below the line, push/pull, advertising/promotion), they all have critical factors in common:

- They originate from the brand owner or distributor, and have the objective of attracting more customers to the brand or store.
- They assume that the potential customer knows less about the product than they do, and makes buying decisions within a limited and controlled market.

However, as any politician or athlete will confirm, it is just when everything seems to be sewn up nicely that some unforeseen change takes place which augurs a step change. One or two fundamental questions need to be asked at the outset:

- If the distribution of consumer goods and services is going to increasingly by-pass physical stores, how will this impact a discipline based on the supremacy of locations?
- If these locations are 're-invented', at least in part, for new roles, how relevant will retail marketing disciplines be to these objectives and activities?
- If customers are better educated, more cynical about media messages and totally capable of informing themselves on every aspect of their lives, what role will there be left for 'persuasion by communication'?
- How realistic will it be for most local brands to achieve competitive superiority in a truly global marketplace using traditional marketing methods?

- If the individual customer is at the centre of commercial activity, then no part of an organization will be able to opt out of the 'customer satisfaction' process. If marketing is 'everyone's responsibility' then it is no one's specific function. Does this explain why many successful retailers do not have a Board level Marketing Director and also why there is such a rapid turnover of Marketing executives elsewhere in the retail industry?

Once suppliers appreciated that they had to position, rather than just sell, their products, the concept of brand management developed, and with it, the idea that 'marketing' should orchestrate the other functions of a business. The 1970s and 1980s saw the growth of large marketing departments and the development of 'strategic' marketing plans by many British retailers. This author was himself appointed to the first marketing designated role in a leading fashion retailer in the early 1970s. During the course of the 1990s, we have seen a fragmentation of consumer markets and the introduction of new technologies which clearly transcend the remit (and often the understanding) of retail marketing departments. As a result, the marketing function has become increasingly sidelined. Emphasis has shifted from promoting the product to capturing and retaining the customer, and decisions on product range, pricing, shop design and so on are seen as too important to be left to the marketing department. Many marketing functions are now routinely implemented using various information technologies, and little judgemental input.

Furthermore, as the pace of change has increased, marketing's emphasis on research and strategy has often been seen as a constraint to innovation. The increasing number of retail companies in the UK controlled by private equity groups has also dictated a lower cost base and faster return on investment than a research-driven culture will allow. So-called 'legacy retailers' like Sears, Boots, W. H. Smith, Littlewoods, Woolworths and Sainsbury have all traditionally been heavy users of management research and consulting, which has not saved them from loss of market share and major restructuring. A philosophy of 'learning by doing' has almost become 'de rigeur' for the retail industry, and even when disciplines are introduced it is accepted that they will have to be executed concurrently with the project rather than prior to its start, as traditionally happens in manufacturing industry. Philip Green and Tom Hunter are examples of the new breed of fleet of foot merchants driving the retail sector forward. Transitory fashion and lifestyle influences are impacting many product sectors beyond the clothing industry. In fact, many would say that they have largely moved on from the clothing industry to influence purchasing decisions in the home and leisure sectors. These days, it is more profitable to be 'roughly right' and on time than 'precisely right' and too late.

Finally, stagnant consumer expenditure and increased competition in many areas has not helped. Expenditure on research, store design, marketing communications and especially the new loyalty schemes can be very high, and hard to justify. Marketing professionals themselves complain that traditional marketing tools 'no longer work' and have been slow to put in place robust measurement techniques which would have enabled them to defend their territory a little better. As profits came under pressure and the accountants and consultants moved in, it was not surprising that not only many Retail Marketing Directors, but entire departments moved out.

These trends have been well recognized by the marketing profession itself (ironically, whose leading individual practitioners were, in the summer of 1998, awarded 'chartered' status). In 1997, the Marketing Society surveyed its members, and under the title *'The Profession Keeping its Grip'*, published a review of members' opinions, from which some of the preceding thoughts have been drawn (Marketing Society, 1997). It concluded with an impassioned plea for 'where marketing should be' essentially a filter or interface between key organizational functions and the customer (Figure 6.1). What this role should involve or how it should be executed was not made clear. Can we justify this view in the context of the retail sector?

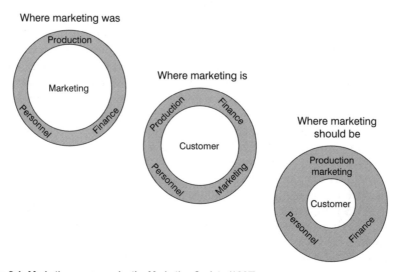

Figure 6.1 Marketing – as seen by the Marketing Society (1997).

The new consumer

The existence of a mass market of homogeneous consumers was always something of a myth. However, in the early years of the 'consumer society', people were more than willing to trade off their individual preferences and personal service for a share of the cheap, high quality products coming on to the market. They needed to be informed about the products, have their features explained and be reassured about their appropriateness for their needs. No more. Except in a few specialist sectors, today's consumer is very different. The pace of social change is faster than it has ever been. UK society today is characterized by: a stagnant, ageing but healthier population; more but smaller families; more women working, but often part time; couples marrying later, and more often; incomes under pressure, but more windfall gains, especially from inheritance; more travel and demand for leisure time; less 'technofear' and widespread computer literacy; diminishing trust in traditional authority figureheads to instance just a few examples. All have relevance for the distribution of consumer goods and services, and hence for the future of retail marketing. They are well documented, especially by The Henley Centre, and will not be detailed again here.

Some significant insights which need to be highlighted include:

- Today's customers virtually defy classification although the more complex they become, the more complex are the psychographic segmentation models created to categorize them. The shopper today reflects the influences of the generation into which she was born, the lifestage she has reached (maybe for the second or even third time), her own income and lifestyle, the attitudes of her reference groups and her own personality. Unlike past times, when there was peer group pressure to conform to a stereotype, today's consumer feels more than ever at liberty to 'be herself' (although admitting to being a little insecure and exposed in this role). The result is that the customer of the new millennium is more individual than ever before. She wants control over her own life, and all the products and services that make it up. She is 'someone not anyone'. Today's family is no longer a 'unit', but a cellular base camp for individuals with their own phones, TVs and computers, front door keys, meal times (and content), dress styles, friends and values. No wonder the mixture is often volatile! No wonder the number of single person households has doubled in the past 25 years.
- There is growing evidence of customer rejection of mass products and cloned stores, in favour of something and some place which is 'right for me'. The rationale for much of the research-based marketing has long been the reduction of risk and the search for an acceptable 'common denominator' segment which can be targeted. It could therefore be said that marketing itself has acted as a brake on innovation, and has partly been responsible for customers turning away from traditional goods and services.
- The evidence for the growing individualism of today's shopper can be seen in the decline of many collective organizations from trade unions to political parties, religious bodies or retail co-operatives. Yet, at the same time, individuals express the need for security and solidarity by coming together in groups or 'tribes' be they Arsenal Supporters, a local neighbourhood watch committee or a PC users' club. The Internet has proved to be a great facilitator enabling like-minded people to form groups, even on a global basis. Brands too (such as, Burberry, Prada or Ben Sherman) can fulfil and exploit this need, becoming the symbolic uniform of choice of groups of 'chavs' and others. This will be further discussed in a subsequent section.
- Shoppers also express their preferences in relation to their needs home needs, leisure needs, work-related needs and 'self-actualization' needs. They exhibit different purchasing attitudes and behaviour according to which situation they find themselves in at any specific time. As Gavin Aldred, former

Managing Director of New Look, said, 'A customer is as likely to buy a CD as one of our blouses. To be honest I've given up trying to fathom out why people buy what they do.' (Aldred, 1998).

- Levels of education are higher than ever before. Perhaps more important, there is the cumulative experience of two generations' exposure to marketing media, press, radio and TV. Shoppers have 'wised-up' to the various marketing strategies and programmes on offer. The media themselves delight in exposing any form of consumer 'exploitation' (especially by retailers or travel companies). Customers are also more willing to try alternative new, often global, providers if they feel they can get a better deal. Hence the growth of businesses like Easy Jet, Amazon.com and the world's most successful new retailer, E-bay.

- Shoppers are more confident than ever before in their capability to solve their own problems. They will write their own wills (on forms bought from W. H. Smith), treat their own ailments (with medicine bought from ASDA), select and book their holidays (from Expedia or Airline Network), plan an instant dinner party (courtesy of Marks & Spencer) and even select a new partner via the Internet. If there is something they cannot do then they go to an evening class or seek help on the 'Net'. The Thatcher years engendered a culture of self-help in the UK which is unique, and which has endured well beyond her demise.

- For many people, incremental Time (and Energy) now has more value than incremental Money. Kurt Salmon Associates' 1998 Consumer Confidence survey reported that, given the choice, 53 per cent of people would opt for more time over more money. Most people are striving to increase their personal time productivity in order to squeeze more activity and more experience into a finite (if longer) life expectancy. 'I want it NOW' has become the cry of today's consumer. Kids cannot understand why supper takes two minutes in the microwave when the package says 'instant'. In the food industry, Proctor and Gamble have invented the 20:20 rule 20 minutes to shop for a meal and 20 minutes to prepare it. Leading retailers like Tesco ('Metro' and 'Express') and Sainsbury ('Central' and 'Local') grow market share and profits by giving customers back their time in exchange for higher prices and margins. Starbucks famously sell a '15 minute experience', rather than coffee and buns.

In the furnishings sector, IKEA has swept all before it by offering instant fashion for the home, while traditional furnishers like Queensway, Maples and Waring & Gillow (now no more) continued to take customers' deposits and deliver a solution 6–8 weeks later. In fashion, much of the independent sector still expects orders to be placed 6 months in advance. 'Fast Fashion' companies like Zara, Hennes & Mauritz and Top Shop are aiming to cut lead times from design studio to store display to as little as 15 days, a model now being emulated by capsule collections from ASDA and Marks & Spencer.

When time runs out, people shift something to another time, making use of time that would otherwise be dead. They video late night films, sports events and educational programmes. They shop for groceries from their home or office and pick them up (or have them delivered) at their convenience. They buy their 'home meal replacements (HMR)' ready prepared from the supermarket. They buy Virgin Vie or Body Shop (and much more) from home sales representatives. They buy birthday presents at the Science Museum shop or the Manchester United superstore. Lifestyles have become a quest for solutions to fulfil multiple needs and desires simultaneously. As Peter Simpson, Commercial Director of First Direct has said, 'The 9 to 5 society has gone, and is as dead as the proverbial Monty Python parrot. It is deceased, it is no more. There is a new definition of time'. (1998, '24 Hour Society' Conference).

- Because of the blurring of activities, people no longer perceive aspects of their life in discrete compartments. Eating in and eating out no longer retain their traditional significance. Sport, fashion and music all overlap so that while the clothing retail sector stagnates, the sports sector explodes, largely by selling clothing. Markets can no longer be defined by product categories, but rather by multi-dimensional lifestyles, which present multi-faceted problems requiring new types of total solution.

So it is no longer enough to target goods and services at demographic or psychographic market segments. A template for determining the appropriateness of a product or service proposition is represented in Figure 6.2.

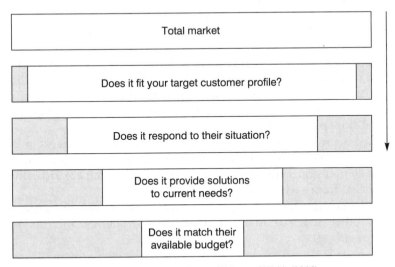

Figure 6.2 Brand targeting in the 21st century. *Source*: Wolny and Webb (2000).

The retail response

As consumers increase the share of their spending devoted to education, health, leisure and entertainment, so they have decreased that devoted to traditional consumer goods groceries, clothes, shoes, furniture and white electrical goods. Even in the innovative electrical leisure sector, falling prices have offset increased sales volumes. Partly, this is the result of saturated markets. An ageing population consumes less calories per head and has acquired a stock of durable items, leaving only a replacement market. Most households have so much 'stuff' that they no longer know what to use or where to store it. Hence the growth in charity shops and car boot sales. In the United States, a growth industry is personal 'lockups' where surplus items can be stored and brought out on a rotating basis. Partly it is because of the improved quality and life expectancy of many products, especially motor vehicles and clothing, which need replacing less frequently, and partly it is because of changing personal attitudes to possessions which are no longer deemed by many to be an indicator of personal success and status. As the American retail commentator Carol Farmer (1995) wrote 10 years ago, 'we have entered the Less Decade'.

However, retailers, and retail marketers in particular, must also accept much of the blame for the performance of their sector. They have been guilty of the very mistake often attributed to Henry Ford offering customers any colour they want as long as it is black. In the drive for centralized control, economies of scale and low operating costs, they have, with a few notable exceptions:

- Reduced the choice available to shoppers, both in terms of available products (too often identical in different stores) and shopping locations, leading to accusations of identikit shopping experiences.
- Confused the customer with proliferation of similar products or products inappropriate to her needs.
- Irritated customers by de-listing favoured products on the basis of new systemized management techniques like DPP (Direct Product Profitability).
- Wasted the customer's time by locating key product categories in remote parts of the store, continuously changing the layout and product presentation, and slow payment processes.
- Explained away 'no-service' as 'self-service', and failed to invest in the calibre and training of store level staff who are in direct contact with customers.
- Created cloned stores and bland shopping centres which are virtually indistinguishable from each other.
- Offered products for sale that are consistently priced more highly than in other national markets (local cost structures and tax regimes notwithstanding).

As Burns et al. (1997) pointed out in a telling article, 'retail renewal' has become the critical issue of the decade. It is an indictment of the past performance of retail marketers, supposedly the customer's champion, that it is only now that some enlightened top managements have decided to truly focus on their customers that these issues have begun to be addressed. What these companies are doing will form the subject of the next section of this chapter.

Current retail initiatives

The pace of change in the UK retail sector continues to increase. Acquisitions, mergers, new ventures and bankruptcies are reported weekly. The UK is the target of a constant stream of new entrants from overseas, and our own retailers, with very mixed results, continue to expand into new territories. The small band of experienced senior retail executives continue to play musical chairs, and attempts to supplement their numbers from abroad, particularly America, have been largely unsuccessful. Analysis of these trends is outside the scope of this chapter, but from them is emerging, not only in the UK but in most markets, a radical new picture of how retailing will look as this century unfolds. For the present, this emerging picture is often described as being 'customer driven' or 'customer focused', but in truth, what we are witnessing is a major shift in power away from conventional retailers in favour of the final consumer. Clearly, this will impact the very nature of 'retail marketing'.

Retailers are responding to the new consumer at five levels:

- Corporate culture.
- Retail organization and management.
- Retail offer or 'proposition'.
- Means of delivery or executing this offer.
- Communications.

Culture

Marketing Week's citation for Tesco, winner of their 1996 'Brand of the Year', stated that 'the real lesson in Tesco's transformation over the past 10 years is that a company can change its culture' (*Marketing Week*, 1997). That Tesco was able to metamorphose from a discount vendor of branded groceries to the poly-faceted solution to most of life's daily problems that it now is, is a tribute to the personal vision and leadership of Lord McLaurin, and those who are continuing his good work. Lord McLaurin realized that 'satisfying the customer' can only be achieved if those at the top have a personal and passionate appreciation of who their customers are and what the needs and desires are that their company aims to satisfy. International retailers such as Nordstrom (USA), Loblaws (Canada) or FNAC (France) have long realized that satisfying the customer is something which the best retailers are, rather than something which they do. In his book '*Crowning the Customer*', Feargal Quinn (1990), founder of the Irish Superquinn Group, wrote 'the centre of gravity of a retail business should be kept as close as possible to the point where the action is where the business meets its customers. If you are customer driven, then the most important place in the company is not the boardroom but the marketplace'. Like Lord McLaurin, Feargal Quinn is an advocate of 'MBWA' Management By Walking About spending time meeting, listening to and talking to customers.

Customer focus is not something which can readily be trained into, or imposed upon, a retail organization. It can only be established through a long-term and consistent example. Julian Richer of Richer Sounds believes that 'culture and people are interchangeable ... A mission statement is not culture; culture comes from the heart' (Richer, 1995). At Richer Sounds, each sales receipt comes with a customer satisfaction counterfoil and assistants receive £3 for each 'excellent' rating (£4 if there is an additional favourable comment and £5 if a letter is received), but lose £3 for every report of 'poor' service.

So it has come to be realized by companies such as Richer Sounds, Carphone Warehouse or Fat Face that a truly marketing driven company does not put its customers first, but rather its own employees. If it fails to recruit, train, motivate and compensate the very best people then there is no chance that marketing and customer satisfaction objectives will be met. It has been demonstrated that staff loyalty and customer loyalty are closely linked in a virtuous (or vicious) circle. In an article in *Retail Week*, consultants Arthur Andersen (1997) reported that it costs £1500–2500 to replace a shop worker and 'three or four times that' for a supervisor or manager. Typically, retailers experience staff turnovers of 15–20 per cent per year. John Ainley, Human Resources Director of W. H. Smith, states that every 1 per cent of staff turnover costs the company £800,000 off the bottom line. As Julian Richer points out, theft and absenteeism are further costs which result from demotivated and disloyal staff.

Retail organization and management

Retail companies have changed the way they work, in order to respond more quickly and more precisely to changing customer demands. As Bernie Marcus of Home Depot is famous for saying 'Being in stock of products that customers want to buy is by far the most important element of customer service.' The critical catalysts for this change have been:

- The development and application of new technologies.
- New management thinking, tools and skills.
- The changing relative cost of people, space and technologies.

In the recent past, we have seen the introduction of Quick Response and Just-In-Time techniques, Electronic Data Interchange, Efficient Consumer Response and Category Management. The application of these interlocking skills has varied from sector to sector, but they are all designed to achieve Bernie Marcus's famous dictum. They have been initiated largely by the financial and logistical experts, usually with little reference to the customer or her representative, the marketing department, so have featured 'efficient' rather more strongly than 'consumer response'. Like their forerunner DPP, they have tended to emphasize the profitability of the 'product' or 'category', often to the detriment of the holistic appeal of the total store or brand. Although they are at least a first step to organizing the store around consumer needs rather than supply-driven product brands, they have also contributed to what the French call the 'banalization' of retailing the convergence towards a lowest common denominator, where customers complain about the lack of inspired, eccentric and personal products in most sectors especially food and fashion stores.

As Figures 6.3 and 6.4 demonstrate, the structure of retail organizations has changed dramatically. Many layers of middle management have been stripped out as store-based technology has simplified merchandising, store operations and logistics. Functions and skills have become more specific, and many which were carried out 'in-house' are now outsourced. This includes many marketing activities from site research to database management. Buying, which was organized by product group to match suppliers' structures, is now more likely to be organized by category (fast food, mobile communications, etc.) or lifestyle (fashion, furnishings, etc.). Companies such as Tesco and Boots use their huge customer databases (see below) to manage their businesses according to customer groups. The *Sunday Times* reported that Tesco is experimenting with dual pricing charging lower prices in stores with catchment profiles of poorer shoppers.

In their mould breaking book, Peppers and Rogers (1993) illustrated how these changes are impacting the marketing function with line management

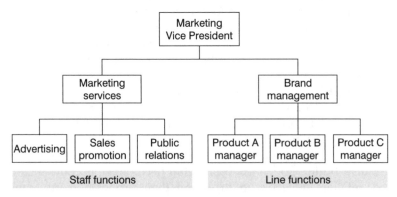

Figure 6.3 The brand management organization chart. *Source*: Peppers and Rogers (1993).

Figure 6.4 The customer management organization chart. *Source*: Peppers and Rogers (1993).

emphasis switching from the product to the customer (Figure 6.3). In this author's view, this analysis leaves unanswered the question of whether customer management can be carried out by the marketing function an issue which will be explored in the conclusions of this chapter.

Proposition

'Proposition' describes the actual 'offer' of goods and services put forward by the retailer. Here too, there have been radical changes both at a conceptual level and in practical terms. Retailers are beginning to appreciate that markets are now better defined in terms of situations and needs (within budgets) than they are by demographic or psychographic descriptors. Thus, food shopping can be utilitarian (for basic needs), convenient (for emergencies and impulse) or stimulating (for entertainment or new ideas). Clothes shopping can also be segmented in a similar way according to intended use. Companies are starting to create and market their products and services as solutions to common lifestyle problems, rather than around product categories. In continental Europe, when the leading French company, Carrefour, remodelled 15 of its largest hypermarkets as 'Universe' stores organized around solutions to needs sales increases of 10–70 per cent (by product group) were achieved and conversion of the remaining 117 stores quickly followed. Albert Heijn's new stores in Holland and Delhaize 'le Lion's' millennium outlet in Brussels (Belgium) are similarly laid out. In the UK IKEA, Urban Outfitters, The Link and Tesco (yet again) are all examples. Even in Germany, 'Lust for Life' (Karstadt) offers a lifestyle concept. This trend has major implications both for the methods of delivery of the proposition, and its branding and communications, which will be discussed below.

As Field (1997) has pointed out, stores are an expensive and inflexible means of distributing goods. As basic retail needs have become increasingly saturated, retailers have begun to extend their proposition into more and more new areas, including catering, financial services, heath and education, and leisure. At the same time, the power and potential profit of retail activities has tempted many compelling non-traditional entrants into the sector from museums and travel termini to sports venues and hospitals. What this suggests is that traditional definitions of retailing were constrained more by the methods of sourcing and distributing products than by a robust appreciation of the evolution of lifestyle needs. Customers' expectations of retailers have changed, and in particular, their definition of 'value' is changing. In the new millennium it is perhaps more helpful to conceptualize the market opportunity not only in terms of the traditional retail content of goods and services, but also in terms of leisure/entertainment and enrichment/self-actualization things to make life fun and things to make life better.

Figure 6.5 illustrates the 'Concept Cube', which represents this picture. Although they will have to acquire new core competencies, retailers are better placed than many of the other organizations and institutions in the cube to move into and dominate the vacant top far right segment of the cube, because of their resources, commercial skills and closeness to the customer. There is

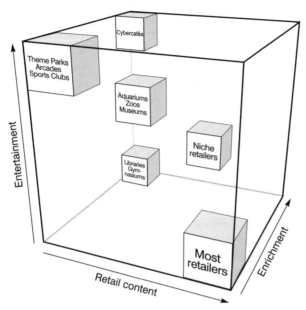

Figure 6.5 New retail brand market positioning matrix. *Source*: Sadleir, Tempus Entertainment (1996).

already considerable evidence that they are extending the range of their offers into new activities:

- The proliferation of pharmacies, post offices and other services in supermarkets.
- The introduction of singles nights, weddings, political canvassing, etc. by ASDA.
- The holding of events, festivals, parties, art exhibitions, etc. by fashion stores, such as Jaeger and Selfridges.
- The opening of restaurants by fashion stores and book retailers (Nicole Fahri, Books, etc., Borders and Waterstones are good examples).
- The development of HMR offers along American lines by Marks & Spencer, Tesco, and to a lesser extent, the other major food retailers.
- The development of DIY workshops, tasting and cooking demonstrations, personal fashion shopping advisors and other educational programmes by leading retailers in all sectors.

When one operator or brand cannot achieve credibility across a sufficiently broad spread of activities, there is a trend towards forming strategic alliances to improve the quality and coverage of the total proposition. The introduction of branded concessions into fashion shops and department stores has long been an example of this. Recent times have seen a succession of link-ups between petrol retailers and supermarket operators for the same reason. The marketing rationale for this is to improve total overall operating competence and benefit from the collective specialist brand reputations. The downside is the dilution of the overall brand impact of the host store (or site).

Another tactic is for stores to purposefully group together with similar traders, thus enhancing the destination appeal of the location. Fashion stores always did this, but it is now common to find furniture or antique shops, DIY stores and electrical shops, and even superstores sited alongside each other. This strategy presumes that the overall local market catchment can be increased, as opposed to conventional analysis of finite product opportunity within a given geographical market.

A linked trend is for entities larger than individual stores to develop and market themselves on the basis that the appeal of the whole proposition is greater than the sum of the parts. Marketing a 'destination' can be simply a street or area (like St Christopher's Place, Covent Garden or Regent Street), it can be a shopping centre, or even an entire town. The highly successful Bluewater regional shopping centre in Kent developed a mission statement, detailed proposition and even a Brand Manual long before it opened. The City of Nottingham launched a civic reward card in 1998 to promote the entire city. More and more UK towns and cities are appointing commercial managers (along the lines of German towns) to carry out this task.

Combining retail businesses with leisure, as suggested by the concept cube, is already under way, especially in the USA. Examples are businesses such as Niketown, Planet Hollywood, The Rainforest Cafe, Disney, REI, Anthropologie, Centex Life Solutions and many other so-called polysensual formats. As yet, there is little evidence that many of these formats cross the Atlantic profitably. European culture (and older populations) seem to demand more sophisticated concepts. Indeed many European experiments by companies like Boots, Oininio, Ipuri and others have not endured. Lifestyle concepts appear to suffer from the twin problems of a high cost base and demanding consumer intelligibility. This is not to say that their intention is misplaced, but rather, like the e-commerce model, implementation will prove more difficult than pioneers envisaged. The German company Tchibo is perhaps the outstanding example of a successful lifestyle concept in Europe. The American futurist Faith Popcorn has identified 'fantasy adventure' as one of the key social trends in western culture. People want the thrills and excitement of adventure without the time or money cost or the personal risk or pain. This was previously only available at theme parks, like Disney World or Alton Towers, but can now be offered in shopping centres thanks to the enabling technologies of virtual reality. Tempus Entertainment pioneered this concept in The Mall of America, and European examples include the Xpo recreation centre in Milton Keynes and the Opel Ride rally driving experience at the Geneva Motor Show. So Charles Revson's insight that he was marketing dreams rather than products turns out to have much wider relevance if we count vicarious experience as dreaming awake.

Delivering the proposition

Changes are also taking place very rapidly in terms of how the retail proposition is made available to customers. Not long ago, 'Location' enhanced by

'Retail Design' was said to be the key to retail success. Retail sales depended on the size and nature of the local 'market' and the quality of site within it. Now, as Tesco has stated, the emphasis has changed from share of the market to customer share – share of the customer's spending power that is. Retail marketing now has to make the proposition available to the customer wherever, however and whenever she finds it convenient. The concept of 'lifetime customer value' has focused attention on alternative routes to market. Thus, Tesco now supplements its food-based superstores with hypermarkets (Tesco Extra, with an enhanced non-food offer), city centre convenience stores (Tesco Metro), convenience stores for the motorist (Tesco Express), Internet shopping on the Tesco Website and a Tesco home delivery service. John Lewis, Next, Lands End, Argos and Boden are just a few UK examples of retailers growing sales and market share through integrated 'multi-channel' retailing strategies involving stores, catalogues and the Internet. According to a 2005 report from Mintel, shopping on the Internet has now overtaken catalogue shopping as the most popular form of home shopping. (Martin, 2005). Forecasts vary on the likely speed, coverage and growth of Internet shopping. All the experts agree that it is growing fast, from a very small base. In the UK the Internet is now (2005) used by 28 million adults and 4.3 million teenagers representing more than 50 per cent of UK households. According to the Interactive Advertising Bureau, it is estimated to have generated retail sales of £14.5b in 2004. Other estimates by the Interactive Media Research Group suggest that some £5b will be spent on Internet purchases for Christmas 2005 alone, up from £3.5b in 2004. By the end of 2004 UK fashion retail sales on the Internet were said to be running at £300m per month. (Newbery, 2004). Some experts such as Stern (1999) have predicted that the life cycle of many e-commerce operators, and the distribution channel as a whole, will be short. Perhaps the most important impact is that it is one catalyst for the acceptance of non-traditional routes to market, by the new generation of shoppers. In total, all these new routes to market will have a major impact on the performance and profitability of traditional retail outlets. In the USA, consultants Kurt Salmon Associates (1999) predict that all 'non-store' retailing will grow from 15 per cent of retail sales in 1994 to 55 per cent by 2010. Already, some 69 per cent of US Internet browsers check out products on-line which they later buy in stores and some 7 per cent of on-line buyers return products to shops. Some important UK initiatives include:

- Following the demise of early fashion e-commerce sites like Boo.com, the launch and rapid move to profitability of a second generation of e-tailers with a clear focus and professional skills. Examples include Figleaves, Bravissimo, ASOS, Net-a-Porter and Boden.
- Introduction of new technology options by the leading mail order retailers, including CD-ROMs, their own e-commerce sites and the use of new mobile phone technology.
- TV-based shopping, based previously on cable or the telephone, but with greatly enhanced potential thanks to digital TV.

- On-site automated shopping including vending machines such as the Belgian-based 'Shop 24' system or Video 24 in Hampstead. This also includes many experiments with kiosks of various kinds.
- With more people based at home, the continued growth in party plan and home selling. Body Shop, Virgin Vie, Ann Summers and Weekender are all prominent in this sector.
- The growing number of manufacturers marketing direct to their customers rather than selling via traditional distribution routes. Examples are Nike, Levi's Swatch and Hagen-Dazs, now joined by brands as diverse as Coca-Cola and Cadbury, Vetrinox and Ben Sherman. As Wileman and Jary (1997) demonstrate, in fashion (or 'repertoire' retailing as they call it) there is a strong case for consumer focused vertical integration as a driver for success-ful brand building, a suggestion more than amply vindicated by the growth of Zara.

Attention is also being put on adding customer value by the quality and manner of the delivery of the retail proposition, as well as the route to mar-ket itself. This means adding back the service factor. All the leading super-market operators have beep recruiting packers people to carry out groceries to the car, and also adding service elements like baby change and toilet facil-ities. Safeway and Waitrose have introduced customer self-scanning in a selec-tion of stores. Somerfield in Partnership with IBM (and Delhaize in Belgium with Alcatel Bell) have experiments in progress whereby company employ-ees can order via the Internet and have their groceries delivered to a secure locker in the company car park. A similar experiment, called Shopping Box, is under way on a wider basis in Munich. In a 1996 initiative, Marks & Spencer launched a customer service drive to re-focus store staff away from company procedures in favour of acknowledging and serving customers although this had little impact given the entrenched management cultures and processes at the time. A fresh initiative by the new CEO, Stuart Rose in 2005, involving all the staff appears to have met with much greater success. The introduction of fitting rooms and counter service meat and deli departments also reflects the awareness of the quality of the customer shopping experience exemplified by the refit of their Marble Arch flagship store, London.

Communication

According to Grey Futures, in 1997 some 90 per cent of all consumer commu-nication was one way from the vendor to the customer. Grey predicted that by the end of the year 2000 this ratio would have fallen to 60 per cent. Facilitated by the explosion of various forms of e-commerce communication is turning into conversation, with customers willing and able to express their needs and views to retailers. This phenomenon has been fully explored by this author in a recent conference paper (Webb, 2005). Internet sites like kelkoo.com, deal-time.co.uk, letsbuyit.com and priceline.com demonstrate how fast and how far the balance of power has shifted in favour of the consumer. Some would argue that this is only reverting back to the pre-technology era when every grocer knew his customers personally. In an article in *Progressive Grocer*, Ryan Mathews (1998) talks about 'a grocer in Michigan who has one store and 26 computers so that he can get to know each one of his customers as well as his grandfather did'.

Instant realtime feedback is increasingly being generated via traditional 'bricks and mortar' retailers. The latest Albert Heijn store in Haarlem includes 'Supplier Hotlines' which customers can use to contact major manufacturers directly. Tesco has been experimenting with an in-store TV information channel with the potential to be extended for interactive communication. However, the Grey forecast highlights just how important direct marketing and the building of customer databases has become to retailers. This is undoubtedly the most important means by which retailers learn about their individual customers' spending behaviour patterns. The idea that retail marketing was largely a blunt instrument for informing and persuading customers on mass to buy things they never knew existed or believed that they wanted is no longer given much credence. Today's customers are too well informed and too street-wise to be taken in by messages which do not accurately reflect a retail brand's culture, offer and delivery performance. Rumbelows found this out to their cost with their 'We save you money and serve you right' campaign. (They did not and could not profitably.) As the American retailer L. L. Bean is fond of saying, it is important to 'make sure the story is never better than the store'.

Both manufacturers and retailers have channelled a larger share of their communications budgets into 'below the line' promotion, as a means of talking to customers individually. This has meant:

- Introducing company branded card schemes of various types and sophistication. The early schemes were largely based on credit accounts, and some have been enduring and successful beyond their founders (e.g. Hepworth, now Next's, Club 24 scheme). The launch of the Tesco Club card, and its role in helping Tesco overhaul Sainsbury, has been well documented. More recently, Shell Select and Boots have introduced cards with much more powerful chips replacing the traditional magnetic stripes. Boots shoppers can obtain personalized promotions and discounts via their reward cards and a network of in-store kiosks.

  The initial rationale for these cards was that it is cheaper and more efficient to retain as many existing customers as possible, rather than continuously replacing them, especially given the current demographic age group profile. However, there is growing evidence that the proliferation of loyalty cards is doing little to change the fundamental habits of shoppers. Promiscuous shoppers are behaving just as they used to only picking up the loyalty bonuses at each store they use. Loyal shoppers are simply claiming a discount.

  The Henley Centre (1998) has called this 'The Loyalty Paradox' and sees the current obsession with customer loyalty as merely the latest in a long line of retail panaceas starting with location, and including EPOS and design, which have their relevance but in themselves cannot make up for shortcomings in the retail proposition. Operators increasingly claim that the real benefits lie in the construction of detailed customer profiles and databases, which enable them to fine tune their assortments and promotions of more accurately reflect their customers' lifestyles and needs.

- Whilst initially flattered at receiving personalized letters from the local supermarket, customers are also finding the constant attempts to build 'relationships' rather irksome, especially when the other party misspells their name, sends them three copies of mailings, downgrades their status when separation or divorce reduces their spending, or connects them to unintelligible voice mail systems. As with people, relationships with stores or brands are discretionary and require the provision of genuine, desired benefits by both sides. Many of the owners of such brands still need to learn the sensitivities of relationship marketing.

- Tailoring communications much more precisely to groups or individuals. Tesco's *Club* magazine was conceived to be published in five issues aimed at different lifestage customers. BT's 'Family and Friends' scheme is a good example of a promotion which retains economies of scale, yet is specific and relevant to each beneficiary. This approach has been called 'mass customization', and we should expect to see more individual tailoring of both products and promotions in the future. Wolny and Webb (2000) have identified the apparel industry as ripe for mass customization initiatives due to the specificity of consumer demand for fit and styling as exemplified by Levi's 'Original Spin' programme.

    Coca-Cola is one company which has recently gone on record as saying that, within its overall brand personality, it must find ways of addressing different customers. Writing in *Adweek*, their ex-Global Marketing Director, Sergio Zyman, explained that they no longer run one campaign, but 20 or more, so that the company can offer customers the choice of many different ways of relating to it.

    Communications strategies are becoming more flexible, with product and store brands being forced to be 'whatever different customers need them to be', when they are targeted at situations and needs rather than people.

- Making use of new media to allow customers to source information for themselves. The growth in retailer websites has been well documented. What is more surprising is the way in which they are being used. Steve Bowbrick (1998) of Webmedia, writing in *Design Week*, stated, 'Website owners have learnt that Internet user are sociable, confident and curious. They want to talk about their purchases to the retailer and to other shoppers, to compare notes and whinge about bad experiences. This is scary for retailers. Allowing customers to talk to each other to compare deals and after-sales service, even to club together to get a better price is anathema to shop owners. The retail business model is actually dependent on ignorance.' He goes on to describe the sense of community generated by visitors to sites such as Garden Escape.com. In the USA a new marketing industry is emerging to harness the power of customers prepared to indulge in 'buzzing' – recommending products to their circle of contacts.

On a wider basis, the availability of intelligent Internet search engines like Yahoo or Ask enables customers to embark on active global searches for choice and value, which is breaking down differential price strategies of global brands wishing to vary prices according to the markets in which they trade.

- Communications are increasingly focused on developing brand values rather than selling products. In their publication *Riding the Wave*, PriceWaterhouse Coopers (1997) wrote 'In the new world, if you haven't got a brand, you don't have a business.' Traditionally branding served a dual purpose to act as a shortcut to understanding a product or service proposition, and defining a system of values to which customers could relate. The tactical benefits of the former are being increasingly eroded, as customers judge brands on the basis of their own experience, but the strategic role of the latter is of growing importance. Virgin is a brand for the young and adventurous whether in music, travel, fashion or financial services.

Many retail brands are seeking to enhance their reputations by espousing good causes what has been called 'Differentiation by Standing for Something'. The Body Shop was an early example of this. More recent examples are fashion companies like Ann Summers supporting breast cancer charities, DIY companies protecting tropical rain forests, Habitat backing art galleries or Tesco running its highly successful 'Computers for Schools' programme. Retailers such as Plannet Organic and Fresh & Wild are exploiting small but growing segments of the food market. In Europe, companies like Migros and Auchan finance entire foundations dedicated to youth and education, whilst Obi runs a technical trade university.

To be credible, brands must deliver against their promises, and increasingly be seen to be authentic as is 'The Original Levis Store' or 'Coke The Real Thing'. This applies both to their physical proposition and any values that they espouse. Writing in the *Sloan Management Review*, Professor Herman Simon (1997) suggests that brands can experience a 'marketing hysteresis'. This means that their reputation suffers permanently from one major lapse in delivering core brand and recovery is only partial. He quotes the example of Shell and their conflict with Greenpeace over the disposal of redundant oil platforms. In the retail sector, Gerald Ratner's famous quip about his products being 'crap' is an example. Others could be the reaction to Benetton's shock advertising (especially in Germany), Hoover's transatlantic flights fiasco, Levi's pulling its Dead Hamster campaign or Esso's quick reversal of its price increase following the end of the September 2000 fuel blockade. Faith Popcorn (1992) talks about 'The Vigilante Consumer', and undoubtedly the guardians of brands (product or store) will need to be much more careful of protecting and delivering their promises, if they are not to be shunned by consumers. 'Best Value' is not the decisive store choice criteria for customers concerned about the fur trade, saving dolphins or trees, apartheid, dictatorships in Burma or Indonesia or child workers in India. Virgin trains (and clothing) for different reasons are high risk strategies for Virgin. The potential upside is great on the one hand, because of the current abysmal repute of rail travel, and on the other because success-ful branding in the fashion and beauty sector elicits the greatest consumer emotional response of any branding. However, the potential impact of fail-ure in either endeavour, and the knock-on effect on Virgin's total credibility, is very high.

Businesses have found that alliances work better when the partners have roughly equal size and strength. So it is proving to be with customers. Mass markets were able to relate to mass producers and distributors. Now, many of the largest companies (including retailers) are losing market share, and it is evident that speed, flexibility, insight and attitude are at least a match for size. Avis was the first to exploit this with 'We try harder'.

Many mainstream retailers too are taking steps to play down their corpor-ate nature and respond to local communities with specific store designs, product assortments and communications programmes. There is clearly a balance to be achieved between the confidence and security of a success-ful brand, and the approachability of a local trader. Wal-Mart, the larg-est and most profitable retailer in the world, takes care to retain its small town, homey origins, both through its staff training and motivation and its communications. It could be argued that some of Sainsbury's difficulties stemmed from that company's psychological distance from its customers.

Conclusions

What can be concluded about the future shape and prospects of retail brand marketing? This chapter has suggested main conclusions, as follows:

1 Definitions of retailing are changing dramatically, and with them the organ-izational roles and skill required to operate retail businesses. Retail market-ing will diverge quickly from physical 'shop' marketing.
2 Marketing has traditionally concerned itself with the removal of barriers, often self-imposed, to consumer satisfaction. It has been largely a compen-sation for deficiencies in the retail system information, offer, delivery and communication. That is why it has sat so uneasily with those responsible for these functions. Step improvements in both supply chain efficiency and consumer demand generation will make most of the operational elements of marketing redundant within a generation. Mitchell (1997) maintains that changed circumstances have caused a 'paradigm crisis for marketing'.
3 As Fred Schneider of Arthur Andersen has written, 'We are moving from a world of consumer choice to consumer control.' Customers will be, already are, doing their own 'reverse marketing'. Let's call it 'specifying' for when that skill replaces 'marketing' in management and academic discussion. Infinite choice, in all aspects of the product and service supply chain, will be something required by consumers, not offered by distributors. Customers will be one part indeed the driving force in a multilateral data exchange embracing 'concept developer', manufacturer and distributor. SINFOS,

an experiment by Rewe, Nestle and Mars in Germany, is a first step in this direction.

4 For the present, as the Danish fashion company In-Wear (1997) wrote in its prospectus, 'The consumer market participants ... may he divided into raw material suppliers, product producers, concept owners, wholesalers and retailers. The concept owners are the driving force in this process. They choose the materials and control the production and delivery process. In addition, they handle a large part of the marketing activities. Consequently it is the concept owners who create, maintain and develop brands, with the effect that the value and goodwill belonging to the brand name is owned by the concept owner.' This means that both upstream manufacturing and downstream selling can be 'outsourced', with the value being attached to the 'needs solution concept'. Marks & Spencer is an outstanding example of a brand that has effectively eliminated any and all value attached to any of its suppliers.

5 Mitchell (1999) argues that customers will identify and select products according to their 'fitness for purpose', value and personal brand values congruity. Eventually, we should expect brands to become redundant, as individuals become their own brands, each and every one of us with our needs and desires individually addressed. In the interim period, the development and communication of brand values will be an ongoing requirement for 'consumer problem solution' businesses (retailers in today's terms), especially for new businesses and new products. This will apply very much more to those 'propositions' positioned against emotional needs (fun, leisure, personal support) than to those positioned against utilitarian or convenient needs, which will lend themselves much more readily to automated solutions. In this respect, the example of fashion marketing, rather than FMCG marketing, will have the most medium-term relevance.

As Professor Peter Doyle (1998) wrote in the Spring edition of *Market Leader*, the business of the future will need to do only three things: to identify opportunities for innovation; create networks which can deliver efficient, fast and marketable solutions; and build and sustain brand equity.

6 Organizations are clearly moving away from hierarchical structures and towards flexible, temporary, teams. Many members are from outside the organization, and may never actually meet other team members. Most retailer 'departments' will become redundant, and with them the functional directors who head them. As the current evidence makes very clear, the marketing function will be the first to be decimated. This will come as a great relief to those many retail companies who have not yet got round to creating one!

7 Only truly customer-oriented businesses will achieve long-term success. The top executives, company culture, and all operational management and staff will truly champion the needs of their customers. The importance of what marketing has been attempting to achieve for the past half century has transcended the abilities and remit of its practitioners. These organizations will be open and transparent to all stakeholders, and enjoy the automatic confidence and trust of their customers.

8 Key activities carried out under the banner of marketing will still need to be executed. These will largely concern the management of information and its transformation into knowledge. Currently, this falls under the remit of category management, but, as Peppers and Rogers pointed out, emphasis is moving quickly towards customer management. Most of these functions are being outsourced to experts; that organizations will need to execute them in a much more integrated manner, with a focus on customers and customer situations, than at present.

9 There is still little evidence that many retail organizations are managing to accumulate and progress their insights. Customers are learning much more quickly than retailers, which is why they gaining control of the process much as retailers wrested it from manufacturers 20 years ago. Possibly it is too late, but a key 'marketing' challenge for retailers in the next millennium will be how to effectively institutionalize a learning process.

References

Aldred, G. (1998). Quoted in *Retail Week*, 13 March.

Arthur Andersen (1997). Counting the cost. *Retail Week*, 24 July.

Bowbrick, S. (1998). Shop talk. *Design Week*, 16 January. London: Cetaur Communications.

Burns, K. B., Enright, H., Hayes, J. F., McLaughlin, K. and Shi, C. (1997). The art and science of retail renewal. *McKinsey Quarterly*, No. 2.

Doyle, P. (1998). Brand equity and the marketing professional. *Market Leader*, Issue 1.

Farmer, C. (1995). The less decade: dream or nightmare? *International Trends in Retailing*, **12** (1).

Field, C. (1997). The future of the store. *Financial Times*.

Henley Centre (1998). *Planning for Social Change*. London: Henley Centre.

In-Wear A/S (1997). *Danish Stock Exchange Listing Prospectus*. Copenhagen: In-Wear A/S.

Kurt Salmon Associates (1999). *Consumer Outlook*. New York: Kurt Salmon Associates.

Marketing Society (1997). *Shaping the Future The Profession: Keeping its Grip*. London: Marketing Society.

Marketing Week (1997). Commentary on 1996 UK Marketing Award Winners, 17 April.

Martin, N. (2005). *Mail Order Left Behind by On-line Shopping*, Daily Telegraph, 18 April.

Mathews, R. (1998). Small big heart. *Progressive Grocer*, 9 February.

Mitchell, A. (1997). Brand strategies in the information age. *Financial Times*.

Mitchell, A. (1999). When the customer finally is king. *Market Leader*, Issue 5.

Newbery, M. (2004). *Trends in Online Apparel Retailing, Forecasts to 2010*, www. just-style.com, Aroq, London.

Peppers, D. and Rogers, M. (1993). *The One-To-One Future*. New York: Piatkus Press.

Popcorn, F. (1992). *The Popcorn Report: Faith Popcorn on the Future of Your Company, Your World and Your Life*. New York: Harper Collins.

PriceWaterhouse Coopers (1997). *Riding the Wave*. New York: PriceWaterhouse Coopers.

Quinn, F. (1990). *Crowning the Customer*. Dublin: O'Brien Press.

Richer, J. (1995). *The Richer Way*. London: EMAP Business Communications.

Simon, H. (1997). Hysterics in marketing a new phenomenon? *Sloan Management Review*, **38** (3).

Stern, N. Z. (1999). The impact of the Internet on retailing. *International Trends in Retailing*, **16** (2).

Webb, W. S. (2005), *Fashion Marketing in the Age of the Empowered Consumer*, Proceedings of the International Fashion Management Symposium, London, London College of Fashion, 27 June.

Wileman, A. and Jary, M. (1997). *Retail Power Plays From Trading to Brand Leadership*. London: McMillan.

Wolny, J. P. and Webb, W. S. (2000). Mass Customisation as an Individualised Value Delivery System. In *Retailing 2000 Launching the New Millennium*, Proceedings of the AMS/ACRA Conference, Vol. IX. Columbus: American Collegiate Retailing Association.

7

Competitive marketing strategies of luxury fashion companies

Margaret Bruce and Christine Kratz

The aims of this chapter are to:

1 understand the tenets of luxury fashion,
2 explore the market dynamics of luxury fashion,
3 identify key elements of marketing strategies,
4 illustrate by case histories.

Introduction

This chapter explores the dynamics affecting luxury fashion brands and documents the strategies of brand owners in managing change. After discussing the concept of 'luxury' and its characteristics, the chapter will focus on the key parameters of the competitive marketing strategies of luxury fashion brand owners. These companies are operating in a turbulent and highly competitive environment, the dynamics of which are discussed here.

Understanding the tenets of luxury fashion

Historically, luxury, style and elegance are commensurate with the French way of life. The first 'grands magasins' were founded in Paris and were synonymous with sensuality, luxury, innovation and premium service. Using architecture to convey a sense of majesty and power, these began to define the shopping experience for wealthy consumers (Zola, 1883). Central to luxury products are coveted products, which are authentic, exude quality and craftsmanship, exclusive (McDowell 2002, Kapferer 1998, Randon 2002), aspirational and timeless. Waiting lists for certain items reinforce the exclusivity and rarity value of fashion luxury, such as a 2-year waiting list for a Hermes 'Kelly' handbag. Such items are accessible at a high price (Erikson and Johanson, 1985) and maintain a premium price differential when compared with other products within the same category (Jackson, 2004). Coco Chanel regarded luxury, as 'the opposite of vulgarity'. Also, the retail environment is prestigious and offers high standards of customer service (Moore et al., 2000). The stores tend to be designed by famous designers and are indulgent and extravagant spaces.

Luxury can be defined from a consumer perspective (Gutsatz, 1996; Dubois et al., 2001), or from a product/brand point of view (Alleres, 2003; Jackson, 2004). From a consumer perspective, Gutsatz (1996) suggests that:

> *'Luxury includes two levels of representation. The first is material, it includes/understands the product and the brand (its history, identity, unique know how, the talent). The second level is psychological. . . and covers representations, which are influenced by our social environment and the brand values'.*

This perspective is reinforced by Jackson (2004) who argues that the luxury fashion brand is: *'characterised by exclusivity, premium prices, image and status, which combine to make them desirable for reasons other than function'.*

Six elements of luxury have been identified by Dubois et al. (2001) as follows:

1 Excellent quality
2 High price
3 Scarcity and uniqueness
4 Aesthetics and polysensuality
5 Ancestral heritage and personal history
6 Superfluousness.

Integral to these elements are iconic product designs, for example Hermes Kelly bag or the Chanel no. 5 perfume; the personality of the creators of the brands (Jean Paul Gaultier); their locations; their brand names and visual symbols associated with these brands and their history. These elements are shown in Figure 7.1.

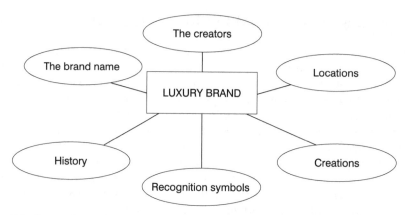

Figure 7.1 Characteristics of luxury brands. *Source:* Adapted and translated from Alleres (2003).

To give examples: Chanel is intertwined with the personality of its creator, Coco Chanel and her lifestyle. Thanks to the creator's image, the brand value ('rente de la marque', Bomsel et al., 1998) is ensured. The logo of Chanel has not changed since its inception and this is commensurate with other luxury brands. Investment in premier locations and the development of flagship stores akin to museums is typical, for example Prada's takeover of the Gugenheim Museum in New York. Luxury retailers are clustered in certain streets in capital cities, like Rue du Faubourg St Honoré in Paris and Fifth Avenue in New York. Burberry tried to reposition itself as a 'credible high fashion brand' by opening a flagship on Bon Street in London (Moore et al., 2004). Heritage of the brand and the history associated with its founder and its craftsmanship are built into the luxury brand (Nueno and Quelch, 1998). The history of the brand is part of its distinctiveness, such as Vuitton's travel cases. As Ivar Björkman, 2002 specified: 'a very important part of the process in creating aura is the stories that surround the company'. The symbolism associated with these brands is instantly recognizable and memorable at an international level (Dubois and Paternaut 1995) and is linked with cultural identity (Dubois and Duquesne, 1993).

In addition, Jackson (2004) suggests that luxury fashion brands are distinguished by:

- Global recognition
- Critical mass
- Core competence and other products
- High product quality and innovation
- Powerful advertizing
- Immaculate store presentation
- Superb customer service.

Indeed, these dimensions serve to build up a relationship with consumers and at the heart of this is a sensorial and experiential basis (Rieunier, 2002).

Product design, marketing communications and retailing are fundamental to the competitive marketing strategies of luxury fashion companies, but how they apply these parameters varies, as the cases show, in this chapter.

The dynamics of luxury fashion

Luxury goods have shown an unprecedented pattern of growth of 14 per cent annual growth rate between 1996 and 2000 (*Financial Times*, 2004). The market for luxury goods is highly fragmented and has four main categories: fashion (couture, ready-to-wear and accessories); perfumes and cosmetics; wines and spirits; watches and jewellery (Jackson, 2004). The three largest companies, LVMH, Richemont and Gucci account for some 10 per cent of the total market. These companies have a portfolio of almost 1000 luxury brands (Euromonitor, 2001). Table 7.1 shows the sales for the top nine luxury goods companies. LVMH (Moet Hennessey Louis Vuitton) is the leading group in both sales and product sector and geographical coverage. This company operates across all four luxury goods categories and includes such brands as Moet & Chandon, Louis Vuitton, Givenchy, Fendi, Christian Dior, Tag Heuer. Fashion luxury brands dominate the luxury sector, as a whole, representing 42 per cent of share of sales in 2003 (Mintel, 2004). In 2003, LMVH, Coach and Gucci had 32.8, 8.4 and 7.8 per cent share of the luxury accessories category and in luxury ready-to-wear fashion, Polo Ralph Lauren, Max Mara and Prada had a 12, 6.9 and 6 per cent market share respectively (Mintel, 2004).

Table 7.1 Major luxury goods companies: sales and profits 2000/2001 (US $ million)

	Sales	Operating profits	Net profits
LVMH	10,932	1,694	784
Richemont	4,002	773	N/a
Gucci	2,258	N/a	336.7
Tiffany and Co	1,668.1	327.4	190.6
Prada	1,420	265	N/a
Hermes	1,090.9	N/a	N/a
Armani	971	117.5	N/a
Bulgari	669.5	N/a	N/a
Versace	390.8	N/a	88.4

Source: Euromonitor (2001).

Luxury brands are a significant part of the French economy, valued at €11.7 billion and 82 per cent of luxury brands are exported, principally to Europe, USA and France. Over the past 10 years, the growth in demand for luxury brands is demonstrated by the doubling of these figures in that timescale. New markets for luxury goods are where a growth in wealth is evident, such as Russia, China, Middle East and South America. At the moment, China is representing a market of about 10 million potential consumers for luxury products (Le Monde.fr) and according to Ipsos Institute (Ipos.com), China will become by 2014, the first client of luxury with 24 per cent of the world market share. For example, for the LVMH group, 'management appears particularly keen on China where the brand has been present since 1992. The company currently operates nine stores with three additional stores to be opened in 2004'. The Chinese consumer already accounts as 'the third largest contributor to sales after the Japanese and the US consumer, if both Hong Kong and Taiwan are included' (Euromonitor, 2004). Affluent consumers in these countries display their wealth through the conspicuous consumption of luxury brands.

Operating in the luxury goods industry can be tough. Strong internal competition exists for each product range and new forms of external competition are evident. These new forms may be offering new services, such as the Vertu mobile phone, or from ready-to-wear fashion groups, like Donna Karan. Also, the production costs for luxury items are high and shorter product life cycles are evident, which reduces profit margins. Within fashion, new products are generated on a twice-yearly basis and speed of obsolescence is high (Jackson, 2002, 2004). A concentration of luxury producers into large financial groups is one approach to survival in a stringent market. The development of luxury brand families covering a range of different markets is evident with companies, such as Donna Koran, Armani, etc. Gucci is characterized by lavish flagship stores, internal manufacturing control and iconic design and has reorganized itself to have a 'parenting advantage' throughout the group, in terms of strategies, structures and processes covering design, communications and retail experience and supply chain (Moore and Birtwistle, 2005). The constant demand to innovate and introduce new products implies that the effective management of the supply chain is required (Moore and Birtwistle, 2005), which integrate different approaches, including licensing, contract manufacturing and joint venture agreements (Moore et al., 2004). The expansion of distribution channels has been evident in the number of luxury store openings (Vickers and Renand, 2003) and also the use of the Internet.

An analysis is shown of the key factors underpinning the turbulent nature of the luxury fashion sector in Table 7.2.

A younger and wider audience for luxury goods, such as the 'nouveaux riches' of the dotcom and IT worlds is evident, indeed 46 per cent of customers of luxury goods are less than 35-year old. Dubois and Laurent (2002) called them 'the Excursionists' because 'they buy luxury goods only in specific circumstances. For them, buying and consuming a luxury item is not an expression of their "art de vivre" but rather an exceptional moment, sharply contrasting with their daily life style'. So the number of 'Excursionists' has increased (Dubois et al., 1996) and the average purchase figures (Table 7.3) show that luxury companies have to deal with these occasional clients (1 to 3 purchases a year) in addition to the traditional 'luxury consumers'.

Consumer lifestyles and profiles for luxury are changing. For younger consumers, brands are absolutely pivotal (Banister and Nejad, 2004) and to afford these brands, younger consumers will continue to stay living with their

Table 7.2 Analysis of factors of market turbulence

Opportunities	Threats
Increasing demand from countries as China, Russia, . . .	Dependance of the political events and tourism (September 11th, terrorism, Iraq conflicts)
Changes of consumer lifestyles (demand from young and senior people)	Importance of counterfeiting
Increasing demand for luxury brands	Newer forms of luxury

Strengths	Weaknesses
Notoriety, brand values	Strong international competition (for instance in fashion with news brands)
Know how, innovation	High production costs
Management of the international channel development (selective and exclusive retailers)	Trend to concentration

Source: Bruce and Kratz (2004).

Table 7.3 Luxury customer (Europe, USA, Japan)

Customer types	USA		Europe		Japan	
	1994	2000	1994	2000	1994	2000
Luxury customers	39	65	40	60	39	62
Occasionals (1–3)	29	44	31	42	25	43
Regulars (4+)	10	21	9	18	14	19
Non-customers	61	35	60	40	62	38

Source: Roux, (2002).

parents, take on high levels of debt and delay entering the housing market. Older consumers are staying younger longer, as reflected in statements, such as 'fifty is the new forty' and the rise in consumption by 'silver surfers' and who are affluent and wish to invest in activities and products to display their wealth and achievements. New purchasing patterns can be observed, as consumers re-define how they use luxury brands. In the past, it was inappropriate to mix luxury products with other brands. Now, it is acceptable to mix a Prada jacket with a pair of blue jeans. To meet the demand from these new consumers, luxury fashion brands have cheaper items to make their brands accessible, such as key-rings, purses, scarves, etc. and to entice new consumers. The danger with this approach is that the brand becomes diluted and looses its exclusivity.

Newer forms of luxury are being generated, which challenge the supremacy of the traditional luxury brand leaders, such as LVHM. These include, luxury mobile phones made out of fine materials and which offer a personalized, global concierge service, travel experiences, etc. Indeed, it has been suggested (*The Economist*, 2005) that: 'the way the rich seek to display status may simply be getting more complex'. So that, 'other motives for luxury purchase are connoisseurship and being an early adoptor'. . . 'Connoisseurs are people whom their peers respect for their deep knowledge of fashion, watches, etc. and early adoptors are those who are first with a new technology'. Fashion companies, such as Commes des Garcons are exploiting connoisseurship through the use of viral marketing and hiring retail sites for very short time periods in out of town locations to promote special editions, which cannot be acquired without being 'in the know' (Doyle and Moore, 2004).

'Copycat' or 'fake' brands are available in every category from perfume to apparel to accessories and objects d'art, so consumers need to be convinced that the 'real' brand has distinctive value; 70 per cent of counterfeits are copies of French products. Burberry has been subject to extensive copying, so that its brand became associated with 'chavs' and has lost its aspirational appeal, especially in certain regions, such as the UK (Moore and Birtwistle, 2004). In France, the 'Comité Colbert' has been established and is composed of 65 luxury brand owners. The mission of the 'Comité Colbert' is to defend the premium quality of their products, their selective approach to retailing, and, to fight against counterfeiting, as this contributes to brand dilution. The counterfeiting represents 300 million Euros (7 per cent of the world trade); 70 per cent of the counterfeits are French product copies (www.comite-colbert.com). One well-known outcome of the 'Comité Colbert' is to defend the title of champagne to that being produced in a particular region of France. This retains the notoriety of the product and reinforces its value.

The country of origin is one factor in value creation (Koromyslov M, 2005, Dubois and Duquesne 1993, Jackson 2004). 'French chic', 'Italian chic', etc. provide a unique national identity and attitude, associated with the brand, such as the eccentricity of the British designer Vivienne Westwood, the 'British classic with a twist' of the British luxury fashion brand, Paul Smith and the elegance and quality of the Italian brands of Prada and Gucci. Such associations contribute to the value of the luxury fashion brand. Jackson (2004) argues that: 'France is considered to be the home of luxury goods because of its heritage, artisan fashion skills and the centre of haute couture'. Although this is being challenged with the advent of Italian and US brands being increasingly associated with luxury (Koromyslov, 2005).

The market for luxury goods has certain discernable undercurrents. One of these undercurrents is the dilution of luxury and its wider accessibility through a growth in credit, wealth, retail expansion, a culture of 'must have' and the development of cheaper entry point luxury items. Another, is a backlash against 'luxury fever' (Frank, 2000) and, more generally, of brand distaste and a concern for social responsibility, as expressed by Klein (2001) in her popular book 'No Logo'. A further trend amongst the super-rich is that of 'conspicuous non-consumption' through philanthropy, dressing down and driving beaten-up cars, ironically, to express an exalted status' (*The Economist*, 2005).

The luxury fashion industry is dynamic. What market strategies are brand owners embraced to manage change in this context? The role of design in brand and channel development is discussed in this chapter.

Marketing strategies in a dynamic context

The key parameters underlying the competitive marketing strategies of luxury fashion companies are identified and discussed here. How these different elements are combined and applied varies and this is shown in the cases presented later in the chapter. The market for luxury fashion is turbulent and dynamic, as the previous section has revealed. This means that there is not a clearly defined approach that luxury fashion companies can adopt to attain a sustainable competitive position.

A new fashion positioning

The growth of premium fashion brands has fuelled a debate as to the true nature of luxury. The development of luxury fashion brands challenges these conventional views of the nature of luxury. Luxury products are timeless and classic. Whereas, fashion is ephemeral and transient. Nonetheless, as Jackson (2004) noted that there is a 'strong association between the notions of fashion and luxury'. Some luxury brands have become 'fashionable' in people's mind because of their product diversification (Chanel, Yves Saint Laurent). Moreover, 'Contemporary designers ... reinforce the fashion association' (Jackson, 2004): Tom Ford and Alexander Mac Queen 'provide creative direction' for Gucci, John Galliano and Marc Jacobs for LVMH. Jackson (2004) adds: 'In essence luxury brands have employed high-profile fashion designers to boost the allure of their products at time in history when more consumers have been able to afford to buy luxury products.'

This perspective is reinforced by Baudrillard (1996) who suggests that fashion brands are an essential aspect of the 'cultural capital' of consumers. They reflect and reinforce a sense of identity and allow for the display of 'conspicuous consumption'.

In the arena of luxury fashion, the role of the designer can gain iconic status. The design signature of Versace, Alexander McQueen, Tommy Hilfilger, Giorgio Armani and so on can override the importance of other qualities, such as country of origin. Their design signature permeates into other related activities, such as perfume and cosmetics, interiors and household products, hotels, restaurants and so on. Internationally renowned fashion designers, such as John Galliano and Marc Jacobs provide a creative direction for the 'grand maison', LMVH and also produce ready-to-wear collections under their own names. These collections court global media attention through fashion shows in New York, Milan, Paris and London. Galliano has responsibility, not only for fashion of Christian Dior, but for the whole brand, including store design, presentation and advertizing. Brand owners, such as Gucci, 'tie-in' notable designers (e.g. Tom Ford and Alexander McQueen) to provide direction across a range of their categories and brands. In other words, the marketing and brand development has a creative direction and is closely connected with design. Indeed, the Annual Report of 1999 states that: 'design and product development are the core of Gucci's success and interact with every other centre of activity . . . We consistently strive to maintain a clear brand image' (cited in Moore and Birtwistle, 2005). The luxury fashion brand becomes a lifestyle statement that permeates across other aspects than apparel. Designers become international celebrities whose personal life is the subject of glossy magazines and their friends and associates are other celebrities, such as shown by photographs in the UK national press of Madonna and Stella McCartney attending a function together. Celebrity endorsement is a form of viral marketing and generates international media interest and awareness.

Role of design in innovation

The turbulent environment and the impact of fashion on luxury have influenced the repositioning and redesign of traditional luxury goods. This leads the luxury companies to innovate (for instance, the new 'cerise' bag designed by Takashi Murakami for Louis Vuitton) and/or to target new kinds of clients (as Dior, Cartier or Dinh Van, developing recently cosmetic ranges or jewellery for men).

Distinctive market segments for fashion luxury can be traced. Alleres (2003) presents this as a luxury continuum (shown in Figure 7.2) with three categories of:

1 Accessible luxury
2 Middle luxury
3 Inaccessible luxury.

Under the influence of demand-led factor, the brands develop accessories, making more these more accessible, like a Mulberry purse, or DNKY's diffusion lines. At the opposite extreme, some companies continue to innovate and to create 'inaccessible' offers, such as Vuitton which launched the limited 'graffiti' line of bags. Despite the success of this creation, Vuitton stopped the production (Catry, 2003).

The Burberry product/brand model in Figure 7.3 (Moore et al., 2004) illustrates this luxury continuum: the accessories target a wide market (demand marketing strategy) while the Burberry Prorsum has been created to 'satisfy the demand for exclusivity' (supply marketing).

Within this turbulent and dynamic context (fragmented market, new purchasing patterns, changing nature of luxury, new emergent markets, external and internal competitions, etc.), Thibaut (2003) argues that: 'the survival of luxury brands essentially comes from permanent incremental innovation.'

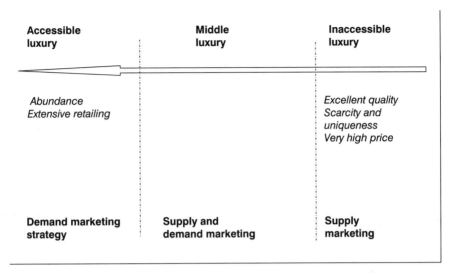

Figure 7.2 The luxury continuum. *Source:* Adapted and translated from Alleres (2003).

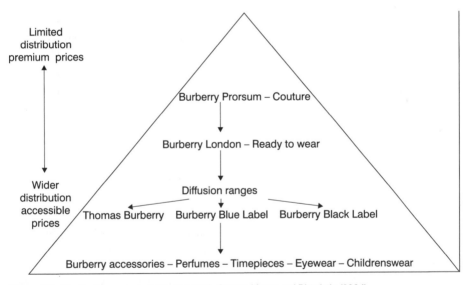

Figure 7.3 The Burberry product/brand model. *Source:* Moore and Birtwistle (2004).

This chapter is concerned with how fashion brand owners, retailers and suppliers are strategically responding to the turbulent market conditions and particularly through investment in design for brand and channel development.

Channel development for luxury fashion

The owners of luxury and premium brands use channels to market that reflect the uniqueness, exquisiteness and rarity of their brands. 'A luxury goods product with an experiential dimension is designed to fulfil internally generated needs in respect to stimulation and/or variety' (Vickers et al., 2003). These need to reinforce the value of the luxury brand from the product itself through to the consumer, so that they will pay a premium price for this (Doyle and Broadbridge, 1999).

Different forms of channels exit, including franchise, licence agreements, wholesaling and own retail sites. An example of the complex nature of channel and distribution for luxury fashion is shown with regard to Burberry (Moore and Birtwistle, 2004) in Figure 7.4. Wholesalers target specific department stores and boutiques with a market profile that matches the brand. These strategies have achieved global coverage effectively (Jackson, 2004).

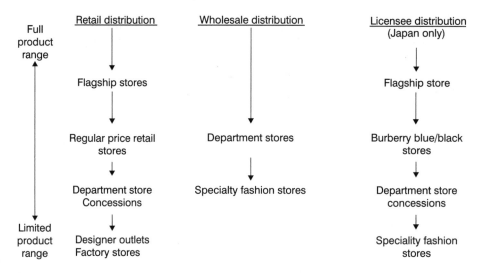

Figure 7.4 Retail and distribution channels for Burberry. *Source:* Moore and Birtwistle (2004).

Increasingly the owners of luxury fashion brands are developing their own channels through extending their own retail outlets (The LVMH group has developed its distribution network from 828 in 1998 to 1,500 stores in 2003, Datamonitor, 2004) and so controlling their extended supply chains from manufacture and design to retailing. Some groups have started to buy back franchises to secure greater control over their brand, as Gucci (Moore and Birtwistle 2005) and Louis Vuitton (Luxembourg Chambre de Commerce Report, 2003) conforming to its strategy 'historically, Louis Vuitton has preferred to sell through its own stores' (Jackson, 2004). The underlying rationale is to ensure that the experience of owning the luxury item is present throughout the purchase experience and that there is coherence in presentation of the brand to the consumer. This is evident for the two company cases described later in this chapter. Investment in flagship stores, personal attention (Gurviez et al., 2000) by the staff in store is all part of the experience of the luxury. Franchise operations may not always deliver this experience. This is exemplified by companies as diverse as the French glass company, Baccarat to the fashion houses of Burberry and Gucci. One aspect of the branding strategies of luxury brands has been that of diffusion lines, such as Armani; building up a 'family of brands', such as Gucci; and brand extension, for example perfume by Stella McCartney.

The Internet is another distribution channel used by fashion luxury companies. The Internet serves as both a communication tool and transaction site, even though it may, arguably, function more effectively as a communication tool (Dall'Olmo and Lacroix, 1997; Nyeck and Roux, 2003). In 2000, LVMH created its own web site called 'eluxury.com' which proposed a luxury selection from more than 80 different luxury brands. It was limited to the US market until recently, when it opened in 2006 to the French market. This is like Hermès, which offers the possibility of purchasing only in the US and in France.

E-commerce can be an opportunity for luxury brands because by this way, they can sell to consumers who have not an easy access to the traditional channel (Kapferer, 2000). Indeed, some luxury companies have are evident on a 'common' site as luxury.com and sell items through this channel. Whereas, others have their own exclusive web site, such as Dior.

According to Marciniak and Bruce (2004), 'the strategic potential of e-commerce can be understood by applying the product matrix of Ansoff'. In the specific case of luxury companies, their Internet strategy can be identified by two segments: market development and market penetration (Table 7.4).

Table 7.4 Ansoff's Product/Market Matrix

Product Market	Existing	New
Present	Market penetration	Product development
New	Market development	Diversification

Source: Ansoff.

Generally, the products sold on the web site are selected from the existing product range and with the intention of targeting: the consumers who are conversant with the brand and wish to purchase through the Internet, and the clients who have difficulties to visit a traditional shop. The survey conducted by Dall'Olmo and Lacroix (2003) identified the type of luxury items the respondents would consider to buy online: the results in Table 7.5 show that the first two categories are food/wine and cosmetics.

At the same time, E-commerce for luxury brands presents a threat of 'commoditization, arising from being referenced by other portals and being pirated' (Kapferer, 2000).

Communications for experiential marketing

Experiential marketing of luxury entails communicating the brand values of the product and its associations, particularly lifestyle aspirations. Luxury

Table 7.5 Luxury items the respondents might buy online

Category	%
Food/wine	37
Cosmetics	33
Accessories	24
Clothes	20
Jewellery	19
Decoration	17
Cars	10
Other items	11

Source: Dall'Olmo and Lacroix, (2003).

brands are aspirational. They are iconic designs. Design is the cornerstone of the experiential marketing of luxury. The product has to reflect the quality of the workmanship, the materials and be sensual to the touch. Communication of the brand means advertizing in premium journals and papers, sponsorship of events, viral marketing and placing the product in exquisite locations, so that the consumer can be immersed in the atmosphere of luxury. Substantial investment is made in marketing communications to maintain high levels of awareness, typically advertizing budgets are between 6 and 12 per cent of sales (Bruce and Kratz 2004; Jackson 2004). For instance, the LVMH group estimates it now ranks in the top 3 in terms of media spending and editorials versus in the top 10 previously. Celebrity endorsement associates the brand with particular lifestyles and can help to reinforce the appeal to certain consumers (such as Emma Thurman for LVMH; Madonna for Jean-Paul Gaultier and Nicole Kidman for Chanel).

World-class retailers renowned for their luxury brands, such as Harvey Nichols and Selfridges are revising their strategies, so as to meet with the needs of suppliers and consumers to provide a shopping experience that is personal and special. Relationship marketing through offering a personal service maximizes the luxury experience (*Financial Times*, 26.3.05). Indeed, 'experiential marketing' (Hetzel, 2002) is recognized as being significant in reinforcing the premium quality of luxury brands. Exclusive contracts for the privilege of retailing luxury brands are one attempt to ensure that rarity and special-ness is maintained. Also, such retailers operate as 'brand police' to allow certain brands into their stores and to keep others out. If new vendors fail to meet with their demands for service, display and product quality, then their contract will be terminated.

With the growth of the Internet as another channel, Okonkwo (2005) asks: 'is it realistic to imagine that the physical luxury retail store environment can be replicated on the Internet?' According to this business analyst, it is feasible to transfer the prestigious atmosphere expected of luxury fashion brick-and-mortar stores to the e-boutique with elements like 'visuals, sound, smell, usability and personalization'. Her analysis is consistent with the Dall'Olmo and Lacroix's findings about the consumer's expectations of a luxury web site (Table 7.6). However, for a common e-commerce site, such as luxury. com, it appears difficult to achieve this and also that is specific to each brand represented on this and other similar sites.

Table 7.6 Features expected in a luxury web site

Feature	%
Aesthetics	60
Communication via e-mail	47
Information on products	44
Easy to navigate	40
Information on brands (PR events)	36
Personalized advice (club, newsletters)	33
Secure connection	32
Community (boards, chat)	31
Clear postage and package charges	28
Real time communication	27
Worldwide	27
Purchase possibility	26

Source: Dall'Olmo, and Lacroix, (2003).

These figures show that the web site for the luxury companies is perceived more as a communication tool, than as a transaction channel. The Internet has become an essential part of the communication strategies of luxury fashion brands and through this channel, it is possible to convey the history and brand heritage and to present products with an appropriate aesthetics. However, whilst information is obtained about the luxury fashion brand from the Internet, consumers still like to enjoy the pampered experience available in a physical store and the opportunity to display their ability to purchase a luxury item.

Case histories

Company A: international fashion retailer

This international Italian company has invested substantially in recent international growth (Moore and Doyle, 2004). The Group is solely owned by the designer, which has provided some latitude in its approach to strategic marketing and implementation. This may not be the case for luxury fashion groups that are subject to shareholders' demands. Fundamental to the marketing strategy has been a focus on key strategic priorities (Giorgio Armani Group, 2003):

1 growth of manufacturing capacity,
2 diversification of the portfolio (including into hotels and leisure),
3 expansion and enhancement of retail store network.

It is worth pointing out that a fourth dimension is that of design. The creative direction, branding, communications and retailing of the brand is controlled by the owner–designer.

Counter to the conventional outsourcing of manufacture, the group has set up a vertically integrated business where the Group 'increasingly takes direct control over all aspects of design, manufacturing, distribution and retail' (Giorgio Armani Group, 2003). The Group has acquired manufacturers, such as Deanna Spa, a specialist of high-quality knitwear, and also four footwear factories in 2002. The Group has manufacturing capability across all of its core product areas. This strategy is to ensure the consistency and 'integrity of the brand around the world' and to ensure design protection and exclusivity. All of the capability is based in Italy, so as to guarantee the value created by country of origin, as discussed earlier. For other items than apparel, such as perfume and eyeware, licence agreements are made.

The Group's brands cover the three main segments of exclusivity to medium to lower end, as outlined by Alleres (2003). The brands and their market positioning are shown in Table 7.7.

Table 7.7 The Brands and their market positioning

Brand name	Positioning
Giorgio Armani	The main line – couture equivalent
Armani Collezioni	Diffusion line of fine-tailoring, sportswear, outerwear and accessories for professionals
Emporio Armani	Young and modern diffusion line for younger customers
AJ/Armani Jeans	Youth line – with a focus on technology and ecology
A/X Armani Exchange	Entry level brand – fast fashion for denim and urban fashion
Armani Casa	Furniture and home accessories ranges

Source: Moore and Wigley (2004).

What is interesting about the brand mix and marketing positioning is the Group's coverage of key customer segments and the management of these to make them apparently exclusive, even though each of these appeal to different groups of customers.

Distribution is divided into wholesale, which represents approximately 50 per cent of the Group's turnover. This approach enables overseas market penetration through recruiting stockists internationally. These stockists are subject to stringent vetting procedures. The Group directly owns a significant minority of retail outlets in its key markets of Italy, Japan and the US. Premier sites, such as Armani Collezioni in Paris and Frankfurt are directly controlled to ensure a premium positioning and all aspects of experiential marketing to build up a relationship with customers.

Company B: luxury brand retailer

Harvey Nichols is a retailer devoted to luxury fashion brands. The company was established in the UK in 1813 and is now owned by Dickson Concepts, a Far Eastern distributor of luxury brands. The company only retails top quality, high fashion brands in apparel, cosmetics, accessories and fragrances, as well as food. As such, the company is a niche player at the highest end of fashion. To achieve this competitive position and to maintain it, Harvey Nichols is very selective with regard to the brands that it retails and the customer experience in store is based on premium service quality, delivery and an atmosphere of rarity and special-ness. Its philosophy is underpinned by: 'right focus, right offer and the right customer experience.' The buying team is well established and has the attitude of personally selecting brands for recognizable customers. Only one or two haute couture items will be selected from fashion catwalks, so that the customer is assured of rarity and special-ness with the fashion items that they purchase from Harvey Nichols. 'Glamour and confidence' are the cornerstone of the retailer's customer appeal. At the same time, the retailer has to be innovative to retain the interest of its customer base. A program of brand renewal is in place and brands are relegated if they fail to be financially effective. This is to ensure that innovation and brand exclusivity meets with changing consumer demands and expectations. The retailer has embarked on a program of international expansion, as well as developing its own brands. The international expansion focuses on store openings in regions where there is a concentration of affluent customers who will purchase luxury brands.

Company C: brand communication

Communicating the values of luxury brand is complex. As the appeal of luxury is to possess an exclusive product and so the promotion of luxury products needs to be understated and retain the notion of specialness and rarity. Even though, in fact, luxury goods are operating in a mass, global market. A luxury brand, like Dunhill sponsors exclusive sports events and tends to use viral marketing. Luxury brands within the Richemont group (e.g. Dior, Patrick Philippe, Tag, Cartier) adopt a communication strategy suitable to the particular brand. Cartier is a recognizable logo and the product design stands out in its own right, Tag is associated with sport and celebrity endorsement is used. Communication is focused on younger end of the market: the wealthy young man who has inherited wealth, or is a 'self-made' man. These consumers may be members of exclusive clubs and so collaboration with the clubs may be feasible to reach these consumers, such as association with Bentley, Black Express club, etc. Low entry products do not exist for brands like Dunhill. The feeling of exclusivity, belonging to an elite group underpins the experience of luxury.

A very different example is that of Comme des Garcons (Doyle et al., 2004). This fashion company is regarded as radical and revolutionary. Its customers are the 'ultimate experientalists' (Anon, 2000) and wish to connect with the fashion company, which is willing to challenge the conventions of retailing through its 'guerrilla stores'. These are unbranded and the consumers have to 'be in the know' to seek out the stores, which are open for a brief period of time. Doyle and Moore (2004) argue that these 'temporary stores ... enable the company to tap into the market "zeitgeist", while not alienating its (main-stream) customers who may be seeking a more hedonistic experience, as offered by its more traditional retail formats'. In addition, this approach to experiential marketing allows the fashion company to quickly test a potential new market opportunity, at low risk. They are in keeping with the spirit of fashion: to be avant garde, innovative and exciting.

Company D: fashion brand

Since the debut of his first line in 1970, Company D has flourished from a menswear designer name into a global designer lifestyle brand. The under-lying philosophy is: 'classic with a twist'. The company's core competencies are derived from its designs and the designers have an excellent technical knowledge of tailoring techniques and historical aspects, which are manipu-lated to create evolutionary products – the 'classic with a twist'. The majority of the fabrics are sourced from Italian mills to guarantee the level of quality required for the luxury items. The design and production staffs are conversant with Italian and treat their suppliers with respect. The relationship aspect of the company culture, not only extends to the customers, but also to suppliers.

The founder of the luxury fashion brand is regarded as being quintessen-tially English, slightly eccentric, but charming. The presentation of the person-ality of the founder is interconnected with the brand values and has become part of the heritage of the company.

The company strategy is to be one of the top names in design, remaining modern and relevant, maintaining the high-quality design profile that they have built. The company hopes to progress by opening more shops, enter-ing into more licensing agreements, catering for the rich and famous to main-tain the companies profile, and through investing in advertizing and Public Relations (PR).

The company is comprised of four complementary sub-brands that address the different lifestyles of the modern individual. Within each sub-brand Company D creates 'a unique world for men, women and children, covering their day, evening, business and casual needs'. In other words, the company has an array of brands, covering the lifestyle needs of the family.

Company D's stores are created to enhance the image of the brand and to reflect the contemporary English lifestyle embedded in the design of the clothes. Whether directly operated or franchised, they are the primary retail vehicles for defining Company D's image. These stores set the standards for presentation and service excellence for all other Company D channels to follow.

The latest flagship store in London's Notting Hill is a remodelled Victorian house. From the bespoke area on the top floor to the women's drawing room on the mezzanine, each room has a different feeling unique to the particular line on display. 'The space is intended to feel so intimate that one feels as if it were the private home of the designer himself'. This reinforces the personalized nature of the purchase experience and is intended to enrich the purchase experience. Control over the presentation of the brand and the retail experience to ensure that the brand values are consistently maintained to provide a distinctive experience for the consumer are central to this fashion luxury brand.

Conclusions

Luxury fashion brands are iconic, aspirational and reinforce the status of the consumer and are deemed to be purveyors of taste. Consumers are increasingly brand aware and are prepared to invest in luxury fashion brands. The overall growth of luxury markets demonstrates this and is reinforced by the development of newer markets in countries like China, India and Brazil. This growth is dominated by luxury fashion. Younger consumers dominate the demand for luxury goods and newer luxury products and services are entering the arena. However, at the same time, luxury fashion brands are facing significant challenges, particularly with an undercurrent of discontent with branding and a concern for social responsibility.

Fashion consumers expect innovation and constant change, and in luxury fashion shorter product cycles have been introduced and investment in innovation has been made to meet the demands of the fast changing fashion market. This has resulted in brand dilution and low entry. But also, has led to the development of a spectrum of market segments in the luxury market, as shown in Table 7.3. A concentration of the ownership of luxury fashion brands has taken place to withstand competition and has resulted in brand families with offerings spanning the luxury spectrum. One example of this was company D.

In this dynamic context, it is evident that the luxury fashion owners are pursuing strategies to enhance further the value of their brands. The sensual feeling of the product – its touch, acoustics and visual nature – contributes to its exclusivity. Clearly, design is fundamental to brand development and communicating brand values to the market. Indeed, internationally renowned fashion designers provided the creative direction of the fashion collection, as well as its packaging and presentation to give this a coherence and integrity across its global markets. This communicates the values of the brand to newer types of consumers and these values are commensurate with a luxury experience.

The uniqueness of fashion luxury is reinforced through the purchase of luxury brands. The retailing of luxury goods has to provide an appropriate atmosphere and luxury brands were clustered in certain locations and types of outlets to achieve this. Luxury fashion brand owners were extending their direct control over the retailing of their products to ensure that a personalized service was provided and to build a relationship with the consumer. The Internet was being used as another channel and as a communications tool.

However, the channel expansion for fashion luxury brands means that luxury is more accessible to more people, which challenges its 'raison d'être' to be rare and special.

The future challenge for luxury fashion vendors is to retain exclusivity in a growing market, where brand dilution has challenged this distinctiveness. However, the distinctiveness of luxury fashion brands can be reinforced through investment in an approach to strategic marketing where a focus on the customer experience is central. This implies investment in design, coherence and integrity in marketing communications and a premier retail environment that reinforces the brand values.

Acknowledgement

We would like to acknowledge the financial contribution and support of the Region Lorraine (France) and EPSRC for the research reported in this chapter.

References

Alleres, D. (2003). Luxe . . . Metiers et management atypiques. *Economica,* Paris p. 177.

Anon (2000). Comme again. *The Guardian*, March 17, http://www.guardian.co.uk (accessed 10th March 2004).

Banister, E. and Nejad, H. (2004). 'Young consumers: the influence of celebrity on clothing choices.' In Bruce, M. et al. (Eds.), *International Retail Marketing*, Butterworth-Heinemann: Oxford.

Baudrillard, J. (1996). *The System of Objects*. Verso: London.

Björkman, I. (2002), Aura: aesthetic business creativity. *Consumption, Markets and Culture,* **5** (1), 69–78.

Bomsel, O., Ducaille, A. and Grumbach, D. 'Le luxe, domaine du rêve', Compte-rendu de la soirée débat des Amis de l'Ecole de Paris, www.ecole.org, 23/03/98

Bruce, M. and Kratz, C. (2004). Turbulent brandscape: retailing luxury brands in the UK and France. *British Academy of Management Conference*, Saint Andrews University (Scotland), August–September.

Catry, B. (2003). The great pretenders: the magic of luxury goods. *Business Strategy Review*, Autumn, **14** (3), 10–17.

Dall'Omo, R. F. and Lacroix, C. (2003). Luxury branding on the Internet: lost opportunity or impossibility? *Marketing Intelligence and Planning*, **21**, 2.

Doyle, S. A. and Broadbridge, A. (1999). Differentiation by Design: The Importance of design in retailer repositioning and differentiation. *International Journal of Retail and Distribution Management, 27* (2/3), 72–81.

Doyle, S. A and Moore, C. M. (2004). Methods of International Market Development: The Guerilla Stores of Comme des Garcons. *British Academy of Management Conference Proceedings*, St Andrews, September.

Dubois, B. and Paternaut, C. (1995). Understanding the world of international luxury brands: the dream formula. *Journal of Advertising Research*, July–August, 69–76.

Dubois, B. and Laurent, G. (2002). Les excursionnistes du luxe, *Les Echos, L'art de l'Entreprise globale*, 09/07/2002.

Dubois, B. and Laurent, G. (1996). The functions of luxury: a situational approach to excursionism. *Advances in Consumer Research*, **23**.

Dubois, B., Laurent, G. and Czellar, S. (2001). Consumer rapport to luxury: analysing complex and ambivalent attitudes, Working Paper 736. HEC School of Management, France.

The Economist (2006). Inconspicuous consumption. December 2005, pp 70–1.

Erikson, G. M. and Johanson, J. K. (1985). The role of price in multi-attribute product evaluations. *The Journal of Consumer Research,* **12** (2), 195–199.

Financial Times (Jonathan Birchall) 2005. Luxury is so last year, says Saks Head, New York FT.com site, March 25.

Frank, R. H. (2000). *Luxury Fever: Money and Happiness in a Era of Excess.* Princeton NJ: University Press.

Gurviez, P. and Besson, M. (2000). Le luxe: de la création à la relation, Actes du 16 ème Congrès international de l'Association Française de Marketing, 253–264, Montréal, 18–20 mai.

Gutsatz, M. (1996). Le luxe: représentations et compétences. *Décisions Marketing*, **9**, 25–33.

Hetzel, P. (2002). *Planète conso, marketing expérientiel et nouveaux univers de consommation*, Editions d'organisation, pp. 380.

Hines, T. and Bruce, M. (Eds.) (2002). *Fashion Marketing*. Butterworth-Heinemann: Oxford.

Jackson, T. (2004). A contemporary analysis of global luxury brands. in Bruce, M. et al. (Eds.), *International Retail Marketing*, Butterworth-Heinemann: Oxford.

Klein, N. (2001). *No logo - La tyrannie des marques*. Ed Actes Sud, juin.

Kapferer, J. N. (2000). How the Internet impacts on brand management. *Journal of Brand Management*, **4** (4), 251–260.

Kapferer, J. N. (1998). *Les marques, Capital de l'entreprise*. Editions d'Organisation.

Kapferer, J. N. (2002). *Ce Qui va Changer les Marques-Remarques*. Editions d'Organisation, Paris.

Koromyslov, M. (2005). Luxury and delocalization. What about the country-of-origin effect? An exploratory study with Russian and French consumers. *13th Annual Conference Marketing & Business Strategies for Central & Eastern Europe*, Vienne (Austria). 1st–3rd December.

Marciniak, R. and Bruce, M. (2004). The scope of e-commerce in retail strategy. In Bruce, M. et al. (Eds.), *International Retail Marketing*, Butterworth-Heinemann: Oxford.

McDowell, C. (2002). He's got it@, *Sunday Times*, London, September 8, pp. 29–31.

Moore, C., Fernie, G. and Burt, S. (2004). Channel power, conflict and conflict resolution in international fashion retailing. *European Journal of Marketing*, **38** (7), 249–269.

Moore, C. and Wigley, S. (2004) The Anatomy of an International Fashion Retailer – The Giorgio Armani Group, *British Academy of Marketing Conf Proceedings*, St Andrew's, September.

Moore, C. and Birtwistle, G. (2004). The Burberry business model: creating an international luxury brand. *International Journal of Retail and Distribution Management*, **32** (8), 412–422.

Moore, C. and Birtwistle, G. (2005). The nature of parenting advantage in luxury fashion retailing – the case of Gucci group NV. *International Journal of Retail and Distribution Management*, **33** (4), 256–270.

Nyeck, S. and Roux, E. (1997). WWW as a communication tool for luxury brands: compared perceptions of consumers and managers. In Van Raiiji, B. et al. (Ed.), *Proceedings of the Second International Research Seminar on Marketing Communication and Consumer Behavior*, La Londe Les Maures.

Nueno, J. L. and Quelch, J. A. (1998). The Mass Marketing of Luxury. *Business Horizons*, **41** (6), 61–69.

Okonkwo, U. (2005). 'Can luxury fashion brand store atmosphere be transferred to Internet', www.brandchannel.com, April.

Randon, A. (2002). The paradoxical relationship between the exclusiveness of luxury goods and profit maximisation. *Working Paper*. School of Business, Stockholm University, March 25.

Rieunier, S. (coordonné par . . .) (2002). Le marketing sensoriel du point de vente, Créer et gérer l'ambiance des lieux commerciaux, LSA Dunod, Paris.

Roux, E. (2002): Le Luxe: au-delà des chiffres, quelle logique d'analyse, *Revue Française du Marketing*, no. 187, 2002/2.

Thibaut, F. (2003). Création et design ou l'innovation dans l'univers du luxe, in D. Alleres, *Luxe . . . métiers et management atypiques*, Economica.

Vickers, J. S. and Renand, F. (2003). The marketing of luxury goods: an exploratory study-three conceptual dimensions. *The Marketing Review*, **3**, 459–478.

Zola (1883). *Au Bonheur des Dames*, Poche – Edition 1971.

Websites:

www.comite-colbert.com

www.lemonde.fr (article from Brice Pedroletti: Comment le luxe français envahit le marché chinois, 29/10/05)

8

Store environment of fashion retailers: a Hong Kong perspective

Alice W. C. Chu and M. C. Lam

Introduction

To survive into and through the next decade, the retail store environment should be better designed, and focused on continuous improvement so as to provide a desirable store environment where consumers want to be during shopping.

Many apparel retailers realize that the design of store environment is an important element of marketing strategy; retailers strive to develop consumer-oriented store environments, which have been identified as a potential competitive advantage. They strive for a differential advantage on variables that are most likely to be store-choice factors as determined by the expectations of consumers in the target market. No wonder many fashion retailers spend millions of dollars periodically designing and refurbishing their stores, because the central challenge lies in understanding the needs of consumers, and hence providing the store environment that appeals to consumers' needs.

With rescheduling of spending priorities and amounts in clothing, consumers are changing the amount of time spent on shopping. Recent research showed that the average time people in the US spend shopping has been declining; the cardinal rule among fashion retailers has been to try to keep customers in the store as long as possible. In this connection, retailers should provide the store environment that makes shopping convenient, relaxing and fun, instead of merely providing racks of clothing for consumers to choose from in the store (Reda, 1997). Otherwise, consumers can use their limited time for other leisure activities which are more enjoyable and satisfying if they find shopping is boring.

Regarding the situation in Hong Kong, it is becoming increasingly difficult for apparel retailers to differentiate their stores solely on the basis of merchandise, price, promotion or location. Hong Kong has been well known internationally as the sourcing centre for most fashion retailers overseas. With the advance in production skills and quick response techniques, clothing styles are easily copied once they have proved to be successful in the retail market. In addition, Hong Kong is just a small city where shops are clustered together; shoppers can easily buy their clothes at a reasonable price by just doing comparison shopping of the nearby stores. Since Hong Kong customers still rank shopping as their favourite pastime, a retailer should provide a retail environment which can lure these customers to enter. Thus, the unique environment offered may be influential to the consumer's store choice decision (Darden et al., 1983). Furthermore, a store's environmental design is particularly important for retailers when the number of competitive outlets increases, or when product entries are aimed at distinct social classes or lifestyle buyer groups. In a study of department store image in Hong Kong and Shanghai, it was revealed that a store's atmospheric design is one of the elements which develop a 'sense of prestigious and high quality' (Chan and Leung, 1996). This indicated that store environment affects the store choice of customers in the upscale market segment.

The purpose of this chapter is to review some of the basic concepts on retail store environment and how Hong Kong consumers react to the retail store environment. A research finding on several Hong Kong casualwear chain stores is included. Results show that social factor in store atmospherics is relatively important compared with other factors such as ambience and function. This is not to say that physical facilities and aesthetic elements are not important in a fashion store environment, rather it indicates that fashion shoppers in Hong Kong are more sensitive to the presence of personnel in the store.

Background

Some retailers can perform well in the competitive fashion retail industry, while some are merely struggling for survival. The reason is that the successful retailers really understand what is the real meaning of 'value' in the consumer's mind. However, many retailers wrongly assume that value means price. Value is the total experience, it means the benefits received from purchasing. Those benefits include pleasant store environment, good sales people service, convenience and quality merchandise. Clearly, price is not equivalent to value, it is just part of the value (Berry, 1996). It implies that not all purchasers are price conscious; some of them are willing to pay more to those stores where the store has nicely displayed merchandise, has a tidy and clean shopping floor together with good customer services, or simply a favourable overall store environment.

Much research has shown that at a time when retailers are finding it difficult to obtain a competitive advantage on the basis of price, promotion and store location, store environment becomes an opportunity for market differentiation (Ward et al., 1992; Kenhove and Desrumaux, 1997). An appropriate store environment catering for the needs of consumers makes for a pleasurable shopping experience. Some researchers found that consumers stayed longer in a shop with a pleasant environment and spent more money than originally planned (Donovan et al., 1994). Keller (1987) also pointed out that many consumers make decisions at the point of purchase, so the store environment can affect people's purchasing behaviour. Most shoppers have shared the experience that, irrespective of the merchandise offered, some stores are more attractive than others, some stores induce a feeling of relaxation, while others may make one feel uncomfortable, or even irritated. Consumers tend to buy more things and spend more money when in a positive rather than a negative store environment. In addition to affecting store patronage choice, a store which has a favourable environment can also achieve a higher customer loyalty (Darden et al., 1983), as well as affecting perceived store image (Lindquist, 1974; Zimmer and Golden, 1988).

The importance of the store and its environment becomes evident when one realizes that 70–80 per cent of customer purchase decisions are finalized when consumers are in the store inspecting the merchandise (Schlossberg, 1992). An appropriately designed store environment where there is good merchandise and services offered can be a powerful means for providing a pleasant shopping experience for consumers, and enables the retailer to obtain a competitive advantage over its competitors. This is the reason why store environment is becoming an increasingly important issue in retail marketing management and retail marketing research. In the past, many retailers took their customers for granted; they merely provided generic goods without much emphasis on store environment. Nowadays, drawing customers into the store and providing a place where they can browse comfortably is the latest strategy which retailers and brand owners are using to enrich consumers' shopping experience.

The consumer's definition of value changes over time, and it can be affected by their past purchase experiences and individual factors such as innate personal needs. Thus, continuous enquiry about the consumer's needs and expectations in the store environment is required. Consumer satisfaction is a function of the closeness between expectations and the store's perceived performance. If the store environment falls short of consumer expectations, the consumer is disappointed; if it meets consumer's expectations, the consumer is satisfied.

In other words, if the perceived store environment can meet their expectations, consumer satisfaction results. Consumers who are satisfied with a retailer may tell an average of five other people, whereas dissatisfied consumers will talk to two or three times more people they meet (Waldrop, 1991), and may never return to the store again. Obviously, the key element to the success of a retailer lies in their ability to identify and define their consumers, and hence cater to their preferences and needs in a distinctive manner (Berman and Evans, 1995).

Store environment

Store environment is critical to a retailer, because it directly affects consumers' total shopping experience. It is also a determining factor in affecting consumers' store choice decision for shopping. Hence, the management of the physical environment is considered as an important element in contributing to a retailer's financial success and a valuable shopping experience for consumers (Eroglu and Machleit, 1993).

The concept of 'atmospherics' was first introduced by Kotler (1973), where a store's atmosphere is defined as the effort to design buying environments to produce specific emotional effects in the buyer that enhance purchase probability. In-store environmental stimuli are positively related to the level of pleasure experienced in the store (Tai and Fung, 1997). Positive store environmental elements can induce a positive experience with the store, and finally contribute to a pleasant response of consumers.

Donovan and Rossiter (1982), using the Mehrabian–Russell environmental psychology model (Mehrabian and Russell, 1974), specified that a store's environmental stimuli can affect the consumer's emotional states of pleasure and arousal, which further affects approach or avoidance behaviours in purchasing. Pleasure refers to the degree to which the consumers feel good, happy, satisfied and joyful in the store environment. Arousal refers to the degree to which consumers feel in control of, or free to act in, the environment. Baker et al. (1992) indicate that, when ambient cues interact with social cues, it can affect consumers' emotional states of pleasure, while social cues influence arousal in the store environment.

More recently, Darden and Babin (1994) indicated that store environment has an emotion-inducing capability. A positive emotion-inducing store can contribute to a consumer's pleasurable shopping experience; stores with courteous and friendly personnel are associated with high levels of pleasure. On the other hand, overcrowded stores are associated with low levels of pleasure.

An elaborate positive store environment can be an effective tool to evoke a consumer's emotion of pleasure or arousal. A positive store environment helps to foster goal attainment, more consumers in a pleasant store environment can easily achieve their goal, and hence attain a pleasurable shopping experience (Spies et al., 1997). Shoppers reporting relatively high pleasure, for example, also report correspondingly high customer satisfaction (Dawson et al., 1990). Thus, there is an important interaction between store characteristics, consumer's mood and satisfaction.

As Parasuraman et al. (1990) noted, consumers compare tangibles of a store with what they think a store should look like. Satisfaction with the store can be increased by minimizing the gap between customers' perceptions and expectations. When expectations were not met, consumers experienced disconfirmation (Churchill and Suprenaut, 1982) and consequently dissatisfaction. If the perception matches the expectations, the customer is satisfied. If the performance exceeds expectations, the customer is delighted and highly satisfied.

Satisfaction can help consumers to identify that a store is worthy of their loyalty. Shopping tends to be a leisure activity and consumers want the shopping experience to deliver something emotional or pleasurable to them (Bromley and Thomas, 1993). Successful retailers need to identify and respond to consumers' expectations (Smith, 1997). There is no doubt that shoppers nowadays want to gain enjoyment and satisfaction when spending their precious time shopping; retailers should therefore acquire a better understanding of consumers' expectation regarding a store's environment.

Store atmospherics

The influence of retail store environments on consumer perceptions and behaviour is a topic that has received relatively little attention since Kotler (1973) introduced the concept of 'atmospherics'. Many researchers became aware of the importance of store environment in creating a differential or competitive advantage in the retailing industry. Researchers started to study a store's influence on shopping behaviour. Consumer satisfaction with the store is greater in a pleasant store environment; customers spontaneously spent more money on merchandise they simply liked if the store environment was pleasant (Spies et al., 1997). Other marketing scholars and practitioners have focused their investigations on the influence of specific atmospheric elements, such as music, social factors or lighting, on shopping behaviour, and the degree of consumer satisfaction and loyalty (Bellizzi et al., 1983; Baker et al., 1992).

Some researchers shifted emphasis to the sensory information of store environmental cues relating cognitive or affective states which can affect shopping behaviours and consumers' product perception (Gardner and Siomkos, 1985). More recent study shows that ambient and social elements in the store environment are more likely to affect consumers to make inferences about merchandise and service quality, and these inferences, in turn, influence store image (Baker et al., 1994). Baker (1986), in her research on the store atmosphere, has developed a three-category framework of store environment, namely store ambient factor, store design factor and store social factor, for evaluating store atmospherics.

Store ambient factor

The ambient factor refers to the background characteristics of the environment that tend to influence consumers at a subconscious level (Campbell, 1983). This includes elements such as temperature, lighting, music and scent (Ward and Russell, 1981; Milliman, 1982; Wineman, 1982; Yalch and Spangenberg, 1990).

All of these elements can profoundly affect how people feel, think and respond to a particular store establishment, and exist below the level of customers' immediate awareness. As a general rule, ambient conditions influence the five senses (Zeithaml and Bitner, 1996). According to Davidson et al. (1988), the ambient factor is felt more than it can be seen and measured.

Ambient conditions are especially noticeable to consumers in extreme circumstances. Undesirable ambient conditions can cause dissatisfaction if the attention of consumers is heightened. For example, a store where the air conditioning has failed, and the air is hot and stuffy, will heighten a consumer's awareness, and dissatisfaction may result. Instead of taking more time to shop, consumers who feel uncomfortable may hurry to make their intended purchases and leave the store (Botlen, 1988).

Background music that is soothing can create a pleasurable atmosphere (Milliman, 1982). Also, soft lighting can create a more pleasant and relaxing mood than using bright lighting (Meer, 1985). Noise that is too loud may make a shopper feel annoyed, and the glare of lighting may lower the consumer's ability to see and cause physical discomfort. Just like noise, unfavourable scent can actually drive consumers away from the store. All these ambient elements can influence whether people stay in or enjoy the store environment.

Store design factor

The design factor refers to a store's environmental elements that are more perceptible in nature than ambient factors. These elements can be aesthetic and/or functional in nature (Marans and Spreckelmeyer, 1982).

Functional elements in stores include layout, comfort and privacy. Aesthetic elements include such factors as architecture, materials, colour and merchandise display; they can contribute to consumers' pleasure in shopping (Baker, 1986). Layout is functional in nature; it helps to route consumers through the entire store in search of merchandise. A wide and uncrowded aisle can also create a better atmosphere than narrow and crowded ones.

Merchandise displays can also be an important aid in helping consumers to make purchase decisions (Dunne et al., 1990). Some apparel consumers regard the dressing room and its facilities as major elements in store selection (Berman and Evans, 1995). As the trend of the store environment becomes more minimalist, the emphasis on the fixtures and fittings will become obvious (Zachary, 1998). Merchandise fixtures help to show the merchandise to consumers, as well as playing a secondary role of aesthetic function. Also, an attractive floor might have considerable aesthetic appeal to consumers (Diamond, 1993).

The design factor is at the forefront of consumers' awareness; it is more visible and perceptible than the ambient factor as consumers can evaluate more easily what they see. The design factor serves as a facilitator in aiding the performances of both employee and consumers in the store, because a well-designed and functional store can help people to be orientated and to find their way. Consumers can more easily locate and obtain the required merchandise/ services (Bitner, 1992). It also helps to improve efficiency and user satisfaction (Greenland and McGoldrick, 1994), and encourages people to browse and look into every corner rather than just standing in the store. If consumers can easily satisfy their goals, the feeling of a pleasurable shopping experience will be enhanced.

Store social factor

The social factor involves people who are present in the store environment. Russell and Snodgrass (1987) note that the number, type and behaviour of both consumers and salespeople are included as elements of the social factor.

Inadequate salespeople can make consumers feel annoyed when they are required to wait for service. Salespeople's performance can also greatly affect consumer (dis)satisfaction. Consumers will evaluate salesperson services based on the personal expectations that they bring to the service encounter (Crosby and Cowles, 1986). As consumers' expectations increase, they expect salespeople to have a deeper product knowledge, and to be reliable and responsive to consumers' needs (Kotler et al., 1996). Frontline employees are assumed by consumers to be not only salespeople, but also consultants (Lovelock, 1991).

In a clothing store, consumers may ask salespeople for suggestions on merchandise selection. Conversations between salespeople and consumers frequently occur in the retail environment (Harris et al., 1995; McGrath and Otnes, 1995). A positive impact of the conversations between consumers and salespeople can achieve consumer satisfaction, which has been well researched and documented (Bitner et al., 1990; Harris et al., 1997).

Research has revealed that one of the three most important factors influencing repeat purchases at a new store was 'helpful personnel' (Schneiderman, 1997). Good salesperson service is about providing the consumer with an efficient, positive and enjoyable purchasing experience (Livingstone, 1997). Similarly, attractive appearance and pleasant behaviour of salespeople can greatly enhance the service experience (Baker, 1986).

The social factor has also been investigated in terms of other consumers in the store, which is exemplified by research on crowding (Harrell et al., 1980). The number of consumers inside a store can have an impact on the shopping experience. Overcrowded stores are associated with low levels of pleasure of consumers (Darden and Babin, 1994).

A consumer in a crowded store finds shopping less enjoyable (Andreoli, 1996). Within a crowded environment, consumers restrict themselves to interacting with salespeople, are less likely to engage in exploratory shopping and will postpone any unnecessary purchase. The behaviour of consumers also affects the experience. A store with ill-mannered consumers would deter shoppers from coming into the store.

A crowded store can also lead to avoidance behaviour, because shoppers perceive that crowdedness can restrict task performance within a store (Stokols, 1976). Mackintosh et al. (1975) found that respondents performing an experiment in overcrowded conditions described themselves as 'tense' or 'confused', whereas positive feelings such as 'pleased' or 'relaxed' were found in less crowded conditions. This showed that physical density and crowdedness may influence consumers' level of satisfaction (Harrell et al., 1980).

Store environment is the overall aesthetic and emotional effect created by the store's physical environment; it is the total sensory experience created by the store. Today's shoppers, regardless of their shopping motives, are more attracted by safe, attractive and comfortable shopping environments. Therefore, a store environment should be tailored to the psychological and physical needs of consumers by creating a focused collection of sensory impressions and shopping experiences (Sullivan, 1992).

An appropriately designed store environment is about providing the consumers with a positive, efficient and enjoyable purchasing experience. Darden and Babin (1994) indicated that store environment has the capability of inducing an effect. A good mood-inducing store will lead to a good shopping experience, which will contribute to positive effects on shopping intentions (Swinyard, 1993).

Store design in the 1980s, with the emphasis on opulence, image and consumption, seems to be outdated (Goldman, 1991). The biggest challenges faced by today's apparel retailers is integrating fashion elements into the lives of consumers and finding ways to make the shopping experience both efficient and entertaining (Reda, 1997).

Retailers now delight in learning more about their target customers than ever before in providing a store environment which can please every possible demand. They want store designs to be flexible enough to respond to changes in merchandise and consumer demographics, as well as being functional and beautiful (Lewison, 1994). Since most store designs are being 'tailored' for this new generation of shoppers, continuous investigation into consumers' needs in the store environment is required.

Current study on the importance of store environment to consumer's casualwear fashion store choice decision in Hong Kong

Importance of store environment to consumer's store choice decision

Using Baker's three-category framework, research was conducted in 1998 in Hong Kong to explore the importance of store environment to consumer's store choice decision. More than 90 per cent of respondents in Hong Kong agreed that store environment is important in affecting their store selection.

Based on the result obtained, the social factor is most important in allowing consumers to have a pleasurable shopping experience. The design factor was perceived as second and the ambient factor third.

Relative importance of elements of the three factors

For the ambient factor, the tidiness of the store was regarded as the most important element in maintaining good ambient conditions. Other remaining elements – lighting, music, scent, temperature and noise level – were of less concern.

For the design factor, most respondents regarded store size as the most important element. The next most important element was also related to size – the size of the fitting room.

For the social factor, a large proportion of respondents considered 'service manner of salespeople' as the most important element in this category. 'Number of people in the store' was also considered as important.

Consumers' expectations on store environment

Nine expectations on store environment, labelled as (1) comfortableness, (2) number and nature of people, (3) recognition by identifiable salespeople, (4) courteous and friendly salespeople, (5) spacious environment, (6) non-irritating environment, (7) minimalist environment, (8) fixtures and displays, and (9) merchandise suggestions, were found.

'Comfortableness' refers to the size of the fitting room, chair availability inside the fitting room, aisle width, clear merchandise arrangement, noise level, temperature and tidiness of the store.

'Number and nature of people' refers to the number and types of customers, as well as the adequacy of salespeople. This includes not only the variables related to the number of consumers and salespeople in the store, but also the nature of shoppers. Shoppers expected that other customers in the store would not be ill-mannered.

'Recognition by identifiable salespeople' suggests that salespeople should wear clothes with similar style and colour, provide proper greetings and wear a name badge. By greeting and saying goodbye to consumers, salespeople can give consumers a feeling that they are recognized and also give them a sense of respect.

'Courteous and friendly salespeople' shows that the attributes of friendliness, courtesy and responsiveness of salespeople are applied.

'Spacious environment' refers to large store size, chairs for resting, large signage and modern window displays.

'Non-irritating environment' of the store refers to store lighting, music and scent.

'Minimalist environment' refers to the background colour (light) and theme colour of the store (white).

'Fixtures and displays' illustrate that merchandise is displayed with hanger appeal, and the use of wooden fixtures was expected by the respondents.

Subsequently, a cluster analysis was employed to see which of the nine expectation dimension(s) was (were) important to each cluster. The largest cluster, comprising a total of 61.3 per cent of respondents, indicated that consumers have a high expectation regarding the social factor.

Most popular casualwear chain store

In order to obtain additional information of consumers' expectations on store environment, respondents were asked to rank four casualwear chain stores in Hong Kong in terms of the most satisfying store environment. The four stores were: (1) Bossini; (2) Esprit; (3) Giordano; (4) U2.

Table 8.1 illustrates that over 70 per cent of respondents were mostly satisfied with the store environment of Esprit. The second most favourable store was U2, with over 50 per cent of respondents ranking this as the second best store environment among the four stores. The third ranked store was Giordano, with a total of 42.8 per cent of respondents rating the store environment in third position. The fourth was Bossini; respondents were comparatively less satisfied with this store environment, with over 55 per cent of respondents ranking it as the least satisfying of the four stores.

Table 8.1 Ranking of the store environment among four stores

Ranking	Bossini (%)	Esprit (%)	Giordano (%)	U2 (%)
1st	4.8	74.3	9.3	11.6
2nd	16.1	8.2	26.0	50.7
3rd	24.0	7.2	42.8	25.0
4th	55.1	10.3	21.9	12.7
Total	100	100	100	100

Favourable store environment and pleasant shopping experience

A majority of respondents agreed that a favourable store environment could lead them to have a pleasant shopping experience. Over 99 per cent of respondents considered that a favourable store environment could achieve a pleasant shopping experience. Less than 1 per cent of respondents denied that store environment could lead them to have a pleasant shopping experience.

Conclusion

The results of this study suggest that store environment is relatively important in affecting consumers' store choice decision when comparing it with other factors such as store location, merchandise assortment and product price. This implies that not all consumers are price conscious; they are willing to select the store for shopping, or just going into the store for browsing if there is a desirable store environment.

According to Zeithaml and Bitner (1996), a well designed and functional servicescape can give consumers a pleasant experience. The present study shows that the majority of respondents agreed that a satisfying store environment could create a pleasurable shopping experience. It is quite clear that the social factor was most important to consumers in leading them to have a pleasurable shopping experience, in comparison with the ambient and design factors.

As noted by Darden and Babin (1994), stores with courteous and friendly personnel correlated with high levels of pleasure to the consumer. This result shows that the 'service manner of salespeople' is the most important element of the social factor in affecting their perception of a pleasant shopping experience, with the social factor regarded by respondents as the most important factor in their having a pleasurable shopping experience.

On the other hand, tidiness of the store was the most important element of the ambient factor, whereas store size was the most important element of the design factor in leading consumers to have a pleasurable shopping experience. Apparently, the ambient and design factors were comparatively less important than the social factor in the consumer's mind. Nevertheless, this does not mean that the above two factors can be ignored; we can only say that these two factors were relatively less sensitive to consumers in helping them to achieve a pleasurable shopping experience.

The results also show that consumers' expectations on the store environment could be further divided into the following nine dimensions: (1) comfortableness; (2) number and nature of people; (3) recognition by identifiable salespeople; (4) courteous and friendly salespeople; (5) spacious environment; (6) non-irritating environment; (7) minimalist environment; (8) fixtures and displays; (9) merchandise suggestions. The results further show the detailed dimensions of consumers' expectations on the store environment. The result of cluster analysis indicated that most of the respondents had expectations regarding the social factor. This implies that salespeople should be rich in product knowledge, and hence that they can be assured of providing quality service, as well as giving individualized suggestions on merchandise selection for each consumer. As Berry (1996) noted, consumers nowadays are concerned with respectful service offered by retailers; they expect salespeople to treat them like royalty, with courtesy, a friendly service attitude and a welcome on their arrival.

More specifically, a satisfying store environment can lead consumers to achieve a pleasant shopping experience. Store environment stimuli can affect consumers' emotional states of pleasure (Mehrabian and Russell, 1974). It is certain that a positive store environment can be an effective tool in evoking the consumer's emotion of pleasure.

Recommendations

Among those areas which consumers would like stores to further improve is the social factor – the service manner of salespeople. This also proves that consumers definitely regard the social factor as relatively more important than the other two factors, and they also have higher expectations in this area. The result supports respondents' concerns on the social factor of a store's environment.

Management of casualwear chain stores will not be surprised to learn that the social factor contributed greatly in achieving consumers' pleasant shopping experience. A desirable store environment can be an important element of achieving a pleasant shopping experience. This influence is likely to be especially pronounced for the social factor of the store environment. Effective retailers can seek a competitive edge in providing a unique store environment that the consumers want, to satisfy their needs and enhance their shopping experience.

The results also indicate that both the ambient and design factors are perceived as less important by consumers. Marketers should be more concerned with the social factor of the store environment, especially the service attitude of salespeople. Hence, it is suggested that casualwear chain stores could provide a desirable store environment by paying more attention to the social factor. As such, special care should be taken with regard to the service manner of sales personnel.

On the other hand, whether there is an adequate number of salespeople on the shop floor can be directly controlled by the retailer. An appropriate number of sales personnel helps to provide a responsive service to consumers. An inadequate number of salespeople will keep consumers waiting for service, and consumer dissatisfaction will result. However, too many salespeople would be wastage. Retailers need to clearly identify the amount of salespeople required to maintain a frontline operation.

Particular care should also be taken by retailers of casualwear chain stores on the expectation of 'recognition by identifiable salespeople' as consumers appreciate a sense of respect by the salespeople when they enter and leave the store. 'Courteous and friendly salespeople' implies that consumers have a high expectation regarding the attitude of sales personnel. Since quality service from friendly, courteous salespeople with an appropriate service attitude does not simply happen, retailers are advised to take particular care to develop a 'service culture' within their organizations. This can enhance the employee's recognition of their responsibilities of customer service. Apart from the development of service culture in the organization, motivation can also be an effective means to achieve this aim. Undoubtedly, financial motivation, including bonuses and commission, is an important means of encouragement.

Particular care should also be taken by the retailers in training the sales-people to be more effective in their interpersonal encounters with consumers, since salespeople are required to be 'friendly and courteous' to consumers. Also, the findings show that consumers expect suggestions on merchandise selection from salespeople. It is suggested that retailers should place emphasis on continuous training of their employees, especially in the areas of being 'courteous and friendly' and having 'expertise' on the products they sell.

Provision of expert sales help can be achieved by enriching the product knowledge of salespeople. Once the salespeople possess sufficient knowledge of their merchandise, the limitations and strengths of the merchandise can be recognized by the salespeople. This enables the salespeople to be highly responsive to all kinds of consumer needs and problems, and assess the value of the merchandise, as well as offering individualized suggestions on merchandise selection. Hence, salespeople with sufficient product knowledge can make more accurate individualized suggestions on merchandise selection based on the different needs of consumers.

In order to provide individualized suggestions on merchandise selec-tion, retailers should not overlook the listening skills of frontline employ-ees. Salespeople who fail to be a good listener fail to understand consumers' concerns, needs, wants and preferences, and in turn fail to give consumers appropriate suggestions on merchandise selection. To fulfil the expectations of consumers, retailers should take particular care in training salespeople to be good listeners.

Although it is suggested that the store manager pays more attention to the social factor of the store environment, the ambient and design factors should not be neglected. A store can have excellent salespeople to deliver high quality service, but if the store plays unfavourable loud music, without much air con-ditioning and space, the overall shopping experience will be affected. Instead of staying longer in the store, consumers will leave the store as quickly as pos-sible. Therefore, the three factors should be well co-ordinated so as to achieve a desirable result.

This study provides a new insight into the relative importance of the three environmental factors, the level of importance of the store environment in affecting consumer's store choice decisions and their expectations on store environment. The study suggests that the social factor is potentially useful in leading consumers to have a pleasant shopping experience. Therefore, dur-ing the refurbishment of the stores, retailers should set aside some financial investment to enhance the social factor of the store environment.

To conclude, fashion retailers that plan to refurbish their stores need to determine in advance the concerns, preference and expectations of the target customer regarding store environment. The better the understanding of the consumer, the better the targeted result of the refurbishment can be obtained. Store environment is just like the packaging of a product; if the package is desirable or attractive to consumers, it can largely enhance the saleability of merchandise. The 1990s were 'value driven'. Retailers are no longer tak-ing consumers for granted; they should maximize the benefits received by consumers. Consumers want a good return on the financial investment they make in their purchasing. One of the most important benefits is a desirable store environment. Consumers, especially those for fashion and clothing, want to have a pleasant shopping experience within the store environment where they can browse and inspect merchandise freely.

References

Andreoli, T. (1996). Hassle-free service the key to repeat biz. *Discount Store News*, 6 May, p. 64. Also see: Goldberger, P. (1997). The store strikes back. *New York Times Magazine*, 8 April, 45–49.

Baker, J. (1986). The role of the environment in marketing services: the consumer perspective. In Czepeil, J. A., Congram, C. A. and Shanahan, J. (Eds.), *The Services Challenge: Integrating for Competitive Advantage*. Chicago, IL: American Marketing Association, pp. 79–84.

Baker, J., Levy, M. and Grewal, D. (1992). An experimental approach to making retail store environmental decisions. *Journal of Retailing*, **68** (Winter), 471–495.

Baker, J., Grewal, D. and Parasuraman, A. (1994). The influence of store atmosphere on customer quality perceptions and store image. *Journal of Academy of Marketing Science*, **22** (Fall), 328–339.

Bellizzi, J. A., Crowley, A. E. and Hasty, R. W. (1983). The effects of colour in store design. *Journal of Retailing*, **59** (Spring), 21–45.

Berman, B. and Evans, J. R. (1995). *Retail Management: A Strategic Approach*. Prentice Hall.

Berry, L. L. (1996). Retailers with a future: the new value equation. *Chain Store Age*, October, 4D–6D.

Bitner, M. J. (1992). Servicescapes: the impact of physical surroundings on customers and employees. *Journal of Marketing*, **56** (April), 57–71.

Bitner, M. J., Booms, B. M. and Tetreault, M. S. (1990). The service encounter: diagnosing favourable and unfavourable incidents. *Journal of Marketing*, **54** (January), 71–84.

Botlen, W. H. (1988). *Contemporary Retailing*. Prentice Hall.

Bromley, R. and Thomas, C. J. (1993). *Retail Change: Contemporary Issues*. UCL Press.

Campbell, J. M. (1983). Ambient stressors. *Environment and Behaviour*, **15** (3), 355–380.

Chan, K. K. and Leung, Y. L. (1996). *A Study of Department Store Image In Hong Kong & Shanghai*. Hong Kong Baptist University, Business Research Centre, Papers on China Series CP96015.

Churchill Jr., G. A., and Suprenaut, C. (1982). An investigation into the determinants of customer satisfaction. *Journal of Marketing Research*, **19** (November), 491–504.

Crosby, L. A. and Cowles, D. (1986). A role consensus model of satisfaction with service interaction experiences. *Creativity in Services Marketing: What's*

New, What Works, What's Developing, Proceedings Series. Chicago, IL: American Marketing Association, pp. 40–43.

Darden, W. R. and Babin, B. J. (1994). Exploring the concept of affective quality: expanding the concept of retail personality. *Journal of Business Research*, **29**, 101–109.

Darden, W. R., Erdem, O. and Darden, D. K. (1983). A comparison and test of three causal models of patronage intentions. In Darden, W. R. and Lusch, R. F. (Eds.), *Patronage Behaviour and Retail Management*. New York: North-Holland, pp. 29–43.

Davidson, W. R., Sweeney, D. J. and Stampfl, R. W. (1988). *Retailing Management*. John Wiley.

Dawson, S., Bloch, P. H. and Ridgway, N. M. (1990). Shopping motives, emotional states, and retail outcomes. *Journal of Retailing*, **66** (Winter), 408–427.

Diamond, E. (1993). *Fashion Retailing*. Delmar Publishers.

Donovan, R. J. and Rossiter, J. R. (1982). Store atmosphere: an environmental psychology approach. *Journal of Retailing*, **58** (Spring), 34–57.

Donovan, R. J., Rossiter, J. R., Marcoolyn, G. and Nesdale, A. (1994). Store atmosphere and purchasing behaviour. *Journal of Retailing*, **70** (Fall), 283–293.

Dunne, P., Lusch, R., Gable, M. and Gebhardt, R. (1990). *Retailing*. South Western Publishing.

Eroglu, S. A. and Machleit, K. (1993). Atmospheric factors in the retail environment: sights, sounds and smells. In McAlister, L. and Rothschild, M. L. (Eds.), *Advances in Consumer Research*, Vol. 20. Provo, UT: Association for Consumer Research, p. 34.

Gardner, M. P. and Siomkos, G. J. (1985). Towards a methodology for assessing effects of in-store atmosphere. In Lutz, R. (Ed.), *Advances in Consumer Research*. Chicago, IL: Association for Consumer Research, pp. 27–31.

Goldman, D. J. (1991). Classic designs return amid economic uncertainty. *Stores*, January, 130.

Greenland, S. J. and McGoldrick, P. J. (1994). Atmospherics, attitudes and behaviour: modelling the impact of designed space. *The International Review of Retail, Distribution and Consumer Research*, **4** (1), 1–16.

Harrell, G. D., Hutt, M. D. and Anderson, J. C. (1980). Path analysis of buyer behaviour under conditions of crowding. *Journal of Marketing Research*, **17** (February), 45–51.

Harris, K., Baron, S. and Ratcliffe, J. (1995). Customers as oral participants in a service setting. *Journal of Services Marketing*, **9** (4), 64–76.

Harris, K., Davis, B. J. and Baron, S. (1997). Conversations during purchase consideration: sales assistants and customers. *The International Review of Retail, Distribution and Consumer Research*, **7** (3), 173–190.

Keller, K. L. (1987). Memory factors in advertising: the effect of advertising retrieval cues on brand evaluations. *Journal of Consumer Research*, **14** (December), 316–333.

Kenhove, P. V. and Desrumaux, P. (1997). The relationship between emotional states and approach or avoidance responses in a retail environment. *The International Review of Retail, Distribution and Consumer Research*, **7** (4), 351–368.

Kotler, P. (1973). Atmospherics as a marketing tool. *Journal of Retailing*, **49** (Winter), 48–64.

Kotler, P., Swee Hoon Ang, Siew Meng Leong and Chin Tiong Tan (1996). *Marketing Management: An Asian Perspective*. Prentice Hall.

Lewison, D. (1994). *Retailing*. Prentice Hall.

Lindquist, J. D. (1974). Meaning of image. *Journal of Retailing*, **50** (Winter), 29–38.

Livingstone, N. S. (1997). Service tips included. *Fw*, May/June, 56–57.

Lovelock, C. H. (1991). *Service Marketing*. Prentice Hall.

Mackintosh, E., West, S. and Saegert, S. (1975). Two studies of crowding in urban public spaces. *Environment and Behaviour*, **7** (June), 159–184.

Marans, R. W. and Spreckelmeyer, K. F. (1982). Measuring overall architectural quality. *Environment and Behaviour*, **14** (November), 652–670.

McGrath, M. A. and Otnes, C. (1995). Unacquainted influencers: when strangers interact in the retail setting. *Journal of Business Research*, **32**, 261–272.

Meer, J. (1985). The light touch. *Psychology Today*, September, 60–67.

Mehrabian, A. and Russell, J. A. (1974). *An Approach to Environmental Psychology*. Cambridge, MA: MIT Press.

Milliman, R. E. (1982). Using background music to affect the behaviour of supermarket shoppers. *Journal of Marketing*, **46** (Summer), 86–91.

Parasuraman, A., Berry, L. L. and Zeithaml, V. A. (1990). Guidelines for conducting service quality research. *Marketing Research*, **2** (December), 34–44.

Reda, S. (1997). Apparel retailers focus on improving shopping experience. *Stores*, March, 38–39.

Russell, J. A. and Snodgrass, J. (1987). Emotion and the environment. In Stokols, D. and Altman, I. (Eds.), *Handbook of Environmental Psychology*. New York: Wiley, pp. 245–281.

Schlossberg, H. (1992). Marketers told to get customers involved and 'take back the store'. *Marketing News*, 13 April.

Schneiderman, I. P. (1997). New retailers' old tricks. *Women's Wear Daily*, 9 September, 10.

Smith, T. (1997). Integrating the cultures. *SEN: The Magazine for Retail Ideas*, May, 33–34.

Spies, K., Hesse, F. and Loesch, K. (1997). Store atmosphere, mood and purchasing behaviour. *International Journal of Research in Marketing*, **14**, 1–17.

Stokols, D. (1976). The experience of crowding in primary and secondary environments. *Environment and Behaviour*, **8** (March), 49–86.

Sullivan, L. R. (1992). Appealing to the technophiles. *Forbes*, 27 April, 52–54.

Swinyard, W. R. (1993). The effects of mood, involvement, and quality of store experience on shopping intentions. *Journal of Consumer Research*, **20**, 271–280.

Tai, H. C. S. and Fung, A. M. C. (1997). Application of an environmental psychology model to in-store buying behaviour. *The International Review of Retail, Distribution and Consumer Research*, **7** (4), 311–337.

Waldrop, J. (1991). Educating the customer. *American Demographics*, September, 44–77.

Ward, J. C., Bitner, M. J. and Barnes, J. (1992). Measuring the prototypicality and meaning of retail environment. *Journal of Retailing*, **68** (Summer), 194–220.

Ward, L. M. and Russell, J. A. (1981). Cognitive set and the perception of place. *Environment and Behaviour*, **13** (September), 610–632.

Wineman, J. D. (1982). Office design and evaluation: an overview. *Environment and Behaviour*, **14** (May), 271–298.

Yalch, R. and Spangenberg, E. (1990). Effects of store music on shopping behaviour. *Journal of Consumer Marketing*, **7** (Spring), 55–63.

Zachary, S. (1998). Into the age of honesty. *SEN: The Magazine for Retail Ideas*, January, 17–18.

Zeithaml, V. A. and Bitner, M. J. (1996). *Services Marketing*. McGraw-Hill.

Zimmer, M. R. and Golden, L. L. (1988). Impressions of retail stores: a content analysis of consumer images. *Journal of Retailing*, **64** (Fall), 265–293.

9

The process of trend development leading to a fashion season

Tim Jackson

'You can't change fashion by parading twenty-five navy suits down the runway'
Anna Wintour, Editor in chief of Vogue magazine

(Foley, 2004, p. 16)

Research design

This chapter is underpinned by primary research drawn from specialist fashion trend prediction businesses and trend scouts. The research comprises a range of data collection that includes information gathered from in-depth interviews with key individuals at two global fashion trend companies, Worth Global Style Network (WGSN.com) and Promostyl. Interviews were tape recorded and transcribed. Each interview typically lasted about 1 hour. The interviews were informed by a set of questions that were sent to the interviewees in advance of the meeting. This was done with the aim of gaining quality information from respondents and allowed further probing to take place during the face-to-face interviews.

Additional material was sourced from regular discussions with senior fashion executives in fashion retailer brands, bi-annual client trend presentations delivered by Promostyl and a series of other fashion trend presentations made by WGSN. Details of the participating companies and dates when the interviews took place are included in the Appendix.

What is fashion?

There is a need to define the term fashion, as this chapter is primarily concerned with the sequence of events that form a process through which trends in fashion clothing and accessories emerge. Breward (2003, p. 9) describes fashion as an important conduit for the expression of social identity, political ideas and aesthetic taste. Perna (1987) defines fashion as 'an expression of the times'. Such broad interpretations fit well with the modern consumer society in which many aspects of peoples' lifestyles are vehicles for reflecting social status and success. This is especially pertinent to products and services that are highly visible when being used, such as mobile phones, watches, cars, clubs, bars, clothing and accessories. In fact it is common for some branded car and mobile phone manufacturers to make reference to seasons' colours and (product) collections in a way that is similar to fashion brands. This wider application was acknowledged by Polhemus and Procter (1978) when they pointed out that the term 'fashion' 'is often used as a synonym of the terms "adornment", "style" and "dress".'

Two characteristics of fashion that impinge on the activity of trend forecasting are the frequency of change and the relative newness or level of adoption that applies to a particular look, style or product. In respect of the latter, many would argue that a fashion manifests itself through mass adoption; hence the terms 'in-fashion' and 'this season's fashions'. Gabrielle 'Coco' Chanel made this point early in the 20th century stating, 'Fashion does not exist unless it goes down into the streets. The fashion that remains in the salons has no more significance than a costume ball', (Charles-Roux, 1981, p. 237).

Change is also a fundamental requirement of fashion. Traditionally change has been framed by seasons although the phenomenon of 'fast fashion' has made bi-annual seasons an irrelevance for some brands as new fashion stories or mini collections are refreshed monthly. Ironically the fickle nature of fashion is not a new concept but one that was well understood at the turn of the 20th century by the couturier Paul Poiret who declared that 'Dress is an industry whose raison d'être is novelty' (Leymarie, 1987, p. 21). The concept of novelty is one, which implies a short lifespan. Reich (2004) draws a distinction between style and fashion stating that fashion has no style it is always just fashion.

Although the term fashion has a very wide frame of reference, the fashion industry tends to be primarily focused on those businesses involved in the design, production, sale and promotion of clothing, accessories and footwear. Indeed, clothing is the most common vehicle used to express fashion issues in the media. Barnard (2001) refers to the need for people 'to be social and individual at the same time' and that 'fashion clothing are ways in which this complex set of desires or demands maybe negotiated'. Additionally, the bi-seasonal changes in fashion clothing have lead to the evolution over many years of a structured sequence of trade shows servicing the various stages of pre-season fashion garment development. Consequently, this chapter will focus on the specific events that contribute to fashion trends in clothing, while recognizing that a similar process applies to the development of other 'fashion' products.

Fashion trends

The term fashion trend refers to aspects of the appearance and construction of fashion products that relate to a particular season. Such trends are manifest in the appearance of fashion products, which are designed and manufactured prior to being delivered in a season. Fashion trends provide insights into the style and colour direction that future fashion products will take in their final form. The notion of a fashion trend will vary according to the kind of business using it, in particular where they are in the clothing supply chain and what their information needs are. For example, yarn producers are more concerned with trends in colour than garment silhouettes, as their business operates at the very early stages of the supply chain. However, a buyer for a fashion retailer own-brand needs to be aware of the complete range of trend information rele-vant to the fashion product category they are responsible for. Also, there are long-term trends that underpin future designs, such as a move to less struc-tured garments or performance fabrics, and short-term trends usually associ-ated with a particular season, for example a particular print or style of bag.

A fashion garment possesses various attributes that can be manipulated to reflect changing fashions. Each attribute is potentially able to reflect a very strong fashion trend in its own right.

- Colour
- Fabric
- Print
- Silhouette
- Styling detail
- Trim.

In the recent past, a fashion garment would sell, all things being equal, if it were the 'right' colour. By the same token, a fashion range would suffer if it did not contain colours that were the right shade for a season. Now it is not so important to have the right shade so long as a version of the 'on-trend' colour palette is included in a season's range. The early 1990s saw many consecu-tive seasons of neutral tones in women's wear, with an explosion of bright and pastel colours occurring in the mid-1990s. The break in the neutrals began with pink and proceeded through lime, orange, yellow and blue through to the millennium. Modern fashion markets are very fragmented and as such a season can carry many different fashion colours and stories to satisfy the diversity of tastes among various consumer segments.

Although trends in fashion are reflected through a variety of design elements, it is believed that customers respond to colour first. There are a number of reasons for this, including strong social and cultural semiotic associations that are learned and, more simply, because a colour is obviously noticeable as it covers the surface of the product. Where fashion products are black, white or neutral in appearance it is common for colour to be used in the packaging or visual merchandising of such products to provide seasonal context. Fashions may also be strongly reflected through fabric qualities (e.g. performance related, faded, sheer), fabric patterns, product silhouette, product styling, trims and packaging. Colour is the attribute that is agreed upon earliest in the trend development process, some 18–20 months prior to a season. During these early stages emphasis is on the context and qualities of colour such as 'a cool colour palette' or 'chalky textures' indicating a range of tones and shades within a particular colour. Typically colours become more specific the closer they are to a particular season. The exact timing varies among trend specialists but two examples include WGSN and Promostyl. WGSN provided their clients with details of colour relating to Spring 2007 in July 2005. Promostyl provided details of colour for the same season in June 2005 but proceeded to reveal their complete view of Summer 2007 (fabric, shape, styling, print and detail) at their client presentation in December 2005.

Fashion trends may vary in longevity, with a particular 'look' crossing many seasons. This could be a colour, a fabric attribute (e.g. sheer) and a garment shape (e.g. neck line or skirt length). It could also be a focus on a part of the body such as the midriff, which may generate a variety of designs utilizing different garment shapes (e.g. low slung hipster pants or tops that are short in the body). Stone (1990) writes of 'rules' where a fashion emphasis concentrates on a part of the body, for example the legs or midriff, until the interest or variety of looks is fully exploited. Through varying emphases and interpretations, this may take a number of seasons. Own-brand fashion buyers will also want to exploit a particularly successful shape or style, which can also extend the longevity of a fashion trend.

Fashion seasons

When examining fashion trends, the issue of fashion seasons emerges as a context in which the trends can be understood. The term 'season' refers to a period of time during which fashion products are sold. The specific period of the selling time associated with a season will vary according to the nature of the fashion business. For example, a fabric manufacturer will sell fabric for production of Spring/Summer (SS) merchandise many months before the SS retail selling season begins.

Historically, there have been two clearly defined and traditional fashion seasons, which are Autumn/Winter and SS. Easy (1995) explains that retailers have organized themselves around consumer demand that has traditionally been influenced by weather patterns. Although factors other than simply the weather are increasingly driving the make-up of fashion product ranges, these seasonal terms are still used because they are firmly ingrained in our culture. Changes to the nature of a fashion season arise partly from changes in consumers' lifestyles. For example, once very seasonal merchandise such as swimwear, traditionally sold from March to July, is now also sold in December and January to accommodate demand from people on winter holidays to the sun. The availability of products on-line at anytime further erodes the rigidity of seasons.

Global climate change is believed to be creating a general warming of the local climates in many northern hemisphere countries and as such fashion retailers and brands can often be caught out by unseasonable weather. The problems seem to be most acute in the autumn as later warm weather means that consumers are reluctant to begin purchasing heavier clothing. Although this maybe a merchandising issue it is likely to have an impact on product design and ranging for autumn collections in the future.

Seasons and user occasions

As peoples' lifestyles have changed, generally becoming more complex and time pressured, so fashion brands have responded by offering greater choice and changing ranges more frequently. Whereas in the past fashion buyers created ranges to satisfy two large periods of demand (SS and Autumn/Winter) it is now normal for fashion brands to buy more quickly and keep ranges focused on what consumers want throughout the year. In marketing terms, it could be said that the brands are 'buying' to satisfy specific consumer 'user occasions'.

User occasions are situations when consumers develop a need for a product either as a result of their attitudes and lifestyle activities or because of a specific event/occasion. Some reflect traditional occasions like beachwear in summer and party outfits for Christmas and the New Year, but increasingly consumer demand is forcing retailers to rethink product ranges around changed consumer behaviour. For example, smart-casual outfits for the office are worn to balance the need to accommodate a relaxed appearance at work with after work socializing. Consumers' awareness of celebrity dressing, as depicted in the media, also drives demand for particular products and styling.

A fashion season has to accommodate predictable periods of demand, such as party dresses at Christmas, with contemporary lifestyle fashion occasions. The traditional SS and Autumn/Winter seasons have inevitably therefore become fragmented.

A more common fashion retail approach to seasons is given in Table 9.1.

Although the structure of a season may have changed and the boundaries between seasons become blurred, a new season still presents a fashion business with opportunities to freshen its stores with new stock. Frequent changes create the perception of 'newness' and provide brands with an opportunity

Table 9.1 The changing fashion retailer seasons in the UK

Sub-season	Period
Early Spring	January/February
Spring (Events – e.g. Valentine's Day)	February/March
Early Summer (Holiday)	April/May
Summer	May/June
Summer Sale	June
High Summer	June/July
Transitional Autumn	July/August
Back-to-school (where appropriate)	August
Autumn	September/October
Party wear	November
Christmas presents/Transitional Spring	December
Winter Sale	December/January

to monitor the performance of early product deliveries. Fast selling styles can be 'repeat ordered', making the rest of the season more profitable. Repeat orders may take the form of a straight replenishment of a fast selling style or a modified repeat where a successful style is changed in a particular way such as colour. A modified version of a successful selling style can stretch sales of the same product and maintain a sense of newness for both consumers and the brand. However, as no one is certain which particular trend is going to take off until the season begins so a fast and efficient supply chain is vital.

Since fashions are fast moving and subject to many influences, it is difficult for a designer to predict and accurately interpret the 'fashion look' for a particular season. As such, the fashion designer and buyer must interpret a range of information and then adapt the key looks for their market.

Retailers'/brands' research

Buyers for fashion brands, whether a retailer or other fashion brand, ultimately determine the look of most fashion apparel, accessories and footwear sold to consumers. Their decisions about the look and fashionability of products are influenced by a variety of events and activities. Many own-brand fashion retailers use the design teams of their suppliers to work on product designs. A small design team working for the retailer then guides these designers, but it is normally the buyer who finally selects the product designs for the range. Buyers work closely with internal design, garment technology and merchandising functions during the early stages of range development, sharing ideas and information. The current and historical sales data of a brand can provide valuable trend information relating to 'best and worst' selling styles, skus (colours and sizes) and price points. However, early fashion ideas come from a synthesis of influences that emerge from a variety of additional sources, including the following:

- Overseas trips to fashionable shopping locations in foreign cities to buy or photograph samples for 'inspiration'.
- Research of competitor channels (stores, catalogues, websites) for information on new styles, pricing and packaging.
- Research from 'out-of-season' shows providing trend ideas ahead of time.
- Trawling through a variety of specialist fashion and style magazines.
- Customized forecasting services/trend books (e.g. Promostyl).
- On-line forecasting services, such as WGSN and style websites such as style. com, stylesight.com, catwalking.com and fashionsnoops.com.
- Specified textile shows such as Premiere Vision (PV) (although knitwear designers and buyers may also attend earlier yarn shows such as Pitti Filatti).
- Specified product shows such as Magic, Bread & Butter and Pitti Imagine Uomo.
- Ready-to-wear (RTW) shows.

The above represents a variety of information sources commonly used by fashion designers and buyers throughout a range development process. It is worth noting at this stage that research from these sources normally occurs pre-season. In other words the shows and other available information clearly relate to a specific and future season. For example the Barcelona 'Bread & Butter' show held in January 2006 relates to the Autumn/Winter 2006/2007 season. Similarly the Paris-based textile trade show PV held in February 2006 relates to SS 2007. However, the increasing trend towards fast-fashion has resulted in some designers and buyers using the shows 'ahead of the season' by incorporating trend information into existing collections (SS begins in January and goes through to June, enabling buyers to bring in new stock influenced by the latest show information). This may occur through adaptation of repeat orders in season or through placing new 'short lead-time' orders for production that can be delivered in a few weeks.

Throughout a season fashion buyers and merchandisers regularly analyse 'best and worst' current and historical sales data to determine the best commercial balance of core and new fashion looks in the range.

On-line sources of fashion trend data are increasingly important as they offer their clients flexible access to current information that is constantly updated. Companies such as WGSN provide comprehensive and global visual information, which is broad in scope and in depth. WGSN provide detailed written reviews and digital images of all trade and fashion shows to subscribers along with summaries of store window displays in foreign shopping locations, views and analyses of future trends (Think Tank). As an on-line provider it is able to update trend information (that begins with Think Tank) and fine tune it closer to a season.

Other fast on-line fashion services include www.style.com, www.stylesight .com and www.catwalking.com. Many such sites post photographs from the runway shows at key fashion weeks almost as they are happening. Some sites also provide invaluable 'behind the scenes' views of hair styling, make-up and the images from parties after the fashion shows.

Role of fashion forecasting

Trend forecasters offer fashion designers objective and early guidance about the changes in fashion colour, fabric and shape. Forecasters explore and ana-lyse changing social, economic, cultural and political influences that are likely to affect fashion. Global and local influences combine to affect the zeitgeist of a season differently in each country. It is the skill of the forecaster to explain how fashion products may best reflect the mood of a moment. Gabrielle (Coco) Chanel stated 'Fashion does not only exist in dresses; fashion is in the air, it is brought in by the wind, one feels it coming, breathes it in the sky and on the pavement, it depends on ideas, customs and happenings' (Charles-Roux, 2005, p. 11). The task of interpreting how the changing world is likely to impact on consumers' desire for fashion products is managed in a variety of ways by brands. Some use trend managers to give direction to their designers, although most fashion retailers use some kind of fashion forecasting service to find out how future season's trends are evolving. Some retailers, however, prefer to research and interpret the trends themselves to maintain their originality.

The process

Forecasters reflect the earliest views on trends some 18–20 months in advance of a season. At this stage, colour is a crucial consideration for yarn mills that need to know what the needs of fabric weavers and knitters will be. It is also the focus of discussion among others who have an interest in very early trend decision-making. An illustration of the sequence of decision-making is shown in Table 9.2 and reflects the wide range of diverse and specialist inputs that contribute to a season's fashion look. These vary from specialists meeting among themselves (e.g. the various colour groups) to a progression of trade and fashion shows. Fashion forecasters combine the views emerging about colour and fabric from the early yarn and fabric trade shows with their own socio-economic and cultural analysis. Major trends in lifestyles, attitudes and culture, in particular music, art, architecture, sports, film and television, are used to predict changing consumer demand.

Trend forecasting businesses

French companies based in Paris have traditionally dominated fashion trend forecasting. Although a number of the larger ones are still French and based in Paris, many with satellite offices around the world, a number of new niche

Table 9.2 Key decision making stages in the development of a fashion season for *Spring/Summer 2007*

Date	Event	Textile shows	Garment/Product Shows
May 05	**Fashion forecasters plan colour**		
June 05	**British Textile Colour Group** (BTCG) meet **Intercolour Group** meets (Paris)		
July 05	**WGSN** Colour palette available		
November 05		**Filo** yarn show (Milan)	
December 05	**Promostyl** client conference Spring/Summer 2007 complete view (variable locations)		
January 06		**European Preview** (USA)	
January 06		**Tissu Premier** fabric show (Lille)	
February 06		**Pitti Immagine Filati** Yarn show (Florence) (mainly for knits)	
February 06		**Moda In Tessuto e Accessori** (Milan)	
February 06		**Prato Expo** Fabric show (Florence)	
February 06		**Texworld** (Paris)	
February 06		**Premiere Vision (Paris) Indigo & Expofil** yarn show (Paris)	
June 06			**Pitti Immagine Uomo** (Florence)
July 06			**Bread and Butter** (Barcelona)
August 06			**Magic** (Las Vegas, USA)
Sept/Oct 06			Designer **RTW** shows
January 07			Designer **Couture** shows

forecasters have emerged offering their own specialist combination of products and services. Some of the better known trend forecasters currently include:

- Promostyl
- WGSN
- Fashion scout
- Sacha Pacha
- Peclers
- Trend Union.

Promostyl is a global trend forecasting business with a client base that extends beyond fashion clothing brands. It offers both a customized consulting service to clients as well as a range of trend books for each season. Their trend books provide detailed forecasts about colour fabric and styling for various market sectors, including women's wear, men's wear and children's wear. The books also provide a quick and effective global overview of major evolving trends.

Tapping into the changing external environment

Social and cultural changes are major determinants of emerging fashions. However, they are themselves affected by other drivers of change that include globalization of world markets and the accessibility of more sophisticated communications technologies. The latter has provided people with fast and flexible access to more ideas and influences from other cultures and societies, driving demand for wider choice in fashion products. The days of a few large retailers producing predictable looks for predictable seasons SS and Autumn/ Winter are long gone.

Figure 9.1 identifies some of the major drivers of change influencing fashion trends today. The model provides an indication of the diverse range of factors impacting on fashion design, rather than representing a complete list of all possible factors.

Although 'globalization' has impacted on the fashion industry in many ways, including sourcing and the spread of international fashion brands, some fashion brands have suffered through not taking into account the differences in demand of local/micro markets. C&A, Etam, Kookai and more recently Morgan have all failed in the UK fashion market after struggling to sell ranges that did not take account of consumers' changing fashion tastes. Similarly, Next, French Connection and Marks and Spencer have all failed in the USA. Fashion styling, ranging, sizing and image can vary significantly across national and cultural boundaries. A mistrust of politics and government linked to globalization has also stimulated the growth of many smaller communities. Some are obviously linked to anti-globalization whereas others are more focussed on rejuvenating local customs, dialects, trade and lifestyles.

Collaborative fashion branding, where a brand is associated with a leading fashion designer, can deliver reciprocal market positioning and differentiation benefits to both. More recent examples of this include Hennes and

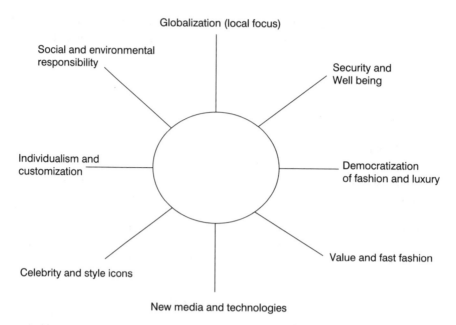

Figure 9.1 Some drivers of fashion change. *Source:* adapted from Jackson and Shaw (2001).

Mauritz's collaborations with Karl Lagerfeld and Stella McCartney. Similarly Adidas collaborated with Yohji Yamamoto to produce its Y3 product. Further fashion collaborations can be expected as a means of driving fresh products and interest in brands.

Promostyl refers to the 'democratization of fashion' to explain the growth of previously ultra-exclusive brands like Gucci into mass market adoption. Phrases such as 'mass to class', 'masstige' and 'massification of luxury' all reflect this growing trend. Burberry has used a similar term, 'accessible luxury', to explain its growth strategy and broader customer base. The term Prada and Primark is used by some UK fashion brands to profile a segment of consumer who mix brands from different market levels to achieve an individual and affordable look that includes an element of luxury. Value fashion and 'fast fashion' have emerged from the more democratic fashion market as consumers purchase products from retailer brands such as Primark and supermarket brands including 'George' (Asda/Walmart) and Tesco's 'Florence and Fred' range. In 2005 Asda and Tesco achieved huge publicity in the UK over the low price of the denim jeans they were selling for £3 and £4 a pair. Although fast fashion is not necessarily always cheap the speed of change does ensure a high stock-turn for brands. Zara, Hennes and Mauritz (H&M) and TopShop are three of the better known European fast fashion brands. In 2005 Robert Polet, President and CEO of the Gucci Group, recognized the importance of this type of fashion when he stated that consumers of luxury products are being 'educated' by fast fashion retailers who offer new products every 6 weeks creating a fast shopping rhythm (Polet, 2005).

The perceived insecurity that has existed in the world since the terrorist attacks of 9/11 is believed to have influenced consumers' tastes towards more conservative dressing. Similarly more money is being spent on 'insperiences' (as opposed to experiences) as consumers prefer to stay in and invest money in their homes through home entertainment systems or interior design. Insecurities have also focused consumer' minds on well-being and the importance of belonging to a family or group.

New technologies are a common driver of fashion change. At fabric level electro-conductive textiles offer a range of product applications for clothing and accessories such as Spyder's ski jacket with iPod controls. Similarly the Air Zoom Moire collaboration between Nike and Apple illustrates the role of technologies in driving new fashion products. Some may well argue that Apple's iPod is itself a fashion product arising from MP3 technology. The Internet provides enormous scope for the production, distribution and consumption of fashion and fashion products. Consumers can engage in free on-line fashion communities such as that provided by the specialist trainer magazine **www.sneakerfreaker.com.** On-line gaming is also providing new opportunities for marketers as in-game advertising offers unique ways for brands to capture the attention of gamers.

Consumers have more knowledge of fashion and brands than at any time in the past. This is in part a result of a burgeoning consumer media that delivers a diet of fashion, celebrity and lifestyle journalism to the mass market. Many fashion brands have to face the fact that their consumers are becoming more knowledgeable and often know more about fashion than brands know about their customers. Coupled with increased competition, this increased sophistication of consumers results in a need to consistently monitor and review the basis of differentiation for fashion businesses. However, greater knowledge is coupled with increased expectations and consumers are more demanding of service and value. Fashion brands need to appreciate the importance of meeting the needs of time pressured consumers through product design, quality, availability and selling. In contrast to the homogeneity of global brands and commodity fashion, many consumers seek out customisation in design as a way of feeling uniquely involved in product or service they buy. Questions are being raised about the sustainability of fast fashion as consumers question the ethics of disposable fashion. There is a general awareness of the importance of recycling which may apply equally to product packaging. Some fashion consumers will be prepared to pay more for bespoke products, which are demonstrably the result of ethical manufacturing processes.

Technological innovations in fibres and fabrics

Frequently, the development of a completely new product is the result of a particular functional need, like a 'trainer sock' or a 'body', but often it is driven by the benefits offered by a new fabric. Specialist forecasters like Line Creative Partners (UK) make the point that technology is changing the range of benefits that designers can build into garment products through the textiles used in construction. As more functions and properties are integrated into their structures, textiles can provide a new range of benefits for garments, including greater protective capabilities, body enhancing qualities and the benefits associated with 'smart textiles' like Amicor, from Courtaulds.

Table 9.3 shows that not all product improvements are derived solely from the development of new fibres, as innovation can occur across the entire textile development process.

Table 9.3 Textile developments

Textile level	Development
Fibre	Amicor – a modified acrylic with anti-bacterial capabilities that is designed to eliminate odour and skin irritation
Yarn	Improved cotton spinning processes producing a softer handle
Fabric	Gore-Tex fabric which uses a hi-tech membrane sandwiched between outer and inner layers of fabric to allow skin to breathe whilst protecting against wind and rain
Finish	Chemicals added to woven fabric to provide crease resistant benefits (e.g. Teflon finish to provide dirt resistant effect)
Colour	Development of vegetable dyes/fox fibre – natural coloured cotton

Source: Jackson and Shaw (2000).

The importance of shows

Buyers and fashion designers are able to predict what is likely to be 'in fashion' through a combination of influences, including reviewing important textile and style magazines, the specialist services of forecasting trend agencies, and visits to textile and garment fashion shows.

Range of shows

The word 'show' is given its widest possible interpretation here to refer to the range of organized textile and fashion garment trade shows, operating over the 15 months preceding a season. Trade shows, whether yarn, fabric or product, have a basic function which is to sell products. The use of these shows for prediction is often a secondary function, although many clearly exploit this aspect. At a basic level, yarn mills sell to fabric weavers and knitters, who sell to garment manufactures and retailers. Fashion buyers may buy direct from fabric or product manufacturers depending on whether they are sourcing on a CMT or factored basis. The different needs arising from the fashion clothing supply chain have resulted in a sequence of yarn, fabric and product trade shows and RTW fashion shows evolving over the years.

Visitors vary according to the nature of the show. A yarn show will attract a range of people, including fabric manufacturers, some retail buyers and designers, although the mix will be more weighted to people involved in fabric production than garment design and buying. Fashion trade press cover the shows, informing those buyers and designers, for whom the shows are too early, of the major trends that are emerging.

The fabric shows perform a more balanced role with great emphasis on the sale of fabrics, but with more retail designers and buyers attending as the products on show have greater direct relevance to garment design and the shows are that much closer to the season.

Garment shows are much more diverse, ranging from the product trade shows through to the high profile RTW Designer shows like London Fashion Week and then the exclusive Paris-based Couture shows.

Lead-times

Lead-time refers to a period of time between specified events. In this case it is used to refer to the period of time prior to a season that a particular show is being held. As a general rule of thumb, fabric shows are held approximately 10 months before a season and garment shows approximately 5 months before a season. The beginning of a season is January for SS and August for Autumn/Winter. However, the transitional Spring ranges are in store late December with Early Spring in January.

The sequence of trade and fashion shows

Table 9.2 shows the sequence of fashion trend evolution, using the season SS 2007 as an illustration. It features the sequence in which a variety of yarn, textile and product shows occur. Although the table is illustrative of the season SS 2007 it is important to appreciate that the sequence and timing of shows may change in the future. Competitive pressures among the various shows and the trend towards fast fashion have influenced some to show closer to the season and others to become more aligned with competitors. For example, the timings of both Expofil and PV shows have changed over recent years. In the past, Expofil was held a number of months before PV. Now the two show simultaneously, although Expofil also provides insights or what it refers to as 'Atmosphere' for the next season. A similar sequence is mirrored for Autumn/Winter at different times.

National and international colour bodies

In the UK, the process really begins with the British Textile Colour Group (BTCG) meeting, where around 25 representatives of a range of companies from different industry sectors, including car, retail and forecasting, meet to discuss colour and their views on factors likely to affect the season's fashion trends. Two representatives are selected to attend the Intercolour Group meeting, which is traditionally held in Paris, but occasionally moves to other countries. Here, the equivalent representatives from many countries around the world, including Europe, Asia and the Far East, meet to exchange views on the likely development of trends and especially the development of colour.

The UK representatives then return to the UK for a review of the global position with the rest of the BTCG. Some forecasters such as WGSN then make their colour palette available for clients.

Textile Shows

These loosely fall into the categories of Yarn and Fabric. Yarn shows tend to exhibit for a season ahead of the large fabric shows as their product is the basis of fabric production. Those interested in using yarn shows for predictive purposes look for colour, texture and blends to understand how fabrics may appear and perform. Following the decisions made by colour bodies one of the earliest signs of SS trends emerges in the Filo show in Milan.

Premiere Vision

PV is one of the world's largest textiles shows. It is held in Paris twice a year, February for the following SS season and September for Autumn/Winter. Dates vary according to strategic decisions about whether to show earlier or later as PV is in competition with others such as Tisssu Premier. In the past, PV has exhibited for SS in February one year and March in another. In 2006 the Paris based SS 2007 show was held in February, the Tokyo show in March and the Shanghai show in April.

PV represents an accurate view of colours and fabric trends approximately 10 months ahead of a season. It is regarded by many to be the 'first sight' of colour and fabric trends for much of the European fashion industry, and is still one of the most important shows in the calendar. Within the vast exhibition halls, approximately 800 European weaver–exhibitors show their fabric ranges to 40,000 visitors over the 4 days. The presentation of key trends on display within the vast exhibition is the result of the combined views of a European Concertation, a body of 65 fashion experts who identify the current trends emerging from around the world, and the PV Fashion team. Colour palettes and key theme statements are signed around the exhibition summarizing the trends, and there is an audio-visual show, which provides an overview of the season at intervals throughout the day. Those visiting who are not trained designers but are trying to obtain a feel for the particular season's trends should realize that PV is not a garment show and so should expect to gain mainly fabric and colour information.

Although PV is an important show, there are other fabric shows like Tissu Premier that are providing earlier insights into colour and fabric trends. Tissu, in particular, is considered a good earlier source of trend information, even though it is not so large and has fewer fabric categories.

Product shows

Continuing the sequence, specialist product trade shows are held after the fabric shows. The product shows are segmented according to broad sector, such as men's or women's wear, and by specialist product category, including sportswear or lingerie. There are many international product shows such as Magic in Las Vegas (USA), Bread and Butter in Barcelona and Berlin, and the various Pitti Immagine shows in Florence. UK-based product shows are less significant than they used to be with purewoneswear one of the few remaining. Product shows are good indicators of colour, fabric, styling and new product categories.

Designer RTW and Couture shows

The RTW garment shows really provide the last opportunity for fashion retailers and brands to incorporate styling changes or overlooked 'must have' items in their ranges. The principal international shows are held during fashion weeks in New York, London, Milan and Paris. However, other international fashion weeks are increasing influential, including Mercedes Australian Fashion Week, and Japan Fashion Week in Tokyo. The shows provide influential fashion media with an opportunity to review and promote the particular season's trends and provide publicity for the designers.

The final set of shows reflecting the season's trends are the Couture shows that are held in Paris in January for Summer and July for Winter. The summer shows held in January have little immediate impact on high street fashion, as Early Spring stock is already in the stores with Summer already being shipped. However, these made-to-measure garments are dominated by occasion wear, including 'after-six' evening wear and ballgowns, many of which are often worn by celebrities at events that carry major media coverage, such as the Academy Awards ('Oscars'). The extensive coverage of celebrities attending high profile events, often given outfits to wear by leading designers, means that new design ideas receive enormous exposure. Frequently, the design themes that emerge seem too forward for most people, but they often have a long-term influence upon future seasons.

Not all the events or shows are directly relevant to all fashion brand designers and buyers. Buyers for own-brand retailers develop products from designs and so are concerned with textile shows. This differs from many boutique and department store buyers who select brands to stock in their stores and so will attend product shows and designer fashion weeks.

Final stage of trend development

The final 'fashion look' for a season is therefore the result of a process of development that combines the evolved views of forecasters, textile and product trade shows, designers, buyers and RTW shows. Like a collage, the final picture emerges after the various layers have come together. Prior to the (fashion week) RTW shows, proposed new looks for a season have not been subject to broad media scrutiny and so are mostly unknown to the end user consumers. Even though the runway shows at the international fashion weeks have an impact on some last minute high street and fast fashion ranges, their major impact is mainly on directing final views of trends close to or within a season. These tend to be the views of fashion journalists writing for a variety of media including specialist fashion glossies, mens' and womens' lifestyle magazines and the fashion/style sections of the press. Crucially, the media coverage of the various RTW and Couture shows is another important dimension in the trend development process as it highlights fashion trends that fashion editors believe will be strong in-season. Such 'authoritative' coverage of the media, focusing attention on aspects of fashion, including 'must-have' looks, colours and products, influences consumers' acceptance of hot trends for a season. As Packard et al. (1983) state, 'Price levels do not indicate fashion, acceptance is the key'.

Magazine coverage of RTW shows

The extensive coverage of the RTW shows by the fashion media provides consumers with their first authoritative views of the new season's looks. This coverage occurs at different times and with **varying** degrees of authority. For example, press and television journalists report headline stories emerging from the shows on a daily basis, whereas the influential monthly women's magazines report in detail some months after the shows. The coverage occurring during the shows tends to be news focused, ranging from stories centred on radical designs to the use of celebrities in fashion shows. As there is little reported analysis of trends during the September/October period of the shows, the consumer does not have a clear picture of what the key fashion themes will be until the New Year.

Trend coverage

Significant and structured 'trend' coverage of the shows is principally delivered to the consumer through the pages of the monthly women's magazines, including *Vogue, Elle, Marie Claire, Cosmopolitan*, Grazia and many more. Table 9.4 shows the relationship between the timing of the RTW shows and the monthly magazines' issue deadlines.

As these magazines work on 3 monthly lead-times, the earliest practical coverage of the September/October shows is in the January issue. The December issues are too focused on Christmas and the completion of the current year to address next season's trends. Furthermore, advertisers in the magazines want to keep SS images close to the relevant selling periods. Although some SS trends are featured in the January issues, with each magazine doing things differently, the major trend coverage will come in subsequent issues. This is because fashion editors tend to wait for the first signs of SS samples, generally arriving in November, before producing significant features.

These 'photo' or press samples are couriered ahead of the rest of production to enable fashion retailers to promote the range. Some magazines will feature a special SS trend supplement in a fixed month, commonly April, with

Table 9.4 UK monthly magazines' production deadlines and coverage of fashion weeks for Spring/Summer season

Month	RTW Fashion Shows	Monthly Magazine Deadlines	Retailer Promotion
September	New York, London	December edition	
October	Milan, Paris	January* edition	
November		February* edition	Press days: Availability of press/PR samples
December		March* & April* editions	

*In the next calender year.

other magazines allowing the trend coverage to trickle out across issues from January onwards to stimulate interest.

Obviously, the interpretation by fashion editors of what the major colours and styling features are for a season has an impact on consumers' belief of what is fashionable. 'Must-have' colours, styles and products are promoted through the magazine features and consumers are educated into an acceptance of what to wear that season. In addition to the specific trend coverage of the RTW shows, the magazines include specific fashion features that focus on a particular aspect of the season. This could be based on an occasion, such as 'holidays', or on a strong fashion theme such as a denim look. Many of these features will include photographs of season's products that are to be in the stores at the time the magazine is published.

In order to take advantage of such opportunities, many fashion brands hold 'press days' during which fashion journalists and editors preview the forthcoming ranges. In the UK these typically occur in July for Christmas and November for SS. This exposure provides magazines with relevant material to shoot for their fashion features and benefits fashion brands by giving them crucial publicity. Brands provide fashion journalists with 'look books' containing photographs of key products from the new ranges and many of the monthly magazines select items from the 'books' to shoot for their own features. As the season unfolds, so the media in all its various forms feature particular looks across their monthly editions, maintaining the 'newness' of the fashions and interest from consumers. Efficient buying departments are able to respond to fast emerging 'hot trends' that supplement the rest of the range.

References

Barnard, M. (2001). *Fashion as Communication*. London: Routledge.

Breward, C. (2003). Fashion, Oxford: Oxford University Press, p. 9.

Charles-Roux, E. (1981). *Chanel and Her World*. London: Weidenfeld and Nicolson, p. 237.

Charles-Roux, E. (2004). *The World of Coco Chanel, Friends Fashion Fame*. London: Thames and Hudson, p. 11.

Easy, M. (1995). *Fashion Marketing*. Oxford: Blackwell Science.

Foley, B. (2004). Marc Jacobs, Assouline Publicity NY. p.16

Jackson, T. and Shaw, D. (2001). *Mastering Fashion Buying and Merchandising Management*. London: Macmillan.

Leymarie, J. (1987) *Chanel, Rizzoli International*, Publications Inc., p. 21.

Packard, S., Winters, A. and Axelrod, W. (1983). *Fashion Buying and Merchandising*. London: Fairchild Publications.

Perna, R. (1987). *Fashion Forecasting*. London: Fairchild Publications.

Polet, R. (2005). *Modern Luxury 2005*. International Herald Tribune Conference, Dubai December 5 and 6.

Polhemus, T. and Procter, L. (1978). *Fashion and Anti-fashion and Anthropology of Clothing and Adornment*. London: Thames & Hudson.

Reich, L. (2004), Questions of Fashion. In Stern, R. (Ed), *Against Fashion Clothing as Art (1850–1930)*. Boston: The MIT Press, p. 151.

Stone, E (1990). *Fashion Merchandising: An Introduction*. Gregg Division McGraw-Hill.

Wintour, A.(2004).

Appendix A: details of interviewees responding to questions for this chapter

Date	Participant	Event
November 2004	Mathew Jeatt – Promostyl Kim Mannino – Promostyl	Interview Interview
March and November 2005	Roger Tredre – WGSN	Interview
November 2004	Anouska Anquetil – Fashion Scout International	Interview
January and June 2005	Promostyl	Client trend presentations: Summer 2006 and Autumn/Winter 2007
October 2004	Roger Tredre – WGSN	Client trend presentation
October 2005	Roger Tredre and Verity McIlreen – WGSN	Client trend presentation
December 2005	Alison Thorne – George (Asda)	Company presentation
May and September 2005	Top Shop Buying Team	Informal discussions
April, June, July	Coast and Oasis	Informal discussions

Date of interview	Respondent name	Company
November 1999	Mathew Jeatt Kim Mannino	Promostyl
November 1999	Bridget Miles	Marks & Spencer
November 1999	Joanna Bowring (written response)	Courtaulds
October 1999	Ros Hibbert	Live
September 2000	Jenny Carrington	*Woman's Journal*
September 2000	Confidentiality retained (written response)	*Company* magazine
September 2000 October 2000	Nicola Griffin Tony Glenville	Selfridges AV Studio

10

Innovation management in creating new fashions

Beatrice Le Pechoux, Trevor J. Little and Cynthia L. Istook

Introduction

Each apparel manufacturer's new collections of garments and accessories are created to satisfy a predicted target consumer demand. These demand predictions are based on target market research and past sales analysis, and input from experienced product merchandisers, designers and buyers. The collections are influenced by trends observed in apparel and related industries (textile, shoes, accessories, home furnishings, etc.), and/or other industries (such as entertainment, sports, music or automotive), as well as wider environmental movements (cultural, social, technological, economical, etc.). All these elements combined help determine the concepts and themes for the new season. Relevant materials, colour palettes and silhouettes are developed and selected accordingly. Trims and details may be added as further embellishments. These former and latter design elements are coordinated and grouped into product lines that meet cost, production and delivery time requirements.

The apparel design process involves gathering and analysing information on fashion trends, markets and past line sales, and editing ideas for successful combinations of fabric, style and price. These ideas are the result of creativity.

The discussion of the role of creativity in today's textile/apparel industry applies to the world's highly developed economies in general, which are entering a new stage of development. For centuries, this growth was based on increases in productivity. However, 'this expansion trajectory is now perceived as unsustainable' (Andersson, 1997). Quantitative growth must be replaced by improvements in quality. 'Wealth creating innovations ultimately substitute knowledge for energy or materials. Knowledge accumulates exponentially, with every innovation creating the opportunity for a greater number of innovations' (Petzinger Jr, 2000). As products are becoming more varied and complex, creativity rather than productivity is becoming the key to business success and survival. In the new knowledge-based economy, Petzinger (2000) concludes 'creativity is overtaking capital as the principal elixir of growth'. Despite the importance of creativity for product differentiation, creativity regarding textile or apparel designers, design teams and the design process has not been widely investigated.

Most of the models reviewed describe the creative process as a problem-solving system. Alexander (1977) recognized that in the architectural design process some problems occur over and over again, in a given environment, with a core (generic) solution. From that observation, he was the first to develop a pattern language for a design process, where each pattern describes a problem/solution combination related to a specific context. The patterns are formulated in such a way that they can be used in different sequences and numbers, many times over, without ever doing it the same way twice. Therefore, the output can always be unique and new, thus defined as creative.

A pattern language for the apparel design process could channel creative efforts and enhance communication between design team members by providing them with a common language for creative fashion design.

Mapping the creative design process

The design process generally includes all the steps involved from generation of ideas and concepts to prototype development of the end product (Secor, 1992). It is a multidisciplinary science that requires teamwork and collaboration between various corporate functions. Marketing and sales information are particularly important in the initial phase of the process. Design, material and process knowledge is necessary to follow through to the next phases and ultimately create new products.

Textile/apparel design processes in the literature are covered from both a theoretical and empirical point of view. Since market and production constraints need to be integrated into the process, a combination of skills and therefore a collaboration of various corporate activities and functions are required. Theoretical models and empirical descriptions attempt to capture the creative design process to make it more tangible for all the design team members and management. The following figures show the product design and development processes from different points of view.

Figure 10.1 shows a theoretical model of the apparel design and development process (Carr and Pomeroy, 1992). Similarly to Carr and Pomeroy's model, Sadd (1996), of KSA, identifies five steps to product development: consumer research, design/concept development, sampling, specification development and finally pre-production sampling. This whole pre-production phase is critical to achieve successful product sell-through. Here, we will focus on the 'origin of styles' phase, which will always be referred to as the creative design or conception phase for the purpose of clarity.

Adapt for Kanye West range!

consider w image + Kanye west.

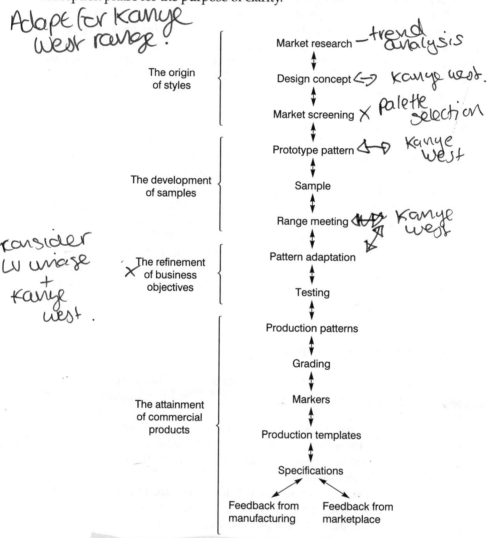

trend analysis

Kanye west.

X palette selection

Kanye west

Kanye west

Figure 10.1 The process of apparel design and product development. *Source:* Carr and Pomeroy (1992).

The following models focus more on this conception phase. The first one is based on a case study run by Gaskill (1992) in order to profile the functional activities performed by two speciality retailers carrying 100 per cent private label merchandise. Having previously observed that retailers were increasingly involved in the process of product design by setting up specialized product development divisions, the objective was to differentiate them by creating unique products that catered to their target consumer's specific preferences. Resulting from the study, the Retail Product Development Model (Figure 10.2) how the sequence of events that take place throughout the creative apparel design process, along with its internal and external influences. This model stops at the line presentation phase.

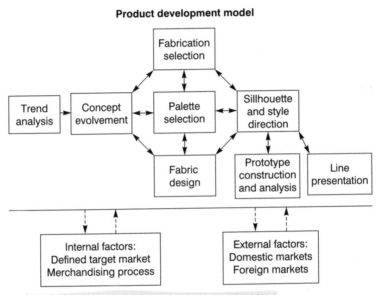

Product development model

Figure 10.2 Retail product development model. *Source:* Gaskill (1992).

Recently, Gaskill, along with Wickett et al. (1999), conducted a new study to support and develop this initial Retail Product Development Model. One of the objectives of these authors was to validate Gaskill's original model by testing it across a broader range of speciality stores. In developing their data analysis tools, they created a guide providing the researcher with a detailed outline of the pre-determined activities included in the product development content areas. Table 10.1 includes the most detailed description of the creative product design process found in the literature. This process can be divided into two basic phases. Initially, information is probed for orientation ideas regarding moods, themes, concepts and product types. In a second phase, all these data are digested and translated into product ideas combining silhouettes, materials and colours.

Early phases include trend analysis and concept evolvement. Influences come from both external and internal sources, both from the environment and personnel related to the design process directly or indirectly. This f·

Table 10.1 Activities guide for apparel product development

Trend analysis

Sources of trend inspiration:
- Shopping domestic markets
- Shopping international markets
- Media (magazines, television, mail order catalogues)
- Fashion support services (trade shows, fabric libraries, styles services, runway shows, colour services)
- Anywhere
- Internal sources (employees, sales tracking information)
- Competition

Employees involved in search for trends:
- Buying area (buyers, general merchandise managers)
- Design team
- Product development manager
- Fashion director
- Chief executive officer
- Merchandising manager
- Product manager

Concept evolvement

How decision on concept emerged:
- Perceptions gained from travelling to markets
- Evaluation of overall trend information
- Assessment of past sales trends
- Information gained from fashion services
- Instinct

Palette selection

How seasonal colour decisions are determined:
- Based on information gained during Trend Analysis

Source of colour information:
- Colour services
- Historical colour data
- Colour testing results
- New 'emerging colour stars'
- Purchased garments
- Trends
- Yarn samples
- Colour swatches
- Colour shows

Fabrication selection

Criteria used in selecting product fabrication:
- Structural fabric characteristics (performance, quality, appearance, draping ability, weight, hand)
- Seasonal theme or timing of the line
- Aesthetics
- Marketplace trends
- Part sales history
- Fabric price
- Perceived customer benefits
- Textile mill availability

(Continued)

Table 10.1 (*Continued*)

Fabric design
Source of fabric design:
- Original designs (prints/plaids) created by the company
- Both pre-developed designs and original designs
- Pre-developed designs from fabric companies

Source of fabric design ideas:
- Books and magazines
- Fabric services (fabric libraries, print services, design services, forecasting services)
- Fabric samples
- Fabric mills
- Market trends
- Textile studios

Silhouette and style directions
Sources of silhouette and styles:
- Original designs
- Branded merchandise ('knock-offs')
- Both original designs and knock-offs

Silhouette and style inspiration provided by:
- Marketplace (domestic and international)
- Current trends
- History (past successful basic style blocks)

Line presentation
Line presentation incorporated:
- Prototype samples
- Sketch boards
- Computerized renderings
- Storyboards
- Paintings
- Pictures
- Swatches
- Fabrications

Line decisions based on:
- Saleability judgements
- Testing results
- Perceived customer reaction
- Cost
- Selling history
- Co-ordination with other apparel groups
- Marketplace trends
- Other (newness, variety, lead-time, quality, colour, instinct)

Intervening factors
Internal factors:
- Needs of the defined customer base
- Sales trends
- Input from employees
- Analysis of store performance
- Specific garments being developed

(Continued)

Table 10.1 (*Continued*)

External factors:
• Fashion trends
• Domestic and foreign markets
• Competition
• Media, quota restrictions and fabric capability

Source: Wickett et al. (1999).

step involves identifying the product styles and categories that are most in demand in the target market. A brief among design team members will usually initiate the process by defining 'the garment type, age group, purpose, climate and rice range which designers should aim at' (Carr and Pomeroy, 1992). Market research is critical to 'starting off right' by capturing the market pulse and direction. The design team needs immersion in 'all current means of communication of fashion ideas' (Carr and Pomeroy, 1992): fashion shows, textile/apparel trade shows, recent technological innovations, colour and fabric libraries, store visits, opinion of buyers, market data services, trade press, product offer from the competition, etc. Cultural, social and political events should also be considered.

The second phase includes palette selection, fabric construction and surface design selection, and silhouette and style directions. These activities are related to more tangible design elements utilizing design principles and skills, along with material and process knowledge to combine them effectively. At this final stage of the creative design process, sketches should include overall silhouettes and details such as collars and pockets, and eventually surface decorations such as pleats or fringes.

Figure 10.3 was taken from a larger model that covers the whole product design and development process for apparel. This 'phase 1' depicts the creative design process of apparel up to the line plan. Figure 10.3 illustrates the various types of research information that can be pulled from the environments, and how they integrate the marketing, merchandising and product development processes to establish a line plan.

At the corporate level, Knox (1989) shows (Figure 10.4) how design interfaces with other company activities providing creative, technological and commercial input in a total market environment. He stipulates that two-way relationships exist between the three types of inputs to develop products that can satisfy future market requirements (Knox, 1989).

Knox then breaks each of these three major fields into groups of activities that directly interface with the designer. In Figure 10.5, he shows how creativity has multi-faceted relationships and affects all areas of company strategy.

Since typically 80–90 per cent of a product's life cycle cost is determined during the pre-production stages, careful planning is a necessary support to successful effective and efficient product design (AICPA, 1998). Inefficient product design can create bottlenecks for improved product quality and time

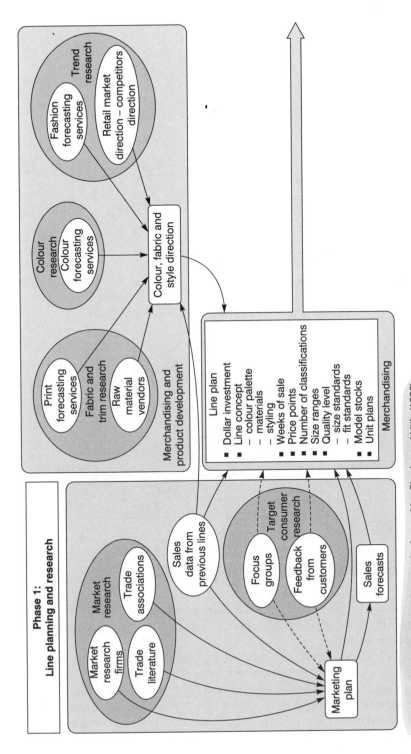

Figure 10.3 Line planning and research. *Source*: May-Plumlee and Little (1998).

Analysis of designer requirements

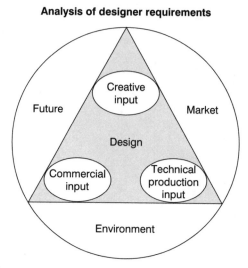

Figure 10.4 Design relationships. *Source:* Knox (1989).

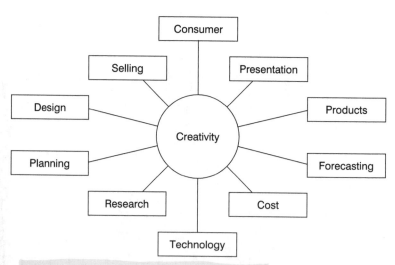

Figure 10.5 Creativity and design activities. *Source:* Knox (1989).

to market. Ineffective product design can lead to poor quality or non-sellable designs. The starting point to successful product design is in the market and trend analyses.

Companies need to set up a research system that enables them to anticipate demographic changes and how lifestyles and expectations of the target market segment are influenced, to 'create a critical path analysis so that the right thing happens at the right time' (Robinson, 1987). Manufacturers seek shorter product development, sourcing, production and delivery cycles. This task is particularly complicated for apparel due to the high number of Stock Keeping

Units (SKUs), the need for constant change, and working on at least three seasons and several lines at a time (Remaury, 1996). Development of new apparel products suffers from low success rates and difficulty in compressing time cycles. Currently, management focus is set on reducing the latter while increasing the former. Compressing time cycles at this stage is crucial to meet calendar deadlines and avoid losing market shares (AAMA, 1991).

Shah (1987) believes that 'timing', that is, getting new styles to the streets at the precise moment the consumer is susceptible and ready for that design message, is related more to market intelligence and understanding the consumer than speed and technology. Though a combination of all three elements really seems key to reaching perfect timing, we agree that design team efforts should particularly focus on and build on this market intelligence. Forecasting is considered critical in apparel and all fashion-related industries. McPherson (1987) suggests that merchandise planning, which translates marketing objectives into specific product lines, can help control potential losses and rapidly take advantage of favourable sales trends.

Marketing and design

Marketing is a two-phase process, which consists of identifying market needs and satisfying them (Carr and Pomeroy, 1992). To reach these objectives, companies need to constantly interact with suppliers, competitors, industry analysts and especially customers to avoid being 'future shocked' (Dammeyer, 1994). 'Now we must invest in consumers . . . Figures alone are not enough: we must understand attitudes, interests, and preferences' (Robinson, 1987).

Identifying market needs

Identifying and understanding market needs is a complicated task, which still needs to be mastered. Currently, most consumers are not satisfied with their shopping experiences. According to Kurt Salmon Associates' 1996 Annual Consumer Pulse Survey, 68 per cent of the apparel shoppers know what they are looking for but 49 per cent claim being unable to find it (KSA, 1996). They seek instant gratification. Satisfying them has become retailers' top concern. Having pushed back in the pipeline some of their actions, they are increasing their operation costs for developing systems to better understand and target their customers, hence increasing responsiveness.

Retailers have shifted their focus from return on investment (ROI) to return on customers (Tandem Corporation, 1997). Instead of trying to increase the number of individual transactions, they now want to increase the value of long-term customer relationships by supplying many 'right' products to one customer rather than one average product to as many customers as possible. The main idea is to increase loyalty, attract old customers back and target new ones more efficiently.

To better focus on specific target consumers, companies develop market segmentation approaches. Initially, market segments were based on product category and simple demographics of the target consumer (such as age, sex, income level and geographic location). In today's intensely competitive environment, products have become increasingly specialized and complex, multiplying the number of definable market segments and blurring the borders between them. To deal with the increasing complexity of market segmentation, marketing has evolved into a new field called 'micro-marketing', which focuses on pinpointing narrow local markets to target customers more efficiently. Based on multi-variable segmentation, micro-marketing requires collecting a wide variety of data incorporating detailed demographic data, as well as consumer information on psychographics, lifestyles and family life cycles, activities, interests, opinions, purchasing and consumption profiles, media used, etc. (Brown, 1997; Pitt, 1997). The information may be based on individual consumers or on households (Carr and Pomeroy, 1992).

This detailed micro-data collected will be used to segment and locate target groups, plan relevant marketing mix, map product potential usage and help customize assortments. As a matter of fact, management focus is shifting from product to category (McCann, 1997), also known as 'consumption constellation' (Solomon and Englis, 1998), taking into account interaction between, rather than within, product categories to offer creative buying incentives and promotional products on a store-to-store basis. This knowledge is particularly relevant to develop different lines of apparel and accessories that may lead to bundled purchases.

Electronic commerce via the Internet will enable manufacturers to directly communicate with and supply consumers, while monitoring and analysing the information each customer is individually pulling down from the World Wide Web. Micro-marketing will become possible on a one-on-one basis. This next stage is already being called 'relationship marketing' (Brown, 1997). The Internet will thus greatly contribute to collecting data on the consumers in addition to that collected through current and past POS and marketing tools such as frequent user programmes.

Response to market demand

Once market needs have been identified and interpreted, response can be given to these defined consumer demands through a mix of marketing elements. The traditional marketing mix factors known as the '4 P' (Kotler and Armstrong, 1994) are product, price, promotion and place. As shown in Figure 10.6, this mix is centred around the target consumer and helps articulate the whole marketing strategy cycle from analysis and planning to implementation and control stages. Product refers to the items and services offered by a company to its target market. Price refers to what will be charged for the purchase of the product. Place refers to where the product will be sold. 'Promotion includes all the efforts of a company to establish the identity and enhance the demand for specific brands and designer name products or to encourage buying from certain retailers' (Jarnow and Dickerson, 1996).

Several authors have given different definitions of the marketing mix, which always include the notions of product, price, place and promotion, while

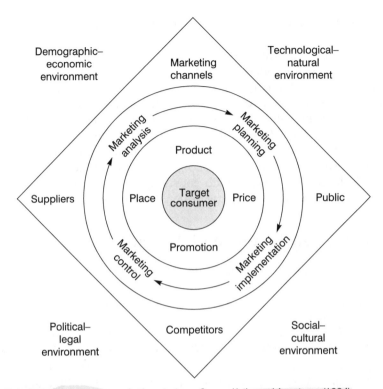

Figure 10.6 Factors influencing marketing strategy. *Source:* Kotler and Armstrong (1994).

classifying design as a category in itself (Rigamonti, 1987; Robinson, 1987; Carr and Pomeroy, 1992; Jarnow and Dickerson, 1996).

Micro- and macro-environments

The marketing environment includes all the opportunities and threats that affect a company's ability to reach its 'goals in developing and maintaining successful business relationships with its target customers' (Jarnow and Dickerson, 1996). For companies to survive they must 'want to change', and this change should be based on knowledge of three main categories: the customer, the market and society. This knowledge can help interpret what lies behind the statistics gathered in market research.

Figure 10.6 shows two types of environments in the inner diamond and the outer square. The micro-environment is closest to the company, affecting 'its ability to serve its target market'. It includes marketing channels, suppliers, competitors and public, such as 'the financial community, the media and the general public'. The macro-environment refers to the larger societal settings in which the company operates. Though there may be a supra-environment that affects all individuals all over the world, note that the environments referred to here may vary from one geographic location to another. Keeping track of the pertinent environments is crucial, especially for a company that designs its product line in New York, sources it in various foreign countries and sells it to global markets.

The marketing of fashion goods is not an isolated process (Rogers and Gamans, 1983). Socio-economic trends prevail and need to be interpreted. Social, political, environmental, technological and even legal events are inter-related to the fashions of a country and shape what will be bought and sold, in both an 'overt and subliminal' manner. Forecasting is based on observation and analysis of all these factors, their potential synergies and correlations, to help determine what influences they may have on future consumer behaviour and fashion (Robinson, 1987). The following section will identify how environmental influences interrelate with consumer wants, fashion cycles, brand image and style, thus influencing the design of new products.

The complex environment of design

Fashion permeates all the environments of the apparel design process. Rogers and Gamans (1983) define fashion as 'any form, custom, usage or style during a particular time that is socially accepted'. 'Fashion is everywhere. We wear it; we use it; we ride in it; we look at it; we read it; we listen to it. Society is per-meated with fashion. ' The list of possible demographic and social influences on fashion is enormous (Shah, 1987) and dynamic. 'Fashion can never stand still' (Rogers and Gamans, 1983). Therefore, fashion changes with everything that is happening around us and is strongly dependent on time and context. Global and local conditions create an atmosphere that triggers feelings, atti-tudes and pressures among the consumer population that require change. Therefore, any industry that is related to fashion must understand the con-stantly shifting consumers' inner emotions at the fastest pace possible. 'It is largely psychological motives that encourage the growth, change, and peren-nial quest for newness in fashion' (Rogers and Gamans, 1983). Burns (1998) concludes that fashion can be studied either as an object or idea, or as a pro-cess of change. 'Although the term "fashion" is often associated with dress and adornment, "fashion" can be related to any object or phenomenon that changes over time based upon individuals' preferences'.

All these contextual and individual factors that affect a person's or a group's selection of what they want their appearance to be, interact with fashion. As with dress, fashion both integrates social factors and is itself a social phenom-enon. 'The cyclic changes of fashion currents are cultural factors which in turn influence culture itself' (Entrada, 1998). Rogers and Gamans (1983) examined fashion in a marketing context. They insist that the fashion cycle must be con-sidered when creating a marketing mix and that market positioning and fash-ion image are interrelated.

Fashion cycle

Fashion is both a product and a stimulus of changing consumer needs and wants through time. Therefore, fashion is evolutionary. 'Acceptance of the new requires a rejection of the old and a period of time before it is embraced by a substantial number' (Packard, 1983).

Figures 10.7 and 10.8 show the process of fashion acceptance and the effect it has on various elements of the marketing mix during the life cycle of a garment style (Packard, 1983). The various stages describe the product's life cycle on the marketplace once it has been designed and developed: introduction, growth, maturity and decline. Today, the introduction stage is increasingly intertwined with the product design and development processes, which integrate continuous market information and consumer feedback. Fashion innovators will adopt the style initially. Opinion leaders and early conformists follow and contribute to increasing the popularity of the style. In the maturity stage, the style becomes widely accepted by mass-market consumers, followed by late fashion adopters at the beginning of the decline stage. Finally, 'fashion isolates' and/or

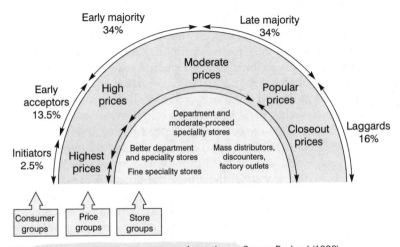

Figure 10.7 Fashion acceptance: consumers, prices, stores. *Source:* Packard (1983).

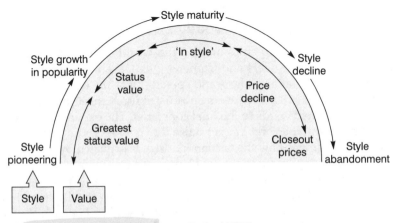

Figure 10.8 Product life span of fashion. *Source:* Packard (1983).

laggards will adopt the style once it has already become obsolete (Kaiser, 1990). Traditionally, these consumer groups were associated with specific types of income levels, social status and lifestyles, as can be determined from the associated price and store groups shown in Figure 10.7. Based on the literature reviewed, these consumer group definitions, based on the trickle down theory of fashion leadership, are no longer restrictively associated with the value, price and store groups defined in Packard's figures.

Style and brand image

Because of their aesthetic component, images have always been important in fashion. 'Dress stimuli' are generally of visual format, such as photographs, drawings, films, video or live encounters (Damhorst, 1990). The visual aspect of clothing is more crucial than ever in today's multi-media 'visual society', here fashion and marketing both focus on image, and where consumers of fashion have become 'consumers of illusion' (Entrada, 1998). Visual images have become more powerful, speaking to a greater number across the globe; aesthetics are critical. Fashion not only focuses primarily on brand image, but fashion has become a mass media in itself. Since 'a picture is worth 1000 words' and is understood internationally, designers who have managed to efficiently market their image have commanded influence and made huge profits in various market categories. Re-targeting or re-launching an image can stimulate total market demand and expand the life cycle of their products and/or their brand(s).

Robinson (1987) believes that since fashion transcends people's lifestyles, distinct brand image and style should transcend corporate culture and structure. To establish a company style, the aim of the business must first be clearly identified, including the target customer, product type and price level. To be successful, the style then needs to be 'consistent'. Building an image can be accomplished with successful marketing and promotion, available time and money, and complete adherence of all company members to the chosen and well-defined style and image.

Environmental sources of creative design

There are now a number of cities around the world considered to be inspirational fashion centres (Rogers and Gamans, 1983). Fashion centres serve as a focal point for new styles and ideas, and spread out to the consumers via retail buyers and fashion media. Producers and distributors meet in order to move the resulting promoted goods to the final consumer. The experts, who populate these fashion centres, interpret market pulse into new styles and predictions.

Perna (1987) illustrates how the fashion industry is activated by various 'gears' which turn in perpetual motion (Figure 10.9), requiring any fashion related company to be plugged into the multiple check points of the fashion information network (Figure 10.10). Shah (1987) claims that it is actually a small group of people who work for trend services or put together exhibitions like Premiere Vision who make fashion. Not only do they research and rationalize all the information, but also 'they co-ordinate their fashion accordingly and they have the muscle and

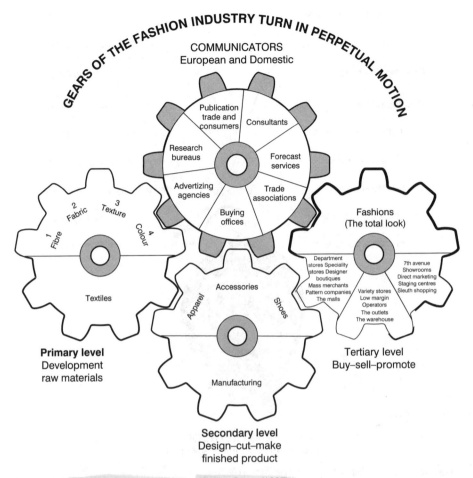

GEARS OF THE FASHION INDUSTRY TURN IN PERPETUAL MOTION

COMMUNICATORS
European and Domestic

Publication trade and consumers

Consultants

Research bureaus

Forecast services

Advertizing agencies

Trade associations

Buying offices

Fashions (The total look)

2 Fabric   3 Texture

1 Fibre   4 Colour

Textiles

Accessories

Department stores Speciality stores Designer boutiques Mass merchants Pattern companies The malls

Variety stores Low margin Operators The outlets The warehouse

7th avenue Showrooms Direct marketing Staging centres Sleuth shopping

Apparel   Shoes

Primary level
Development
raw materials

Tertiary level
Buy–sell–promote

Manufacturing

Secondary level
Design–cut–make
finished product

Figure 10.9 Gears of the fashion industry. *Source:* Perna (1987).

influence to pass on these ideas in a pure and more personalized format to their own clients, magazines, etc'. According to him, this is what makes Paris the styling centre rather than the individualistic Italy.

According to Kurt Salmon Associates' vision of textiles markets in the new millennium, the consumer who has developed a strong sense of individuality, making him or her loyal to only his or her wants, will play an active role in the apparel design process. The industry activities will be redistributed into a 4-D model: designers, developers, distributors and displayers. The first, second and fourth Ds will become 'co-designers' in a virtual network which will ultimately integrate the consumer as well. Consumers will test new designs, colours and sizes via the Internet and in-store direct consumer response. They will actually activate demand when and where they choose. New forms of competition will arise from the potential gain of successfully editing this massive information (Smith, 1995).

It appears that both the consumer and the designer are creative. The designer in the styles imagined, the consumer in the selection and combinations applied.

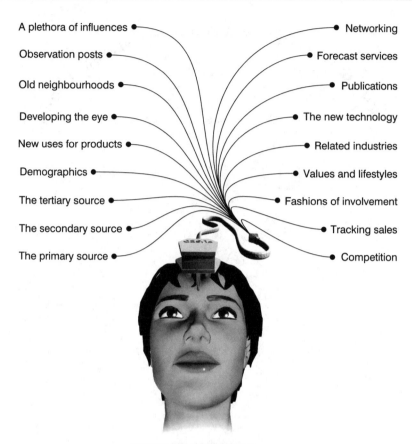

A plethora of influences

Observation posts

Old neighbourhoods

Developing the eye

New uses for products

Demographics

The tertiary source

The secondary source

The primary source

Networking

Forecast services

Publications

The new technology

Related industries

Values and lifestyles

Fashions of involvement

Tracking sales

Competition

INFORMATION NETWORK –
are you plugged into the check points?

Figure 10.10 Information network. *Source:* Perna (1987).

Consumers are potential wearers and/or viewers. These three categories of people (designer, wearer and viewer) influence each other in their personal critical evaluation of a certain way to dress (Figure 10.11). All three are individuals who are part of a specific environment interpreting appearance and dress as forms of expression using all their five senses (Kaiser, 1990).Consumer behaviour and design creativity are affected by multiple factors. Fashion is both a consequence and an inspiration to the interaction between consumers and designers, where aesthetic traits are extremely relevant and changes occur at a rapid pace. Companies must therefore be able to mine available data for adequate information on consumer preferences in design, and establish differences in relation to competitors through creative design that incorporates continuously updated market intelligence.

The model presented in Figure 10.12 shows the various levels of contexts, embedded within one another and defining the perception of clothes. The model attributes a title at each level along with a few non-exclusive examples of

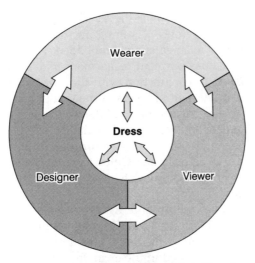

Figure 10.11 Critical framework for evaluating dress. *Source:* Adapted from Bryant and Hoffman (1994).

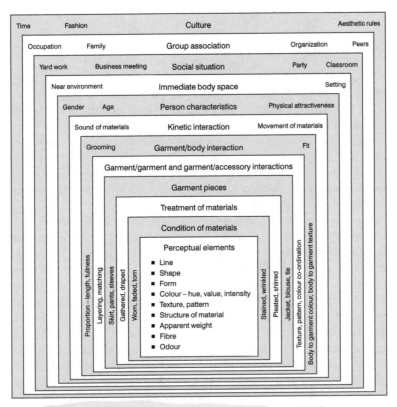

Figure 10.12 Contextual model of clothing sign system. *Source:* Damhorst (1990).

factors influencing that specific context level. The inner layers refer specifically to the complete dress appearance. Clothing, including garment pieces, materials and all perceptual elements are embedded in the larger context of appearance, which includes garment to garment and/or accessory combinations. These are viewed in conjunction with the wearer's body and personal attributes as defined in the central layers of the model. The outer layers represent the micro- and macro-environments of the user, referring to his or her roles and identities. Immediate body space and 'social situation in which a person is observed provides a context for viewing his or her appearance, which may be framed in terms of group associations. Culture provides a larger framework for interpreting that appearance according to aesthetic rules, historical context, and fashion' (Kaiser, 1990).

Identifying the linkages within and across contexts is necessary to understand the similarities and differences in the assignment of meaning to clothing. Defining the contexts that affect the target consumer and understanding their interactions should be integrated in the creative design process because of the impact they have on the consumer's perception and selection of dress elements. The processes explained in this model help understand the dynamics that lie behind fashion and product life cycles, as well as the creative design process. The success of new products builds on the success of previous products.

Creative design

In today's competitive environment, creativity has a prominent place as it is what differentiates market leaders from the runners up (Sheasly, 1996). Creative thinking is the raw material of innovation, which enables a company to do things better, more cheaply, more effectively and more aesthetically (Bati, 1994). If creativity is indeed the main factor that helps differentiate one brand from another, two essential questions need to be addressed. The first is to figure out a way to measure the value of creativity in a product according to the target consumer's perception. Second is to develop a process to achieve this value most effectively and efficiently.

Creativity involves three components: *skills*, *newness* and *value* (Young, 1998). These components make up what is known as the creative product. It is difficult to distinguish between 'the creative product's social value versus its intrinsic value, the simplicity versus complexity criteria, and the distinction between creative achievement, creative skills/abilities/talent, and creative dispositions' (Kato, 1994). Eysenck (1997) distinguishes four general fields of creativity: product, process, person and environment. After briefly reviewing the multiple definitions of creativity and design, these terms will be analysed in a marketing context. This last section will show how the dimensions of value and newness are associated with the product and the market, while the skill component relates more to the process, the environment and of course the person or team who can achieve such a product successfully deemed creative by the target consumer.

'The target consumer could be an individual or a group of individuals (target market)'. Both the designer and the consumer interact with a greater circle denoting culture. In the outer circle, the FEA design criteria are interrelated in various ways depending on the target consumer and use situation. They may be complementary or contradictory, dominant or negligible. The authors suggest pairing the three types of criteria to assess their relative importance. Functional criteria include fit, mobility, comfort and protection. Expressive criteria refer to values, roles, status and self-esteem. Aesthetic concerns deal with art elements, design principles and body/garment relationship. All these criteria could be determined and evaluated using the contextual model of clothing sign system presented in Figure 10.13.

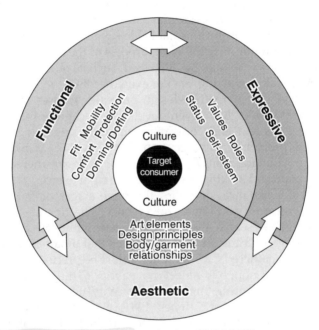

Figure 10.13 FEA consumer needs model. *Source:* Lamb and Kallal (1992).

According to Kato (1994), Besemer and Treffinger's (1981) evaluative criteria defined previously as novelty, resolution, and elaboration and synthesis, can be assimilated with the design criteria of the FEA model. Functionality relates to utility features, which are part of the resolution criteria. Expressiveness is one of the elaboration and synthesis criteria, which refer to 'the particular style the product transpires'. Finally, Kato contends that aesthetics in Western society include such notions as originality and uniqueness, which are classified as novelty criteria.

As stated previously, there is no one formula to creativity. 'Creativity always goes beyond any definition of it', because 'creative behaviour always goes beyond any codification of it' (Young, 1998). It all starts within a person. Tools, models and technology can only support the creative system, but it initially depends on a special blend of inner qualities (Ditkoff, 1998). Creativity results from synergistic interaction of intellectual, intuitive and emotional intelligence (Myers, 1998). Therefore, the creative mind combines a complex combination of various abilities, knowledge, skills, traits and needs.

By definition, creative output should be a surprise outcome, but according to several authors the process leading to successful creative design is predictable. Based on skill, knowledge, inspiration, motivation, experience and problem-solving techniques, designers seek something new by creating change or finding new solutions to old and new problems. The design process transforms ideas into reality and occurs from conception of an idea until the development of a workable solution (van Praag, 1987). LaBat and Sokolowski (1999) believe that by following a structured process it is possible to develop a project in an orderly fashion so as to ensure maximum product design effectiveness and efficiency. It is also useful in establishing realistic timelines and providing a means of communicating the work process of the design team among its members and anyone who may be interested, such as other department managers (marketing, sales, sourcing, etc.) or even the CEO.

Most research done on creative design processes focuses on the cognitive approach. Several models have been developed to capture the sequence and associations of divergent and convergent thinking stages logically used to solve identified problems. 'Divergent thinking involves thinking in different directions or drawing from a wide range of options, whereas convergent thinking focuses on and synthesises toward one right answer' (Kato, 1994).

Jones (1981), for instance, describes the three stages of industrial design as divergence, transformation and convergence. The first stage requires the designer to actively research the entire problem without many constraints. The following stage of transformation 'requires that a pattern be imposed on all the information gathered . . . The pattern must be precise enough to lead to a solution, but broad enough to reflect the realities of the situation'. This stage is the most creative, requiring 'high-level creativity, flashes of insight, changes of set, and inspired guess work' (Jones, 1981). Convergence then reduces the range of options after application of all the required criteria and constraints. According to LaBat and Sokolowski (1999), industrial design processes are most similar to textile design processes because designers in both cases have to 'combine in-depth knowledge of the physical nature of materials and processes with keen awareness of the aesthetic sense of the object'.

Kato (1994) stresses that little research exists on the implementation stage and that most of the research on evaluation deals with evaluating the finished product. How the designer conducts the evaluation is neglected, even though it is an integral part of this individual's creative progress. Kato also highlights that incubation is not addressed in the creative process models applied to apparel design. Many authors contend, however, that time is essential to nurture and stimulate idea generation and thus activate the creative process (Kim, 1990; Turner, 1991; De Bono, 1992; Guilford, 1950). In her doctoral thesis, Secor (1992) confirms that designers complain about having 'too little time to create'.

Design follows a visual thinking pattern (Kato, 1994; Finke, 1997), which comprehends 'ideas in parallel rather than one after the other: shapes, colours and textures as an integrated whole rather than separately' (Carr and Pomeroy, 1992). 'Because apparel is multi-dimensional and experienced through sight, sound, and touch, apparel designers may be particularly sensitive to these sensory modalities as they create apparel'.

Design creativity is a multidisciplinary science on several levels, especially now that much of the creative process is done in teams including designers, stylists, merchandisers and sometimes even buyers. Design creativity interacts with fashion and trends of the times, with the style of the designer, design team and/or company, as well as with the target consumer's needs and wants. Design creativity is personal to the creator's inner qualities or the creative team's synergies.

In their 1992 publication, Lamb and Kallal asserted that any design project requires market intelligence for analysis of FEA criteria of target consumer needs (Figure 10.14): 'success is judged by how well these needs are met in the final product'. However, after comparing their 1992 model with industry practice (Kallal and Lamb, 1993), they realized they had neglected a different category of criteria relative to merchandising and retail needs of the retail customer. Based on their field study, they collected the following criteria cited by selected apparel companies: ability to retail, brand image, calendar, company

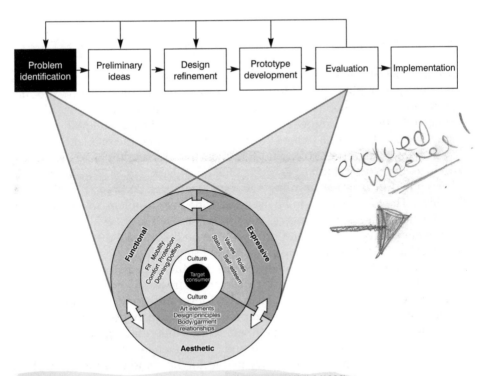

Figure 10.14 FEA design process framework. *Source:* Lamb and Kallal (1992).

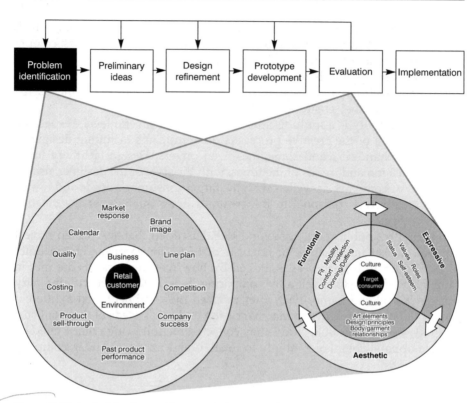

Figure 10.15 Product development framework. *Source:* Kallal and Lamb (1993).

success, competition's past performance, costing and availability of resources and skills, line plan, past product performance, product quality, product sell-through and response to market changes. Therefore, they revised their framework, shown in Figure 10.15, to illustrate that the apparel manufacturer actually caters to two customers, the final consumer and the retailer.

Lamb and Kallal (1992) contend that their model contributes to evaluating products in the marketplace and can thus be considered 'as part of the merchandising function, specifically planning, developing and presenting a product line'. The FEA model can be used to define new problem-solving projects for developing seasonal concepts and styles, as well as to evaluate the suitability of existing products and product lines on their target markets and their potential for adaptation to new target market segments.

Figure 10.16 illustrates how the textile product design process has been delineated into distinct phases by the various researchers. Designers must pursue free flow of ideas with both short-term and long-term solutions in mind. Each season they must design products that satisfy the target consumer or even maybe attract new market segments, while making sure that these products correspond to, perpetuate and/or rejuvenate the company's style and brand image. They must also try to develop new and existing products in a way that will optimize their respective life cycles.

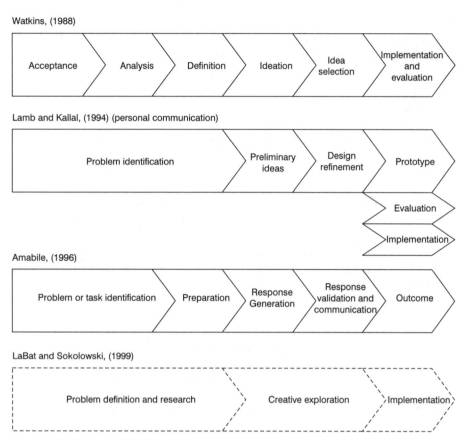

Figure 10.16 Comparing the phase of creative design process models. *Source:* Le Pechoux (2000).

The creative exploration is the least well-defined stage, referred to as the 'creative leap' by Watkins (1988) or 'black box' design by Jones (1981). However, Jones believes this phase can be described, if not explained, in detail and communicated to all design process participants. This 'glass box' approach to design, as he calls it, is a systematic, visible and analytical approach in which sub-functions and links between functions are mapped out, and where patterns are imposed on all the information gathered in the initial stage of the design process. The models reviewed fail to focus on this initial stage, its components and its dynamic structure. A pattern language could provide the tool to map out and move through the archetypal model of this creative process (Le Pechoux, 2000).

Future innovation management practices

The current state of knowledge in the area of creative fashion design teaches us that the dynamics of the industry are a complex system of interactions in the turbulent and unpredictable climate of the *fashionsphere*. Managing innovation poses significant challenges for the practitioners. The knowledge available can be synthesized as follows (Le Pechoux, 2000):

- In the textile and apparel product design and development models reviewed, design emerges as a multidisciplinary science, which is most generally achieved through teamwork.
- Marketing strategy models place design as an integral component of the marketing mix.
- The target consumer is always at the centre of the *fashionsphere*, guiding and constraining the design process and output.
- Consumer-related issues deal with defining personal profiles, social influences, decision processes and the impact of context and perception on product evaluation.
- When fashion is analysed in a marketing context, it becomes a major environmental factor influencing both the consumer and the companies related to textile and apparel design.
  - Fashion affects a product's life cycle and all of the elements of the corresponding marketing mix.
  - Fashion is subject to multiple global sources and movements.
  - Each brand name has a style and image associated with it, which will evolve to a certain extent with overall fashion trends.
- Fashion is a major external source of inspiration and constraint for the creative design process. The design process also depends on the company's internal resources, such as design professionals, design team management and co-ordination with the company's marketing activities.
- The design process aims to create a product that satisfies a target market demand. Consequently, buyers and target consumers define the creative value of the product to be designed.

Developing a pattern language for innovation management

Research (Le Pechoux, 2000) shows that the creative apparel design process can be greatly improved through the development of a generic pattern language by developing a set of interrelated patterns that describes the initial creative phase of the apparel design process. Using the product development, marketing strategy and creative design process models presented earlier in this chapter, along with the internal and external factors that influence these processes, it is possible to build an archetype of this creative process that will incorporate all of the following:

- Focus on the creative phase of the apparel design process.
- Definition of the design and marketing components within that phase.

- Identification of the links between these components and the various stages of the process.
- Dynamic structure based on these links.
- Consideration of environmental factors.
- Evaluation method of the created output.
- Combination of logical thinking, 'educated' processes and sensory 'naive' processes.

The pattern language developed articulates the dynamic structure of the archetype. Patterns describing the links between all the components and stages of the creative apparel design process have been established (Le Pechoux, 2000). The pattern language enhances the understanding of the creative design process and provides a common language for all design professionals practising a 'glass box' approach. However, it can be foreseen that this pattern language can be used to develop a software tool, customized to the needs of design team members, which will help channel creativity in apparel design and optimize the process. Different design teams developing unique styles could use the pattern language describing apparel design creativity. Their creativity will depend on their own interpretation of each individual pattern, and their selection and sequence of patterns composing their personal language. They may even add some patterns of their own making to this language. As prescribed by all pattern language experts, patterns developed by one design professional should be shared with others in order to speed up the process of establishing a comprehensive pattern language for apparel design, and thus benefit the whole apparel design community and its related industries.

References

Alexander, C. (1977). *A Pattern Language: Towns, Buildings, Construction.* Oxford: University Press.

Amabile, T. M. (1996). *Creativity in Context.* Oxford: Westview Press, Harper Collins.

American Apparel Manufacturers Association (AAMA) (1991). The impact of technology on pre-production activities. *TAC Report: The Impact of Technology on Apparel*, pp. 63–68. Washington: AAMA.

American Institute of Certified Public Accountants (AICPA) (1998). Product lifecycle management. *Center for Excellence in Financial Management Business Management Issues.* AICPA/CEFM Publication <http://www.aicpa.org/cefm/plcm/index.html>

Andersson, A. E. (1997). Creativity, complexity and qualitative economic development. In Sahlin, N.-E. *The Complexity of Creativity* (Andersson, A. E. and (Eds), pp. 139–151. Dordrecht: Kluwer Academic.

Bati, A. (1994). Ideas. *Textile Horizons*, **14** (3), 48–50.

Besemer, S. and Treffinger, D. (1981). Analysis of creative products: review and synthesis. *The Journal of Creative Behavior*, **15**, 158–178.

Brown, A. (1997). Micro marketing, relationship marketing. *Class Notes*, Chapter 10 <http://www.udel.edu/alex/chapt10.html>

Bryant, N. O. and Hoffman, E. (1994). A critical framework for exploring the aesthetic dimensions of wearable art. In DeLong, M. R. and Fiore, A. M. *Aesthetics of Textiles and Clothing: Advancing Multi-Disciplinary Perspectives, ITAA Special Publication No. 7* (Eds), pp. 84–96. Monument, CO: International Textile Apparel Association.

Burns, L. D. (1998). *Fashion Theory* <http://osu.orst.edu/instruct/aihm577/fthome.html>

Carr, H. and Pomeroy, J. (1992). *Fashion Design and Product Development*. Oxford: Blackwell Scientific.

Damhorst, M. L. (1990). In search of a common thread: classification of information communicated through dress. *Clothing and Textile Research Journal*, **8** (2), 1–8.

Dammeyer, M. A. (1994). Marketing research: pinning down change. *Industrial Fabric Products Review*, **71** (3), 22–23.

De Bono, E. (1992). *Serious Creativity – Using the Power of Lateral Thinking to Create New Ideas*. New York: Harper Business.

Ditkoff, M. (1998). Qualities of an innovator. *Personal Creativity* <http://www.thinksmart.com/articles/MP_3-4-2.html>

Entrada, J. J. (1998). *Fashion: A Cultural Communication of Image* <http://home.earthlink.net/~entrada/writing/Fashion.html>

Eysenck, H. J. (1997). Creativity and personality. In Runco, M. A. *The Creativity Research Handbook* (Ed.), Vol. 1, pp. 41–66. Creskill, NJ: Hampton Press.

Finke, R. A. (1997). Mental imagery and visual creativity. In Runco, M. A. *The Creativity Research Handbook* (Ed.), Vol. 1, pp. 183–202. Creskill, NJ: Hampton Press.

Gaskill, L. R. (1992). Toward a model of retail product development – a case study analysis. *Clothing and Textile Research Journal*, **10** (4), 17–24.

Guilford, J. (1950). On creativity. *The American Psychologist*, **14**, 444–454.

Jarnow, J. and Dickerson, K. G. (1996). *Inside the Fashion Business*. Upper Saddle River, NJ: Prentice Hall.

Jones, C. (1981). *Design Methods: Seeds of Human Futures*. New York: John Wiley.

Kaiser, S. (1990). *The Social Psychology of Clothing – Symbolic Appearances in Context*. New York: Macmillan.

Kallal, M. J. and Lamb, J. M. (1993). Linking industry practice with apparel design education. In Sillanpaa-Suominen, H. and von Knorring, M. *Lectures and Writings from the International Conference on Fashion Design*, 25–27 May 1993 (Eds.), pp. 253–258. Helsinki: University of Industrial Arts Helsinki UIAH, the Department of Clothing and Fashion Design.

Kato, S. L. (1994). An investigation of the creative process and application to apparel design models. In DeLong, M. R. and Fiore, A. M., *Aesthetics of Textiles and Clothing: Advancing Multi-Disciplinary Perspectives, ITAA Special Publication No. 7* (Eds), pp. 48–57. Monument, CO: International Textile Apparel Association.

Kim, S. H. (1990). *Essence of Creativity, A Guide to Tackling Difficult Problems.* New York: Oxford University Press.

Knox, S. (1989). Design management. *Textile Horizon*, February, 59–61.

Kotler, D. and Armstrong, G. (1994). *Principles of Marketing.* Englewood Cliffs, NJ: Prentice Hall.

Kurt Salmon Associates (KSA) (1996). *KSA Annual Consumer Pulse Survey Results.* KSA Publications, New York.

LaBat, K. L. and Sokolowski, S. L. (1999). A three-stage design process applied to an industry – university textile product design project. *Clothing and Textile Research Journal*, **17** (1), 11–20.

Lamb, J. M. and Kallal, M. (1992). Conceptual framework for apparel design. *Clothing and Textile Research Journal*, **10** (2), 42–47.

Le Pechoux, B. (2000). A pattern language describing apparel design creativity. *Textile Technology and Management Ph.D. Dissertation*, College of Textiles, North Carolina State University, Raleigh, NC, USA.

May-Plumlee, T. and Little, T. (1998). No-interval coherently phased product development model for apparel. *International Journal of Clothing Science and Technology*, **10** (5).

McCann, J. M. (1997). The evolution of marketing systems. *Generation Marketing Insights* <http://www.duke.edu/~mccann/mwb/12partnr.html>

McPherson, E. M. (1987). In Needles H. L. *Apparel Manufacturing Management Systems* (Ed.). New Jersey: Noyes.

Myers, N. (1998). What is this thing called 'Heart Intelligence'? *Personal Creativity* <http://www.thinksmart.com/articles/MP_3-1-1.html>

Packard, S. (1983). *The Fashion Business – Dynamics & Careers.* New York: CBS College Publishing.

Perna, R. (1987). *Fashion Forecasting – A Mystery or a Method?* New York: Fairchild.

Petzinger Jr, T. (2000). There is a new economy out there – and it looks nothing like the old one. *The Wall Street Journal*, 1 January, s. R, 31.

Pitt, T. (1997). 'Advanced' target marketing. *Segmenting and Targeting Markets*, Ch. 6 <http://www.pcola.gulf.net/~tonypitt/mk6.htm>

Remaury, B. (1996). Levolution de la fonction produit/collection. In *Rep`eres Mode & Textile 96*, pp. 178–188. Paris: Institut Français de la Mode.

Rigamonti, A. (1987). Second-generation marketing in the textile industry. In *World Textiles: Investment Innovation Invention*, pp. 229–248. The Textile Institute. Papers presented at the Annual World Conference, 4–7 May 1987, Como, Italy.

Robinson, H. (1987). Fashion: the way forward. In *World Textiles: Investment Innovation Invention*, pp. 249–258. The Textile Institute. Papers presented at the Annual World Conference, 4–7 May 1987, Como, Italy.

Rogers, D. S. and Gamans, L. R. (1983). *Fashion – A Marketing Approach.* New York: CBS College Publishing.

Sadd, D. (1996). Structuring product development for higher profits. *Bobbin*, October, 68–73.

Secor, L. C. (1992). *Computer Usage in Apparel Design and its Effect on Styling and Creativity*. UMI, USA.

Shah, D. R. (1987). Timing: the key to success. In *World Textiles: Investment Innovation Invention*, pp. 269–282. The Textile Institute. Papers presented at the *Annual World Conference*, 4–7 May 1987, Como, Italy.

Sheasly, W. D. (1996). The essence of creativity. *Chemtech*, March, 15–16.

Smith, T. (1995). Vision of changes in textile markets. *Indian Textile Journal*, **105** (4), 166–167.

Solomon, M. R. and Englis, B. G. (1998). Consumer preferences for apparel and textile products as a function of lifestyle imagery. *National Textile Center Briefs*, March, 28.

Tandem Corporation (1997). Decision support in retail: unlocking the power of retail data. *Retail Solution Brief* <http://www.tandem.com/INFOCIR/HTML/BRFS_WPS/DSSRETSB.html>

Turner, J. D. (1991). Activating the creative process. *Textile Chemist and Colorist*, **23** (2), 21–22.

van Praag, L. (1987). Managing design. In *World Textiles: Investment Innovation Invention*, pp. 303–308. The Textile Institute. Papers presented at the Annual World Conference, 4–7 May 1987, Como, Italy.

Watkins, S. (1988). Using the design process to teach functional apparel design. *Clothing and Textiles Research Journal*, **7**, 10–15.

Wickett, J. L., Gaskill, L. R. and Damhorst, M. L. (1999). Apparel retail product development: model testing and expansion. *Clothing and Textile Research Journal*, **17** (1), 21–35.

Young, J. G. (1998). What is creativity? *Adventures in Creativity, A Multimedia Magazine* <http://www.volusia.com/creative/2mag1.htm>

11

Consumers and their negative selves, and the implications for fashion marketing

Emma N. Banister and Margaret K. Hogg

Introduction

The primary focus of this chapter is the interaction between consumers' views of themselves and their use of fashion products and brands as symbols to enhance these views, and more specifically the 'non-choice' or avoidance of other products, and the relationship of these products (or brands) with the self. In its discussion of self-congruency theory, this chapter primarily concentrates on the purchase of clothing brands, the choice of fashion retailers and the selection of images in accordance with views of the self. However, the theory and ideas put forward should be of relevance to any product or product category that can be considered to be high in symbolic meaning. Initially, existing literature concerning symbolic consumption, the self-concept and congruency theory will be outlined. This will be followed by a discussion of the negative aspects of symbolic consumption and a consideration of the influence of *negative selves* on consumption decisions.

Symbolic consumption

Product and brand symbolism recognizes the inability of the economic value of an object to fully capture the actual value of products or brands for many consumers (Levy, 1959; Hirschman and Holbrook, 1980; Solomon, 1983; Richins, 1994), and represents value above the functional value of the product (or brand).

In order to convey symbolic meaning, a minimum of two conditions must be present – a symbol should be identified with a group, and within this group it should communicate similar meanings (Hirschman and Holbrook, 1980; Ligas and Cotte, 1998). The product and brand symbolism literature reflects the idea that aspects of the consumption process allow others to make certain inferences about consumers (Grubb and Grathwohl, 1967, p. 24; Solomon, 1983, p. 320; Freitas et al., 1997; Belk, 1988) and that psychological needs can be achieved through consumption choices (Escalas, 1997). Clothing is a highly symbolic product category and its high visibility means that individuals will often make assumptions about others purely on the basis of their clothing. The symbolic nature of clothing can incorporate clothing styles, brands, retailer outlets, uniforms, membership of particular subcultures and so forth.

> For example, Calvin Klein. When someone buys an item of Calvin Klein branded clothing, they are unlikely to buy items by the label solely as a means of ensuring warmth and cover. Wearing the Calvin Klein label hints at the sophistication and design consciousness of the consumer. The label might be worn by people who want to communicate an element of wealth in addition to an uncluttered lifestyle (the simplicity of the designs) and an appreciation for quality and the finer things in life is likely to be assumed by others.

Symbolic consumption is not limited to the purchase and wearing of fashion items, but includes all social practices. The purchase of products, newspapers and magazines, visiting museums, watching films, even the food that we eat – all these practices are saturated with meanings and values. The meanings and values combine to contribute to consumers' sense of who they are (and who they are not) and what they represent (or do not represent).

Self-concept

Any discussions about identity and the relationship between consumers and their possessions should feature the notion of the *self-concept*. A fairly early definition by Rosenberg (1979, p. 7) is perhaps the most widely used, and considers the self-concept to denote the 'totality of the individual's thoughts and feelings having reference to himself as an object'.

A number of different dimensions of the self-concept have been identified. The most widely explored components are the actual or current self (how a person perceives him or herself), the ideal self (the qualities that an individual would like to possess but falls short of) and the social self (how a person believes that others will perceive him or her). The self-concept is essentially a dynamic structure that changes according to the nature of the social surroundings or situation. Possible selves (which include both hoped for and feared possibilities) can function as incentives for future behaviour (Cross and Markus, 1991; Markus and Nurius, 1986). The central idea, and the importance of possible selves to consumption decisions, is based on the premise that what an individual is striving for is as important as what they currently are. Consumers will make use of negative possible selves as incentives to change their current self or as a motivation to act and consume in a certain way.

The audience

In addition to the self-concept, the notion of an audience plays a significant role in the communication of products' and brands' symbolic properties. The idea of an audience of 'significant others' draws upon Bearden and Etzel's (1982) research concerning reference[1] groups. Consumers will form associations with certain groups that will then influence their behaviour. Consumers will also form stereotypes of the generalized user of the product and form product images, which will then serve to influence the consumer decision-making process (Erickson, 1996). Positive reference groups will encourage consumers to consume in a certain way, while negative groups will discourage the consumption of certain items, with consumers making negative associations on the basis of the negative reference group.

> For example, in schools, cliques of children often exist who tend to dress in similar ways to each other. The style of dress is often informed by other consumption decisions common to the group (e.g. the type of music favoured by group members). Often other pupils (outside of the group) will form general assumptions about the personality of the group rather than relying on the cues of individual group members. The influence of the group therefore functions in two directions. On the one hand, individual group members will be influenced by others within the group, and so their clothing and appearance may be similar. In addition, others (outside of the group) will make certain assumptions about group members on the basis of the generalized group image.

Product and brand imagery

When consumers interpret the imagery associated with a product or a brand, it is often highly linked to the stereotype of the generalized user of the product – Sirgy et al. (1997) refer to this as the product – user image. It is

---

[1]Reference groups are defined as 'a person or a group of people that significantly influences an individual's behaviour' (Bearden and Etzel, 1982, p. 184). For a more detailed explanation of group influence on consumers' behaviour, see Solomon et al. (1999, pp. 268–298).

this image (often informed by the views of the audience) that is considered by Sirgy et al. (1997) to be the most significant in the generation of self-congruency theory. Consumers therefore make judgements and consumption decisions regarding fashion products and brands based on their stereotypical opinions about products and the 'typical consumers' of those products.

> For example, at an airport the observation of others' choice of luggage alone might lead us to make certain assumptions about consumers' lifestyles and even their holiday destinations. A Louis Vuitton luggage set could communicate wealth and style, and observers might assume that the owner is jetting off to an exclusive resort. An old rucksack may be used by someone with a considerably smaller budget, and could indicate a sense of adventure – perhaps someone intending to backpack around the world. The symbolism that consumers attach to these brands would become confused if contradictory messages were communicated (e.g. if the old rucksack was carried by someone wearing an Armani suit).

Self-image/product image congruency

The theory of self-image/product image congruency proposes that connections exist between an *individuals' self-image* and their *consumption decisions* (Erickson and Sirgy, 1992; Kleine et al., 1993; Grubb and Grathwohl, 1967). The *image congruency hypothesis* (Grubb and Grathwohl, 1967, pp. 25–26) links the evaluation and interpretation of product and brand imagery with the self-image and the views of an audience (Figure 11.1). In effect, products and

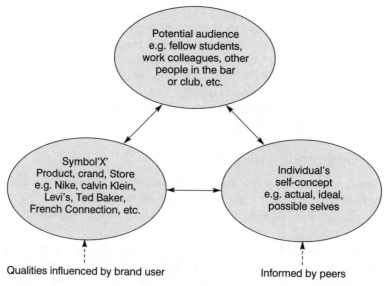

Figure 11.1 The image congruency hypothesis. *Source:* Adapted from Grubb and Grathwohl (1967).

brands are used as instruments to improve individuals' self-image, and the socially attributed meanings of the product are then transferred to individuals through consumption.

An important assumption of the image congruency hypothesis is that the self-concept is valuable to consumers and that individuals therefore will seek to protect and enhance it (Sirgy, 1982, p. 289). This means that if, for example, you are purchasing an item of clothing, you are likely to select a brand name or retailer that conjures up a positive image for you. Often, this positive imagery will be formed on the basis of the *typical user stereotypes* that you associate with that brand. So, for example, you may have a certain set of brands – termed the evoked set – that you would consider acceptable. You would hope (consciously or subconsciously) that by purchasing and wearing an item of clothing identifiable to others as being one of these brands, that the qualities associated with the brand will then be identified with you and effectively communicated to the potential audience.

In essence, the relationship between products and brands (including fashion items) and consumers' identities functions in two directions. On the one hand, the products purchased help consumers to define who they are. On the other, individuals will seek to *maintain* their self-concepts by purchasing items perceived to be congruent with their identity. Therefore, we can see that both the actual self and the ideal self are important players in this relationship.

Self-congruency theory supports the existence of a system of *appearance management*, whereby individuals use clothing as a flexible means to negotiate their identity (Kaiser et al., 1991). We can see from Figure 11.1 that the 'chosen' identity could vary depending on the potential audience (and the situation). Therefore, different sets of brands or fashion retailers would be deemed appropriate in different situations.

Negative symbolic consumption

So far, we have considered how individuals use their identities and the positive images of products and brands to influence their consumption decisions. However, it is also important for fashion marketers and manufacturers and those studying consumer trends to form an understanding of those items, brands and trends which are not attractive to consumers, and more importantly to appreciate *why* items acquire the images that they do. It is suggested that *what we choose not to consume* is an important aspect of both individual and group identity (or identities). Consumers' rejection of fashion items and brands often says as much about them personally and socially as that which they opt to consume. A framework has been developed that incorporates the negative aspects of symbolic consumption, along with congruency theory, in an attempt to understand consumers' rejection of fashion items for symbolic reasons (see also Banister and Hogg 2004; Hogg and Banister 2001).

Possible selves were presented in the self-concept section as *a set of imagined roles* or states of being that can be either positive or negative (Markus and Nurius, 1986). Negative selves work in a conflicting manner operating as (dis)incentives for future behaviour – representing selves to be rejected or avoided (Markus and Nurius, 1986).

Much is made of the concept of taste (e.g. tastes in clothing, furniture, and art) yet it is significant that tastes are often asserted in negative terms. Consumers usually have less difficulty talking about products that they dislike and would not consume than they do in expressing their desires and preferences (Wilk, 1997). Consumers also tend to have little difficulty identifying and articulating the negative product–user stereotypes and the negative inferences that can be associated with product cues.

Similarly to the positive self-concept, a number of negative selves exist. These negative selves operate within the context of possible selves. Two categories of negative selves have been identified, the *undesired* self (Ogilvie, 1987; Banister and Hogg, 2001) and the *avoidance* self (Banister and Hogg, 2001). The characteristics of these and their influences on individual consumption activities will be discussed.

Framework

A framework (Figure 11.2) is depicted which seeks to identify the means by which consumers attach undesirable qualities to items and the likely negative influence of these on their purchase decisions (i.e. rejection or avoidance). This complements the work of Grubb and Grathwohl (1967), who looked at the purchase of products and brands as a means of *self-enhancement*. The framework seeks to understand how *individual* consumers use the consumption process (i.e. in terms of those products they decide to avoid consuming) as a vehicle for creating meaning.

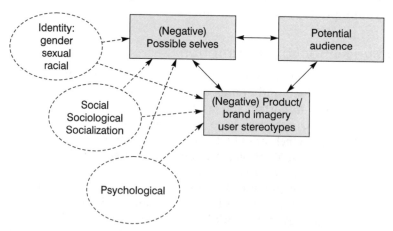

Figure 11.2 Conceptual framework: consumers' interpretation of (negative) product and brand meanings.

The framework (Figure 11.2) depicts the means by which product and brand meanings are interpreted by consumers in the context of (negative) possible selves, and the product and brand user imagery that these negative selves activate. The spheres on the left and the broken arrows depict the probable influences on individual consumers' (negative) possible selves and the stereo-types that are important to them. These influences reflect the fact that different consumers interpret products and brands in different ways, and that much of this variety will depend on their particular identity, as well as social forces and their psychological make up.

Two main facets of negative possible selves will now be outlined; these are the undesired self and the avoidance self. One of these selves, the undesired self, was identified by Ogilvie (1987) and the other was identified by Banister and Hogg (2001). The main difference between the two facets is the more extreme and permanent nature of the undesired self, as opposed to the some-times temporary or transient nature of the avoidance self.

The central idea of these negative selves is that they function as important reference points for consumers, and therefore are significant aspects of iden-tity creation. They will be used by individuals to assess how close or distant they are from being like their most negative (or worst) images of themselves (Ogilvie, 1987; Eisenstadt and Leippe, 1994). Ogilvie (1987) made compari-sons between the undesired self and the ideal self, and found the push (of the undesired self) to be more effective than the pull (of the ideal self) in terms functioning as a standard for measuring one's present place in life.

The undesired self: 'so not me!'

The *undesired self* represents those images that consumers consider to be the most alien to their identity, that is 'so not me! '. The *undesired self* is the most extreme view of the negative self, compared with the *avoidance self*. It is less abstract than the ideal self and consumers often have clear views of the type of people (i.e. the negative user stereotypes) that they would associate with this image (i.e. those consumers who would wear the outfits, brands or retail-ers that they are rejecting). Some of the characteristics associated with the *undesired self* will now be discussed.

Stereotypes

Consumers make use of negative product stereotypes as a means of under-standing the product and brand imagery that accompanies fashion items. These negative stereotypes used by consumers are often labelled, with ideas and assumptions about consumers' lifestyles and their consumption activities accompanying the stereotypes. In this way, negative stereotypes form an inte-gral aspect of the undesired self, and a means by which to express why par-ticular brands, images and retailers are 'so not me! '.

Behavioural and personality assumptions

The main difference that exists between the *undesired self* and the *avoidance self* is the notion that specific 'undesirable' qualities accompany the undesired self.

These behavioural and personality assumptions are informed by the negative stereotypes that are identified with the undesired self, and in certain cases adversely affect individuals' behaviour towards others (Feinberg et al., 1992). It should be remembered that what represents a negative image for one person may well be interpreted positively by a different individual (with a different set of influences on their consumption decisions).

It is not always complete images, but even small details of a person's dress that can communicate fairly specific messages about consumers. For example, an individual with their shirt untucked from their trousers could be assumed to be disorganized on the basis of the lack of organization of their clothing. Where these negative comments concern personality traits, they often serve to ensure that the observer would not consider dressing in a similar way, illustrating the 'push factor' of Ogilvie's (1987) argument concerning the undesired self.

Experience related

It was argued by Ogilvie (1987) that the undesired self is more experience based and less conceptual than the ideal self. Negative images that are connected with clothing are often formed on the basis of previous experience. This previous experience can relate to (usually disliked) others, or it might be defined by a past image that individuals once had – for younger consumers the 'past image' will often have been influenced by their parents. Sometimes, undesired selves that are informed by 'past experience' translate into not making previous 'fashion mistakes' again.

The avoidance self: 'just not me!'

The *avoidance self* can be contrasted with the *undesired self*. The undesired self is *always* viewed negatively – whether in relation to the individual or in relation to someone else. The avoidance self is viewed negatively in relation to the individual, but might well be viewed positively on someone else who has a different lifestyle, is at a different life stage, a different appearance, personality and so forth.

A different set of criteria is significant when looking at the avoidance self – specifically age, body image, character/personality, situation – and many of these are less permanent characteristics than those that are associated with the undesired self.

Age related

The age dimension is one of the most important characteristics of the *avoidance self*. Clothing is often used by others to indicate the age of the wearer, and consumers tend to have established ideas about what form of dress is appropriate for particular age groups. When clothing is worn that is considered to be inappropriate to an individual's age, it is often interpreted to be 'bad taste' and forms an aspect of the avoidance self. The age dimension functions in two directions. On the one hand, individuals are ridiculed for wearing clothing that could be considered as too 'young' for them – 'mutton dressed as lamb'. In addition, much is made of children (especially girls) wearing clothing that is considered to be too old, and therefore inappropriate. In some ways, the 'choice' associated with fashion items is reduced as consumers become older and more concerned about their body image, and this is perhaps again particularly true for women.

The avoidance self recognizes that, throughout an individual's life, different patterns of consumption will be deemed appropriate (and this is particularly the case with clothing), and consumers will adjust their image accordingly, sometimes with items that a few years before represented an avoidance self for them.

Body image

Consumers' body images are relevant to their avoidance self and the associated avoidance of clothing items, brands and images. In many cases, consumers' body image is related to their age. It is usually important to individuals that they wear clothing that is flattering to their body shape, as well as appropriate. Rules about appropriateness will differ between cultures and will also depend on individual lifestyles.

Character/personality

It is important for consumers that the clothing that they wear is considered to be congruent with their character or personality (an aspect of the self-congruency theory). Wearing clothing which does not 'suit' the individual, in terms of their character or personality, is perhaps the major way in which clothing could be considered negatively (activating the avoidance self), in spite of its recognition as a positive image on someone else.

Therefore, individuals need to be aware of what their image is and the type of dress that they can 'get away with' and, linked to this, the particular 'limitations' that exist for them.

> For example, outrageous designs might be considered acceptable for someone with a vibrant and outrageous personality, although on someone a little more reserved they might be viewed as inappropriate or ill suited.

In this way, it is likely that some items/images may be rejected for symbolic reasons (i.e. because of the messages they communicate), but without negative connotations becoming attached to the clothing.

Situational

The clothing that consumers purchase is likely to reflect their individual life situation and the contextual nature of consumption. Davis (1985) saw the relevance of wearer, occasion, place and company to the meanings that clothing communicates.

Consumers' life situations will be partly dictated by occupation, life stage, age or simply their priorities at a particular point in time (Martineau, 1957). Often, situational influences will be a reflection of an individual's very specific ideas about what represents 'me' and therefore by contrast 'what is not me'. At times, what can be termed 'situational not me' will become relevant. Situations which deviate from the 'norm' for individuals, such as job interviews, functions (e.g. weddings and other formal dress occasions) will represent occasions when participants may 'play' a role that is different from their usual (and often preferred) one. In these situations, it becomes necessary for consumers to embrace an image which might normally be associated with their avoidance self.

> For example, a successful job interview could result in a student most happy in jeans and a T-shirt becoming accustomed to wearing a suit on a daily basis. What might have initially represented an 'avoidance self' for the student essentially becomes a part of their positive image or at the very least a 'situational self', that is part of their image in specific situations.

The work environment is a particularly relevant factor in decisions about what to wear in many countries and employment situations. It is often felt to be imperative that the correct signals (e.g. formal, professional, non-sexual) are communicated at work.

The negative self: a summary

Different aspects of the negative self can be identified and classified under two headings. The undesired self ('so not me') embodies the most extreme notions of what is 'not me' and can be linked to the rejection of products/brands and product/brand user stereotypes. The avoidance self ('just not me'), in comparison, embodies less strong views about 'not me' and can be linked to feelings of aversion and the avoidance of products/brands and product/brand user stereotypes. What clearly differentiates the undesired from the avoidance self is that the latter incorporates images that are negative when the images are applied to ourselves, but these images could be viewed positively on someone else (for further reading please see Banister and Hogg 2001; Hogg and Banister 2001; Banister and Hogg 2004).

Implications for fashion marketing

A greater understanding of negative symbolic consumption and knowledge about the different facets or criteria identified with negative selves is important for fashion marketers attempting to understand consumers. Rather than concentrating solely on the positive aspects of product or brand selection, it would be beneficial for those involved in fashion to understand the negative stereotypes and symbolism that is (or becomes) associated with brands, retailers and images. This information can be used in decision-making right the way through the supply chain: from design, buying and merchandising, through to the formulation of effective promotional strategies.

It is important that designers, buyers and manufacturers do not produce or attempt to sell clothing and fashions which conjure up negative associations to their intended customer base. The implications for promotional strategies are two fold. On the one hand, it is important for advertisers to ensure that negative stereotypes and associations do not become associated with products, brands or retailers by consumers within their target market. It should also be possible for advertisers to use a knowledge of negative symbolism or negative selves in advertising campaigns that *encourage* consumers to attach negative stereotypes to the competition. This aim can be achieved without alluding directly to competitors but through the use of slogans[2] and images that play on their target consumers' undesired and avoidance selves.

In order to fully appreciate the 'make-up' of their customer base and potential customers, it is important for companies, particularly those involved with the fickle world of fashion, to begin to form an understanding of this area. It is essential for them to be aware of not just who their customers are, but who they are not, enabling a greater insight into fashion and clothing consumption.

References

Banister, E. N. and Hogg, M. K. (2001). Mapping the negative self: from 'so not me'. . . to 'just not me'. In Gilly, M. C and Meyers-Levy, J. (Eds.), *Advances in Consumer Research*, Vol. XXVIII. Utah: Association for Consumer Research Conference.

Banister, E. N. and Hogg, M. K. (2004). Negative symbolic consumption and consumers' drive for self-esteem: the case of the fashion industry. *European Journal of Marketing*, **38** (7), 850–868.

Bearden, W. O. and Etzel, M. J. (1982). Reference group influence on product and brand purchase decisions. *Journal of Consumer Research*, **9** (September), 183–194.

Belk, R. W. (1988). Possessions and the extended self. *Journal of Consumer Research*, **15** (September), 139–168.

Cross, S. and Markus, H. (1991). Possible selves across the life span. *Human Development*, **34**, 230–255.

Davis, F. (1985). Clothing and fashion as communication. In Solomon, M. R. (Ed.), *The Psychology of Fashion*. Lexington Books, pp. 15–27.

[2]To some extent, this is already being done, through the usage of such slogans as 'beware of cheap imitations' or 'stand out from the crowd'.

Eisenstadt, D. and Leippe, M. R. (1994). The self-comparison and self-discrepant feedback: consequences of learning you are what you thought you were not. *Journal of Personality and Social Psychology*, **67** (4), 611–626.

Erickson, M. K. (1996). Using self-congruity and ideal congruity to predict purchase intention: a European perspective. *Journal of Euromarketing*, **6** (1), 41–56.

Erickson, M. K. and Sirgy, M. J. (1992). Employed females' clothing preference, self-image congruence, and career anchorage. *Journal of Applied Social Psychology*, **22** (5), 408–422.

Escalas, J. E. (1997). Meaningful self-brand connections: the incorporation of brands into consumers' self concepts. Unpublished paper.

Feinberg, R. A., Mataro, L. and Burroughs, W. J. (1992). Clothing and social identity. *Clothing and Textiles Research Journal*, **11** (1), 18–23.

Freitas, A., Davis, C. H. and Kim, J. W. (1997). Appearance management as border construction: least favorite clothing, group distancing and identity . . . not! *Sociological Inquiry*, **67** (3), 323–335.

Grubb, E. L. and Grathwohl, H. L. (1967). Consumer self-concept, symbolism and market behaviour: a theoretical approach. *Journal of Marketing*, **31**, 22–27.

Hirschman, E. C. and Holbrook, M. B. (1980). Symbolic consumer behaviour. *Proceedings of the Conference on Consumer Esthetics and Symbolic Consumption*, May. New York: Association for Consumer Research.

Hogg, M. K. and Banister, E. N. (2001). Dislikes, distastes and the undesired self: conceptualizing and exploring the role of the undesired end state in consumer experience. *Journal of Marketing Management*, **17** (1–2), 73–104.

Kaiser, S. B., Nagasawa, R. H. and Huttton, S. S. (1991). Fashion, postmodernity and personal appearance: a symbolic interactionist formulation. *Symbolic Interaction*, **14** (2), 165–185.

Kleine, R. E., Kleine, S. S. and Kernan, J. B. (1993). Mundane consumption and the self: a social-identity perspective. *Journal of Consumer Psychology*, **2** (3), 209–235.

Levy, S. J. (1959). Symbols for sale. *Harvard Business Review*, **37** (4), 117–124.

Ligas, M. and Cotte, J. (1998). The process of negotiating brand meaning: a symbolic interactionist perspective. *ACR Competitive Paper* (1999), *Proceedings*.

Markus, H. and Nurius, P. (1986). Possible selves. *American Psychologist*, **41** (9), 954–969.

Martineau, P. (1957). *Motivation in Advertising: Motives that Make People Buy*. New York: McGraw-Hill.

Ogilvie, D. M. (1987). The undesired self: a neglected variable in personality research. *Journal of Personality and Social Psychology*, **52** (2), 379–385.

Richins, M. L. (1994). Valuing things: the public and private meanings of possessions. *Journal of Consumer Research*, **21** (December), 504–521.

Rosenberg, M. (1979). *Conceiving the Self*. New York: Basic Books.

Sirgy, M. J. (1982). Self-concept in consumer behaviour: a critical review. *Journal of Consumer Research*, **9** (December), 287–300.

Sirgy, M. J., Grewal, D., Mangkeburg, T. F., Park, J., Chon, K., Claiborne, C. B., Johar, J. S. and Berkman, H. (1997). Assessing the predictive validity of two methods of measuring self-image congruence. *Journal of the Academy of Marketing Science*, **25** (3), 229–241.

Solomon, M. R. (1983). The role of products as social stimuli: a symbolic interactionist perspective. *Journal of Consumer Research*, **10** (December), 319–329.

Solomon, M., Bamossy, G. and Askegaard, S. (1999). *Consumer Behaviour: A European Perspective*. London: Prentice Hall Europe.

Wilk, R. R. (1997). A critique of desire: distaste and dislike in consumer behaviour. *Consumption, Markets and Culture*, **1** (2), 175–196.

12

Fashion retailer desired and perceived identity

Tony Hines, Ranis Cheng and Ian Grime

Questions of identity are clearly central to fashion marketing. In the chapter on segmentation identity is an important issue for targeting customers. However, a theory of identity is difficult in the sense of certainty as was demonstrated in that chapter. Most identities are socially constructed rather than possessing clearly discernable characteristics that are universally observable. Even when individuals consider themselves and others it is difficult to say with any certainty what the identity of themselves and others might be. Consider your own position sometimes you may observe others and draw conclusions about others from their observable appearance. However, judgements are coloured by who we are and how we interpret what we see. We collectively and individually are products of our time, formed by our experiences of being in the world. We have reference groups such as friends, colleagues, family and we often characterize these relationships temporally. Time becomes a locator an identifier for who we are and for who they are. The 'I' of this moment is present in the 'me' of the next moment (Mead, 1934). Thus Mead locates the self in two parts related temporally. 'I' is what you were and are in a Heidegerrian sense 'being' whereas 'me' is what you are 'becoming'. The key point is that 'I' can alter through social interaction and 'me' is the result.

In fashion all human life is observable. We refer to lifestyle as a concept, 'she is a minimalist, he is contemporary, they are so 1960s' are representative of our everyday language identifiers for particular lifestyles. We are always searching consciously and/or unconsciously for differences and similarities between individuals and groups of people. Our point of reference is often ourselves or groups to which we belong and identify with. We like to categorize and label what we think we see through judgements we make. It is the empiricist in us all that allows us to do this without necessarily being trained to do so although some of us may be trained tacitly or explicitly through our own life-being. Many of us continually people watch and from observed interactions make judgements relating to human characteristics that provide us with key identifiers: age, gender, size, dress sense, intelligence, class, beliefs, attitudes and so on. Not many of us would acknowledge complete certainty in these contextual judgements. Many of us might recognize multiple identities for any single person: Mother, wife, professional, fashionable, young, old, sister, dancer, student, sportswoman, musician and so on. These multiple identities then become identifiers in particular contexts with particular individuals and groups of others. These multiple identities lead to multiple marketing opportunities for fashion retailers if they can create a match between identity and products they wish to supply. However, as we have witnessed in the segmentation chapter this is not an easy task. Our social constructions of who we are and who others are shifts through time and so in effect creates a moving target for the fashion marketer. Perhaps this singular observation has led fashion retailers to concentrate more on product than market. In other words if you develop products and place them on offer in stores customers find them. Whereas the marketing concept refers to notions of understanding who customers are and what they buy with the purpose of creating products to satisfy the discernable demand. If retailers follow the first route to market focusing on product and place then this has implications for identity. In this context it is the retailer identity that is important rather than the customer identity. This is so because customers identify with the retailer and their products to build parts of their own multiple identities manifested through what they wear. This notion of retail identity and its importance in fashion markets is what the rest of this chapter will focus on.

Corporate identity

Corporate identity is increasingly popular within the retailing industry. This is because the sector depends heavily on its staff at the store level to interact and communicate the identity to customers (Kennedy, 1977; Burghausen and Fan, 2002). Nevertheless, there is limited empirical research on corporate identity (Balmer, 1998; 2001a; Cornelissen and Elving, 2003), and more particularly within a retailing context (Burt and Sparks, 2002). Although the literature which considers how audiences recognize corporate identity has developed in recent years; for example, Balmer and Soenen (1999), Kiriakidou and Millward (2000) and van Rekom (1997), their research tends to focus more on the gap between desired identity and actual identity. There is a paucity of research related to how customers perceive corporate identity. Therefore, the purposes of this paper are to examine the role of corporate identity within the context of UK fast fashion retail industry. The aim is to analyse the gap between desired corporate identity [D] and perceived corporate identity [P] by uncovering the top management and customers' perceptions towards the concept of corporate identity.

Perspectives on the development of corporate identity research

Corporate identity first came to light with Lippincott and Margulies's (1957) and Margulies's (1977) studies which have coined the concept with organization's visual identity and corporate image, respectively. Since then, the popularity of corporate identity has risen and there have been a plethora of corporate identity definitions and theories, which have been developed by both practitioners and academics. To many corporate identity consultants and scholars, corporate identity is *'a visual statement of who and what a company is'* (Gregory and Wiechmann, 1999: 64) and it *'must be visible, tangible and all-embracing'* (Olins, 1994: 7). What corporate identity is concerned with is how these visual elements can distinguish one organization from the others and how they are related to corporate image (Gregory and Wiechmann, 1999). Corporate identity can be seen as visual arrangement of elements which include the corporate name, logo, tagline (Alessandri, 2001), company housestyle (van Riel and Balmer, 1997), building and advertising (Gregory and Wiechmann, 1999) and other publicity components (Cornelissen and Elving, 2003). In this sense, corporate identity is closely related to organizational symbolism in which consistency is emphasized (Bernstein, 1989; 1996; Balmer, 1998; Leitch and Motion, 1999). Practitioners from North America, including Margulies (1977), have brought an extra dimension into corporate identity management which includes graphic design and the symbolism and have associated the concept of corporate identity with corporate image. This visual notion is then supported by some British writers, such as Olins (1978; 1978–1979) and Bernstein (1989), who also assert the importance of corporate identity to organizational values and organizational culture, especially in communicating to internal stakeholders (Balmer, 1998).

There is growing interest amongst academics and practitioners who advocate the idea that corporate identity should not merely be described in visual terms, Balmer (1995, p. 25), for instance, refers the corporate identity as *'the distinct attributes of an organization'*; Topalian (1984), explains corporate identity can articulate what an organization is; and Harris and de Chernatony (2001, p. 268), denote corporate identity as *'organization's ethos, aims and values which create a sense of individuality which differentiates a brand'*. Hence, corporate identity has been conceptualized as an organizational focus concept that is multidisciplinary in nature (van Riel and Balmer, 1997; Balmer and Dinnie, 1999;

Knox and Bickerton, 2003). The evidence suggests that there are divergent views within the literature defining and theorizing corporate identity (Balmer and Wilson, 1998; Kiriakidou and Millward, 2000; Alessandri, 2001; Cornelissen and Elving, 2003). Corporate identity is defined as *'the set of meanings by which an object allows itself to be known and through which it allows people to describe, remember and relate to it'* (van Rekom, 1997, p. 411). Corporate identity does not simply refer to what an organization is, it is related to how an organization delivers its identity to the public and how its stakeholders perceive its identity. van Rekom's definition is an appropriate definition to use when addressing the identity gap due to its broad description of corporate identity.

Identity gap

Corporate identity is about how an organization presents itself to the public and the stakeholders and how an organization distinguishes itself from other organizations (Markwick and Fill, 1997). With this in mind, corporate identity can be described as ways that an organization delivers its identity, that is, what an organization is to its stakeholders (Balmer, 1995).

An increasing number of studies are concerned with the differences in the ways that audiences recognize corporate identity (van Rekom, 1997; Balmer and Soenen, 1999; Hatch and Schultz, 2000; 2001; Kiriakidou and Millward, 2000; Balmer, 2001b). van Rekom's (1997) study, for instance, was the first to pinpoint different types of corporate identity. There is a notable divide between how the management wants the organization to be that is desired identity (van Rekom, 1997, p. 412; Balmer and Soenen, 1999, p. 82), and what the organization actually is (there is variation in the literature regarding the terminology used to describe what the organization actually is, for example, what the operational reality of organization is (Kiriakidou and Millward, 2000), its factual identity (van Rekom, 1997, p. 412), or as Balmer and Soenen (1999, p. 82) call it, its actual identity (Balmer and Soenen, 1999, p. 82)).

While many studies have focused on the gap between desired identity (management's vision) and actual identity (how employees perceive corporate identity), there is lack of attention towards how customers perceive on organization's identity, (i.e. perceived identity). If corporate identity as previously defined as how an organization presents itself, in other words, what the organization is, to its internal and external audiences; then it is equally important to understand how these audiences perceive its identity. This article echoes Hatch and Schultz's (2003, p. 1047) views on the success of corporate branding based on the interplay between strategic vision, organizational culture and corporate image. We argue that the interplay between various concepts of corporate identity perceived by different audiences, including the top management, organizational members and external stakeholders, can also contribute to the effective corporate identity management. In this discussion, we particularly focus on the interplay and gap between desired identity and perceived identity.

Based on Hatch and Schultz's model, the concept of vision, culture and image indicate that there are gaps between these interfaces, which can be termed as the vision–culture gap, the image–culture gap, and the vision–image gap. Amongst these three interfaces, vision–culture gap (desired identity and actual identity gap) has attracted the most attention while the vision–image gap (desired identity and perceived identity gap) has been neglected. For example, in Kiriakidou and Millward's (2000) study, they examine the 'degree of fit' between the desired and actual identity based on employees' perceptions. However, despite an increasing number of studies in this area, there is still a paucity of empirical research which explores the desired – vis-à-vis perceived identity gap. Therefore, the focus is to identify the gap between the desired identity and perceived identity. More specifically, we investigate the gap between the corporate and management visions of the organization, which are often decided by the top management team (desired identity) and customers' perceptions towards the organization's identity (perceived identity).

Corporate identity constructs

The extant literature has considered a number of dimensions of corporate identity as presented in Figure 12.1. Schmidt (1995) proposes five main constructs of corporate identity, including corporate culture, corporate behaviour, products and services, communications and designs and market conditions and strategies; van Riel and Balmer (1997) suggest that the way for organizations to obtain favourable corporate reputation and better organizational and financial performance is to use corporate identity mix which consists of behaviour, communication and symbolism (Stuart, 1999). Balmer and Soenen (1999) introduce a novel corporate identity mix as being composed of the soul, mind and voice. Melewar and Saunders (2000) propound that Balmer and Soenen's corporate identity mix should also include the body of the organization, such as the location, building and the nationality of the corporation. The above studies suggest that although various authors identify and categorize the identity constructs and components in different ways, their views harmonize with each other. Although there are different notions on the terminology and elements of the corporate identity constructs, they should not be regarded as stand-alone constructs; they should be viewed from a holistic perspective, as integrated mixes of corporate identity. Our approach here mainly adopts Schmidt's (1995) corporate identity constructs as they largely coincide with and overlap with other authors' constructs, as seen in Figure 12.1.

Corporate culture

Some authors may argue that corporate culture is notably the most import-ant element of corporate identity formation (Baker and Balmer, 1997) and the corporate culture should reflect organization's missions and ethos. In order to have a successful corporate brand, an organization should understand its corporate

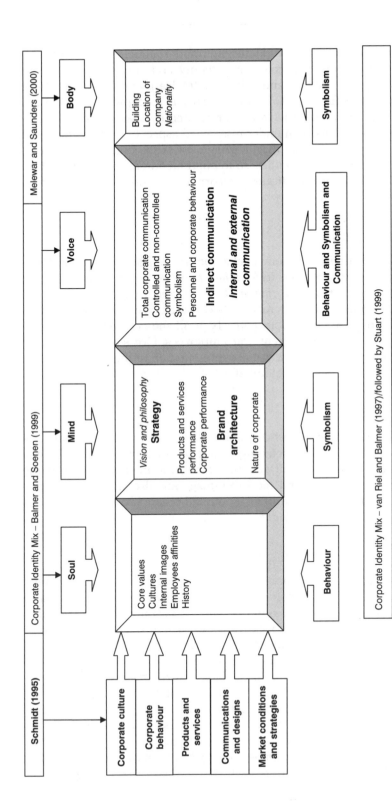

Figure 12.1 Components of corporate identity mix, from Schmidt (1995), van Riel and Balmer (1997) Balmer and Soenen (1999), Melewar and Saunders (2000).

identity and its corporate culture (Hankinson and Hankinson, 1999; Balmer, 2001a). There is no doubt that corporate identity and corporate culture are interrelated (King, 1991; Balmer and Wilson, 1998; Harris and de Chernatony, 2001; Cornelissen and Elving, 2003) as the former is an expression of the latter. Personnel play a crucial role in corporate identity management as they mediate the messages. This is an under researched aspect of identity in a retail context. Therefore, it is essential that management of the organization makes attempts towards minimizing conflicts so to build favourable corporate culture and avoid any dilution relating to desired corporate identity (Suvatjis and de Chernatony, 2005).

Corporate behaviour

Schmidt (1995, p. 36) defines corporate behaviour as *'the sum total of those actions resulting from the corporate attitudes which influence the identity, whether planned in line with the company culture, occurring by chance or arbitrary'*. These actions are important in determining an organization's corporate identity (Melewar and Jenkins, 2002). Corporate behaviour consists of all the behaviours within an organization including management and employees. Occasionally, corporate behaviour sometimes can act as a visual representation of the organization to the public (Suvatjis and de Chernatony, 2005).

Products and services

Products and services must reflect corporate mission and organizational philosophies (Balmer, 1995). In the retailing sector, products and service designs are not the only determinants of success, rather, the interior design of the stores, visual merchandising and the store image are also critical influences. Perhaps this is even more so within fashion retail where image and identities play a significant role in marketing.

Communications and designs

Communication plays an important role in corporate brand management (Bickerton, 2000), both at internal and external levels. Organizations need to transmit their policies to employees through internal communication channels; employees, then, can collect feedback from external stakeholders and report back to the organization (Kennedy, 1977). Suvatjis and de Chernatony (2005) suggest this is a two-way communication channel which transmits and receives information from both within and outside the organization. Internal communications can take different forms, such as formal, informal, written, oral, verbal and non-verbal (Rode and Vallaster, 2005). There are also relationship management communications which mainly target non-customer stakeholders and market communication which use corporate designs, corporate advertising, corporate events and corporate sponsoring to communicate to stakeholders (Einwiller and Will, 2002). Some organizations use their logos to communicate their identities to the public (Foo and Lowe, 1999). Corporate design consists of all the visual elements of an organization; its corporate logo, trademark, symbol, colour, shapes and typeface, sometimes may be called visual identity (Baker and Balmer, 1997).

Market conditions and strategies

According to Melewar and Woodridge (2001), the nature of the industry and the products and services the organization offers have an impact on its corporate strategy. It should include all the marketing strategies and how organization differentiates itself form the competitors in the industry.

Introducing the cases

Two illustrative cases were selected with the aim of investigating how top management within the fashion retail sector present their corporate identities to the public and how customers perceive these identities. Burt and Sparks (2002) suggest that the retailing industry lacks sufficient empirical work on corporate identity. This is particularly the case within the fast fashion retail sector. Furthermore, this is perhaps an industry where image and identity concepts are arguably more important than any other (Hines and Bruce, 2001). This research has focused on two of the most popular international clothing retailers, Hennes and Mauritz (H&M) and Zara both of which operate in fast fashion.

The main criterion for individuals to participate in this study is that they must have experienced shopping in either of the two retail chains. All selected participants were professionals aged between 21 and 39 years which are congruent with the two fashion retail chains' target audiences who are between 20 and 45 years old (Mintel, 2002).

The 'fast fashion' mantra has become a significant phenomenon throughout the UK clothing industry. Many clothing retailers have shifted their attention to fast and disposable fashion (Mintel, 2004). Fast fashion has a number of characteristics identified by Hines (2004, pp. 89–90) which in summary are: fast store throughput time which in turn attracts increased footfall through more frequent store visits, replenishment lead times are not an issue because retail organizations operating in the fast fashion sector do not replenish but rather move on to something new – hence fast fashion is new fashion. Both H&M and Zara have been selected as case studies to illustrate this phenomenon of retail identities due to their popularity and profile within the UK and in the international fast fashion clothing market. These two retailers are often viewed as potentially similar in their identities, merchandise, target audiences and their operations in the fast fashion clothing market.

The unit of analysis in each case is the organization's corporate identity. Each case consists of two embedded units of analysis, including how customers perceive an organization's identity (perceived identity) and how the organization presents its identity to the public (desired identity).

Case studies can adopt different types of quantitative and qualitative research paradigms (Eisenhardt, 1989), and select multiple data sources, such as detailed observations, interviews, documents, archives, and participant observations (Stake, 1995; de Weerd-Nederhof, 2001; Rowley, 2002; Yin, 2003). Furthermore, case studies may also be used to build theory and are particularly useful in this context when the phenomenon under examination is underexplored (Eisenhardt, 1989; Stake, 2000).

Desk research was carried out to establish the desired identity and in-depth interviews were conducted to establish perceived identity. Two evidence sources were used in the present study: documentary evidence and customer interviews. The retailers' websites, press releases and other public materials such as fashion magazines and market reports were used to compile an understanding of desired identities (Sinkovics et al., 2005). Essentially these evidence sources reflect what the top management of the retailers wants the companies to become.

The fundamental process of analysis used *a priori* thematic codes drawn from the literature review for development of a corporate identity mix, shown in Figure 12.1. Five main constructs were identified and they were:

1 corporate culture;
2 corporate behaviour;
3 products and services;
4 communications and design;
5 market conditions and strategies.

The purpose of this research being to identify the gaps between each retailer's desired and perceived identity.

What did we learn from the cases?

This section examines the gap between organizations' desired identity and perceived identity. The results have been compiled by focussing on the key components of the corporate identity mix identified in Schmidt's (1995) framework. The key findings for the two case studies are presented in Tables 12.1 and 12.2.

Hennes and Mauritz's case

The (H&M), is also known as Hennes and Mauritz AB. It was founded in 1947 and it is originated in Sweden. H&M is considered to be one of the fastest growing clothing retailers that sell cheap and chic fashion. H&M operates its business mainly within Europe, the US and Canada (Mintel, 2005). H&M sells its own label clothing. Its products are all under the H&M logo and a variety of sub-brands. According to Mintel's (2004), H&M has established a strong brand image and reputation for affordable fashion clothing in the UK H&M has become increasingly popular. Seven percent of all women, mostly from the ABC1 social group, have bought clothing from H&M (Mintel, 2004).

Table 12.1 Case Study 1: Hennes and Mauritz (H&M) – desired identity and perceived identity

	Desired identity[a]	Perceived identity[b]
H&M's Corporate Identity?	'Provides fashion and quality at the best price'	'H&M is just like a brand, it does not tell the public anything about it. . .it sells bags of cheap disposable clothes to women, men, teenagers and children' 'What I think of them is they are highly fashionable' 'They offer the latest, most trendy things at affordable prices' 'A very cheap, fast, low quality organization'
Corporate culture	'H&M was established in Sweden in 1947 by Erling Persson' Adopts direct communication approaches with staff 'Open door spirit' 'Provide fashion and quality at the best price'	H&M is German/French/Dutch/Swiss/British 'The staff are trendy, young most of the time and they are relaxed' 'I wouldn't say it looks like Scandinavian and Swedish in terms of culture' 'I mean in terms of culture, they are quite informal as well' 'In terms of quality of clothing, I wouldn't say they are really good quality' 'It's cheap, perky, disposable fashion I would say, rather than quality fashion'
Corporate Behaviour	'Everyone works towards the same goal – give customers unbeatable value through fashion, quality and price' 'Our customers' shopping experience will be formed by their personal reception from our employees as well as other impressions' 'H&M provides internal training in customer care'	'I don't think the staff management is very good because if you go to H&M on any day, there is always massive queue at the checkouts' 'The interaction that I have in the past seems that the staff are not organized. They do not always know where thing are, they are not always helpful' 'Customer services hasn't seem to be high on their agenda'
Products and Services	'Giving the customer unbeatable value through the combination of fashion, quality and price . . . provides internal training in customer care' 'All garments in H&M's collection go through a number of quality and security tests'	'I don't think they are very good at customer services, not something that they are actually focusing on a lot' 'Variety, massive variety. You got lots of styles and themes' 'I'm more conscious of buying clothes from H&M because the quality aspects'

(Continued)

Table 12.1 (*Continued*)

	Desired identity[a]	Perceived identity[b]
Communications and Designs	'Creates a comfortable and inspiring atmosphere in the store. . .great efforts have been put into the layout of stores and the way in which the goods are presented. . . shopping in H&M should be an easy, pleasant and inspiring experience' 'Communicate what H&M stand for and what they offer customers'	'I've never really thought about the décor, all I though about is how the hell you are going to find anything in here, it's just crammed out' 'The clothes are fashionable, the designs are there' 'The store is very messy and they have too many clothes' 'When I see the logo, I would be like – Yuk! It's not fashionable, it's not nice. It doesn't say anything. What is H&M? You can't associate it with anything.'
Market Conditions & Strategies	Advertising campaigns around Europe & in parts of US Has one of the fastest turnaround time. Products can move from drawing board to store shelves in as little as 3 weeks	'Given the age group, I would say their competitors are Topshop, Miss Selfridge, I wouldn't necessarily say Zara, Mango or River Island because they are slightly better quality and better organized'

[a] Desired identities taken from documentary sources in the public domain
[b] Perceived identities generated from interview data with customers

Table 12.2 Case Study 2: Zara – desired identity and perceived identity

	Desired identity[a]	Perceived identity[b]
Zara's Corporate Identity?	Refer its corporate logo as the company's corporate identity	'You can't really tell by looking at the logo what Zara is about, unless you actually go into he stores and have a look around to see it yourself'
Corporate Culture	'Corporate culture is characterized by teamwork in a horizontal structure, where open communication and accountability at all levels are the foundations for motivation and personal commitment to customer satisfaction'	'Zara's culture is clearly defined. They want to have high quality clothes appealing to specific audiences, to young professionals' 'The culture of Zara emphasizes the importance of high quality clothing at reasonable price. You can see the mentality has been transmitted to the staff as well. They are very helpful and professional'

(*Continued*)

Table 12.2 (Continued)

	Desired Identity[a]	Perceived Identity[b]
Corporate Behaviour	'Inspires staff to motivate themselves to satisfy customers' 'Keeps business transparent and build relationships with all groups that hold a stake in Zara' 'Responsible and socially committed company' 'Offers customers a standard of excellence in all its products'	'The managers are all well trained. If you ask the staff questions, they are always there to help you. They always know the information about the products' 'I think the staff have an idea of what the image of Zara is, the brand and the managers want them to portray' 'The staff certainly have trainings. They are quite laid back but helpful'
Products and Services	'Designs are inspired from prevailing trends in fashion market and from customers' Provides quality clothing to customers Have a strong customer focus	'Their clothes are generally very stylish, but not practical' 'They sell fashion smart and fashion casual ranges to customers' 'They have variety of clothes' 'The quality of clothes are good, excellent, but it does not always fit though' 'Services, I think it's excellent. I've never had a complaint, and I've never encountered a problem'
Communications and Designs	'The store are designed to create a special atmosphere that will allow the client to feel the pleasure of buying fashion' Encourages horizontal communication within Zara Customers are free to express views and opinions on fashion	'Zara's logo is one of the most recognizable logo in fashion industry, along with a couple of others, like H&M, very strong brands' 'The logo is just the name really. I don't know what Zara means' Their communications are very structured. The staff know when and where to call the managers'
Market Conditions and Strategies	Target customers from all generations Uses fashion to bring people together 'The ability adapt the offer to meet customer desires in the shortest time possible'	'I don't think they target students really, young professionals are certainly one' Competitor could be FCUK because recently they are trying to look very smart casual' 'It may have competitions from two different angles, one is coming from high end, like Austin Reed, Reiss, Ted Baker, FCUK, the other one is Topman, River Island and may be H&M, but I'm not sure'

[a] Desired identities taken from documentary sources in the public domain
[b] Perceived identities generated from interview data with customers

Corporate identity

Customers perceive corporate identity of fashion retailers different than other sectors. Participants have expressed how they perceive corporate identity, as one customer from the H&M's case explained:

> . . . I think corporate identity refers to how people look at the stores externally and internally. I don't know, the concept is probably associating with the whole experiences of shopping in the stores, so the staff, the services, the atmosphere of the stores should be part of it.
>
> H&M Interviewee no. 3

Although H&M presents itself as a clothing retailer in its website and press release as:

> Provides fashion and quality at the best prices.
>
> Hennes and Mauritz, 2006

Participants' views contradict the desired identity of H&M, as one customer said:

> H&M is just like a brand, it does not tell the public anything about it . . . it sells bags of cheap disposable clothes to women, men, teenagers and children.
>
> H&M Interviewee no. 6

Corporate culture

According to Hennes and Mauritz (2006) website, H&M is a Swedish clothing retailer with its head office based in Stockholm. However, the participants either recalled H&M's nationality as 'Dutch', 'German', 'British' or 'French' and portrayed H&M's culture as *'they are relaxed'*, *'it's quite informal'*, *'continental European'*, *'trendy and pop'*. In fact, H&M describes its communication approach with employees as direct. The retailer outlines its philosophy on its website as:

> To give the customer unbeatable value by offering fashion and quality at the best price.
>
> Hennes and Mauritz, 2006

Most recently, H&M's online press release described its mission as:

> To offer new fashion concepts and good quality at exceptional prices

Conversely, participants perceived H&M as a low quality fashion retailer that sells clothes at cheap price, as one of the participants said:

> In terms of quality of products, I wouldn't say they are really good quality, because most of the time they keep the production costs low, and the clothes don't last long and they keep shrinking.
>
> H&M Interviewee no. 4

Corporate behaviour

H&M acknowledges that its staff is the most important channel to deliver its identity to the customers and the retailer offers internal training to its employees, as indicated on its website and public releases:

> Our customers' shopping experience will be formed by their personal reception from our employees as well as other impressions . . . H&M provides internal training in customer care, displays, textiles, leadership and H&M's basic values.
>
> Hennes and Mauritz, 2006

In spite of this, participants had negative perceptions towards the employees' behaviour of H&M. H&M's staff are not well trained and there is lack of communications between the company and the staff. The employees do not have sufficient knowledge on the products, one participant from an interview pointed out:

> . . . I mean what kind of training do they need if they have a relaxed approach? I don't think the part-time staff know about the products. I mean, let's be realistic, they only come to work once or twice per week, so would they know all the products' information? . . .
>
> H&M Interviewee no. 5

It was widely believed that H&M has insufficient and inefficient staff and the staff do not pay attention to its customers which is demonstrated by their impolite and unfriendly attitudes, as a participant put it:

> . . . they don't really pay much attention to the customers . . . customer services doesn't seem to be high on their agenda . . . the staff don't seem to care, they are just there walking around chatting . . . they are not always been helpful.
>
> H&M Interviewee no. 2

Products and services

Participants agreed that H&M offers wide ranges of fashionable products in various concepts to different audiences, including women, men, young customers and children. Nevertheless, participants were not impressed with H&M's customer services, as one specified:

> I don't think they are very good at customer services, not something that they are actually focusing on a lot, and I think that's because they have very young staff and mostly work on part time basis . . . it suggests to me that they have high staff turnover . . .
>
> H&M Interviewee no. 4

Participants' views are inconsistent with H&M's desired identity on products and services, as the company expressed in its website:

> . . . giving the customer unbeatable value through the combination of fashion, quality and price . . . provides internal training in customer care . . .
>
> Hennes and Mauritz, 2006

Further complaints were made towards H&M that it had poor quality offerings. While acknowledged that H&M offers fashionable clothing at low price to customers, but its products quality is below standard, especially when H&M had been compared to other clothing retailer, such as Primark, as is evidenced in the comments of one participant:

> . . . I mean you can go to Primark, you pay for less but you get similar products. I would definitely say no to the quality aspects. Most of the time, over ninety percent of the time, H&M does not equate quality, definitely not.
>
> H&M Interviewee no. 6

Participants' perceptions and experience were not parallel with H&M's business concept and its quality control policy as outlined on its website:

> To give the customer unbeatable value by offering fashion and quality at the best price . . . all garments in H&M's collections go through a number of quality and security tests.
>
> Hennes and Mauritz, 2006

Communications and designs

H&M's website indicates that it has put considerable efforts in its store designs and its aims to:

> Creates a comfortable and inspiring atmosphere in the store . . . great efforts have been put into the layout of stores and the way in

which the goods are presented . . . shopping in H&M should be an easy, pleasant and inspiring experience . . .

Hennes and Mauritz, 2006

However, participants' opinions were discordant with H&M's desired identity. Participants felt that the stores are untidy and they give customers very unpleasant shopping experience as one explained:

The checkout is not well organized . . . sort of in the middle of the stores . . . I think the reality in store is just looking like a mess, it's cluttered, you can't find things, a lot of displays aren't displayed very well . . .

H&M Interviewee no. 7

Participants' views on displays were conflicting with how H&M top management wants to achieve, as the company says on its website:

The way goods are displayed and our use of mannequins provides customers with inspiration for how our clothes can be put together.

Hennes and Mauritz, 2006

Despite of participants felt that there is lack of communication between the company and the employees, H&M believes that they have put great efforts in internal communication, as it demonstrates on its website:

. . . face-to-face meetings remain one of the most important ways of communicating . . . our in-house magazine H&M News is issued four times a year . . . we communicate and strengthen the corporate culture as well as updating our staff on what's going on within the group.

Hennes and Mauritz, 2006

H&M explains its communication purpose is to 'communicate what H&M stand for and what they offer customers' even though the participants could only recall the logo of H&M and failed to identify what H&M really stand for, as one participant pointed out:

I think in terms of recognising the brand, oh yes, that's H&M, but in terms of meaning, they read H&M logo doesn't really say anything to anybody, does it?

H&M Interviewee no. 1

Participants noticed only a few advertisements of H&M. Some of them could only remember a few H&M's billboard campaigns a couple of yeas ago. Although they felt that the campaigns have successfully informed the customers what are the company's latest products, participants did not agree that the campaigns have reflected the company's advertising aim, as it is written on the website:

> . . . to show who we are and what we stand for.
>
> Hennes and Mauritz, 2006

Market conditions and strategies

In terms of target audience, Participants felt that H&M's target customers are mainly *'students'*. Conversely, H&M has shown that in its website (Hennes and Mauritz, 2006) and public documents that the company has put great efforts on promoting itself as a clothing retailer who tailors fashion conscious customers of all ages with wide ranges of clothes.

Although H&M does not explicitly indicate its main competitors on the websites and company documents, one of the participants referred Primark and Topman as H&M's main competitors, as specified:

> Topman's stuff in terms of products is better quality, designs are better, and quality looks better. Primark obviously is cheaper than H&M, and it has more choice, but the quality seems to be quite similar to H&M.
>
> H&M Interviewee no. 3

Case analysis

The above findings have shown that there is significant gap between desired identity and perceived identity in H&M's case. There are differences in how H&M describes its identity to its stakeholders and on how customers perceive H&M's identity. There are apparent gaps on each corporate identity constructs, as shown in Table 12.1.

On one hand, H&M promotes itself as a clothing retailer offering fashion and quality at the best price to its customers. It provides internal training to its employees in customer care and establishes effective internal communication with its staff at all levels. It carries out quality control and tests on its products. H&M also claims that it creates a comfortable and inspiring store environment for its customers. The retailer uses its advertising campaigns to inform customers of who H&M is and what H&M stands for. The company targets customers of all ages and gender.

On the contrary, the reality of the stores and the experiences of the participants contradict with H&M's desired identity. They perceived H&M as a fashion retailer selling clothing that they judge as inferior quality because of its low-price points. There is lack of internal communication between the company and the staff, and there perception is of insufficient training for its employees. These have been reflected from staff's poor and inefficient customer services, perceived unprofessional attitudes, and insufficient knowledge on company's products. Participants also described the store environment of H&M as unpleasant with stores that are untidy and cluttered with large volumes of clothing. Visual merchandising is ineffective. Participants failed to identify who H&M really is and what H&M really stands for from its advertising campaigns.

Zara's case

Zara is known as part of Inditex in Spain. Inditex has over 2,500 stores across 400 cities in 58 countries generating sales of €66 billion. During 2005, alone, Inditex opened 323 stores and by 2009 aims to nearly double its total. Zara is one of the fastest growing and successful clothing retailers. Zara had more than 500 stores located all over the world, including Europe, the US, the Latin America, the Middle East and the Asia-Pacific region (Mintel, 2005). According to IGD (2006) they are reported to now have 816 stores worldwide. The first UK Zara store was opened in 1998 in Regent Street, London. Since then, Zara has always been perceived as a strong retail brand (Mintel, 2004). Zara offers high fashion clothing to men, women and children. The most successful store opening was said to be Dublin's 20,000 square feet retail space in Henry Street. Zara's highly responsive supply chain can get product to store in weeks whereas traditional clothing retailers measure time in months. Unlike many other retailers Zara manufactures about sixty per cent of its product and outsources the remainder. This provides it with greater flexibility. The marble floors in its own stores are sourced from its own quarry.

Corporate identity

Zara, on its website (Inditex, 2006) referred its *corporate logo* as the company's corporate identity. However, participants had different opinions:

> Zara's logo does not tell the public what Zara is about I think . . . I mean it is a well-known international brand and it sells clothes to different customers.
>
> Zara Interviewee no. 1

Furthermore, participants felt that the concept of corporate identity in the fashion industry do not only advert to visual designs, logos and graphic elements, as one participant expressed:

> The company's logo does not really tell the public anything about it, I mean people have to go into the stores in order to understand the identity. It is the whole store package . . .
>
> Zara Interviewee no. 6

Corporate culture

Nearly all the participants acknowledged that Zara is a Spanish fashion clothing retailer. They tend to agree with Zara's philosophy on Inditex's website:

> Offers quality clothing at affordable prices that keep us in step with the latest international trends each season.
>
> Inditex, 2006

On its website, Zara described its corporate culture as:

> . . . corporate culture is characterized by teamwork in a horizontal structure, where open communication and accountability at all levels are the foundations for motivation and personal commitment to customer satisfaction.
>
> Inditex, 2006

Participants' views harmonious with Zara's desired identity on corporate culture, as one of the participants expressed:

> I think they are quite structured . . . I find them quite professional, looks very professional. They sort of have that professional look on it. The staff always look professional, the shop layout and the designs are professional. So the culture centre to them is being professional and value customers. You know, I feel good as a customer.
>
> Zara Interviewee no. 3

Corporate behaviour

In contrast with H&M, participants had positive perceptions towards Zara's employees' behaviour, as one illustrated:

> I think they are quite friendly . . . the staff working in Zara, they seem to be well educated . . . they are well trained . . . they try to be helpful as much as possible.
>
> Zara Interviewee no. 4

Participants' views correspond with Zara's desired identity, as the company described on its website:

> . . . corporate culture is characterized by teamwork, open communication and a high level of demand . . . offers its employees a dynamic and international environment that values their ideas. Inditex values job stability, training and internal promotion.
>
> Inditex, 2006

Participants felt that Zara's personnel are well trained and are working towards the same goal. Moreover, some had impressions that the staff in stores provide customers with a comfortable and constraint free environment, this was expressed by one participant:

> ... the staff working in Zara, they seem to be well educated and sort of immersed in that kind of culture that Zara tries to put forward in the stores and also the image. Because they don't really interact much with the customers, they only come to you if you want something ... it's quite a nice thing because I don't want the staff to come and observe me, or ask me all the time whether I'm okay. The staff are very discretely placed in the stores. I think to me, it's a big plus ...
>
> Zara Interviewee no. 1

Products and services

Zara's clothing quality has been praised by participants. Many of them have described it as 'it's good', 'the quality is excellent' and 'I think they are proud of themselves as offering high quality products at a reasonable price'.

Although Zara promotes itself as a clothing retailer who provides fashion to everyone despite their culture and generation differences (Inditex, 2006), a few participants felt that some of Zara's products do not tailor to individual's needs, such as sizes, as one explained:

> ... Zara only sells trousers in a certain length and sizes, I'm quite short, which means whenever I go to Zara and buy a pair of trousers, I have to add on another ten pounds for shortening the trousers.
>
> Zara Interviewee no. 4

Participants were satisfied with the customer services in Zara, as put it:

> Services, I think it's excellent, I've never had a complaint, and I've never encountered a problem.
>
> Zara Interviewee no. 2

Participants' opinions accordant with Zara's desired identity on services as the company commits itself to customer satisfaction through its employees.

Communications and designs

Zara has a nicely planned store designs and layouts as it indicates on the website:

> The store are designed to create a special atmosphere that will allow the client to feel the pleasure of buying fashion ... the key

element in the organization is the store, a carefully designed space conceived to make customers comfortable as they discover fashion concepts . . . eliminating all barriers between the garments and the customers.

Inditex, 2006

Participants tend to agree with that, as one explained:

The designs of the stores are very nice, it's very bright, the design focus in on the clothes, so the clothes are the main thing that you look at . . . it's always tidy . . . it's very contemporary . . .

Zara Interviewee no. 7

Zara described its window display on its website as:

Authentic advertising for our chains in the world's main shopping streets.

Inditex, 2006

Most of participants felt that the windows informed customers of Zara is, as one participant said:

I see the display, I know it's Zara because of the clothes they present, how they put it, the colour, the designs . . . The display tells people, you know, we sell clothes, accessories, cosmetics for the kids, for children, for men, for women.

Zara Interviewee no. 5

Participants did not understand what Zara stands for. On the company's website (Inditex, 2006), the company directly refers its corporate logo as its corporate identity. However, participants felt that an organization's corporate identity is more than just a logo, as one participant expressed:

I mean the logo doesn't really tell me anything about a company. Identity is about everything. It's the whole package. It's about the whole philosophy of the company. It's about what they do and how they act in the society.

Zara Interviewee no. 2

Market conditions and strategies

Participants had the impressions that the target audiences of Zara are *'those young professional with some disposable income'*. However, Zara did not explicitly indicate on its website and public documents. Rather, Zara has attempted to provide fashion to everyone in the society:

> There's something of Zara in all of us . . . Zara is in step with society, dressing the ideas, trends and tastes that society itself has developed. That is the key to its success among people, cultures and generations that, despite their differences, all share a special feeling for fashion.
>
> Inditex, 2006

Some participants regarded Zara as a rather up-market retailer who competes with established fashion brands. However, a few participants felt that H&M could potentially be seen as Zara's leading rivals due to its market position, as one customer explained:

> Zara is offering something very high quality at a reasonable price. Because of the image of the stores, people associate it with expensive and high end sort of stores and some high street stores as well, so it may have competitions from two different angles, one is coming from high end, like Austin Reed, Reiss, Ted Baker, FCUK, the other one is Topman, River Island and may be H&M, but I'm not sure.
>
> Zara Interviewee no. 4

Zara's fast turnaround time means that the retailer can bring in the fashion clothing from the drawing board to the store shelves within a short period of time:

> . . . the ability to adapt the offer to meet customer desires in the shortest time possible . . . vertical integration enables us to shorten turnaround time . . . new articles reach the stores twice a week . . .
>
> Inditex, 2006

Participants strongly agreed with Zara's desired identity on its market strategy, as one participant expressed:

> The stock keeps changing, it gives me a fresher feel. Every time I go there, I always find something different. I know if I don't like anything this month, I'm sure I will find something new next month.
>
> Zara Interviewee no. 3

Case analysis

There is a narrow gap between desired identity and perceived identity in Zara's case. There is only disparity in some of the corporate identity constructs, including the concept of corporate identity, Zara's products and Zara's market condition, as shown in Table 12.2.

Zara referred to its corporate logo as the company's identity. However, participants believed that the logo of Zara does not inform customers of Zara stands for. Zara's corporate identity should include its products, the store environment, its staff and to create and communicate identity. Moreover, participants felt that the window displays of Zara can act as a more powerful tool in communicating with customers as the window shows what Zara is, a clothing retailer selling fashion to men, women and children. Although Zara offers fashion to customers across boundaries, with different backgrounds and culture, participants did not feel that Zara tailors its products to individual needs of customers, such as the lengths and sizes are not suitable for petite customers. Furthermore, participants believed that Zara's target audience are young professionals due to its high quality clothing and pricing.

Cross case comparative analysis – H&M and Zara

Discussion

The findings from the case studies have identified that Zara have a desired–perceived identity gap but it is relatively smaller than the gap observed at H&M. There are differences between how the top management of the retailers present their identities to the public and how customers perceive the identity of the companies. The desired–perceived identity gap is particularly significant in H&M's case. This section will discuss in more detail the gaps and implications for retail identity.

H&M and Zara have been compared as competitors in the fast fashion market intensively (Mintel, 2002). This is not surprising if one takes into account some of their overlapping target audiences and their recent success in Europe and in the US. Their stated philosophies are similar which is to provide fashion and quality to customers. However, the participants have perceived H&M as an inferior fashion retailer due to its low price and poor quality offering. Most of the participants in this study were not satisfied with H&M's clothing quality, especially with some of the clothes shrinking after just one wash. Fast fashion is often referred to as disposable fashion but one wash may be just too disposable. Zara, on the other hand, is perceived differently due to the high quality merchandise and reasonable price points customers identified. The results emerging from the case studies have indicated inconsistency between desired identity and perceived identity. In H&M's case, the disparity has become more apparent. This is because customers perceive H&M's corporate identity as a fashion retailer offering cheaper, lower quality and disposable clothes. Consumers drew comparisons with discount retailers, such as Primark and other fast fashion retailers, such as Topshop/Topman.

Two important concerns discussed by customers in evaluating the retailer's identity focused on price and quality constructs.

The results indicate that there is only a narrow gap between desired identity and perceived identity in Zara's case. Therefore, Zara would be a good exemplar for H&M and other similar companies attempting to closely align their perceived and desired identities. Zara has delivered its desired corporate identity to the employees within the organization. Its corporate culture, company's philosophy, employees' behaviour, quality of products, customer services and store designs have reflected Zara's desired identity to the participants. From the case studies, it seems that Zara has an efficient internal communication channel, which communicates its missions to its employees across all departments to ensure that they reflect the desired identity to the public. For instance, the staff at the store level have the appropriate attitudes and behaviour towards the customers. The staff are polite and friendly. They have professional attitudes towards the customers. Foo and Lowe (1999) explain that some organizations may use their logos to communicate their identities to the public and it is certainly the case in Zara. However, many participants felt that a logo can only act as a recognition purpose, and it cannot act as the whole of corporate identity. The other minor drawback of Zara is that its product offerings are not tailored for all customers, as they desire. Although Zara aims to bring fashion to all people despite of their differences in culture and background, its products sometimes are not suitable for petite sized customers as observed by customers interviewed.

There are ways that H&M could reduce its desired–perceived identity gap. Firstly, H&M should improve its product quality with tighter quality control and testing to avoid problems like shrinkage identified by some customers. According to Balmer (1995), a company's products and services must reflect corporate missions and philosophies. At present, the poor quality of the products does not correspond to the retailer's desired mission on quality offering. Secondly, H&M should enhance its store images by designing a better layout and providing a more comfortable environment to its customers. These can be achieved by displaying fewer clothing in stores and recruiting more staff to tidy stores more frequently. These would give customers pleasure in shopping in H&M stores. Moreover, H&M should communicate more effectively with its staff and train them in its policies and missions (Kennedy, 1977) and acknowledge the attitudes the employees hold before the company presents its identity to the public. The company could have a more defined core values and clearer missions and well-planned internal communication with its employees. It should make sure that both its full-time and part-time staff have appropriate trainings in customer care and product knowledge. H&M should ensure that its staff fully understand the corporate missions and make sure that they can reflect company's mission to the customers. This could help to minimize any conflicts and misalignment between employees and the company, and most importantly, it could reduce the gap between the desired identity and the perceived identity. For instance, in Zara's case, Zara motivates its employees at all levels to achieve customer satisfaction. Participants could identify the professionalism of Zara from staff's friendly and helpful behaviour and attitudes towards customers. Furthermore, H&M should have more effective advertising campaigns and should aim to deliver clearly what the company is and what the company stands for to its customers. By carrying out these suggested measures, H&M should be able to minimize its desired–perceived identity gap. The findings from the two cases highlight the differences rather than similarities which one might have expected when we set out to explore identities of these two (rather similar in many respects as we thought when we chose to examine them) retail organizations.

A number of propositions emerge from the cases:

P1: Retail identities rely on customer perceptions, which may be formed without reference to the retailer's desired identity.

In any market customer perception is of paramount importance. After all it is customers that demand products, generate profit and ensure existence for retail organizations. Customers may or may not be aware of the retailer's desired identity or statements about that identity may be paradoxical, misleading or confused. This has implications for marketing communications. Customers need to be informed and they need to believe the messages. There is a disconnection between the desired and perceived identity as a consequence in store influences become dominant in the formation of perceived identity. This leads to a second proposition.

P2: The most important influences on customer perceptions and customer belief is product, followed by store environment and staff interaction with the customer.

Customer opinion can be transformed quickly if any of their encounters are negative in relation to these three factors.

P3: Product attributes most important to customers were fashionability, quality, price and value.

Customers generally accepted trade-offs between these aspects. It would be of interest to explore the impact of these factors in perceptions of identity.

P4: Corporate communications can only influence perceptions of identity if customers experiences are congruent with the desired identity statements.

In the H&M case study in particular customers observations and sense experiences did not match with the statements for desired identity. Customer experience is perhaps the most important influence on perceived identity in this context.

The final section draws conclusions and considers implications for identity theory, retail management and further research.

Conclusion and implications

In this investigation, two case studies were conducted in an attempt to contribute to the corporate identity research area by introducing how top management's presents its corporate identity to the audiences (desired corporate identity) and how customers' perceive the company's identity (perceived corporate identity), with reference to Hatch and Schultz's (2003) original framework on vision–image gap. This research has theoretical implications and contributes to an empirical side of the corporate identity management research. As van Rekom (1997) notes, corporate identity is about how an organization allows itself to be known and how it allows people to describe, remember and relate to it. Although existing literature has identified that there is gap between desired identity and actual identity, that is, whether the reality of organizations reflect the top management's vision, and how important this gap is to the corporate identity management, for example, (Balmer, 2001b; Balmer and Soenen, 1999; Kiriakidou and Millward, 2000). The results of the present research, using the case of the UK's fast fashion sector, show that organizations cannot primarily focus on the desired–actual identity gap and ignore the desired–perceived identity gap. Perceived identity has appeared to be equally important in this study. Organizations should take into account customers' perceptions towards their identity when they promote themselves to the audiences. The findings of this study identifies the case companies have disparity between top management and customers' perceptions towards an organization's corporate identity.

This chapter has a number of managerial implications for fashion retailers. First, it demonstrates a significant divergence of insights into how customers perceive corporate identity and how the retail organizational decision-makers present it. We argue that an organization cannot simply present its corporate mission statement to its employees at all levels (Kiriakidou and Millward, 2000) and expect them to promote this identity to its customers. Organizations have to have effective internal communication channels and offer appropriate training programmes to staff. The case studies for H&M and Zara, provide some useful insights into the identify gap between desired and perceived identity the next stage for retailers would be to consider appropriate strategies that might reduce it.

References

Alessandri, S W. (2001). Modeling corporate identity: a concept explication and theoretical explanation, *Corporate Communications: An International Journal*, **6** (4), 173–182.

Baker, M. J. and Balmer, J. M. T. (1997). Visual identity: trappings or substance? *European Journal of Marketing*, **31** (5/6), 366–382.

Balmer, J. M. T. (1995). Corporate branding and connoisseurship, *Journal of General Management*, **21** (1), 24–46.

Balmer, J. M. T. (1998). Corporate identity and the advent of corporate marketing, *Journal of Marketing Management*, **14**, 963–996.

Balmer, J. M. T. (2001a). Corporate identity, corporate branding and corporate marketing, *European Journal of Marketing*, **35** (3/4), 248–291.

Balmer, J. M. T. (2001b). From the Pentagon: a new identity framework, *Corporate Reputation Review*, **4** (1), 11–22.

Balmer, J. M. T. and Dinnie, K. (1999). Corporate identity and corporate communications: the antidote to merger madness, *Corporate Communications: An International Journal*, **4** (4), 182–192.

Balmer, J. M. T. and Soenen, G. B. (1999). The acid test of corporate identity management, *Journal of Marketing Management*, **15**, 69–92.

Balmer, J. M. T. and Wilson, A. (1998). Corporate identity. there is more to it than meets the eyes, *International Studies of Management and Organization*, **28** (3), 12–31.

Bernstein, D. (1989). Advertising voices: corporate void, *International Journal of Advertising*, **8**, 315–320.

Bernstein, D. (1996). *Company Image and Reality. A Critique of Corporate Communications.* London: Cassell.

Bickerton, D. (2000). Corporate reputation versus corporate branding: the realist debate, *Corporate Communications: An International Journal*, **5** (1), 42–48.

Burghausen, M. and Fan, Y. (2002). Corporate branding in the retail sector: a pilot study, *Corporate Communications: An International Journal*, **7** (2), 92–99.

Burt, S. L. and Sparks, L. (2002). Corporate branding, retailing, and retail internationalization, *Corporate Reputation Review*, **5** (2/3), 194–212.

Cornelissen, J. P. and Elving, W. J. L. (2003). Managing corporate identity: an integrative framework of dimensions and determinants, *Corporate Communications: An International Journal*, **8** (2), 114–120.

de Weerd-Nederhof, P. C. (2001). Qualitative case study research. The case of a PhD research project on organizing and managing new product development systems, *Management Decision*, **39** (7), 513–538.

Einwiller, S. and Will, M. (2002). Towards an integrated approach to corporate branding – an empirical study, *Corporate Communications: An International Journal*, **7** (2), 100–109.

Eisenhardt, K. M. (1989). Building theories from case study research, *The Academy of Management Review*, **14** (4), 532–550.

Foo, C. T. and Lowe, A. (1999). Modelling for corporate identity studies: case of identity as communications strategy, *Corporate Communications: An International Journal*, **4** (2), 89–92.

Gregory, J. R. and Wiechmann, J. G. (1999). *Marketing Corporate Image. The Company As Your Number One Product.* Chicago: NTC Business Books, NTC/ Contemporary Publishing Group.

Hankinson, P. and Hankinson, G. (1999). Managing successful brands: an empirical study which compares the corporate cultures of companies managing the world's top 100 brands with those managing outsider brands, *Journal of Marketing Management*, **15**, 135–155.

Harris, F. and de Chernatony, L. (2001). Corporate branding and corporate brand performance, *European Journal of Marketing*, **35** (3/4), 441–456.

Hatch, M. J. and Schultz, M. (2000). Scaling the tower of Babel: relational differences between identity, image, and culture in organizations, In Schultz, M., Hatch, M. J. and Larsen, M. H. (Eds.), *The Expressive Organization. Linking Identity, Reputation and the Corporate Brand,* Oxford University Press, New York, pp. 11–35.

Hatch, M. J. and Schultz, M. (2001). Are the Strategic Stars Aligned for your Corporate Brand? *Harvard Business Review*, February, 129–134.

Hatch, M. J. and Schultz, M. (2003). Bringing the corporation into corporate branding, *European Journal of Marketing*, **37** (7/8), 1041–1064.

Hennes and Mauritz (2006). About H&M, available at http://www.hm.com

Hines, T. (2004). *Supply Chain Strategies: Customer Driven and Customer-Focused*. Oxford: Elsevier Butterworth-Heinemann.

Hines, T. and Bruce, M. (2001). *Fashion Marketing: Contemporary Issues*. Oxford: Butterworth-Heinemann.

IGD (2006). *Managing International Supply Chains*, Watford, Institute of Grocery Distribution.

Inditex (2006). available at www.inditex.com

Kennedy, S. H. (1977). Nurturing corporate images – total communication or ego trip? *European Journal of Marketing*, **11**, 120–164.

King, S. (1991). Brand-building in the 1990s, *Journal of Marketing Management*, **7** (1), 3–13.

Kiriakidou, O. and Millward, L. J. (2000). Corporate identity: external reality or internal fit? *Corporate Communications: An International Journal*, **5** (1), 49–58.

Knox, S. and Bickerton, D. (2003). The six conventions of corporate branding, *European Journal of Marketing*, **37** (7/8), 998–1016.

Leitch, S. and Motion, J. (1999). Multiplicity in corporate identity strategy, *Corporate Communications: An International Journal*, **4** (4), 193–199.

Lippincott, J. G. and Margulies, W. (1957). The corporate look: a problem in design, *Public Relations Journal*, **13**, 27.

Margulies, W. (1977). Make the most of your corporate identity, *Harvard Business Review*, July–August, 66–77.

Markwick, N. and Fill, C. (1997). Towards a framework for managing corporate identity, *European Journal of Marketing*, **31** (5/6), 396–409.

Mead, G. H. (1934). *Mind, Self and Society*. University of Chicago Press: Chicago.

Melewar, T. C. and Saunders, J. (2000). Global corporate visual identity: using an extended marketing mix, *European Journal of Marketing*, **34** (5/6), 538–550.

Melewar, T. C. and Woodridge, A. R. (2001). The dynamics of corporate identity: A review of a process model, *Journal of Communication Management*, **5** (4), 327–340.

Melewar, T. C. and Jenkins, E. (2002). Defining the corporate identity construct, *Corporate Reputation Review*, **5** (1), 76–90.

Mintel, UK. (2002). Clothing Retailing in Europe – UK, Mintel International Group Limited.

Mintel, UK. (2004). Womenswear Retailing UK, Mintel International Group Limited.

Mintel, UK. (2005). Clothing Retailing – UK – July 2005, available at http://reports.mintel.com/sinatra/reports/my_reports/display/id=114754&anchor=atom/display/id=170726

Olins, W. (1978). The Corporate Personality. An Inquiry into the Nature of Corporate Identity. London: Design Council.

Olins, W. (1978–1979). Corporate identity: the myth and the reality, *Journal of the Royal Society of Arts*, **127**, December 1978–November 1979, 209–218.

Olins, W. (1994). Corporate Identity. Making Business Strategy Visible Through Design. London: Thames and Hudson.

Rode, V. and Vallaster, C. (2005). Corporate Branding for Start-ups: The Crucial Role of Entrepreneurs, *Corporate Reputation Review*, **8** (2), 121–135.

Rowley, J. (2002). Using Case Studies in Research, Management Research News, **25** (1), 16–27.

Schmidt, K. (1995). *The Quest for Identity: Corporate Identity, Strategies, Methods and Examples*. London: Cassell.

Sinkovics, R. R., Penz, E. and Ghauri, P. N. (2005). Analysing textual data in international marketing research, *Qualitative Market Research: An International Journal*, **8** (1), 9–38.

Stake, R. E. (1995). *The Art of Case Study Research*, London, Thousand Oaks: Sage Publications.

Stake, R. E. (2000). Qualitative case studies, In Denzin, N. and Lincoln, Y. S. (Eds.), *The Sage Handbook of Qualitative Research*, Sage Publication, London, Thousand Oaks, pp. 443–466.

Stuart, H. (1999). Towards a definitive model of the corporate identity management process, *Corporate Communications: An International Journal*, **4** (4), 200–207.

Suvatjis, J. Y. and de Chernatony, L. (2005). Corporate identity modelling: a review and presentation of a new multi-dimensional model, *Journal of Marketing Management*, **21**, 809–834.

Topalian, A. (1984). Corporate identity: beyond the visual overstatements, *International Journal of Advertising*, **3**, 55–62.

van Rekom, J. (1997). Deriving an operational measure of corporate identity, *European Journal of Marketing*, **31** (5/6), 410–422.

van Riel, C. B. M. and Balmer, J. M. T. (1997). Corporate identity: the concept, its measurement and management, *European Journal of Marketing*, **31** (5/6), 340–355.

Yin, R. (2003). *Case Study Research. Design and Methods*, London: Sage Publications.

13

Fashion e-tailing

Ruth Marciniak and Margaret Bruce

Introduction

The Internet is gradually becoming more mainstream as a retail distribution channel. It is also a compelling channel for fashion goods (Beck, 2004) as it not only provides a excellent means for a fashion retailer to display their most up-to-date lines via photograph, video and sound technology, the use of web sites has also enabled them to sell direct to their customers. Despite continued speculation about the ability to sell clothes online, the volume of sales of clothing and footwear sold via the Internet has grown steadily. For instance, figures from the Interactive Media in Retail Group (IMRG, 2005) indicate that online revenues for fashion goods have been growing at 25–30 per cent a year since 2000. Indeed they estimate that 24 million people spent £1.6 billion online in September 2005 alone. Indeed according to Ebay a piece of clothing sells every 7 seconds on their site (Morrell, 2006) and Top Shop's web site is believed to be its second largest outlet after its Oxford Street flag shop store (Dudley, 2005). In all, fashion has been identified as the fastest growing online sector in the UK representing 9 per cent of all online British retailing (Ashworth et al., 2005). The significance of the sales of clothing products within the economy cannot be ignored. For instance, the retail fashion market in the UK in total amounted to £37 billion in 2004 (Mintel, 2005b) whereas the total value for the book retail market in the same year was a mere £3.62 billion (Mintel, 2005a).

In line with the increase in consumer spend on fashion goods online, there is gradually beginning to emerge increasing academic interest in fashion electronic retailing (e-tailing). Of this much of the work relates to consumer behaviour issues, for example identification of consumer characteristics that may lead them to make online clothing purchases (Goldsmith and Goldsmith, 2002; Goldsmith and Flynn, 2004; 2005; Kim and Kim, 2004) and; examinations of cross channel shopping behaviour involving fashion purchases via the high street, catalogue and online (Lu and Rucker, 2006; Nicholson et al., 2002; Koontz, 2002). Other work has focussed upon the components of fashion web site design and fashion web site quality (Jang and Burns, 2004) together with consumer perceptions of these (Siddiqui et al., 2003; Kim and Stoel, 2004). Whilst much of this work adopts a consumer perspective, literature focussing on a fashion retailer's online strategy is much less common. Neverless, again work is beginning to emerge in this area. This work includes Marciniak and Bruce's (2004) examination of fashion retailer online levels of commitment and identification of specific retailer characteristics in terms of market positioning and product focus. Other work includes Ashworth et al.'s (2005) empirical work, which investigated the stages in development of fashion web sites. Work has also been undertaken with regard to the nature of the decision-making process of fashion retailers developing web sites (Marciniak and Bruce, 2005; Salmeron and Hurtado, 2005).

The purpose of this chapter is to offer a comprehensive review of the above literature and in doing so, provide both academic and practitioners alike with a foundation on which to form specific fashion sector insights with regard to its involvement in electronic retailing. Areas addressed in this chapter include identification of fashion retailers who are involved in e-tailing; consumer perceptions of fashion web sites; consideration of how fashion retailers develop web sites; and finally, examination of characteristics of consumers who shop for fashion online.

Who Sells Online?

Jang and Burns (2004) suggest that online fashion retailers generally fall into one of four categories; virtual e-tailers, bricks and mortar retailers and catalogue companies who have expanded their operations to include online retailing and multi-channel retailers who sell products in stores, through catalogues and online. Alternatively Marciniak and Bruce's (2004) offers a classification of online fashion retailers based upon product focus and market positioning. This classification, based upon a web survey undertaken in 2003, includes product specialists or niche retailers (e.g. maternity wear), fashion designer retailers (e.g. Paul Smith), general merchandise retailers who sell fashion (e.g. House of Fraser) and general fashion retailers (e.g. Diesel). Evident in this classification is that e-tail interest is representative of various fashion retailers regardless of their product focus or market position. The findings of their survey also identified, of those web sites that were transactional, product specialists were the most well represented. For instance, most pure play retailers were product specialists. This supports the view that by the very fact these retailers are specialists, makes it easier for them to generate traffic to their web site (Huizingh, 2002). For example, keying in the term 'ski wear' into a search engine will take one directly to a list of outdoor clothing retail specialists.

However whilst product specialists have the advantage of having a specific product category to exploit online, other fashion retailers may have their own distinct brand name to attract customers, for example well-known multiples such as The Gap, Top Shop and French Connection. Nevertheless Marciniak and Bruce's (2004) study identified that at the time of the study a high number of these own brand multiples were 'information only' therefore indicating that these retailers were not exploiting the virtues of the Internet as much as other fashion retailers. It was only the own brand high street general fashion retailers who also sell via a catalogue, such as Next and Laura Ashley, who were transactional. Therefore indicating that these multi-channel retailers were exploiting their competences in direct delivery and logistics to sell online. Indeed Next Plc is highly focussed on their 'one brand, three ways to shop' proposition, being one of the first UK retailers to realize the potential of a multi-channel approach. Reportedly the company is probably the most successful example to date within the UK of fashion retailers who have made efforts to penetrate e-commerce (Mintel, 2005b). For instance according to Nielsen/NetRatings (*Retail Week*, 2003), one of the most popular sites visited on the Internet by British women is Next. Adopting a market penetration strategy, as a multi-channel approach is, induces consumers to purchase more. This makes sense given that the market for fashion goods within the UK is mature evidenced by intense competition (Mintel, 2005b).

Alternatively, according to Marciniak and Bruce's (2004) survey, fashion designers are least likely to be transactional retailers. Various explanations for why this may be are offered. First, they may wish to protect their image, considering that having a further channel to market may dilute such an image. Second, given that typically fashion designers are international they may not wish to commit the resources required in running an international online operation. Finally, they may perceive that the high level of customer service incurred selling high-price fashion items would be difficult to replicate online. However there exist a number of pure play retailers including the UK retailer Net-a-porter and the Italian company Yoox who are doing well-selling designer clothing online (Corcoran, 2005; Howell, 2005). These fashion retailers focus is on the designer clothes that are highlighted in magazines, but are often difficult to find in independent retail outlets because they may be considered 'risky' (Corcoran, 2005).

Independent fashion retailers are the least likely group of retailers to utilize the Internet to sell their goods (Marciniak and Bruce, 2004). This may not be a surprise as these small retailers, who typically will serve local markets, may not see the need to invest in e-commerce initiatives. Such a decision further serves to widen the gap between small stores and major national chains. One initiative to rectify this has been Ready2Shop, a fashion advice business co-founded in 1999 by fashion gurus Trinny Woodall and Susannah Constantine, which was to include a 'boutiques' selling fashion goods from independent retailers, which would then have to handle their own delivery (Hall, 1999). However the company had to scale back its ambitions for its web site after failing to attract enough venture capital and subsequently was forced to dissolve in 2001.

In all, in terms of who sells online, whilst product specialist fashion retailers, designers, general merchandisers and general fashion retailers all have a presence on the Internet, at this current time, transactional retailers are predominantly product specialists. Whilst branding has become an increasingly important feature of fashion retailing (Moore, 1995), in terms of online selling, it is product focus that is significant.

What makes a good fashion web site?

A company's web site is a key tool for communication (McGolderick et al., 1999). To this end, web site quality is understood to be significant. Researchers such as McGolderick et al. (1999) have devised an instrument, webqual, employing scaling techniques for capturing consumer perceptions of the online service provision environment. Secondly, the level of information and organisation relating to the degree of information provided in order that a consumer can fulfil a desired task on a web site. Thirdly, web appearance, which relates to the visual appeal of the web site and the extent to which web pages are easy to navigate and control (Chen and Wells, 1999). In terms of fashion retail web sites, Kim and Stoel (2004) undertook an empirical investigation to examine web site attributes that favourably affected consumer satisfaction. Respondents, evaluations were based upon experiences of females' favourite apparel web sites. Their findings indicated informationess (or what they referred to as information fit to task), transaction capability and response time were dimensions that were significant predictors of customers' fashion web site satisfaction. Further to this, their study indicated that neither visual appearance, aesthetic aspects of a fashion web site, nor provision of entertainment were seen as significant contributors to satisfaction. Kim and Kim (2004) supports these findings as their empirical work identified transaction cost factors (including credit card security, fast delivery time, privacy assurance, money back guarantees) rather than web design features (e.g. ability to zoom in on a specific fashion product) were the most significant contributors to overall perceptions of online clothing shopping attributes.

However in contradiction to both Kim and Stoel's (2004) and Kim and Kim's findings Siddiqui et al.'s (2003) work, which examined web sites of fashion retailers, reported that respondents indicated that they were looking for a particular online experience wherein they can view clothes close up and in 3D, have greater interactivity and more excitement. Siddiqui et al.'s (2003) findings are supported by Then and Delong (1999) who identify three important visual aspects for successful web sites for clothing shoppers, which include, images of the online product in its closest representation of end use, displays in conjunction with similar items and views from various angles. In

Then and Delong's view, retailers have not demonstrated successful Internet penetration because the majority of clothing sites cannot provide the kinds of rich experience consumers are looking for. This is further supported by Stockport et al. (2001) and Damesick (2002).

With regards to web site components characterized by retailer type, Jang and Burns (2004) study of fashion web sites identified that it is the virtual or pure play retailers who focus more on providing detailed information about their goods. This may be expected as these retailers have no physical store to display their products, and as Jang and Burns (2004) indicate greater information contributes to reducing consumers' perceived risk associated with non-store shopping. Further to this their study indicated that both catalogue and multi-channel retailers typically provide a greater number of customer service components, for example ordering options, than other retailer types. Given that a catalogue company's core competence is in distribution and direct delivery, higher levels of customer services compared to other online retailer types would be expected. Catalogue companies were also more likely to provide additional promotional services to the consumer, for example two for one offers. However Jang and Burns (2004) found that multi-channel retailers provided a more convenient returns policy than catalogue companies. An explanation for this being multi-channel retailers such as Next allow consumers who have purchased goods from their web site to return them to their nearest physical store if they wish (Nicholson et al., 2002), thereby enhancing customer service through the increased options for how a consumer makes returns on goods bought. A summary of Jang and Burns (2004) study is offered in the Table 13.1 below. As can be seen the table shows that different retailer types have different strengths in terms of services they provide to the consumer.

Table 13.1 Component of fashion retailer web sites: what they do best by retailer type

	Product detail information	Promotional services	Multiple options for ordering	Convenient returns policy
Catalogue		*		
Pure play	*			
Bricks & mortar				*
Multichannel			*	*

Note: Retailer competences.

In terms of presentation, typically consumers that currently purchase fashion online base their purchase and size-selection decisions mostly on 2D photos of garments and sizing charts (Beck, 2004). However various industry attempts have been made to solve issues of online product evaluation in terms of colour, quality of fabric and style of garment. For instance, US retailer Lands' End has created 'my virtual model'. This function enables consumers to create models in their own image through inputting information regarding height and weight. Subsequently they can dress the virtual model of themselves with the items they have selected. Based on this information provided, Lands' End automatically then makes recommendations on matching items (Moin, 2004). In all, this technology goes towards ensuring long-term loyalty by reducing dissatisfaction associated with the uncertainty whether to buy the product due to fit (Beck, 2004).

In all, in terms of what makes a good fashion web site is undecided. Whilst some researchers' findings consider that functionality in terms of efficient and effective transaction procedures is important, others view that functionality in terms of product presentation is more important. The disparity between these results may be explained by differences in nationality and culture of the samples used. Whilst Kim and Stoel's and Kim and Kim's empirical work was based on US females, Siddiqui et al.'s (2003) sample was UK residents. Evidence to support the notion that culture plays a part in consumer behaviour online is borne out by the work of Lu and Rucker (2006) who in comparing and contrasting US and Chinese students' channel preferences for purchasing fashion identified that different factors played a part in influencing each group of students in regard to which shopping channel they chose to select. Nevertheless in terms of the future, advances in Internet technologies will further permit online multi-sensory engagement between consumer and products thereby enhancing presentational aspects of existing online marketing channels (Barlow et al., 2004).

How do fashion retailers develop web sites?

Despite evidence to suggest that strategic decisions surrounding e-commerce are rarely planned (Salmeron and Hurtado, 2005), various planning models exist to explain how e-commerce comes about within an organization. Typically such models present a staged approach to implementation and development online (e.g. see Quelch and Klein, 1996; Coleman, 1998; Stroud, 1998; Martin and Kambil, 1999). Common to these models is that they suggest a company moves from developing an information only web site, wherein it has a web presence supplying product and company information, to a transactional site dealing in selling directly to customers. Ashworth et al. (2005) estimate that time scales for movement along these stages are between 4 and 7 years. However problematic with such models is that they are generic and as Reynolds (2002) points out, no models exist within the literature to explain specifically how the retail sector develops an online presence.

To redress this, Ashworth et al.'s (2005) empirical work has identified an alternative model exclusively focussing upon small- and medium-sized fashion retailers (SMEs). Moreover, in contrast to the generic models, their model captures the evolution of web site development wherein profit is made from the outset. Based upon case studies of both pure play and bricks and mortar retailers, Ashworth et al.'s (2005) model identifies five development stages of web site evolution, which are identified in Figure 13.1 below.

STAGE ONE
Develop a web presence
↓
STAGE TWO
Develop information competence
↓
STAGE THREE
Develop value integration and creative market development
↓
STAGE FOUR
Enhance integration of skills, processes and technologies
↓
STAGE FIVE
Leverage experience, learning and knowledge to maximise business value

Figure 13.1 Five stages of the development of fashion e-tail web sites.

Ashworth et al. (2005) indicate that routes to online success lies in bridging knowledge gaps as the fashion retailer progresses through each of the five stages. Gaps identified include:

> 'maximising economies in the supply infrastructure, conversion of added value into commercially viable units of response, keeping the customer happy whilst adding income direct to the bottom line and building an integrated operational system that best utilises synergies within the organisation' (Ashworth et al., 2005, p. 10).

These findings contrast with larger fashion retail chains who retain information only web sites (Marciniak and Bruce, 2004). More research is called for in order to capture the experiences of larger fashion retail organizations in order to confirm or adjust Ashworth et al.'s (2005) model, which is based solely on SMEs.

Whilst Ashworth et al.'s (2005) work examines the stages in the development of a fashion web site, alternatively Salmeron and Hurtado (2005) have investigated the strategic objectives pursued by a fashion retailer when developing e-commerce provision. This empirical work was achieved through the examination of top management's decision-making processes. Their results indicated that top managements reasons for developing business to consumer (B2C) e-commerce were to increase revenue, facilitate purchases from customers and amplify brand recognition.

Whilst Salmeron and Hurtado (2005) captured the thinking of top managers in terms of rationales for e-commerce development, Marciniak and Bruce (2005) sought to examine various planning styles adopted by fashion retailers. The examination of how decision-makers plan for e-retailing is relevant as the environment in which these technologies exist is dynamic (Kearns, 2005). The definition of a dynamic environment being one in which uncertainty exists, there is an absence of pattern and change is evident (Dess and Beard, 1984). Various strategy writers hold opposing views to how strategy should be planned within dynamic environments. For instance, both Porter (2001) and Ansoff (1991) argue that planning should be explicit, whilst Chaffee (1985) and Harrington et al. (2004) indicate that it should be more emergent. The findings of Marciniak and Bruce's (2005) study identified different approaches to decision-making in developing e-commerce initiatives of fashion retailers and found that no one approach to strategy making was dominant. For instance, whilst one of the case study companies exhibited a greater propensity towards a more explicit, formal and deliberate approach to decision-making, another company exhibited a more emergent style of planning. Further to this, both companies exhibited more than one planning style within the same organization. These results indicate that no one single mode of decision-making was employed by these fashion retailers working within this dynamic environment as would be assumed by Porter (2001), Ansoff (1991), Chaffee (1985) and Harrington et al. (2004).

Who buys online?

Whilst retail literature suggests that some consumers will avoid shopping via mail order catalogues due to concerns regarding security of money transactions (Schoenbachler and Gordon, 2002), with e-tailing this is compounded due to perceived greater security risks associated with the Internet (Lu and Rucker, 2006). In terms of characteristics of consumers who are motivated to shop online for fashion goods, Kim and Kim (2004) identified that gender, income, education and number of children were significant predictors. However alternatively, Goldsmith and Flynn (2004) point out that it is important to go beyond demographic descriptions as such figures are transitory. For example in 1998 Breitenbach and Van Doren (1998) reported that Internet users tend to be better-educated, business-oriented, young male consumers. However this profile no longer holds. For instance a study of UK and German females undertaken by Iris Female in 2005, reported in New Media Age (2005), indicated that females make up 52 per cent of the online population with the average female shopper spending £500 a year online, 5.3 per cent more than men (New Media Age, 2005). Further to this, both Goldsmith and Flynn (2004) and Phau and Chang-Chin (2004) suggest that being an enthusiastic clothes shopper does not necessarily incentivise consumers to shop for fashion online. Rather,

> 'better predicators were an enthusiasm and adventuresomeness for online buying in general and a history of buying clothes from catalogues' (p. 92).

These results indicate that perhaps the reason for which shoppers buy via a catalogue, such as time pressure or limited access to high street stores, would also be the same reasons for them to buy fashion goods online. Goldsmith and Flynn's (2004) findings are supported by Donthu and Garcia (1999) and Jones and Vijaysarathy (1998), Beaudry (1999) and Eastlick and Feinberg (1999) who all identify motives for online shopping as being the convenience of shopping from home. Certainly catalogue retailers have been proactive in terms of developing e-tail initiatives exploiting the fact that customers with experience of well-established catalogue retailers may be less wary of buying online. Undoubtedly, at this current stage in the development of e-tailing, familiarity and trust are key factors in deciding with whom to shop with online as along with catalogue retailers, high street retailers such as Argos, Next Plc and John Lewis are also exploiting their brand awareness to a competitive advantage (Mintel, 2005d). In all, Goldsmith and Flynn (2004) conclude that the e-tailer does little that is different from a mail order company, rather what is crucial to both is good databases and good logistics and distribution systems. Such similarities indicate that the motive is driven by a desire to purchase clothing and not an interest in a specific channel to market.

More recent evidence suggests that those who do shop via mail order may be transferring their purchasing online. As a Mintel (2005d) survey indicates Internet shopping overtook mail order as the most popular form of home shopping in the UK in 2004. The report suggests that mail order has failed to change or diversify sufficiently to appeal to today's 'more demanding and sophisticated home shopping audience'. Hence whereas previously early predictions indicated that e-tailing would replace traditional bricks and mortar stores, there is now growing consensus that Internet technologies will supplement catalogue retailing. Therefore bricks and mortar retailers should fear the Internet as a shopping alternative less than originally thought (Goldsmith and Flynn, 2005).

In all, in examining who buys online for fashion goods, there is a difference in findings between different researchers in terms of the significance of demographic characteristics. However what is established is that consumer characteristics are short-lived given that the Internet is a rapidly evolving technology with increasing number of users, the profile of who is a 'typical' online user will change. What is evident is an interest in fashion is not a motive to shop online, rather experience of home shopping together with an interest in making purchases online are factors that give confidence to consumers to purchase fashion goods via the Internet.

Who engages in cross channel shopping?

Whilst there is an association between catalogue and online shopping, as outlined above, there is also considered to be an association with high street shopping and home shopping. For instance Kim and Kim (2004) consider that using multiple channels to market can reduce consumers' perceived risks associated with online transactions in terms of garment fit, style, colour, feel and both quality of fabric and garment. The reason being, consumers can evaluate these attributes in the physical store, try on the garment then subsequently make the purchase from home. In addition, Lipke (2002) identified that consumers who shop from more than one channel to market typically spend more overall than store only shoppers, thereby making them a more attractive prospect to target. These consumers are what Koontz (2002) refer to as 'supper shoppers', who quoting from the Retail Federations 'Multi-channel Retail Report 2001' define them as:

> 'more likely to be customers of all three channels and purchase four times more frequently online than the average online shopper. Super shoppers also purchase from a retailer's store seventy per cent more frequently than the average store customer and one hundred and ten per cent more frequently from the retailer's catalogue' (p. 381).

This is borne out by Goldsmith and Flynn's (2005) empirical study of fashion shoppers, which indicated that heavy buyers of clothing tend to be more interested in fashion, more fashion innovative and more innovative in terms of engaging in online buying compared to light and medium buyers of fashion goods. Further to this, consumers who frequently choose to purchase fashion goods remotely, either via catalogue or the Internet are less fashion involved. Hence Goldsmith and Flynn (2005) suggest retailers using remote channels may be most successful by selling 'standard' clothing items online rather than high-fashion items.

Whilst multi-channel marketing strategies by definition seek to encourage multi-channel consumer behaviour (Nicholson et al., 2002), the challenge for researchers is to attempt to identify the situational factors such as the time of day and presence or absence of others that prompt multi-channel consumers to select from a particular channel at any one point in time. Nicholson et al. (2002) attempt to do this in their study of consumer shopping channel selection for fashion goods when faced with multiple retail channels. Theoretical underpinning for their research was provided by through Belk's (1975) taxonomy of situational variables affecting consumer behaviour. In this taxonomy five dimensions are identified, which are physical surrounding, social surrounding, temporal perspective, task definition and antecedent states. Each of these are defined in Table 13.2 below together with Nicholson et al.'s (2002) application of these variables in context to a retailer's web site.

Results obtained from Nicholson et al.'s (2002) study suggest that differences exist in the importance of particular situational variables between shopping channels. For instance, they identified that mood reflected strongly in the target purchase as consumers were more likely to select a physical store when shopping for hedonic fashion goods or what the researchers described as 'treats'. With regard to this, they conclude:

> 'a strong physical environment serves as a powerful reinforcer in such circumstances, elevating the mood state further via enhanced opportunities for social interaction, product evaluation and sensory stimulation' (p.141).

Table 13.2 Belk's taxonomy of situational variables applied to retail web sites

	Belk's (1975) definition of five situational variables	Nicholson et al.'s (2002) application to retail web sites
Physical surroundings	The geographical and institutional location of a retail store. Also store decor, fixtures and fittings, sounds, aromas, lighting and visible configurations of merchandise.	Environment in which the consumer views the web site. Visible configurations of merchandise and provision of information including use of colours, illustrations and music in web design.
Social surroundings	People present in the retail situation, their characteristics, roles and interpersonal interactions.	Any interaction with telesales staff and online consumer communities associated with the web site.
Temporal perspective	Time of day, season of the year, pre- or post-lunchtime, pro- or post-payday.	Consumers can shop online anytime of the day, any day of the week.
Task definition	The requirement to select, shop for or obtain information about a general or specific purchase (e.g. task may be a gift purchase).	Purpose of shopping task may influence consumer's choice to shop via a retailer's web site.
Antecedent states	Mood when shopping (e.g. anxious or excited) and condition of shopper (e.g. unwell or tired).	Choosing to shop via a web site may be influenced by a consumer's mood.

As in shopping in physical stores, consumer accounts of shopping via catalogues were also dominated by mood factors as respondents saw the catalogue as a relaxing read and something to 'unwind' with or indulge in. Hence temporal factors had little influence on the decision to shop both within a physical store and using a catalogue. This was not the case with online shopping. Rather temporal factors exerted a positive influence on the decision for the respondents to shop online. For instance a task to purchase functional clothing exhibited a lower motivation to devote the time to shopping as respondents indicated that they would prefer to purchase these kinds of clothing items online because it took less time.

A further finding by Nicholson et al. (2002) was that whilst respondents were making consumer purchases online, they were not actually shopping online. Rather purchase selections were being made by the retailer's catalogue and only the ordering stage of the purchasing process was being made online. This finding is supported by a report in *Retail Week* (2000), which indicated that Next customers were using a combination of the Internet and Next

Directory to shop. The article further reported that customers using both in combination spent on average 20 per cent more than customers using the catalogue alone.

Nicholson et al. (2002) conclude that it is naïve to think of the various shopping channels to market in isolation. Rather they should be seen as three different types of shopping experience as consumers are combining the various channels and making a channel selection based upon mood and lifestyle demands. Ultimately physical store shopping is viewed as a mood-enhancing experience and online shopping is viewed as a vehicle to make repeat purchases for standard or functional items of clothing. In addition to this, consumers will use remote channels to market in combination with each other.

Conclusion

Internet shopping for fashion goods is still in its infancy and researchers' conclusions based upon the empirical work reported in this chapter may not hold for long, given the current rapid developments of e-commerce technologies and the increasing number of computer savvy consumers (Kim and Kim, 2004). The current empirical work being reported within this subject area is summarized in Table 13.3 below.

Evident from the research being undertaken is that e-tailing has gradually moved from being a curiosity towards becoming a mainstream retail channel. This research has captured this movement within a specific retail sector, fashion. However whilst it has made an important contribution to the subject area, a number of limitations can be identified. First, the use of university or college students as convenience samples. Whilst this group provide access to large numbers of consumers, plus a high proportion of university students are fashion leaders (Behling, 1992) who will be well practised in using the Internet, there is a need to examine how far such results are generalizable across the population. Further to this, a number of studies drew upon female consumers only. Whilst benefits for using females are that they shop for fashion goods more often than men (Mintel, 2005b), such studies neglect to capture the total picture with regard to consumer clothing purchasing behaviour online. With regard to studies that have focused upon how retailers go about developing their web sites, and web site strategies adopted, again limitations are identified as these studies have drawn on small sample sizes, typically one or two case study companies only; again making it difficult to generalize the findings.

In conclusion, roads are being made through exploratory research to understand better both consumer behaviour with regards to e-tail shopping and fashion web site presence and development, however further empirical research is called for in order to give the subject area more academic and commercial value; in addition to this, theoretical models need to be developed.

Table 13.3 Empirical work on fashion e-tailing

	Aim of Study	Findings	Sample
WEB SITE PRESENCE & DEVELOPMENT			
Ashworth et al. (2005)	Conceptualize & contrast the stages in development of a fashion retail web site.	Identifies a five stage e-tail Internet strategy model.	Comparative case study based on one pure play and one bricks and mortar UK SME fashion retailers.
Jang and Burns (2004)	Differences between types of online fashion retailers and components of their web sites.	Competition among web sites is based upon how information is provided as oppose to what information is provided on fashion retailers' web sites.	36 apparel retailing web sites.
Marciniak and Bruce (2004)	Fashion retailer use of web sites	Product specialists have greater levels of involvement in e-commerce.	990 fashion retailers operating within the UK.
Marciniak and Bruce (2005)	Identification of planning styles adopted by fashion retailers.	No one approach to strategy planning is evident within e-retailing. More than one approach can be adopted within the same organization.	Two case study companies, both multi-channel UK fashion retailers
Salmeron and Hurtado (2005)	Strategic objectives pursued by a fashion retailer when developing e-commerce provision	Increase in revenue, facilitation of purchases from consumers & amplification of brand recognition are the most important factors associated with establishing a B2C web site.	Case study company of one top European fashion design/ retail business.

(continued)

Table 13.3 (Continued)

	Aim of Study	Findings	Sample
CONSUMER BEHAVIOUR & ONLINE CLOTHING SHOPPING			
Goldsmith and Flynn (2005)	Compare & contrast consumers who buy fashion goods in stores, from catalogues and online.	Consumers who shop more frequently & spend more on clothing do so via all three shopping modes. Buying online is closely related to buying from a catalogue.	Questionnaires to 805 male & female students in studying marketing at a US university.
Goldsmith and Flynn (2004)	Identification of demographic & psychological characteristics of consumers that may lead them to make online clothing purchases.	Being an adventurous online buyer & heavy catalogue shopper has the most impact on online clothing buying.	Questionnaires to 805 male & female students in studying marketing at a US university.
Goldsmith and Goldsmith (2002)	Identification of characteristics that distinguish consumers who have purchased online and those who have not.	Demographic variables of age, sex & race are unrelated to online buying behaviour. Online apparel buyers do not differ from non-online buyers in terms of enjoyment of shopping & frequency of purchases.	Questionnaires distributed to 263 men & 303 women students in the US.
Kim and Kim (2004)	Predictors of the intention to purchase clothing online	Transaction/cost and incentive programs factors are important predictors in determining the intention to purchase clothing online.	Mail survey using questionnaires to 303 US male and female adult consumers.
Kim and Stoel (2004)	Dimensions of web site quality as significant predictors of customer satisfaction.	Information fit-to-task, transaction capability & response time are significant predictors of shopper satisfaction.	273 questionnaires to US female online apparel shoppers.

Author	Purpose	Findings	Method
Lu and Rucker (2006)	Identification of predictors of channel choice for apparel acquisition.	The intention to use multiple channels is positively related to convenience orientation & Internet connectivity for Chinese consumers, whilst age is negatively related for US consumers.	Focus group interviews plus 203 questionnaires using female college students at large state universities in China & US.
Nicholson et al. (2002)	Understanding of consumer selection between available channels for clothing purchases.	Different shopping methods are selected individually in different situations. Consumers combine & integrate channels as part of the decision-making process for one clothing purchase.	Longitudinal qualitative case study of one UK fashion retailer's 48 female customers who all shop via multiple channels using focus groups & shopping diaries.
Phau and Chang-Chin (2004)	Fashion innovator behaviour	There is no difference between fashion innovators and non-innovators in Internet purchase behaviour.	Questionnaire via mall intercept to 225 male & female Australian consumers.
Siddiqui et al. (2003)	Online activities of established fashion retailers captured through both retailer & consumer perceptions of fashion retailers' web page designs.	Fashion retailers are 'failing to create an exciting online offer'.	25 interviews with consumers plus 1 consumer focus group and 1 interview with fashion retail organization.

References

Ansoff, H. I. (1991). Critique to Henry Mintzberg's The design school: reconsidering the basic premises on strategic management. *Strategic Management Journal* **12** (6), 449–461.

Ashworth, C. J., Schmidt, R. A., Pioch, E.A. and Hallsworth, A. (2005). An approach to sustainable 'fashion' e-retail: a five-stage evolutionary strategy for 'Clicks-and-Mortar' and 'Pure-Play' enterprises. *Journal of Retailing and Consumer Services, In Press, Corrected Proof, Available online 12 October 2005.*

Barlow, A. K. J., Siddiqui, N. Q. and Mannion, M. (2004). Developments in information and communication technologies for retail marketing channels. *International Journal of Retail & Distribution Management,* **32** (3), 157–163.

Beaudry, L. M. (1999). The consumer catalog shopping survey. *Catalog Age,* **16** (6), A5–A18.

Beck, B. (2004). Key strategic issues in online apparel retailing [http://tc2host.com/techexchange/thelibrary/online_fit.html] *accessed 24th January 2006.*

Behling, D. U. (1992). Three and a half decades of fashion adoption research: what have we learned? *Clothing and Textiles Research Journal,* **10** (2), 34–41.

Belk, R. W. (1975). Situational variables and consumer behaviour. *Journal of Consumer Research,* **2** (3), 157–165.

Breitenbach, C. S. and Van Doren, D. C. (1998). Value added marketing in the digital domain: enhancing the utility of the Internet. *Journal of Consumer Marketing,* **5** (6), 558–575.

Chaffee, E. (1985). Three modes of strategy. *Academy of Management Review,* **10** (1), 89–99.

Chen, Q. and Wells, W. D. (1999). Attitude toward the site. *Journal of Advertising Research,* **39** (5), 27–37.

Coleman, K. (1998). Make your web site a business success. *E-Business Advisor.* pp. 12–17.

Corcoran, C. T. (2005). Ghost in the machine, *Women's Wear Daily,* **189** (51), 5.

Damesick, P. (2002). E-commerce and UK retail property: trends and issues. *Briefings in Real Estate Finance,* **1** (1), 18–27.

Dudley, D. (2005). Arcadia focuses online as a key growth area for Topman brand. *New Media Age,* November 13th.

Donthu, N., Garcia, A. (1999). The Internet shopper. *Journal of Advertising Research,* **39** (3), 52–58.

Eastlick, M., Feinberg, R. A. (1999). Shopping motives for mail catalog shopping. *Journal of Business Research,* **45** (3), 281–290.

Goldsmith, R. E. and Goldsmith, E. B. (2002). Buying apparel over the Internet. *Journal of Product & Brand Management,* **11** (2), 89–102.

Goldsmith, R. E. and Flynn, L. R. (2004). Psychological and behavioural drivers of online clothing purchase. *Journal of Fashion Marketing and Management,* **8** (1).

Goldsmith, R. E. and Flynn, L. R. (2005). Bricks, clicks, and pix: apparel buyers' use of stores, Internet, and catalogs compared. *International Journal of Retail & Distribution Management,* **33** (4), 271–283.

Hall, J. (1999). Ready2Shop to consider offline stores. *Retail Week* December 3rd.

Harrington, R. J., Lemak, D., Reed, R. and Kendall, K.W. (2004). A question of fit: the links among environment, strategy formulation and performance. *Journal of Business and Management,* 10(1).

Howell, N. (2005). Dressed to impress. *New Media Age,* March, 31st pp.16–17.

Huizingh, E. K. R. E. (2002). The antecedents of Web site performance. *European Journal of Marketing,* **36** (11), 1225–247.

Interactive Media in Retail Group (2005). E-retail 2006: *Annual Report,* Executive Summary [http://www.imrg.org/8025696F004581B3/(search)/414001EACDDC483180256FD9002AF69E?Opendocument&highlight=2] accessed 20/1/06.

Jang, E., Burns, L. D. (2004). Components of apparel retailing web sites. *Journal of Fashion Marketing and Management,* **8** (4), 375–388.

Jones, J. M. and Vijaysarathy, L. R. (1998). Internet consumer catalog shopping: findings from an exploratory study and directions for future research. *Journal of Internet Research: Electronic Applications and Policy,* **8** (4), 322–330.

Kearns, G. S. (2005). An electronic commerce strategy typology: insights from case studies. *Information & Management,* **42** (7), 1023–1036.

Kim, E. Y. and Kim, Y. K. (2004). Predicting online purchase intentions for clothing products. *European Journal of Marketing,* **38** (7), 883–897.

Kim, S. and Stoel, L. (2004). Apparel retailers: website quality dimensions and satisfaction. *Journal of Retailing and Consumer Services,* **11** (2), 109–117.

Koontz, M. L. (2002). Mixed reality merchandising: bricks, clicks – and mix. *Journal of Fashion Marketing and Management,* **6** (4), 381–395.

Lipke, D. J. (2000). Mystery shoppers. *American Demographics,* **20** (12), 41–43.

Lu, Y. and Rucker, M. (2006). Apparel acquisition via single vs. multiple channels: college students' perspectives in the US and China. *Journal of Retailing and Consumer Services,* **13** (1), 35–50.

Marciniak, R. and Bruce, M. (2004). Identification of UK fashion retailer use of web sites. *International Journal of Retail & Distribution Management,* **32** (8), 386–393.

Marciniak, R. and Bruce, M. (2005). Planning for e-commerce in fashion retailing. In Greenland, S. and Caldwell, N. (Eds.), *Contemporary Issues in Marketing,* London: Metropolitan University, pp. 34–51.

McGolderick, P., Vasquez, D., Lim, T. Y. and Keeling, K. (1999). Cyberspace marketing: how do surfers determine website quality. In Broadbridge, A. (Ed.), *10th International Conference on Research in the Distributive Trades.* Institute for Retail Studies, University of Stirling, Stirling, Scotland, pp. 603–613.

Martin, L. and Kambil, A. (1999). Looking back and thinking ahead: effects of prior success on manager's interpretations of new information technologies. *Academy of Management Journal,* **42,** 52–61.

Mintel (2005a). *Books* – UK – June 2005.

Mintel (2005b). *Clothing Retailing* – UK – July 2005.

Mintel (2005d). *Home Shopping* – UK – March 2005.

Moin, D. (2004). Sears brings fashion mix to the Internet. *Women's Wear Daily*, **188** (56).

Moore, C. M. (1995). From rags to riches: creating and benefiting from the fashion own-brand. *International Journal of Retail & Distribution Management*, **23** (9), 19–27.

Morrell, l. (2006). Big story: ebay – watch and learn. *Retail Week*, January 13th.

New Media Age (2005). Brands should focus on female shoppers. *New Media Age* June 23rd p.15.

Nicholson, M., Clarke, I. and Blakemore, M. (2002). One brand, three ways to shop: situational variables and multichannel consumer behaviour. *Review of Retail, Distribution & Consumer Research*, **12** (2), 131–148.

Phau, I. and Chang-Chin, L. (2004). Profiling fashion innovators: a study of self-concept, impulse buying and Internet purchase intent. *Journal of Fashion Marketing and Management*, **8** (4), 399–411.

Porter, M. (2001). Strategy and the Internet. *Harvard Business Review*, **79** (3), 62–79.

Quelch, J. A. and Klein, L. R. (1996). Internet and International Marketing. *Sloan Management Review Spring*, pp. 60–75.

Retail Week (2000). Next customers spend more online. March 31st.

Retail Week (2003). Next is the first choice of women on the Internet. June 27th.

Salmeron, J. L. and Hurtado, J. M. (2005). Modelling the reasons to establish B2C in the fashion industry. *Technovation, In Press, Corrected Proof, Available online 19 July 2005*.

Schoenbachler, D. D. and Gordon, G. L. (2002). Multi-channel shopping: understanding what drives channel choice. *Journal of Consumer Marketing*, **19** (2002), 42–53.

Siddiqui, N., O'Malley, L., McColl, J. and Birtwistle, G. (2003). Retailer consumer perceptions of online fashion retailers: web site design issues. *Journal of Fashion Marketing and Management*, **7** (4), 345–355.

Stockport, G. J., Kunnath, G. and Sedick, R. (2001). Boo.com: the path to failure. *Journal of Interactive Marketing*, **15** (4), 56–70.

Stroud, D. (1998). Internet Strategies MacMillan Business.

Then, N. K., and Delong, M. R. (1999). Apparel shopping on the web. *Journal of Family and Consumer Sciences*, **91** (3), 65–68.

Weir, L. (2005). Catalogue sales drop as e-tailers expand. *Retail Week*, November 18th.

14

The international flagship stores of luxury fashion retailers

Christopher M. Moore and Anne Marie Doherty

Introduction

Luxury fashion retailers are among the most prodigious of the international retailers. Their commitment to international participation is evidenced by the breadth and diversity of the foreign market coverage and the contribution of foreign sales to their overall business income. For example, the Giorgio Armani Group is represented in over one hundred countries and in 2004, 82 per cent of their sales were from foreign markets (Gruppo Armani S.p.A, 2004a). The internationalization strategies that they adopt are often complex and appear impenetrable, dependent as they are upon multi-layered business networks. Yet, despite their often complicated international arrangements, most, if not all of the international luxury fashion retailers are committed to maintaining international flagship stores.

In what is now regarded as the 'experience economy', where the experience of acquiring a product is as important as ownership of the product itself, the flagship store plays a pivotal role in communicating the retailer's values and market positioning to prospective consumers. If executed well, it offers a managed luxury consumption experience which coherently and consistently supports the status of the luxury fashion retailer, their brands and their values. Little has been written about the purpose and status of the international luxury fashion flagship store. In this chapter we offer some observations and comments with respect to this important dimension of luxury fashion retailer internationalization.

Definitions of luxury are varied and extensive (see Beverland, 2004 for a comprehensive review of these). However, definitions of luxury fashion retailing are difficult to locate. We define luxury fashion retailers as those firms that distribute clothing, accessories and other lifestyle products which are:-

- exclusively designed and/or manufactured by/or for the retailer;
- exclusively branded with a recognized insignia, design handwriting or some other identifying device;
- perceived to be of a superior design, quality and craftsmanship;
- priced significantly higher than the market norm;
- sold within prestigious retail settings.

An illustrative, but not exclusive list of the luxury fashion retailers that fit our categorization would include Chanel, Louis Vuitton, Giorgio Armani, Prada, Hermes, Burberry, Gucci, Lanvin, Chloe, Mulberry, Fendi, Dunhill and Jil Sander.

International flagship stores

The maintenance of an international network of flagship stores can, on the face of it, seem like an unnecessary extravagance on the part of the luxury fashion retailer. While no company will admit to a loss-making flagship, the significant capital investment required to open a new store and the high operating costs associated with their day-to-day running, has led many commentators and analysts to predict that these stores are loss-making showcases which in the majority of cases fail to deliver a contribution to company profitability. If it is the case that international flagship stores are not directly profitable, then it may be the case that that is not their function. While perhaps breaking the rules of prudent business management, these costly outlets provide a return to their business in other, more indirect ways: ways that would justify their continuance, even if their costs outweigh their income.

A generic definition of flagship stores was provided by Kozinets et al. (2002) who identified three characteristics as follows:-

1 They carry only a single brand of product:
2 They are company-owned:
3 They operate with the intention of building brand image rather than solely to generate profit for the company.

We will return later to consider whether this definition sufficiently represents the dimensions of the international luxury fashion flagship. Figure 14.1 provides a scheme for the examination of the international flagship store, of which four core dimensions are identified as follows: location and place; the strategic purpose; the place of the flagship in the distribution hierarchy in a foreign market and the language of flagships.

The remainder of this chapter will examine each dimension in detail.

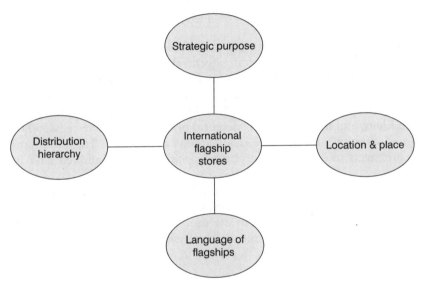

Figure 14.1 Dimensions of the luxury fashion flagship store.

The strategic purpose of a flagship store

As a preliminary to understanding the strategic purpose of the luxury fashion flagship store, it is important to return to the initial definition. While it is typically the case that the three definitional dimensions are relevant to luxury fashion retailers, a definition within this sector must also incorporate other important dimensions and recognize significant distinctions. First, not every international store, even if is the only store that a luxury fashion retailer has in a particular foreign market, can be classed as a flagship store. Instead, luxury fashion flagship stores are only to be found in those markets that are currently – or promise to be – the most financially lucrative for the luxury retailer. For example, the British luxury retailer Burberry operates stores in Europe, the USA and Asia, but identifies only four – in London, New York, Barcelona and Tokyo – as flagship stores. For Burberry, the flagship stores are confined to its most important revenue markets (Moore and Birtwistle, 2004).

Second, the luxury fashion flagship store is further defined by its physical scale – particularly when compared to the retailer's other international stores. For example, the Armani Group's flagship in Hong Kong measures 8,700 square metres, while their principal stores in other cities, such as Barcelona and Athens, are much smaller, measuring 515 square metres and 825 square metres respectively. Within a crowded and highly competitive market, luxury fashion flagships need to impress – principally in terms of architectural scale. The very essence of luxury requires an association with extravagance and space, confidence and stability. The flagship store therefore serves as the physical manifestation of these intangible, yet vital brand characteristics through the provision of what may seem an excessive consumption space. The availability of what appears to be excess space becomes a defining element of a luxury consumption experience.

Third, and crucially, these flagship stores are physical declarations of luxury as communicated through their architectural features and the quality of the materials used. Consequently, it is now common for luxury retailers to commission celebrated architects to design their flagship stores. Notable collaborations include Rem Koolhaas who has designed for Prada; John Pawson for Calvin Klein, and the leading architectural practise, Future Systems, who have designed flagships for Comme des Garcons and Marni. The importance of these architects to luxury fashion brand positioning is examined later in this chapter.

Other than underlining their luxury market positioning, the significant financial investments that are made with respect to flagship stores are an important indication of their strategic role in the process of developing and supporting international expansion. The strategic significance of the flagship store within an international context can be categorized in four ways as delineated below:

1 as a market entry method;
2 as a conduit and support for partner relationships;
3 as the focus for marketing communications;
4 as a blueprint for store development.

Flagships: as a market entry method

As has been previously indicated, international luxury flagships are an expensive and on the face of it, a potentially uneconomical distribution method. However, for many luxury fashion brands, the flagship store marks their first direct investment within a foreign market. The role of flagships as the first means of entry into a foreign market has been unrecognized within the academic literature (Moore et al., 2000). However, recent developments within China, in particular, have shown that luxury fashion retailers open landmark flagship stores in strategic locations at the earliest stages of their business development within foreign markets. For example, by opening a flagship on Shanghai's Bund, the Armani Group proposed that this 'demonstrates our long-term commitment to this fast growing market, in which we plan to develop comprehensive distribution and retail channels for each of the Group's main brands and product lines' (Gruppo Armani S.p.A., 2004b). In the same communiqué, the Group also stated that after the launch of the Shanghai flagship, their corporate plan is to have a network of between 20 and 30 free-standing stores throughout China's most important cities by 2008.

Flagships as a market entry mechanism apply not only to greenfield locations but also to mature luxury markets – such as Japan – and to mature brands – such as Fendi. For example, after having acquired control of the Fendi business from Prada in 2001, the LVMH Group opened a Fendi flagship store in Tokyo in September 2003 (LVMH, 2003). Given that Japan accounted for 34 per cent of all LVMH fashion and leather goods sales in 2003, the development of a Fendi retail network in Japan – commencing with a flagship store opening in Tokyo – appears to make sound business sense.

Entering a foreign market with a flagship store communicates the retailer's commitment to a long-term participation within that market and indicates their expectations of market viability and development potential. Critical to the realization of these expectations is the need to develop credible relationships with business partners, opinion formers and target customer groups.

Flagships: a conduit and support for business relationships

Flagship stores serve as an important mediator in the development and management of collaborative relationships that must exist between the retailer and their partner/stockists within a foreign market. While many luxury fashion retailers, such as Gucci, Burberry, Fendi and Ralph Lauren, have sought to increase control over product distribution through the securing of direct ownership over their retail store networks, most rely upon franchise partners and third-party wholesale stockists for sizeable proportions of their sales income. For example in their 2004 Annual Accounts Ralph Lauren reported that 51.8 per cent of their total income was from wholesaling, while Burberry reported a figure of 52 per cent. Given the financial importance of wholesaling partners, it is critical that the internationalizing retailer establishes adequate devices to nurture and support these relationships.

Research by Doherty and Alexander (2004) has examined the range and diversity of formal and informal mechanisms that internationalizing fashion retailers use in order to support and develop franchise activity. Predominant among these are those initiatives which seek to improve the resource management and business development skills of local partners.

Similarly, flagship stores play an important role in partner relationship formation. As already noted, a flagship indicates a commitment to the foreign market by the internationalizing retailer and raises the profile of the brand in the mind of local consumers. Furthermore, this marker also attracts stockists and franchise partners to the brand since the flagship indicates internal resource capability on the part of the internationalizing retailer and suggests the availability of some form of market development strategy.

Flagship stores which are usually meticulously controlled in terms of operating standards and merchandising methods, provide a tangible guide and direction to stockists in terms of brand presentation. Typically, flagships hold the complete brand offer in terms of the various sub-brands and total product options. By encouraging partners to make flagship visits, the luxury fashion retailer is able to communicate and inculcate the positioning and values of their brands.

Moore et al. (2000) found that prospective partners of premium fashion brands identified the availability of a flagship store as an important criterion for determining which brands they stocked. From their perspective, the flagship was an important communications tool which attracted the attention of the media and other opinion formers, as well as current and potential customers.

Flagships: a focus for marketing communications

As will be discussed in the section which examines the language of luxury fashion flagship stores, these exist as tangible manifestations writ large of the brand within the foreign market. This is perhaps best exemplified in the opening of a 900 square metre flagship store in Shanghai by Louis Vuitton in late 2004. The largest luxury store yet opened in China, the store has a 10-metre high glass façade etched with the brand's house insignia – the Damier check (LVMH, 2004). This store is a confident and extravagant statement by the Louis Vuitton brand of its aspirations within the Chinese market. Its purpose is also to attract public attention and to generate interest, and hopefully sales, from Shanghai's brand aficionados.

Flagships, such as the theatrically dramatic Donna Karan flagship store on London's Bond Street, are statement pieces which stimulate interest, attract attention and ensure that the brand appears and remains on their target customer's shopping list. These sales may come through the flagship store or instead through the business' other retail outlets and third-party stockists. For some retailers however, such as the Italian luxury menswear brand Ermenegildo Zegna, the majority of sales in a foreign market come via the flagship store. In Zegna's case, 45 per cent of the company's UK sales are from their Bond Street flagship store (Foster, 2004).

However, in most cases, the majority of sales are derived from other channels – such as department store concessions and third-party wholesale stockists. In these cases, a primary purpose of the flagship is to promote and support sales within these other outlets. These other stockists need not be located in the same city as the flagship store in order to benefit from its effect. For example, British wholesale stockists located outside of London recognize the positive effect of the London 'flagship' upon demand for fashion goods. An important impact may also be derived from press coverage of new store openings or celebrity events hosted at the flagship. Furthermore, with more of their customers having a greater awareness of the London flagship stores, as well as the means of visiting them on a regular basis, the increased exposure stimulates luxury brand purchasing at the local level. As a caveat to this apparently symbiotic relationship, the role of the independent stockist may become less tenable in the future as a result of the increase in the number of provincial stores directly operated by the luxury brand retailers in the UK (Foster, 2004).

Flagship stores also provide an important place for the luxury brand to be promoted to luxury fashion opinion formers. The importance of celebrity endorsements and close associations has long been recognized by luxury fashion companies (Breward, 2003), and the flagship store provides the opportunity for celebrities to be feted and then photographed as they leave the flagship with their possibly free gratis products. Other than providing a space to host celebrity events, the flagship store also provides the opportunity for the company to showcase their entire collections to the fashion press – especially at the launch of a new season.

The creation and nurturing of positive relationships with the fashion press is critical for the luxury fashion brand. And while editorial coverage within the leading monthly fashion magazines is determined by the brand's level of advertizing spend with that publication, newspaper coverage is more at the discretion of the fashion editors and writers. In an effort to influence these fashion reporters, many luxury fashion companies will establish and staff a local Press Office. The purpose of this office is to represent the brand to the local media through the provision of corporate photography (that can be used for publication); corporate and product information, as well as press samples of their 'must have' products of the season which can be used for photo shots. Working in conjunction with the Press Office, the flagship store because of its placement within the primary fashion districts, ensures that the brand remains in the memory of local fashion reporters.

It should not be forgotten that the flagship store plays an important role in creating and maintaining customer loyalty. Through such initiatives as exclusive fashion shows, private shopping evenings and public relations events – such as book launches – the flagship serves as a place where the relationship between the brand and the key customer is established and enhanced. Within this context, the Armani Group recently announced that 5 per cent of their flagship customers generated 52 per cent of sales. Using a year's worth of credit card data, Armani found that unlike other businesses where 20 per cent of customers account for 60 per cent of turnover, for the company, the figure was 80 per cent (Ody, 2005). Consequently, the Armani Group is committed to a strategy which encourages more frequent flagship store visits by its highest spending customers.

Flagships: blueprint for store development

As a naval term, a flagship was the most impressive and important, and its purpose was to lead and direct the lesser ships in the fleet. It is not far-fetched to suggest that the luxury fashion flagship store plays a similar role within foreign markets. In response to an increase in consumer demand for luxury goods, the international fashion brands have extended their retail coverage beyond capital cities and the leading commercial centres to include a greater regional participation. For example, Louis Vuitton, the leading luxury brand, has extended its UK retail store network from its Bond Street flagship to include stand-alone stores and major department store concessions within Edinburgh, Manchester, Birmingham and Dublin. This has resulted in sales of the brand doubling in the past 4 years – with the brand's concession in Selfridges in Manchester reaching £4 million in 2003–2004 (Foster, 2004). All of these Louis Vuitton satellite stores share a common store fit – in terms of fixtures, fittings and décor – that replicates the brand identity portrayed by the Bond Street flagship.

As brands such as Louis Vuitton, Armani and Mulberry extend beyond their flagship stores to open smaller outlets locally or in other cities within a foreign market, their flagships exert an important influence over these satellites. In operational terms, it is the blueprint for management procedures, information technology processes and stock handling methods. Staffing and other human resource policies are typically developed there and then extended to the satellite stores.

But perhaps the most obvious and arguably most important flagship store influence is in terms of the architecture and design of the satellite stores. A central tenet of luxury brand success is the need for consistency and coherence in terms of how the customer experiences the brand. The flagship store affords the visitor the opportunity to 'experience' the values of the luxury brand. Therefore, it offers a formula of how the luxury brand ought to be presented, communicated and experienced in all outlets within the market. As a result, the format is faithfully replicated – but in a more modest scale – within the satellite stores and concessions that the brand operates elsewhere in the market.

The extent to which a flagship serves as a retail formula – or in some instances identified as a retail footprint – is perhaps best exemplified by the Armani Group's strategy. The Armani Group is comprised of six lifestyle brands – of which the Giorgio Armani brand is pre-eminent. The world flagship for this brand is located in Milan on Via Sant' Andrea. Designed by the internationally acclaimed architect, Claudio Silvestrin (2001), this flagship has served as the prototype for the other Giorgio Armani flagship stores the Group has opened in Paris, Moscow, Vienna, Dubai, Hong Kong and Barcelona. The influence of the world flagship upon the other flagship stores is acknowledged by the Group in the Press Communiqué for the launch of the refurbished Giorgio Armani Flagship in London as follows:

'The interior will echo the beauty and simplicity of the Silvestrin-designed flagship boutique in Milan. Each Silvestrin-designed boutique has a unique feature and in London it is the construction of an impressive water sculpture five metres high'

(Gruppo Armani S.p.A. 2003b).

As identified in the above statement, the Armani Group, like many of the other luxury fashion retailers, adopt a standardized approach to flagship store development. Central to this standardization is the influence of the world flagship and the design direction of one architect. This standardization represents yet another dimension of the global marketing strategies that luxury brands adopts – the primary purpose of which is to present a consistent brand identity regardless of the geographic or cultural context.

In an effort to expand their market reach and manage market volatility, the leading fashion houses have developed diffusion brands, of which the Armani Group has been among the most successful. From the main Giorgio Armani Collection, the group has developed a number of diffusion brands as detailed in Table 14.1 below:

Table 14.1 Armani Group Brands

Group brands	Positioning	Date of establishment
Giorgio Armani	Main line – couture	1975
Emporio Armani	Younger – affordable	1981
Armani Exchange	Younger – trendy – entry level prices	1991
Armani Collezioni	Diffusion of main line	1997
Armani Jeans	Denim offer	1997
Armani Casa	Home furnishings	2003

Source: Gruppo Armani S.p.A. (2003a).

For each of the diffusion brands, the Armani Group has developed a retail distribution network that fully replicates the strategy developed to support the distribution of the main Giorgio Armani brand. As such, each of the diffusion brands has a number of strategically placed flagships within their key trading markets. The format for each of the diffusion flagships is then carefully replicated in all satellite stores.

There are some exceptions to the standardized flagship design rule and two notable examples, at Prada and Comme des Garcons, will be examined at the end of this chapter.

Location and place

Alongside their having a heightened status within the retail store hierarchy of the luxury fashion retailer, flagship stores share some common locational characteristics. These can be considered at the macro and micro levels, as well as in terms of occupancy costs.

Macro-level features

At the macro level, flagship stores are almost always situated in the capital city – or in the most important commercial city – of the retailer's most important foreign markets. To illustrate this latter point, while Milan is not the capital of Italy, nor New York the capital of the USA, both play host to the vast majority of the foreign flagship stores located in each country. This concentration in the non-capitals of Milan and New York is inevitable. Both serve as the commercial centres for fashion in their respective markets and each outweighs their capital city counterparts in terms of economic and social significance. However, both are perhaps high profile exceptions to the rule. In most other cases, flagship stores are a capital city phenomenon. Hollander (1970) described this citing of the flagship stores as the 'New York, London, Paris syndrome'. In most cases, the luxury fashion brands adhere to Hollander's description. However, as new and lucrative markets have emerged the geographic spread of these stores has widened to include Moscow, Shanghai and Hong Kong.

While it would appear that no study has examined cities in terms of flagship store density, the sheer proliferation of these stores in Tokyo would suggest that this is the luxury fashion flagship capital of the world. This density is perhaps best explained by the fact that Japan accounts for approximately one-third of all luxury goods sales (Mintel, 2004). Another important flagship city is Milan. British fashion houses, such as Burberry, Paul Smith, Vivienne Westwood, Alexander McQueen and Pringle of Scotland have all established flagship stores in Milan in recent years. Anecdotal reports from industry commentators suggest that Milanese fashion shoppers are not especially interested in British or other non-Italian brands – so the decision to open a flagship is not in response to significant local market demand. Instead, companies such as Pringle of Scotland have maintained that a flagship in Milan is an important strategic investment. Having a presence in Milan helps secure a reputation as a credible fashion house – particularly in the premium menswear market – which is all but based in Milan where most of the menswear selling shows take place. A presence on the Via Monte Napoleone or there-abouts helps secure international media coverage, as well as the attention of buyers from the leading department stores in the US, Japan and Europe.

Micro-level features

At the micro level, flagships are concentrated within specific streets or closely knit districts that are geographically and socially proximate and accessible to 'high net worth individuals', fashion-aware consumers and international visitors/tourists. In most cases, these flagships cluster together to create luxury enclaves that are recognized as such by the wider community. These streets – such as Bond Street in London, Madison Avenue in New York and Via Monte Napoleone in Milan – provide a prestigious address which supports the luxury credentials of the retailers located there. The high concentration of luxury flagships within these very confined locations serves to augment and enhance the exclusivity and allure of the luxury brands. Perhaps, more importantly, this concentration assures these areas as important shopping destinations for local and visiting consumers. Indeed, it has been noted that in cities such as London, the majority of flagship customers are tourists and business visitors to the UK (Mintel, 2004). The emergence of these luxury enclaves as powerful tourist attractions has not gone unnoticed by the local civic authorities. For example, Visit London – London's Tourist Agency, rigorously promotes the city's luxury fashion offer as a principal reason for visiting the capital.

The allure of the luxury flagship is further enhanced by the status and heritage of the building that it occupies. For example, the Giorgio Armani store in Shanghai is located in an early 1900s neo-classical building; while Louis Vuitton's Manhattan flagship is built in the New York Trust Company building. The decision to establish new flagships within landmark buildings has a practical benefit in that it helps to locate the premises for locals and visitors. But perhaps most importantly, the acquisition of imposing residencies – such as the Rhinelander Mansion in New York by Ralph Lauren or former bank buildings such as the former Royal Bank of Scotland Building by Jil Sander at Burlington Gardens, London – help to create, support and reinforce the premium positioning of the luxury brand. For example, the connotations of the Rhinelander Mansion support Lauren's brand proposition with its aristocratic associations, while the austerity of the Sander flagship reflect the clinical purity of that brand.

High occupancy costs

Access to these prestigious locations comes at a high cost. Fernie et al. (1998) noted a significant variance in the rental and operating charges of the luxury flagship districts in London and New York compared to other comparable commercial districts. Other studies have noted that premium occupancy costs for luxury districts are a feature of other world centres. Tracking the retail rental charges of 229 shopping districts in 45 countries, Cushman and Wakefield, and Healey and Baker's (2004) reported the dominant position of streets with a high proportion of luxury brand tenants. New York's Fifth Avenue – with its high proportion of luxury fashion brands – was found to be the world's most expensive street – with rents at £5,680 per square metre in 2004. Bond Street, which has a concentration of luxury fashion brands, was found to be the third most expensive street in Europe with an average rental charge of £3,036 per square metre in 2004.

Consequently, luxury analysts and other commentators have proposed that only a minority of these flagships are profitable. For example and as mentioned previously, Ermenegildo Zegna operates a flagship in London, alongside a small store in the City and a concession in Harrods. In 2003 these cumulatively generated sales of £8.7 million, but made a loss before tax of £111,000 (Foster, 2004). The high occupancy and operating costs and the low levels of profitability may explain why most flagship stores are directly owned by the international retailer and not a franchise partner (Moore et al., 2000).

Yet, despite the astronomical occupancy and operating costs, tenant turnover in these districts is typically low and the retailer mix tends to remain constant. This consistency in luxury tenant profile is as a result of strict landlord tenant controls and prohibitively high occupancy costs. But for whatever reason, it is also clear that access to these areas is not available to the smaller/fledgling luxury firms. Their lack of resources means that they are denied access to these prestige locations and the rich customers that these attract.

Flagships and the distribution hierarchy

Thus far it has been established that the flagship store plays a critical role in the luxury fashion retailer's internationalization strategy. In particular, it acts as a showcase for the full merchandise range and for this reason it takes precedence in the distribution hierarchy in three main ways.

First, in merchandising terms, the flagship store will usually stock the brand's full merchandise assortment which is allocated in advance of any other outlet or stockist within the market. This prioritization enables the flagship to fulfil the expectations of its key customers and maintain high levels of customer service. The fact that these stores face considerable scrutiny from the media, celebrities and competitors is a further reason for a commitment to high stock levels. In the case of the largest flagships where sales demand is high, it is not unusual for the flagship to have a dedicated warehouse to assist in efficient stock replenishment.

The stock assortment of the other satellite outlets will be less extensive. These assortments are edited to match the size of store, its sales history and the competitive environment in which it operates. Third-party stockists will offer the narrowest assortment – although variations will exist among customers depending upon the scale of their buying. For example, buyers representing prestigious department stores may be able to access products from the full assortment in order that the luxury brand can secure the best location within that store. And while these department stores may be able to negotiate access to the brands most covetable products, they would not stock the breadth and depth of the collection available within the brand's flagship store.

In recognition of the special status of certain department stores and other stores within important trading markets, many luxury brands now develop products that are exclusive to these third-party stockists. For example, the British department store chain Harvey Nichols has secured an exclusive range of accessories from the luxury brand Bottega Veneta. These goods were marketed by Harvey Nichols as a marker of their status as a leading department store. Similarly, the niche luxury store Corso Como in Milan has secured exclusive ranges from a number of luxury brands, including Burberry, Prada, Gucci and Comme des Garcons. In this case, it could be argued that the cult status encouraged these luxury houses to develop collections marketed as 'Designed for Corso Como'.

Second, not only are new collections launched within flagship stores, but often these are allocated exclusive products which are not available through other channels. For example, the Gucci guitar, which was emblazoned with the Gucci double G insignia, was available only within the company's flagship stores including London, Milan, New York and Tokyo. It is not uncommon for luxury fashion firms to limit their most expensive and daring items in this way. It is not solely due to a desire to enhance the prestige of the flagship that motivates such limitations. Recognition of the limited nature of demand also explains the restrictions. The development of limited edition ranges – in product categories such as handbags and shoes – that are only available within flagship stores are a further development of a strategy which seeks to increase the volume of customer traffic passing through flagship stores.

Third, because flagship stores are usually owned by the luxury retailers and are therefore under their direct control, these stores benefit from greater levels of investment in areas such as technology and visual merchandising devices. For example, Prada has installed in their New York Epicentre Store a video device in their changing rooms which not only lets customers view the whole collections, but also allows them to view themselves wearing the ranges from whichever angle they so choose. Prada has also invested in Radio Frequency Identification Technology (RFID) which was designed to enable sales associates to capture information from a garment tag or a customer card with an RFID chip and gain access to a library containing information concerning the shopper's previous buying patterns. As we identify later, commentators have questioned whether these sorts of initiatives are commercially viable, but the important point to note at this stage is that these types of expensive technological investment are usually confined only to flagship stores.

The language of flagship stores

Retail atmospherics is a well-established area of academic research and various studies have sought to explain the impact of colour, scale, olfactory devices, texture, visual display methods and store layout techniques upon consumer mood and behaviour. From a practitioner perspective, luxury fashion retailers have come to recognize that their customers expect to be stimulated, entertained and excited within their retail stores. These customers have become expert in the skill of reading, decoding and understanding the various visual messages and cues that are embedded in the language of the luxury fashion retail experience. The technical specification and details of this language belong to the domain of architecture and design and are therefore beyond the scope of this chapter. However, in broad terms, this luxury flagship language is comprised of a number of signals, some of which relate to the scale of the building, the utilization of superior building and furnishing materials, the integration of innovative architectural and technical devices and the adoption of advanced lighting devices.

The purpose of the flagship store is to declare, communicate and enhance the values of the luxury fashion retailers and their brand(s) with respect to their target audience. The flagship store tells the story of the luxury fashion retailer. In order to better understand how that story is told, the remainder of this section will consider two important dimensions:

1 The role and function of the 'celebrity' architect.
2 The relationship between flagship store design and luxury retailer positioning.

The chapter concludes with a review of Prada's innovative approach to flagship store development – the Prada Epicentre store concept.

The role and function of the 'celebrated' Architect

Just as sales for Mulberry's Gisele, Roxanne and Bayswater bags have benefited from the endorsements of A-list celebrities such as Keira Knightley, Scarlett Johansson and Sienna Miller, then in a similar way the luxury flagship stores have gained in terms of prestige as a result of their associations with the leading architects of the day. Architects, such as John Pawson – as famous for designing a Cistercian Abbey in Burgundy as he is for the Calvin Klein flagship in Madison Avenue New York and Rem Koolhaas, who has designed for Prada, as well as the HQ for Central China Television and Seattle Public Library – contribute to the kudos and status of the flagship stores they design. Not all of those commissioned have experience of retail projects. For example, for his London flagship store on Bond Street, Ralph Lauren commissioned the American architect Thierry Despont. Despont had no previous retail design experience. However, he did have an extensive domestic design portfolio and an impressive client list that included such notables as Bill Gates, Calvin Klein, Conrad Black and the CEO of Warner Brothers, Terry Semel (Niesewand, 1999). By commissioning Despont, Ralph Lauren was not only accessing a significant design talent, he was also securing a credibility and kudos for his latest London venture as a result of this association.

The close relationship between leading architects and leading luxury designers is now well recognized. Sudjic (2000) noted a particular concentration of activity on one of London's principal luxury retail districts, where it was possible to find 'more high – profile, heavyweight, contemporary architects in Sloane Street than anywhere else in Britain' (p. 7). That street serves as an architectural 'Who's Who?' and includes work undertaken by such notable architects as David Chipperfield – for Dolce and Gabbana; Future Systems for Marni and Nigel Coates for Katherine Hamnett's store before it was acquired by Gucci.

There are three principal reasons for commissioning a noted architect to design a flagship store. First, these commissions provide access to talented, innovative, experienced and reliable designers who can make a significant contribution to the advancement of the business through their development of a memorable flagship experience. Second, their involvement helps to secure coverage of the flagship in the 'quality' press and among the cognoscenti – which in turn engenders interest in the company among lucrative target customer groups. Third, by commissioning a 'celebrated' architect, the retailers benefit from the development of a store design template which, as suggested previously in this chapter, can be used to direct the design of their other retail outlets in the home market and abroad.

Flagship store design and positioning

The way in which a flagship store is designed and subsequently looks is inextricably linked to the luxury retailer's positioning strategy. For example, Comme des Garcon assure control of their corporate image through the maintenance of a strict control regime for their flagship store design. Reflecting upon their strategy, Davey (1999) suggested that any change in the strategic positioning of Comme des Garcons is first manifest in the changes to their flagship store design. For example, with a positioning guided by what Davey (1999) described as 'rampant individuality and experiment', the design of the company's flagship store in New York clearly reflects these themes from the outset: the entrance is a silver tunnel made of aluminium panels which culminates into a store comprised of bright white, enamelled steel walls. The architects, Future Systems, have created a store which not only disorientates and challenges but also entices the customer. These characteristics lie at the heart of the Comme des Garcons philosophy and it is the architectural language of the flagship which provides the first clues to their design aesthetic.

It is the role of the architect to understand clearly the strategy, positioning and image of the luxury fashion retailer and to then interpret and communicate these core dimensions through their design and materials choice. The American architect, Peter Marino, who was the first architect to be awarded the prestigious Master of Design award from the Fashion Group International in 1997, is credited as being the pioneer in the development of the luxury flagship language. Having designed stores for Valentino, Christian Dior, Giorgio Armani, Louis Vuitton, Calvin Klein, Chanel, Yves Saint Laurent, Fendi and Donna Karan, his work recognizes the need for the language of the flagship store to quickly and efficiently communicate the positioning of the company to the passing customer.

The mechanics of Marino's design language is best evidenced in two of his stores situated on London's Bond Street. For the younger, urban ready-to-wear DKNY store, he sought, according to Niesewand (1998) to place a chunk of New York precinct straight into the very heart of traditional New Bond Street. Recognizing the DKNY brand positioning to be dynamic, energetic and inextricably linked to the vibrant values of New York, Marino's store front interprets these qualities by being deliberately open and unobstructed – plate glass is all that distinguishes the street from the store. With an electric white interior, an atrium penetrating four floors, a clear glass roof and an espresso bar at the entrance, the mood of the store is modern and cosmopolitan. Images of yellow NYC cabs are emblazoned on the back wall. The flagship environment harmonizes with and compliments the mood of the brand.

Across the street, Marino's design for the Donna Karan store is markedly different. Reflecting the brand's premium status, this flagship store is grander in scale and opulent in its fittings and furniture. The Portland stone frontage, the large scale windows and the solid and wide entrance, combine to indicate that entry to the store herald's an event, a truly memorable experience. Donna Karan's positioning is confident and dramatic, and the store interior is reminiscent of a film-set. A grand staircase rising from the front of the store moves the customer–actors between floors, while the black walls, dark furniture and the studio-style lighting generate the excitement of a Hollywood premiere. The distinction between the two stores is startling. The DKNY store is urban ready-to-wear, while the Donna Karan is the essence of American glamour.

Two further case examples illustrate the communicative function of the flagship store.

As noted earlier, the Giorgio Armani label holds the premium brand positioning within the Giorgio Armani Group. The special status of the brand is reflected in the exclusivity of its distribution, its premium price points and the high quality of the fabrics used. Commissioned to design the brand's Milanese flagship store in 2001, Claudio Silvestrin sought to reflect the understated and refined luxury inherent to the collection in this new venture. In his own review of the new store, he noted that his use of architecture attempted to communicate the brand's luxury values through the 'opulent use of empty – and commercially inactive – space' (Silvestrin, 2001). With an exterior clad in cream stone and with a sheer glass, apparently frameless front window, entry to the store is via a long stone ramp. Within the store, the linearity of the design is achieved by the use of ebony shelving against creamy stone walls. The simplicity of the merchandise display system and the precision embedded in the linearity of the layout scheme, serve to emphasize the simplicity and purity of the design inherent to the Giorgio Armani brand. Silvestrin's design augments, but never over-powers the impact of the merchandise assortment.

The second case example is the Marc Jacob's store in Japan. This store was the first to include both the luxury main line brand, Marc Jacobs Collection, with the Marc by Marc Jacobs diffusion line. The architects, Stephan Jaklitsch Design, faced a formidable challenge in having to develop a unified and coherent design scheme which also maintained and clearly communicated different brand identities for the two brands. The architects achieved this through differences in colour choice, materials, textures and furniture. A distinction was made between the brands in terms of where each was located in the building. The exclusivity of the Marc Jacob's Collection is underlined by its more private and discrete placement on the first and basement floors, while the diffusion brand, aimed at a younger customer, is sold on the ground floor to allow for maximum access. To further distinguish the two, the ground floor has a navy blue stained wood floor, a denim-covered sofa and high gloss white wall panels. The shelving and display systems, made of stainless steel and glass, seek to replicate the brand's vibrant and modern image. In contrast, the environment for the premium line utilizes subdued colours and more luxurious materials. Dark walnut veneer walls, the lacquered wood fixtures, the use of subdued lighting and the integration of leather furnishings, project a sense of affluence and extravagance. This store, in particular, illustrates how the language of the luxury flagship, with its array of design cues and signals, can effectively and efficiently communicate the very essence of the luxury brand.

Prada's epicentre stores

Described as a modern-day Medici for her architectural patronage, Miuccia Prada, co-owner of the Prada fashion house, has challenged the formulaic and standardized approach to international flagships with what she describes as Epicentre stores (Chow, 2003). Devised in the late 1990s as part of a strategy to protect the cutting-edge image of Prada, the company has continued to search for ways in which it could break away from the typical store design model and so create a new form of consumption experience. When asked whether the individualistic nature of each epicentre may undermine the cohesiveness of the Prada brand, Patrizio Bertelli, co-owner of the company suggested:

'Prada has such an old identity that it doesn't need the same space all the time. The market has become more selective, the customer more cultured. They expect this. It's all about communication'

(Irving, 2003, p. 26).

At a news conference in Spring 2004 arranged to announce the opening of the latest epicentre store to opening in Los Angeles, its architect, Rem Koolhaas proposed that the store gives people the freedom not to shop by devising alternative sources of interest (Glasiter, 2004).

Regardless of their definition and the intention to break away from the restrictions of the flagship formula, Prada's three Epicentre stores that have been opened since 2001 retain some of the core features of the traditional model. First, each was designed by 'celebrated architects' – what *The Architectural Review* (Chow, 2003) described as a 'select stellar cabal of avant-garde designers'. For the American stores – in New York and Los Angeles, they commissioned the Office of Metropolitan Architecture, led by Rem Koolhass. For the Tokyo store, Prada chose the leading Swiss practise – Herzog and de Meuron. Second, all three are located within each city's prestigious shopping districts – for example, the Los Angeles store is located on Rodeo Drive. Finally, each store, as we have reported earlier in the chapter, was expensive to design and build, the budget for the Japanese store was reported to be £52 million (Chow,

2003) – and each is in luxury retailing terms an exceptionally large retail space – the New York store is 24,000 square feet.

There are however some important deviations from the typical flagship formula, arguably the most significant of which is that each is entirely unique in its design and execution. A review of the features of each illustrates this point. At the New York site, the defining feature is the 'wave', a curving floor that connects the ground floor to the basement – where the majority of the merchandise is presented. The connecting wave has steps to one side – which the architects intended could be used for display, as well as for customers to try on shoes. Perhaps, most memorable in this store is the use of technology – such as in the changing rooms where cameras and plasma screens record customers trying on garments and through an instant replay facility, allow customers to play these back in order to inspect themselves from all directions. Recently, commentators, such as Reda (2004), have suggested that much of the technology used in the store has been either removed because of negative customer feedback and/staff resistance or because of its failure to integrate with Prada's existent IT system.

The Tokyo Epicentre offers a very different consumption experience. The exterior, which could be described as being like a string vest with concave and convex glass panel inserts, offers no focal shop window. Instead, the whole store operates as a large display case. Internally, every aspect provides hints of the Tokyo cityscape and externally, the store offers tantalizing glimpses of merchandise from the ground to the fourth floor.

The Los Angeles Epicentre seeks to invert and subvert all flagship expectations. From its Rodeo Drive setting, the store has no obvious store frontage. According to Glasiter (2004) the lack of a door entrance embodies the architect's thoughts on the informality of Los Angeles and is a pragmatic response to the temperate climate. Instead, the entrance is entirely open and underfoot displays set under transparent discs offer glimpses of the merchandise within. The Architectural Record noted that the only apparent external architecture was in the form of a plain aluminium street-facing elevation, which is supported by a truss one full story above street-level (Giovanni, 2005). There is no external signage – there is nothing to indicate this to be a Prada stage. Throughout the store are plasma screens which offer a collage of colliding and disparate images – these might range from Renaissance ceilings to recordings of President Bush.

Prada has sought to challenge the thinking around the form and function of the luxury fashion flagship and has provided some innovative architectural enhancements to the luxury consumption experience. It is important to note however that these innovations have been extremely expensive and may have contributed to Prada's reported high debt levels.

Whatever the impact upon Prada's financial health, a final question with respect to luxury flagship stores inevitably arises. Given that these are ultimately no more than clothes shops, are these worthy of all this financial and creative investment? Or is luxury fashion immune from the demands of prudent business management and old fashioned common sense!

References

Beverland, M. (2004). Uncovering 'the theories-in-use': building luxury wine brands. *European Journal of Marketing*, **38** (3/4), 446–466.

Breward, C. (2003). *Fashion: Oxford History of Art Series*. Oxford: Oxford University Press.

Chow, P. (2003). Under the net. *The Architectural Review*, October, 46–51.

Cushman and Wakefield Healy and Baker (2004). Main Streets Across the World, 2004. CWHB, London.

Davey, P. (1999). Garcons a la Mode – Comme des Garcon's design. *The Architectural Review*, October.

Doherty, A. M. and Alexander, N. (2004). Relationship development in international retail franchising: case study evidence from the UK fashion sector. *European Journal of Marketing*, **38** (9/10), 1215–1235.

Foster, L. (2004). *Poor Little Rich Stores – Design Independents, Drapers*. June 5th, pp. 28–29.

Foster, L. (2004). *Elegantly Waisted – Ermenegildo Zegna, Drapers*. August 21st, pp. 24–26.

Foster, L. (2004). *I Love Louis Drapers*. August 14th, pp. 32–34.

Giovanni, J. (2005). Prada Los Angeles epicenter. *Architectural Record*, February.

Glasiter, D. (2004). Down with shopping. *The Guardian*, July 20th.

Gruppo Armani S.p.A. (2003a). *Annual Report 2003*.

Gruppo Armani S.p.A (2003b). 'Press Communiqué: Giorgio Armani unveils new concept boutique in Sloane Street, London', 18/09/03.

Gruppo Armani S.p.A. (2004a). *Annual Report 2004*.

Gruppo Armani S.p.A. (2004b). 'Press Communiqué: Armani Group Announces Agreement with House of Three for Shanghai Flagship Store', 16/02/2004.

Hollander, S. C. (1970). Who are the multinational retailers? In *Multinational Retailing*, Michigan State University: MI, pp. 14–53.

Irving, M. (2003). Being muccia. *Financial Times Magazine*, June 21, 25–27.

Kozinets, R. V., Sherry, J. F., Deberry-Spence, B., Duhachek, A., Nuttavuthisit, K. and Storm, K. (2002). Themed flagship brand stores in the new millennium: theory, practice, prospects. *Journal of Retailing*, **78** (1).

LVMH (2003). *Annual Report 2003*.

LVMH (2004). *Press Communiqué: Louis Vuitton Opens Largest Ever Luxury Store in China*. 06/10/04.

Moore, C. M. and Birtwistle, G. (2004). The Burberry business model: creating an international luxury fashion brand. *International Journal of Retail and Distribution Management*, **32**(8), 412–422.

Moore, C. M., Fernie, J. and Burt, S. (2000). Brands without boundaries – the internationalisation of the designer retailer's brand. *European Journal of Marketing*, **34**(8), 919–937.

Mintel (2004). *Luxury Goods Retailing*. Mintel International Group Ltd., London.

Niesewand, N. (1998). Donna Karan wanted someone to make her look good. *The Independent*, January 15th, p. 20.

Niesewand, N. (1999). Shopping in contemporary style: Ralph Lauren chose the man who refurbished the statue of liberty to design his New London Store. *The Independent*, May 3rd, p. 10.

Ody, P. (2005). Armani tills to track high spenders. *Drapers*, November 20th, p. 35.

Reda, S. (2004). Prada's pratfall. *Stores*, May.

Silvestrin, C. (2001). Fashion show. *The Architectural Review*, June.

Sudjic, D. (2000). Dress to impress: London's hippest designers have found the perfect showcase for their talents. *The Observer*, October 1st, p. 7.

15

The making and marketing of a trend

Martin Raymond

The fashion business has come a long way from the days when trend predictions were all about attending the industry's key trade fairs and catwalk shows and coming away with a set of sketches or complimentary kit of trend boards with appropriate fabric swatches attached. Certainly this still happens, at events like Premiere Vision, Pitti Filati or indeed the twice yearly catwalk extravaganzas in London, Paris, New York and Milan, but more and more, the industry is moving away from this rather inaccurate and intuitive model of trend prediction, and onto more ethno- and socio-graphic versions. Ones where a whole battery of marketing tools, observation methods and techniques are being used to underpin the looks and lifestyle gambits promoted by an ever increasing number of brands and labels.

Yes, middle market retailers and department stores still use mood boards and fabric swatches to brief their studios, the Urban Nomad Look, the Techno-Warrior look, the City Sophisticate or, if they have less imagination and a dull fashion sense, comparative shoppers who travel the globe and bring back key items to deconstruct and copy. But these techniques are happily on the wane. At the branded end of the market at least, designers more and more realize that fashion is no longer a matter of clothing, but one of lifestyle – a multi-faceted, multi-purpose entity where fashion is just one part of a heady, highly complex way of living. One that requires the true designer to look to the houses we live in, the furniture we sit on, the clubs we go to, the bars we socialize in, or indeed the office environments we spend our days or nights in before he or she can be confident that the collections they are working on have any value or real meaning.

More and more we require these things from our clothes if we are to part with the ever-increasing amounts of money designers and retailers demand from us. Meaning, justification, a sense that the jacket we desire, or the dress we cherish, is not just going to clothe us, but send out the required social and sexual messages as well – here is a man or woman who is a player, a doer, a party animal; someone who knows not just what the latest fashion is, but *why* it is.

To do this properly, trend prediction agencies (really trend research agencies) braille[1] the culture, as in reaching out to touch, feel and sense its emerging subcurrents – which, for the moment, and the immediate future (a core or extreme trend can boil for a year before the mainstream even gets wind of it) is about glamour, irony, optimism, retro power dressing or the idea that we are living a 24-hour day.

We know from futurologists like James Gleick (1999) and Leon Kreitzman (1999) (author of *The 24 Hour Society*) that the current zeitgeist is also about speed, compression culture, urbanity, being plugged in and part of that great Western rush towards a notion called the New Economy – hence clothes, clubs, labels and lifestyle choices that are all about the super-casual, the super-sexy, but also the super-utilitarian: garments and accessories made from neoprenes, plastics, rip-stop nylons, fabrics that are streamlined (shark-skin bodysuits from Speedo) fast forward, with pockets, closures, linings and shell outer layers that tell others you are part of a new mood, a new world order that works a 24-hour clock, that lives a portable, ever on the move lifestyle.

All this explains why we are beginning to see clothes with pockets and smart fabrics that can accommodate wrapround communications (Levis and Philips ICD+ range of jackets with wireless mobiles and MP3 connections), diagnostic interfaces (shoes from Fuseproject that can tell manufacturers and retailers just how comfortable or otherwise they are when you wear them), wearable computers (Charmed Technology's embroidered mainframes with keypads), magic skin macs (Sofinals self-healing fabrics that can be repaired with a brush of the fingers), aromafabrics (Elizabeth de Senneville's Cosmetic Concept collection that allows you to deliver moisturizers to the body), medi-fabrics (Soldier Systems Center, a research unit with the US army, are currently testing smart fabrics which detect gun wounds on the body and alert medics to the depth and dangers of the wound via remote wireless access), sonic fashions (fabrics that carry positive and negative charges in filaments that work together when crushed to play music or to whisper soothing sounds) or indeed the more familiar multi-purpose ones that have been given a new

---

[1] Brailling, term coined by futurologist Faith Popcorn.

lease of compression culture life by labels like Vexed Generation, CP company or artists like Lucy Orta, whose garments can become tents, sleeping bags or indeed pods to accommodate up to five people.

In many cases, the above began as socio-artistic experiments, as blue skies research, or as ideas that started on the counter-cultural periphery and worked their way in to become part of the accepted mainstream. Think combats, sushi, Pokemon toys, Hello Kitty memorabilia, G-shock watches, or labels like Abercrombie and Fitch and you get the idea, now quite commonplace, 10 years ago were the first stop choice of the informed few.

How we find out about these things, and how they are subsequently catapulted into the greater culture, is what trending is really about – not seeing into the future, but searching the present for potentially viral items that are set to infect and pollute tomorrow's fashionscapes. So not a matter of crystal ball gazing then, but a careful mix of judicious research and knowing where and how to look. And this is what the best trend analysts do; look, listen, search and ask the right questions about what they are seeing. Go back to the clothing types we listed above and ask yourself this: As a trend where did they come from? Were they inspired by music? Increased casualization of the work ethic? Shifts in the way we view work (from a career-based activity to a project-specific one), or the ways we are altering how we break up and negotiate our day – from the old economy nine to five model, to the new 24-Seven option inventions like the Internet have thrown up?

The answer of course is all of the above. I know this from searching and surveying this particular part of the culture. Likewise, if I am to look at the job categories of the people who adopt this look, or catapult it on (in trending argot this is also known as sneezing), I get a fuller and more in-depth picture of their lives and lifestyle activities. Club promoters, DJs, start-up tsars, designers, illustrators, drum and bass musicians, bar owners, club owners, models, fashion photographers, fashion designers, and zine publishers and editors – job categories that have quite a lot in common, wouldn't you say? Media, music, modelling and fashion; in other words plugged-in, in the know, ahead of the posse. Now, when I look closer at these categories, I notice something else, where their businesses are located, in the Hoxton, Shoreditch, Commercial Road triangle.

Again, I ask myself why, and again the answer only becomes clear when I actually visit the area. Victorian and Edwardian warehouses, open plan walk ups, a rundown terrain of dingy streets, dilapidated shops and now desolate factories once upon a time inhabited by immigrant sweatshops, artisan workshops and a succession of ethnic minority groups from Lithuanian Jews, to Chinese coolies, to Irish, Somalian and Bangladeshi refugees, all of whom have left a unique and highly charged stamp on the area.

They also left the kind of infrastructure the people we are brailling like – a place of low rents, high ceilings, easy to convert buildings and a 24-hour access policy that is denied in most other parts of a city that follows fairly traditional and increasingly outmoded work practices. Creatives are inevitably lured to this kind of place – in Paris it is the sentier, in New York the lower east side, in Dublin Temple bar – and here studios are opened, bars, late night clubs, galleries, design ateliers, Internet companies, recording studios, magazine publishers and all slotting into a routine and a way of life that develops its own social codes, work practices, and way of eating and chilling out.

And out of this, of course, comes the *look*, the Hoxton look, if that's what you want to call it, or as Richard Benson, a one-time editor of *Arena* magazine and now head of lifestyle consultancy, Bug, named it, the flexecutive look, or to give this tribe its now accepted name, Generation Flex.

The look is now all too familiar, but 5 years ago it was still on the fringes, still boiling. As Benson explains it, it consisted and still consists of combat trousers, fleeces and all-terrain trainers – but the labels are consciously flash. Sure, there was Nike, Adidas, New Balance Caterpillar, the North Face, Berghaus, Clarks, Spiewak, ironic Kappa and genuine army surplus, but there was also US only Carhartt, Prada, Sport, Napapijri, Helmut Lang, Left Hand, DKNY, 6876, a little Merrill footwear and some Jacqueline Rabun jewellery, etc. (Benson, 1998).

As this look solidified, many who did not live in the area, or indeed worked in those industries we have mentioned, began to copy it, replicate the sense of the look without living the life of it, even down to the goatee, the one shoulder rucksack and now ubiquitous micro-scooter. This is what fashion is really about, and why trend analysis and trend prediction is no longer done with mood board and fabric swatches but on the street, in the club, around and about fashion flash points, or lifestyle hotspots (Pillot de Chenecey, 2000).

For lifestyle as a concept and as a badge of social office has completely reversed the flow of design and trend prediction and how these things are done. Once, in the 1950s, it came from Paris, and the twice yearly couture shows there, and trickled down, via a slow process of copying and adjusting to the average man or woman's wardrobe, She of Slough and He of Hanley finally getting to wear a version of the original look long after designers, retailers, manufacturers, or the local tailor or seamstress diluted it down to whatever was deemed acceptable for the class or social category they were selling into. Now the look, key ones at least, start on the street and work their way up and are copied, adjusted or cleansed of any subversive element by the designer or manufacturer, who makes them more palatable for their target market group.

More to the point, the look, as we have seen with the flexecutive, springs out of a lifestyle choice (flexecutive fashions are all about function, portability, the idea that the person wearing them would not be seen dead in the City, in a suit or a dead-end nine to five job), or from shifts and subtle movements in that part of our social or leisure lives that may not be initially visible to the retailer, designer or manufacturer caught up in the endless cycle of production, distribution and retailing.

This is why we now have cool hunters – connected, plugged-in researchers who scan the culture or travel the globe for early signs of activities that are set to become key and major trends brand leaders and designers need to know about and incorporate into their design philosophy – futurologists, ethnologists, cultural analysts or lifestyle consultancies such as The Future Laboratory, Promostyl, The Intelligence Factory, BrainReserve, Trend Union, Bug, The Henley Centre, Captain Crikey or Media Street Network, all of whom eschew the instinct-only approach to trend analysis in favour of a more scientific, and less problematic, methodology of making lifestyle predictions.

These can vary from the more traditional tools used by market research companies – telephone polling, focus groups, data mining, face to face interviews, Q&A surveys – to ones that borrow heavily on the procedures and techniques used in the not unrelated fields of ethnology and anthropology – the use of urban hides, field researchers, culture scouts, hidden cameras or cultural brailling, a reading of the culture via its magazines, TV programmes, Internet sites and chatrooms, that requires the analyst to have a thorough and in-depth knowledge of current and emerging trends, and how these are likely to impact on the cultural mainstream, or indeed fragment, and mutate into something new. Dress Down Friday, and the subsequent fall-off in suit sales in the UK and US, is a good illustration of this.

In the 1980s and early 1990s, suits were symbolic of power, position and taste (if you wore designer ones), but also of a sense of purpose, privilege and status. Silicon Valley, the rise of dotcom culture and the sartorial attributes associated with it – jeans, casual shirt, no tie, cross trainers – changed all this. Here were people who were creative, cool, engaged in some wacky and wonderful social and societal adventure, and look, no suits! Better still, they were *wealthy* with no suits. More pointedly, they looked like they were enjoying the jobs they did, in Seattle, in Silicon Valley, in Hoxton, and yes, they seemed to work at them longer (where our current 24-Seven culture came from), make few distinctions between when they played at the office, or indeed when their offices became a place for playing and partying in, and certainly when you saw them out in bars, at Starbucks (the original dress down coffee shop), or at a Nirvana gig, the one thing they had in common (apart from platinum Amex cards) was the fact that they did not wear suits.

Imagine that, no suits and yet they were still earning, still respectable members of society, still being wined and dined by old world players. But, and this was a big but, they actually seemed to be having a good time. So much so, many opted out and joined them – lawyers, PRs, advertizing agencies, financial houses, venture capitalists and so on. Which made the business behemoths of the old economy sit up and take notice. How to stop the drain? How to keep their embattled, embittered employees happy? By making their offices fun places to work in? By making them more egalitarian? By making them more casual and less corporate? All of this – hence offices that now have communal work stations, chill out areas, sleep seats, or companies that have stakeholders instead of shareholders, many of the stakeholders being valued employees they want to keep. But, on top of this, they also allowed people to dress casual, to feel creative by looking creative. In other words, imitating the dress sense of the Silicon Valley set.

In trend reporting and analysis, this kind of behaviour is called mirroring, or the placebo effect – where one socio-economic group hopes that wearing the clothes or looks of another will somehow endow them with the other's lifestyle choices. In other words, if you want to look the part, dress it. Fashion then has less and less to do with the sometimes bizarre dictates of designers, and it has to be said even less to do with manufacturers copying the look for half the price, or indeed retailers offering discounts or blue cross sale days. If anything, it has to do with shifts in the greater culture that impact on something as ordinary and everyday as the suit in a way that not only affects how we view it sartorially, but also how we view it sociologically – from being an object of desire, respect and stability to one that suggests a lack of imagination, a personality that is dull, colourless, truculent and all that was stodgy and backward looking about the old economy.

Indeed, this general revolt towards casualization on one hand and individuality on the other by the consumer has left much of the middle market retailers and brands in turmoil – Marks & Spencer, Arcadia, Moss Bros. Ironically, these are the very groups that continue to cling to the mood board method of trend prediction, continue to use the comparative shopper, the inhouse studio that visits all the right fabric fairs and catwalk shows, that continues too to use outmoded class and social categories to sell clothing, continues to their peril to ignore the science of trend and societal analysis and prediction – that which replaces what the customer wants with what the customer desires, that which allows for individual input, which turns shopping into a relationship-based activity, and one that is highly interactive and immersive, rather than one based around the idea of exchange, money being handed over for a product handed back.

However, good trend analysis is also about knowing the realities of how the population is broken up, not only by new social categories (Flexecutives, Soft Lad, Ladettes, Grit Girls, SINDIES, The New Tasteocracy, Hedonists, The Limelight Generation, etc.) (*Viewpoint*, 2000), but by group trend consultants know as Antenna groups, Early Adopter groups, Late Adopters and Laggards.

Antenna people are those who see new ideas, or indeed invent them or place them into a particular social context. Adopters are a larger, more sociable group of people who take the ideas introduced by Antenna people and make them more widely visible and less threatening in appearance. They are also known as sneezers, people who literally spread ideas, like germs, at an incredible and highly volatile rate. Then comes the Early Adopters, those of us who see ourselves as fashion-orientated, and change and tweak things to suit ourselves, and then, we have Late Adopters, the high street mainstream who need to be reassured that what they are wearing is not too outlandish, or likely to go out of date so quickly they will not get enough wear out of it. Finally come the Laggards, who talk about clothes rather than fashion, and who mysteriously believe that clothes are about looking tidy, presentable or/ and never worn to stand out.

It is by surveying these groups that the new generation of trend consultancies or viral marketeers get a feel for how a specific trend, that is, a clothing trend, or a more lifestyle-orientated one (a growing demand for organic foods,

foods that are GM free, for ethically sourced clothes or products, for adventure holidays, easy Internet access), is set to move and trickle through the culture.

But they also look at context, at how the trend or life change is most likely to be transmitted or passed on, by word of mouth (also known as viral marketing), word of mouse (on the Internet, in chatrooms and on bulletin boards) via music, clubs, in fashion magazines, in the office, through advertizing, by one ethnic or socio-economic group mimicking or aping the look, characteristics or coolness factor of another. Think here how clothes associated with ragga, gansta rap, skateboarding, the Spice Girls, punks, Neo Romantics, Grunge or bands like Oasis filtrate across or down and become part of the visual, fashion or cultural aura of groups who are far removed from the originators of the look.

In his book, *The Tipping Point*, Malcolm Gladwell (2000a) breaks these categories down into specific types of people: mavens, connectors and salesmen; in short, those who know (mavens), those who pass ideas on (connectors) and, most importantly perhaps for the mainstream, those who sell ideas in ways that are more culturally and socially acceptable – body modification, tattooing and piercing are good examples of this. Once they were badges of the fetishistic fringe, extreme activities associated with sexual branding, gang membership or a criminal past. Now, thanks to the way we have mitigated piercing and tattoos through music (the Spice Girls), fashion (Naomi Campbell and Kate Moss), or by selling it as something celebrities do (Madonna, David Beckham, Brad Pitt), it becomes more widely acceptable, if not a desirable passport to a world that we want to be part of, the *beau monde*, the celebrity party. These processes and procedures of such trend progressions are all part and parcel of the new way of measuring, brokering and ultimately predicting them.

But to understand how trends spread (from the cultural extremes inwards to the suburban mainstream), we also need to understand why. And nowhere is this more compellingly explained than in Gladwell's *The Tipping Point* (2000a), a book, along with Naomi Klein's *No Logo* (2000), Paco Underhill's *Why We Buy* (1999) and Seth Godin's *Unleashing the Ideavirus* (2000a), that has become core to understanding how trends work, and how these new generation forecasting groups function as a consequence.

Gladwell (2000a) explains it thus. Occasionally a book, a building or a fashion look impinges on our culture and we have no idea where it came from or why. One day nothing, then the next, you are on the underground and there's that book everybody seems to be reading (*Divine Secrets of the Ya Ya Sisterhood, Harry Potter and the Goblet of Fire, The Tipping Point*). Or maybe it's a pair of shoes, Hush Puppies say, or a one shoulder rucksack; an odd kind of way to design a bag, but look about you and from Hoxton, to TriBeCa, Barbés, to Berne, there they are. Everywhere. And yet there has been no advertizing for them.

And what of Palm Pilots and the WAP phone, the i-Mac or Dyson cleaners, sushi bars or stainless steel kitchens, wood floors or the New Tasteocracy's obsession with wallpaper, soft-form furniture, Pilates, micro-scooters or fashion labels like Abercrombie and Fitch? Invisible then rampant like a disease, a virus. Because they are new? Perhaps, but not all the time. Gladwell (2000a) and Godin (2000a) have a much different theory, and one that has given rise to trendland's latest buzz phrase, viral marketing, and the launch of a whole new generation of trends and guerrilla marketing agencies: The Future Laboratory, Media Street Network, Captain Crikey, Cake, Mother, Headlight Vision.

And in many ways the job of the viral marketeer and the trend analyst is interchangeable; each, after all, is chasing after the same thing, the Big Idea – for if Gladwell's book is about locating the trend and explaining its spread, Godin's is about locating it and then telling you how to spread it. And if you look at trends closely you will see that a trend can only become a trend if somebody somewhere wants to adopt or adapt it.

Take the Hush Puppies thing (Gladwell, 2000a, pp. 5, 7, 8). Comfortable, the kind of shoes dad wore at weekends to look casual in. Not exactly a hip and happening fashion statement, but there you go. And there they went. By 1995, sales were down to 30,000 a year and falling. Even the backwoods outlets in America's mid-west could not get rid of them. Then one fine day, a miracle. At a fashion shoot two Hush Puppies executives, Owen Baxter and Geoffrey Lewis, ran into a stylist from New York who told them that the classic Hush Puppies had suddenly become hip (*Viewpoint*, 2000), that there were re-sale shops in the Village, in Soho, where the shoes were being sold. People were going to the Ma and Pa stores, the little stores that still carried them, and were buying them up.

As Gladwell (2000a) tells it, these two hard-bitten sales reps were puzzled. Then came calls from designers like Issac Mizrahi (I think it's fair to say that at the time we had no idea who Issac Mizrahi was), John Bartlett, Anna Sui and LA designer Joel Fitzgerald, all asking for Hush Puppies for their forthcoming shows. Joel was even opening a Hush Puppies store he told them, gutting a place next door to his Hollywood boutique he said, and putting a 20-foot inflatable Basset hound on the roof (the Hush Puppies symbol) because the demand for Hush Puppies in that area had gone nuclear and he wanted people to know his was the shop that could satisfy all their cravings.

Naturally, the Hush Puppies people were thrilled, but they still did not get it. Had no idea why sales had rocketed from 30,000 pairs per year in the Autumn of 1995, to four times that amount the following year, and the year after that still more, until Hush Puppies were once again a fashion staple in the wardrobe of with-it kids from Seattle to St Louis. The publishers of *The Divine Secrets of The Ya Ya Sisterhood* were to see similar patterns in how the book shot from obscurity to become a runaway international best seller overnight. Ditto Bloomsbury, who publish the Harry Potter tales, and Fendi, whose Baguette has revived the fortunes of that company almost single-handedly. Nothing. Then bang. Like a plague, a virus, a hyper-infectious contagion.

And that, according to Gladwell (2000a) and Godin (2000a), is exactly what it is; not a trend, not a fad, not a mood board idea being slavishly replicated down the line, but a sartorial or intellectual virus. And Gladwell should know; for years he did the science and medicine beat for *The Washington Post* and encountered viruses and infectious diseases aplenty. What he was not banking on, however, was how areas of interest such as epidemiology or virology would impact so profoundly on his other interests: why trends as in social or fashion trends happen the way they happen, how movements or ideas run through the culture the way they do.

We think, for instance, that they happen slowly, he says, and over a long period of time, moving carefully and measurably through those categories cool hunters or trend forecasters are so fond of using – from innovators, to Early Adopters, to Early Majority, to Late Majority and finally onto the Laggards – as each one of us takes it on when we are ready, familiar with the shape of that shoe for instance, or comfortable with the textures and surfaces of that chair or that house (Gladwell, 2000b).

But no, Gladwell, with his knowledge of virology, noted that the opposite was the case. That ideas and products and messages and behaviours spread just like viruses do. More bizarrely, he noticed that the spread corresponded to characteristics found in all infections, that they were not slow to infect, but did so rapidly and in strict geometric progression. More peculiarly, he observed that it only took one or two people or carriers to spread the disease, and that once this infection process began, it showed up as a dramatic and upward curve. The point at which this curve hits critical mass has been named the Tipping Point, the title of his book.

For Godin (2000a), it is a similar procedure. For him, in future all ideas and fashion statements will be spread this way. His book is a perfect example of this. Launched with no advertizing budget, it is a paradigm of that process; you can download it from the Internet (at www.ideasvirus.com) and, when you do, it tells you how the book can be spread like a virus via chatrooms, e-mails to friends, by firestorming bulletin boards or by word of mouth (Godin, 2000b). This of course is how fashion and lifestyle trends can be spread most effectively. All of which throws into doubt much of what we have always believed about how trends spread, why they spread, and the part or otherwise advertizing, the media and big budget marketing play in spreading them.

The latter not a lot, if you are to believe the central plank of Gladwell or Godin's thesis. Indeed, for both, word of mouth (viral marketing) is by far the best way for trends or ideas to spread, and this happens best and most effectively – not by TV, by advertizing (interruption marketing) or niche advertizing as one would suspect – but via a network of people Gladwell calls mavens, connectors and salesman, yes, by word of mouth.

These are a small but influential (his Law of the Few) group of men and women who, because of their positions (connectors), the way they garner and store information (mavens), or indeed disseminate such information in a way that is more palatable to the slow to catch on majority (salesmen), are core to the whole process of how tastes, trends and ideas are brokered or spread to the rest of the population. Media Street Network, a successful US trends consultancy and media marketing agency run by 23-year-old Reggie Styles, does this by recruiting teams of teenagers from the street who will either tell him what's hot and what's not, or if his company already has a hot trend, product or music idea to promote, it will use these teenagers to connect with

Early Adopters and transmit or pass on the required idea. This is known as firestorming, or trend salting (Godin, 2000b).

There are other factors to be considered, however: the Stickiness Factor, for example, and the Power of Context. The former is of course that elusive Holy Grail all trend analysts, marketing and advertizing agencies are obsessed with identifying and isolating, the thing or tick that makes us recall a product, place or fashion moment instantly and with the corresponding need to purchase it. The latter is the context in which we surround things so that they become sticky or appealing in the first place.

Again, look to Hush Puppies; they were always there, dormant, or in decline, like quite a few of our current social illnesses, then something happens, a stylist (maven) maybe at a particular downtown club (context) sees one or two people wearing them and thinks, that's a tip, that's a thing I can take and promote, so they do, telling their friends, or one particular friend who is a heavy socializer, gets to all the other downtown hotspots (a connector) and tells everybody he/she meets about the Hush Puppies thing, and since they are unaffiliated, not seen to be a representative of the company or advertizing agency, everybody says, hey, that's cool (the stickiness factor) and starts telling others, and so on, until the rest of us are saying very much the same thing as well.

What's fascinating about this is that it is true for all areas, not just fashion, but design, technology, art, politics, media and modes of behaviour; why, for example, hedonism has become such a Big Thing at the moment, or endurance holidays, or vigilante consumerism, or Intellectual capital, or such notions as social and ethical responsibility. They are not new, merely finding their moment, their way in from the counter-cultural fringes.

In fashion terms then, it is easy to not just predict the next big trend, but to get it right; we know that chatrooms, bulletin boards and target youth groups are live with the re-emergence of the brand as king. We know too that it is a lifestyle issue rather than a fashion one. Furthermore, we know that words and phrases like ethical responsibility are in the air, ditto sustainability, accountability, the hollow corporation, relationship selling, so the next big trend must surely be towards the citizen brand concept or trend, products, looks or ideas that reassure us, and do not disappoint us across all categories.

Nike and Adidas, for instance, may be gods in fashion, but there is a query about their third world working practices and labour rights issues. This of course taints how we view the brand, and offers us one less reason for buying the brand. Tommy Hilfiger has suffered a similar fate, ditto Gap and Starbucks. This does not tell us, however, what specific trends will appear – we need to survey the culture closely for this – but it can tell us what categories they will or should fall into. We know too from research that health and leisure are among the largest growing sectors of profit, that the over fifties – Silver Surfers – are among the wealthiest and the most leisure orientated. We know too that thirty-something women, Grit Girls as they are called, are now one of the most powerful economic forces to be reckoned with – women own 9 million companies in the US alone, and within a decade will employ half the

US workforce – so we can look to these sectors to throw up the next big trends (Popcorn and Marigold, 2000).

We also know that biogenetics, biotechnology, our concerns about global warming and our planet's increased lack of water are increasingly occupying our thought processes – which can only have a knock-on effect in what we wear or how we wear it. Take the colour blue for instance, in, out, in, out, but over the next 5 years, as water becomes an issue between the have and the have nots, the depletion of the ozone layer a more strident reality, blue is certainly the colour most likely to dominate not just the sense and sensibilities of fashion designers, but designers and architects everywhere.

Blue is also about spirituality, poetry (other words being picked up in chatrooms), the sky and the sea, but also in its darker shades, about science (electricity), mystery and some would say evil – biotechnology, genetic modification. So blue then would be a safe colour to choose as the most dominant colour of the next decade – just like beige was the colour of the 1990s (minimalism, softness) and black the key colour of the power-suited 1980s. How do we know? The greater indicators are there, but also smaller, quieter ones on the cultural periphery. It is only a matter of seeking them out – not guessing them out – a case of applying science to the requirements of futurology, along with instinct, intuition and a broader appreciation of things from other aspects of our cultural roots besides fashion. Fashion, after all, is a reflective medium not a proactive one.

References

Benson, R. (1998). Flexi living. *Viewpoint*, (6), 77.

Gladwell, M. (2000a). *The Tipping Point*. London: Little Brown.

Gladwell, M. (2000b). Interview by Martin Raymond. *Viewpoint*, (8), 36, 37.

Gleick, J. (1999). *Faster; The Acceleration of Just About Everything*. London: Little Brown.

Godin, S. (2000a). *Unleashing the Ideavirus*. Published from www.ideavirus.com

Godin, S. (2000b). Interviewed by Tim Adams. Culture section, *The Observer*, 6 November, 4.

Klein, N. (2000) *No Logo*. London: Flamingo/HarperCollins.

Kreitzman, L. (1999) *The 24 Hour Society*. London: Profile.

Pillot de Chenecey (2000). Captain Crikey, interview by Martin Raymond. *Viewpoint*, (8), 61.

Popcorn, F. and Marigold, L. (2000). *Evolution: The Eight Truths of Marketing to Women*. London: HarperCollins Business.

Underhill, P. (1999). *Why We Buy, The Science of Shopping*. London: Orion Business Books.

Viewpoint (1999). New social categories for measuring lifestyles against. (8).

Viewpoint (2000). The limelight generation, October 2000.

16

Approaches to doing research

Tony Hines

The various chapters in this book have hopefully given readers a good insight into the variety of issues facing people and organizations in the contemporary global fashion industry when identifying, analysing and taking decisions related to marketing. It is essential that the research agenda and research designs considers a rich variety of issues that face fashion marketing decision-makers and that different researchers with their different perspectives are able to make their contributions to the field. There is no single best method to do research. Social science research has acknowledged differences between the ways in which the scientific tradition views the world and ways in which social researchers view the world (Blaikie, 1995). The approach taken must reflect upon your views of the world, the phenomena under investigation and the research questions you want to address. In addition you will also want to consider practical aspects of doing research such as how can I address the question, what data sources are available to me, are my questions focused enough, will they tell me what I want to know, do I have the necessary resources to do the research and so on. Most researchers refine their plans when they answer such questions. Research questions often begin with a wide-angle lens and need to very quickly focus zooming in on the phenomena of interest. What you do will also be determined by how much time you have and the research skills and knowledge you possess.

Critical thinking requires the researcher to conduct a thorough critical review of the literature covering the topic under investigation. Research rigour is a necessity for scholarly research. If we are to capture cumulative knowledge within our own study we must be thorough in doing our literature review. The literature plays an important part in identifying areas of interest that we might want to research. It provides guidance in terms of questions we want to ask and it can inform us of how previous researchers have tackled similar problems in order that we can make appropriate choices and justification of methods in our own work. The literature also acts as a stimulus for discussion and argument. Our own thought trials often engage with relevant literature that we have read and this is how we can make sense of phenomena under investigation (Weick, 1995).

It is not just the literature that is important in shaping what we do but other considerations related to being, doing and knowing. This final short chapter will consider some of the issues critical to doing research in fashion marketing. We begin by considering some criticisms of the marketing discipline in relation to research.

Criticisms levelled at the marketing discipline

A number of criticisms have emerged in the discipline domain of marketing by those inside and those outside of the discipline. The main criticisms focus on selection of phenomena to study, relevance to practice, ontological stance, use of theoretical frameworks and appropriate choice and justification of method. Research in marketing is haunted by Bartels's (1951) widely cited question: 'is marketing a science?'. Some critics have argued that there is only one scientific method and that is used in the physical sciences. Essentially there are three parts to the scientific method of doing research and they are: observation, conjecture as to the cause and effect of the facts observed, and verification through renewed observation.

The initial debates centered around a proposed definition of a scientific marketing method (Buzzell, 1963; Halbert, 1965; Hunt, 1976; Deshpande, 1983). However, this dominant view was challenged during the 1980s and arguments for methodological pluralism were promoted (Anderson, 1982, 1983; Arndt, 1983). More recently the question of dominant logic in research in marketing has been revisited (Sheth and Sisodia, 1999; Vargo and Lusch, 2004). The major problem for researchers and for ways of knowing that follows on from a singular dominant approach to doing research may not in the first instance be clear and you may wonder what all the fuss is about. However, it is quite serious if you consider three aspects of having a dominant logic. Implicit in the scientific method are assumptions about the ways we view the world (ontology), ways of doing research (methodology) and ways of knowing (epistemology).

Table 16.1 illustrates three approaches and the conditions that influence research: ways of being, truth claims, ways of doing research, ways of

Table 16.1 Conditions that influence research: three approaches compared

Condition	Scientific method	Social constructionist	Pragmatist
Reality – ways of being	A world out there of objects, properties and processes. A Cartesian split (after Descartes).	Socially constructed realities, that is the product of social factors and not the result of some objective reality of how things are independent of social interests. May not be a Cartesian split.	Ontological oscillation Accept that the subject matter of the social is socially constructed but for practical purposes follow the lines of scientific orthodoxy.
Methodology – ways of doing research	Observation Measurement Verification Usually requires quantitative approaches.	Qualitative approaches Grounded theory Interpretive repertoires Hermeneutics Discourse analysis Narrative 'linguistic' turn.	Methods leaning towards the scientific reporting styles.
Epistemology – ways of knowing	Science (i.e. knowledge) is cumulative and is based on sensory experience. Research questions such as what are the distribution and attitudes of opinion. Statistical sampling.	Science is one form of construction and other forms are equally legitimate. Research questions such as what lies behind this phenomenon. Purposive or theoretical sampling. Natural groups in setting. Open ended dialogue and probing. Qualitative data analysis.	Mixed approaches dependent on context.
Truth claims and concerns – what we know	Absolute (e.g. scientific laws – certainty) Validity (internal & external) Reliability.	Relative (e.g. plausibility) rather than certainty Confirmability Credibility Dependability.	Relative (e.g. probability) Validity Reliability.
Usefulness – when is it most appropriate?	Testing extant theories.	Generating new theories.	More concerned with testing extant theory rather than developing new theory.

knowing and usefulness in terms of research purpose. There are clearly implications for the way we do research based upon our world-views. Ontological stance determines our truth claims and both methodology (including research design, method and tools employed) and knowledge purpose and what we learn are a consequence of our world-views.

Influence upon doing research

If you take the example given in the chapter on segmentation in this book you will see that our world-view informs the research questions posed, the ways in which we set about conducting research into segmentation and the way knowledge about the phenomenon is generated and interpreted (Hines and Quinn, 2007). Thus ways of being, ways of doing and ways of knowing are clearly interrelated in the research process.

A further brief example from Kathy Charmaz in relation to grounded theories may also serve to illustrate the point and I have taken a quote and used it to explain what I mean.

> 'Grounded theory serves to learn about the worlds we study and a method for developing theories to understand them. In the classic grounded theory works, Glaser and Strauss talk about discovering theory as emerging from the data separate from the scientific observer. Unlike their position, I assume that neither data nor theories are discovered. Rather, we are part of the world we study and the data we collect. We construct our grounded theories through our past and present involvements and interactions with people, perspectives and research practices'.
>
> (Charmaz, 2006, p. 10)

I don't usually approve of, or use long quotes but the statement made by Charmaz is critical to our understanding of how world-views impact upon the research we do and what we will know after the research is completed. There is an acknowledgement in the first sentence of the quote that we enter different worlds when we choose a phenomenon to study. The second sentence makes references to the founders of grounded theory Glaser and Strauss who use *discovery* in relation to grounded theories. Discovery is a loaded word and its meaning has implications for their [G&S] nature of realty. It implies that there is a world waiting to be discovered that we are separate from. This world exists independently and is separated from us, the researchers. Hence Glaser and Strauss saw themselves as scientifically detached. Charmaz on the other hand sees it differently and views herself as part of the world she is researching and recognizes that this may influence the data gathered. Thus, ways of knowing are affected by ways of being in the world and ways of doing research.

The value of research

The value placed upon research depends upon your own assessment of worth and the contributions you think you have made given the evidence as well as the audience it is aimed at and the value they place upon it. In addition the academic community will make evaluations through critiques of your work. As a rule of thumb research should follow four major canons in this respect: it should be rigorous, it should be useful to the potential users, it should be timely and it should provide the academic community and practitioners with 'food for thought' by way of knowledge disseminated.

Common sense in the research process

It is with this in mind that I would like to leave you with a final thought which is not to lose sight of how important it is to be grounded in reality in your search for new concepts and new applications. This will avoid any criticism regarding relevance of your work. There are very seldom, general solutions to specific problems and one size does not fit all. Context is important. Capturing the zeitgeist, searching for new customers, new markets, applying new business models or simply trying to understand existing customers, consumer behaviour and the impact or opportunities that globalization or e-business presents is not easy. It is always useful to take a common sense 'reality check' after considering the various pieces of data including advice from practitioners, academics and consultants.

Let us reflect...

S-commerce: a new B2C retail craze?

They're calling it shops or 'S-Commerce' and it's being rolled out in towns and cities nationwide. It's a real revelation, according to Malcolm Fosbury, a middleware engineer from Hillingdon. 'You just walk into one of these shops and they have all sorts of things for sale.' Fosbury was particularly impressed by a clothes shop he discovered while browsing in central London. 'Shops seem to be the ideal medium for transactions of this type. I can actually try out a jacket and see if it fits me. Then I can visualize the way I would look if I was wearing the clothing'. This is possible using a high definition 2D viewing system, or 'mirror' as it has become known.

Shops which are frequently aggregated into shopping portals or 'high streets' are becoming increasingly popular with the cash rich time poor generation of new consumers. Often located in densely populated areas people can find them extremely convenient. And Malcolm is not alone in being impressed by shops. 'Some days I just don't have time to download huge Flash animations of rotating trainers and then wait five days for them to be delivered in the hope they will actually fit,' says Sandra Bailey, a systems analyst from Chelsea. 'This way I can actually complete the transaction in real time and walk away with the goods'. Being able to see whether or not shoes and clothing fit has been a real bonus for Bailey, 'I used to spend my evenings boxing up gear to return. Sometimes the clothes didn't fit, sometimes they just sent the wrong stuff'. Shops have a compelling commercial story to tell too, according to Gartner Group Retail Analyst, Carl Baker. 'There are massive efficiencies in the supply

chain. By concentrating distribution to a series of high volume outlets in urban centres typically close to where people live and work
businesses can make dramatic savings in fulfilment costs. Just compare this with the wasteful practise of delivering items piecemeal to
people's homes'.

Furthermore, allowing consumers to receive goods when they
actually want them could mean an end to the frustration of returning
home to find a despatch notice telling you that your goods are waiting in a delivery depot the other side of town.

But it's not just convenience and time-saving that appeals to
Fosbury, 'Visiting a shop is a real relief for me. I mean as it is I spend
all day in front of a bloody computer.'

Source: Anonymous (June 2000)

The views expressed in this short piece demonstrate some of the myths and
realities surrounding e-business applied to fashion retailing and support the
need for critical thinking when conducting research or in applying new business ideas.

I hope that this brief final chapter has provided you with some important
insights into ways of being in the world and the influences we are subjected to
as researchers. It demonstrates importantly that our own understanding about
ourselves as researchers has an impact upon the research we choose to do, the
ways we set about doing it and what we will eventually find out and claim as
our contributions to knowledge.

References

Anderson, Paul F. (1983). Marketing, scientific progress, and scientific method.
    Journal of Marketing, **47** (4), 18–32.
Anderson, Paul F. (1982). Marketing, strategic planning and the theory of the
    firm. *Journal of Marketing*, **46** (Spring), 15–26.
Arndt, J. (1983). The political economy paradigm: foundation for theory build-
    ing in marketing. *Journal of Marketing*, **47** (4), 44–55.
Bartels, R. (1951). Influences on the development of marketing thought, 1900–
    1923. *Journal of Marketing*, **16** (1), 1–19.
Blaikie, N. (1995). *Approaches to Social Enquiry* (Reprint ed.). Cambridge:
    Blackwell Publishers Ltd.
Buzzell, Robert D. (1963). Is marketing a science? *Harvard Business Review*, **41**
    (1), 32–40.
Charmaz, K. (2006). *Constructing Grounded Theory: A Practical Guide Through
    Qualitative Analysis*. London: Sage.
Deshpande, R. (1983). Paradigms lost: on theory and method in research in
    marketing. *Journal of Marketing*, **47** (4), 101–11.
Halbert, M. (1965). *Meaning and Sources of Marketing Theory*. New York:
    McGraw Hill.

Hines, T and Quinn, L. (2005). Segmenting Fashion Consumers: Reconstructing the Challenge of Consumer Complexity. In Hines, T. and Bruce, M. (Eds), *Fashion Marketing Contemporary Issues*, 2nd Edn. Oxford: Elsevier.

Hunt, S. D. (1976). The nature and scope of marketing. *Journal of Marketing*, **40** (July), 17–28.

Sheth, J. N. and Rajendra S. Sisodia (1999). Revisiting marketing's lawlike generalizations. *Journal of the Academy of Marketing Science*, **27** (1), 71–87.

Vargo, Stephen L. and Robert F. Luseh (2004). Evolving to a new dominant logic for marketing. *Journal of Marketing*, **68** (1), 1–27.

Weick, K. E. (1995). *Sensemaking in Organizations*. Thousand Oaks: Sage Publications.

Index